Global Institutions and Responsibilities:
Achieving Global Justice

ℳ METAPHILOSOPHY

METAPHILOSOPHY SERIES IN PHILOSOPHY

Series Editors Armen T. Marsoobian and Brian J. Huschle

The Philosophy of Interpretation, edited by Joseph Margolis and Tom Rockmore (2000)
Global Justice, edited by Thomas W. Pogge (2001)
Cyberphilosophy: The Intersection of Computing and Philosophy, edited by James H. Moor and Terrell Ward Bynum (2002)
Moral and Epistemic Virtues, edited by Michael Brady and Duncan Pritchard (2003)
The Range of Pragmatism and the Limits of Philosophy, edited by Richard Shusterman (2004)
The Philosophical Challenge of September 11, edited by Tom Rockmore, Joseph Margolis, and Armen T. Marsoobian (2005)
Global Institutions and Responsibilities: Achieving Global Justice, edited by Christian Barry and Thomas W. Pogge (2005)

Global Institutions and Responsibilities: Achieving Global Justice

Edited by

Christian Barry
and
Thomas W. Pogge

Blackwell
Publishing

First published in *Metaphilosophy* 36, nos. 1–2 (January 2005), except for "The Preventive Use of Force: A Cosmopolitan Institutional Proposal," "Just International Monetary Arrangements," "The New Liberal Imperialism: Assessing the Arguments," and "Whose Sovereignty?: Empire Versus International Law."

BLACKWELL PUBLISHING
350 Main Street, Malden, MA 02148-5020, USA
9600 Garsington Road, Oxford OX4 2DQ, UK
550 Swanston Street, Carlton, Victoria 3053, Australia

First published 2005 by Blackwell Publishing Ltd

Library of Congress Cataloging-in-Publication Data

ISBN 1-4051-3010-5 (paperback)

A catalogue record for this title is available from the British Library.

Set in India
by Macmillan
Printed and bound in the UK
by TJ International, Padstow, Cornwall

The Publisher's policy is to use permanent paper from mills that operate a sustainable forestry policy, and which has been manufactured from pulp processed using acid-free and elementary chlorine-free practices. Furthermore, the publisher ensures that the text paper and cover board used have met acceptable environmental accreditation standards.

For further information on Blackwell Publishing, visit our website:
www.blackwellpublishing.com

CONTENTS

Part 3: Responsibilities

Notes on Contributors

Christian Barry is editor of *Ethics & International Affairs*. He served previously as a contributing author to the United Nations Development Program's *Human Development Report*. He received his Ph.D. in philosophy from Columbia University. His recent publications include "Understanding and Evaluating the Contribution Principle" (in *Real World Justice*, Kluwer, forthcoming), "Redistribution" (in *Stanford Encyclopedia of Philosophy*, 2004), "Global Justice: Aims, Arrangements, and Responsibilities" (in *Can Institutions Have Duties?* Palgrave, 2003), and "Education and Standards of Living" (in *Blackwell Companion to the Philosophy of Education*, 2003). He is currently working on a book (with Sanjay Reddy) on trade and labor standards.

Allen Buchanan is James B. Duke Professor of Philosophy and Public Policy at Duke University. His research and teaching are mainly in two areas: political philosophy, with an emphasis on ethical issues in international relations and the philosophy of international law; and bioethics, with an emphasis on ethical issues in genetics. His most recent books are *From Chance to Choice: Genetics and Justice,* cowritten with Dan W. Brock, Norman Daniels, and Daniel Wikler (Cambridge, 2000), and *Justice, Legitimacy, and Self-Determination: Moral Foundations for International Law* (Oxford, 2003).

Jean L. Cohen is professor of political theory in the Department of Political Science at Columbia University. She is the author of several books, including *Class and Civil Society: The Limits of Marxian Critical Theory*; *Civil Society and Political Theory,* cowritten with Andrew Arato, and *Regulating Intimacy: A New Legal Paradigm*. She has published more than forty articles in various journals of political theory as well as in law reviews. She is currently working on a book on rethinking sovereignty and international and imperial law.

David Singh Grewal received a J.D. from the Yale Law School, where he focused on international law and legal theory. He is currently a graduate student in the Department of Government at Harvard University, where he is studying political theory and the history of political thought. His book *Network Power and Globalization* is forthcoming from Yale University Press.

Bashshar Haydar is associate professor of philosophy at the American University of Beirut, with research interests in the areas of moral and political philosophy as well as aesthetics. Publications include "The Moral Relevance of Cost," in *Philosophical Studies*; "Consequentialism and the Doing-Allowing Distinction," in *Utilitas*; and "Aesthetic Principles," in the *British Journal of Aesthetics*.

Robert Hockett is assistant professor of law at the Cornell Law School in Ithaca, New York. He has worked both at and as an outside consultant to the International Monetary Fund in Washington, D.C. His recently completed doctoral work at Yale lies at the intersection of international economic law, distributive justice theory, and financial theory. He teaches, researches, and writes in those three fields and is a reviewer for the *American Political Science Review* and the *Journal of Theoretical Politics*.

Robert O. Keohane is professor of international affairs at the Woodrow Wilson School of Public and International Affairs, Princeton University. He is the author of *After Hegemony: Cooperation and Discord in the World Political Economy* (1984) and *Power and Governance in a Partially Globalized World* (2002). He is the coauthor (with Joseph S. Nye Jr.) of *Power and Interdependence* (third edition, 2001) and (with Gary King and Sidney Verba) of *Designing Social Inquiry* (1994). He has served as the editor of the journal *International Organization* and as president of the International Studies Association and the American Political Science Association.

Nancy Kokaz teaches international relations and peace and conflict studies at the University of Toronto. She is currently completing her first book, where she develops a civic conception of global justice that can effectively address the pressing challenges of global poverty and inequality in a plural world. Building on this general theory, her second book will explore international fairness in relation to practices of collective justification that regulate the world economy in concrete issue areas.

Darrel Moellendorf teaches philosophy and directs the Institute for Ethics and Public Affairs at San Diego State University. He is the author of *Cosmopolitan Justice* and various articles on related topics. His current research projects concern issues of justice, trade, and development and issues of reconciliation and socioeconomic rights in South African constitutional jurisprudence.

Thomas W. Pogge has been teaching moral and political philosophy at Columbia University since receiving his Ph.D. from Harvard. His recent publications include "The First U.N. Millennium Development Goal," in the *Journal of Human Development* (2004), *World Poverty and Human Rights* (Polity Press, 2002), and, as editor, *Global Justice* (Blackwell, 2001). Pogge's work has been supported by the MacArthur Foundation, the Princeton Institute for Advanced Study, All Souls College, Oxford, and the National Institutes of Health. He is a member of the Norwegian Academy of Science and is currently Professorial Research Fellow at the Australian National University Centre for Applied Philosophy and Public Ethics.

Jedediah Purdy is assistant professor at Duke Law School. His most recent book is *Being America: Liberty, Commerce, and Violence in an American World* (Knopf, 2003). He is also the author of many articles and essays, including "A Freedom-Promoting Approach to Property" in the *Chicago Law Review* and "The Ethics of Empire, Again" in the *California Law Review*.

Sanjay G. Reddy is assistant professor of economics at Barnard College, Columbia University. His areas of research include development economics, international economics, and economics and philosophy. He has a Ph.D. in economics from Harvard University, an M.Phil. in social anthropology from the University of Cambridge, and an A.B. in applied mathematics with physics from Harvard University. He has worked extensively as a consultant for development agencies and international institutions, has been a member of the "advisory panel of eminent experts" of the U.N.'s *Human Development Report*, and is a member of the U.N. Statistics Division's Steering Committee on Poverty Statistics.

David Rodin is Leverhulme Research Fellow at the Oxford Centre for Applied Ethics and Senior Research Fellow at the Centre for Applied Philosophy and Public Ethics at Australian National University. His research interests cover business ethics, international justice, and the ethics of war and conflict. His first book, *War and Self-Defense* (Oxford University Press, 2002), was awarded the American Philosophical Association Frank Chapman Sharp Prize for the best monograph on the philosophy of war and peace.

Juha Räikkä teaches philosophy at the University of Turku, Finland. After his studies at the University of Turku and the University of Miami, Florida, he earned his Ph.D. in 1992 with a dissertation entitled "An Essay on International Justice." He visited Southwest Texas State University in 1994 and the European University Institute in Florence in 1999, 2001, and 2003. His research interests focus on issues in political theory, philosophy of law, and ethics. Recently he has written on such topics as global poverty and population theory.

Ingrid Robeyns was trained as an economist at the Universities of Leuven, Göttingen, and Cambridge, where she obtained her doctorate with a dissertation on gender inequality and the capability approach. She was a visiting scholar in the Department of Philosophy at Columbia University and is now a research fellow in political theory at the University of Amsterdam. Her research interests lie at the intersection of welfare economics, political theory, and normative political philosophy.

Kok-Chor Tan received his Ph.D. in philosophy from the University of Toronto in 1998 and is currently assistant professor of philosophy at the University of Pennsylvania. His area of research is in moral and political philosophy, and he has special interests in global justice, nationalism, and human rights. He is the author of *Toleration, Diversity, and Global Justice* (Pennsylvania State University Press, 2000), which was a joint runner-up for the Canadian Philosophical Association 2003 book prize, and *Justice Without Borders* (Cambridge University Press, 2004). His essays have appeared in such series or journals as the *Journal of Philosophy, Monist, Ethics*, the *Canadian Journal of Philosophy*, and *NOMOS*.

John Tasioulas is Fellow and Tutor in philosophy at Corpus Christi College, Oxford. His research interests are in ethics, political philosophy, and the philosophy of law. His recent work has focused on the morality of law and questions of global ethics. Recent publications include "Human Rights, Universality and the Values of Personhood: Retracing Griffin's Steps," in the *European Journal of Philosophy* (2002), "The Legal Relevance of Ethical Objectivity," in the *American Journal of Jurisprudence* (2002), and "Mercy," in the *Proceedings of the Aristotelian Society* (2003).

1

INTRODUCTION

CHRISTIAN BARRY AND THOMAS W. POGGE

The aim of this collection is to help close some gaps between theory and practice, between theorists and practitioners, by integrating rigorous thinking about principles of global justice into debates about existing institutions in ways that can enrich each.

Global justice concerns the moral assessment and reform of global institutions. These include markets in capital and labor, international fiscal, labor, and property law, international trade and monetary arrangements, rules governing the use of force, and constitutive features of the modern state, such as its sovereign rights to tax, to bind its citizens through treaties, to control the use of natural resources within its territory, and to represent their interests in international bargaining and rule setting. Various concepts, such as the "global basic structure," the "international regime," the "global institutional scheme," and the "social and international order," have been used to characterize these institutional arrangements.

These social rules and arrangements have great moral significance, as decisions about their specific design have a tremendous impact on human lives. Moreover, global justice assessments are increasingly important normatively as guides for individual and collective action. This is so not only because individual and collective agents bear ultimate moral responsibility for the justice of social rules but also because the ethical assessment of even mundane conduct options, such as purchasing and consumption behavior, increasingly requires an informed evaluation of such institutional arrangements as labor markets and trade rules.

These observations are becoming commonplace. Yet, most philosophical discussions of global justice have remained quite out of touch with the concerns of activists, journalists, and policy makers engaged in evaluating global institutions and in advocating for their reform or outright replacement. With a few notable exceptions, theorists of global justice have focused on individual obligations to donate for the distant needy, on unspecific duties of affluent states to assist poor countries, or on generic and abstract "duties of justice" to promote fairer global rules and institutions. They have generally failed to illuminate difficult and pressing questions concerning specific responsibilities with respect to the design and conduct of such existing organizations as the World Bank, the International Monetary Fund, the United Nations, and the World Trade Organization, or the justice of such institutional arrangements as rules governing taxation, labor markets, and the use of force. This has led, unsurprisingly, to accounts of normative responsibilities with respect to global justice that have tended to be thin, obscure, and sometimes rather unrealistic.

This charge may perhaps seem unfair and to miss the point of political theory. Political arguments that are presented in everyday politics, after all, have a purpose different from that of those which constitute political theorizing, and many writers have rightly stressed the importance of distinguishing these purposes. They address different audiences, and to engage in political theory is not necessarily to engage in politics—nor should it be. Such distance becomes problematic, however, when it is so great that it undermines the capacity of theories to provide useful insights into the evaluation of institutional arrangements, social practices, and the nature of moral argument about them. Indeed, the very meaning of competing principles of global justice and obligation will remain obscure if they cannot be shown to have different implications for concrete policy issues.

Theorizing about global justice must maintain a critical distance from policy discussion but must also illuminate it—avoiding both uncritical acceptance of the status quo and endorsement of unrealistic and under-specified utopian alternatives. We should not expect such theorizing to yield theories that will translate obviously or algorithmically into rules of conduct for individual persons or collective agents, or into fine-grained institutional rules. The essays in this collection suggest, however, that it can give at least some rough guidance to agents who are working out what to think and do about pressing practical dilemmas while taking account of the nonideal circumstances of political life, such as noncompliance, incomplete or apparently conflicting evidence, and the need to reach and enforce individual and collective decisions in the face of disagreement.

Rational argument about what is needed to achieve global justice can be of three kinds. It can concern the ends—the goals, values, and ideals—that global institutional arrangements ought to be designed to achieve or embody. It can be about institutional arrangements that would realize these aims or about the allocation of responsibilities to promote, support, or defend such arrangements. Although all of the ensuing essays at least touch on these interconnected questions, each tends to emphasize one or another of them. We have grouped and ordered them accordingly.

In addition to the contributors, we would like to thank those who have given us help and support while preparing this collection, especially Paige Arthur, Eva Becker, Joel Rosenthal and Lydia Tomitova at the Carnegie Council on Ethics and International Affairs, Otto Bohlmann and Armen Marsoobian at *Metaphilosophy*, Alexander Grossman for designing the cover, and Rekha Nath for her work on the index.

2

GLOBAL JUSTICE WITHOUT END?

JOHN TASIOULAS

1. Introduction

Are there any principles of distributive justice with global reach? In addressing this question, we can usefully distinguish international justice from transnational justice.[1] Principles of transnational distributive justice regulate distributive relations *within* political communities, for example, among members of the same state or between the government of a state and its members. Thus, it might be asserted that the difference principle should be implemented by all states in relation to their members, so that social and economic inequalities are to the greatest benefit of the representative least advantaged citizen. Principles of international distributive justice, by contrast, regulate distributive relations among agents that are not members of the same political community (or, perhaps, that are not members of any political community or that do not stand in the relationship of governed to government within a political community). So, for example, it might be claimed that relations between states ought to be subject to the difference principle in order to ensure that any inequalities serve to maximize the position of the representative least advantaged person or society in the world.

I shall be primarily concerned with principles of international distributive justice of a specific kind: those that supposedly apply between political communities. And my aim will be to offer a qualified defense of John Rawls's position in *The Law of Peoples* (Rawls 1999, especially 105–20). According to Rawls, we should not acknowledge any principle of international distributive justice, whether in ideal or nonideal theory. Instead, he advocates a duty of assistance in nonideal theory—a duty to "assist other peoples living under unfavourable conditions that prevent their having a just or decent political and social regime" (37). My defense of Rawls's position is rather heavily qualified, however, because I conceive of the duty of assistance as a more exacting standard than he does. As I go on to argue, Rawls's sound insights about international distributive justice are betrayed by his flawed, intervention-driven account of human rights. This leads him to characterize the duty of assistance in a way that is insufficiently responsive to the asymmetry of intervention and assistance.

---

[1] I borrow the distinction from Buchanan (2004, 190–91).

Of course, some believe that the very idea of international distributive justice is fundamentally misguided from the very start because it rests on presuppositions that are not now met and that are highly unlikely ever to be satisfied in any realistically foreseeable state of the world. So-called realists advance this skeptical thesis on the grounds that supposed principles of international distributive justice fly in the face of the maxim that "ought" implies "can." Their idea is, roughly, that principles of this kind are hopelessly utopian, given certain entrenched features of the global political environment, such as the ineradicable propensity of states to pursue their self-interest and the impotence of international institutions authoritatively to formulate, apply, and enforce norms of distributive justice.

But it is far from obvious that the ideal theory of international distributive justice is to be condemned *ab initio* as an exercise in naïve utopianism. As Rawls himself insists, for any account of international justice to be acceptable, it must be *possible*—"somewhere and at some time" (127)—for political communities to comply with its standards, given the relatively immutable psychological, social, and institutional facts of human life. This is why Rawls's global ideal is characterized as a "*realistic* utopia." Moreover, what is possible in the relevant sense is not set by a factual parameter of capability fixed independently of our considered value judgments. What falls within the realm of practical possibility depends, in part, on how inspiring are the options that we confront. And why should not the goal of international distributive justice be a powerfully attractive one, especially if Rawls is correct in tracing the "great evils of human history" to political injustice (126)?

At this point, the self-styled "realist" might respond that even if a principle of international distributive justice can be implemented, the conditions under which this would be the case—the establishment of a world government able to gather the necessary information, issue authoritative pronouncements, and deploy coercive power to enforce them—would pose an unacceptable threat of global tyranny. Indeed, this threat might even render the very idea of international distributive justice practically self-defeating, since its attempted realization would spell the demise of the politically independent societies whose relations were to be governed by it. The answer here, of course, is that the costs of implementation depend on the precise content of the relevant principles, and one factor that will significantly influence the latter is the cost of any feasible implementation scheme. What this sceptical argument yields, at best, is a compelling reason for adopting a moderate principle of international distributive justice, one whose fulfillment does not require that power be concentrated in the hands of a potentially tyrannical agency.

A different form of preemptive skepticism about international distributive justice draws on the communitarian idea that the very applicability of distributive justice presupposes the existence of a genuine community, one that is conspicuously lacking in the international context. On one interpretation of this view, what is vital is the absence of communal solidarity among the members of different political communities that might provide both a justification and an effective motivation for those better off to make the necessary sacrifices demanded by redistribution. On another interpretation, it is the absence of a widely shared, tradition-based understanding of the "meanings" of the various goods to be distributed that is invoked (Walzer 1983, 28–30). Since any broadly acceptable distributive criterion would have to be responsive to such an understanding, the undeniable fact of pervasive global dissensus on the latter score is said to entail the nonexistence of any such criterion.

Again, it seems to me that this line of thought misses its target. Tempering the demands of a principle of international distributive justice can help intercept both the objections from communal solidarity and shared understanding. In the former connection, for example, Rawls rightly stresses that the content of the Law of Peoples is constrained by the psychological principle that "social learning of moral attitudes supporting political institutions works most effectively through society-wide shared institutions and practices" (112 n. 44). But another line of response is that these objections, even if they have some weight, are living on borrowed time. Thus, the requisite solidarity can only gain strength through processes of cooperative interaction and in the light of the gathering prospect of an unwanted backlash of terrorism, illegal population movements, and the global spread of diseases like AIDS (112–13). Similarly, in a globalizing world, the idea that we can achieve a consensus on basic elements of a worthwhile life seems increasingly plausible (see, e.g., Nussbaum 2000, ch. 1). For reasons of this kind, Walzer has himself acknowledged the provisional nature of his argument for sidelining considerations of international distributive justice (1995, 293).

2. Rawls contra International Distributive Justice

Rawls pursues a less ambitious, but considerably more promising, strategy than either realists or communitarians in resisting the claims of international distributive justice. Rather than attempting to uncover a devastating flaw in the very idea of distributive justice between societies, he urges the attractions of an alternative understanding of how inter-societal relations might be ordered. His argument has two components. (1) As part of ideal theory, a "realistic utopia" is outlined in which all societies are liberal or decent, and it is claimed that in this situation, which is the best we can realistically hope for, no duties of international distributive justice obtain. (2) As part of nonideal theory, that is, the segment of normative theory concerned with conditions of noncompliance and unfavorable conditions, Rawls contends that well-ordered peoples bear a duty to assist burdened societies to become decent or liberal societies, but not any duty of international distributive justice.

Rawls's theory takes as its normative subjects well-ordered peoples, which are of two kinds, liberal and decent. He speaks of peoples, rather than states, because peoples lack the traditional powers of internal sovereignty and abide by moral constraints, such as respecting the independence of other peoples, in pursuing their self-interest. These general features of peoples, which constitute their moral nature, qualify them to be represented in the second-level original position that leads to the construction of a Law of Peoples. Regarding transnational justice, both liberal and decent peoples comply with Rawls's minimalist schedule of human rights, which includes a right to subsistence (65). This is the only explicit individual socioeconomic entitlement decent peoples are required to meet qua decent. Liberal societies need to secure more than the conditions of physical subsistence, of course, since their basic structure guarantees for all their citizens "sufficient all-purpose means to make intelligent and effective use of their freedoms and to lead reasonable and worthwhile lives" (114). Famously, Rawls's preferred way of giving effect to that guarantee is the difference principle.

When it comes to international distributive justice, however, Rawls denies that any principles of this sort should be acknowledged. Their Achilles heel is that they do not incorporate a target or cut-off point beyond which they cease to operate. For example, the difference principle does not require the meeting of some absolute threshold, such as a guaranteed minimum of primary social goods, beyond which any further inequalities are to be treated as inherently unproblematic from the standpoint of justice. Instead, it sets the continuous task of ensuring that any inequalities serve to maximize the position of the worst off. Rawls takes the absence of a target and cut-off point to characterize "most" principles of distributive justice (106). It is vital to a fair evaluation of his argument against the internationalization of distributive justice to appreciate its circumscribed range: it is essentially directed at principles that belong to this supposed majority group.[2] For the sake of convenience, when I refer to distributive justice, I shall follow Rawls in having this specific category of principles in mind. Those who find this terminological stipulation unduly restrictive may instead simply interpret Rawls's argument as directed against the regulation of relations between political communities by a certain *class* of principles of distributive justice. Prominent members of this class are egalitarian distributive principles, like the difference principle, that is, those according to which

---

[2] Allen Buchanan's critique of Rawls suffers from failing to take this restriction into account. Buchanan appears to equate "distributive" justice with positive rights to social and economic goods (especially to goods necessary for a living standard beyond subsistence level). See Buchanan 2004, ch.4.

there is always at least a *pro tanto* reason to eliminate material inequalities, since their existence is always intrinsically bad.

Rawls's rejection of international egalitarianism is best understood as tempered in two main ways. First, it is compatible with the existence of nonegalitarian reasons for restricting global socioeconomic inequalities, since they can bear on values—such as the relief of suffering, self-respect, and procedural fairness—that are distinct from distributive equality, and nothing in Rawls's argument prevents him from endorsing them (113–15; see also Beitz 2001). His main concern, I suggest, is to oppose ascribing *intrinsic* significance to any international redistributive principles that lack a target and cut-off point. Second, Rawls allows the possibility of an "egalitarian principle with target," which treats material inequalities as sometimes inherently bad, but not when the position of the individuals or societies being compared exceeds a defined target. Depending on how its target is specified, Rawls admits that such a principle might not differ greatly from his duty of assistance, leaving largely practical matters of administration to differentiate them (119). The implication of his argument, however, is that reflection on the merits of the duty of assistance undercuts the motivation to endorse even this sort of international egalitarian principle.

The duty of assistance is owed by liberal and decent societies to burdened societies. Unlike "outlaw states," the other chief concern of nonideal theory, their salience stems not from culpable noncompliance with the Law of Peoples but from unfavorable conditions preventing full compliance. Irrespective of whether they are materially well off or poor, burdened societies "lack the political and cultural traditions, the human capital and know-how, and, often, the material and technological resources needed to be well-ordered" (106). The target of the duty of assistance is to help them achieve well-orderedness, to become societies with liberal or decent institutions that, inter alia, secure human rights and meet the basic needs of their members. Once that long-term target is reached, a cut-off point comes into operation for each formerly burdened society so that no further assistance is owed under the duty (111, 118–19). Any surviving inequalities among well-ordered peoples—considered simply as such—are a matter of indifference from the point of view of international justice.

Of all the eight principles that make up the Law of Peoples, Rawls regards the duty of assistance as "especially controversial" (37 n. 43). In contrast to those other principles, it is not derived from "the history and usages of international law and practice" (41, 57), which partly explains why it is given a more sustained defense than most of those other principles receive (105–20). In the course of this defense, Rawls readily admits the considerable initial appeal of a global difference principle in the present circumstances of the world, with its "extreme injustices, crippling poverty and inequality" (117). But the fact that it is meant to apply continuously without target or cut-off point, even in a hypothetical world in which the duty of assistance is fully satisfied, shows that it should be rejected. This is brought out by the following thought experiment:

> Two liberal or decent countries are at the same level of wealth . . . and have the same size population. The first decides to industrialize and to increase its rate of (real) saving, while the second does not. Being content with things as they are, and preferring a more pastoral and leisurely society, the second reaffirms its social values. Some decades later the first country is twice as wealthy as the second. Assuming, as we do, that both societies are liberal or decent, and their peoples free and responsible, and able to make their own decisions, should the industrializing country be taxed to give funds to the second? According to the duty of assistance there would be no tax, and that seems right; whereas with a global egalitarian principle without target, there would always be a flow of taxes as long as the wealth of one people was less than that of the other. This seems unacceptable. (117–18)

(Rawls also offers a second thought experiment, which focuses on differential rates of population growth and their bearing on the status of women.)

As I interpret it, a key objective of Rawls's thought experiment is to highlight the importance of political self-determination. The value of individuals and associations being attached to their culture and taking an active role in its common public and civic life justifies "preserving significant room for the idea of a people's self-determination" (111). This being the case, his thought experiment prompts the question why a political community's self-determination should be compromised for the sake of ameliorating inequalities between societies that are already well ordered. Rawls's contention is that no such compromise is required, because once the duty of assistance has been satisfied "each people adjusts the significance and importance of the wealth of its own society for itself" (114).[3] The conclusion here is a radical one: it is not that considerations of international distributive justice are defeated by the countervailing value of self-determination but that there are no valid demands of this sort to begin with.

It is not just the political autonomy of the potential contributor societies that is at issue but also that of potential beneficiaries. The duty of assistance certainly liberates the former from the obligation to assist less advantaged societies provided the latter are well ordered, and that is perhaps the most conspicuous way in which it respects their political autonomy. But the duty of assistance also bears on the autonomy of potential beneficiary societies. It clearly does so positively,

---

[3] Elsewhere, he says that the role of the duty of assistance is to assist burdened societies to become full members of the Society of Peoples "and to be able to determine the path of their own future for themselves" (118). For an insightful discussion of the tensions between (national) self-determination and global distributive justice, see Miller (2000, 167ff.).

insofar as its discharge helps them become effectively self-governing liberal or decent peoples. But it also does so negatively, and this not just because such societies might themselves one day graduate to the status of duty-bearers with an interest in avoiding subjection to a redistributive principle.

We can see how this is so if we interpret Rawls's duty of assistance as a "default duty," to use Henry Shue's phrase, one that obtains where the primary duty-bearer has failed to fulfil its duty. In the present context, the primary duty-bearers are political communities, all of which are obligated to become well-ordered peoples by establishing just or decent institutions. But burdened societies are incapable of fulfilling that primary duty because of the obstacles they confront. In consequence of that failure, liberal and decent societies come under a default duty—the duty of assistance—to help them meet their primary duty. The target at which the duty of assistance is set, therefore, reflects the standards that a society must meet in order to be in good standing as a member of the Society of Peoples. And the level at which the latter standards are fixed clearly impinges on the self-determination of all political communities, including potential beneficiaries of the duty of assistance. It seems naturally to follow, on this analysis, that burdened societies have a general duty to accept assistance to become well ordered. But even this duty preserves some leeway for their autonomy, since they may remain free to decide whether to become liberal or decent (assuming both options are feasible), and they also presumably retain some discretion as to the form assistance should take.

On Rawls's account, the duty of assistance operates against the significant assumption that societies are under no obligation (of transnational justice) to achieve a higher standard than decency. This accords them greater autonomy than any account of international justice that presupposes a more demanding standard of transnational justice, for example, one that requires all societies to adopt the difference principle internally. The implications of this are particularly significant in the context of Rawls's wider theory, according to which certain kinds of failure to achieve well-orderedness can deprive a society of immunity from legitimate intervention (where, for example, the failure is due to its violation of the human rights of its members).

Now, Rawls's argument might be attacked by questioning two presuppositions of his thought experiments. The first is the empirical assumption that the most significant determinants of a people's economic condition lie in their political culture, their moral and other traditions, and the attitudes and virtues of their members (108, 117, 119). It follows according to Rawls that, marginal cases like the Arctic Eskimos aside, no society exists lacking the natural resources needed to become well ordered. It is this supposed fact that makes differential endowments of natural resources an inadequate basis for justifying a redistributive principle in the international case. Contrast here differential endowments of natural talents in the domestic case, the arbitrariness of which helps motivate Rawls's difference principle in the context of a liberal society. But, of course, it is a highly contestable assumption, both as to its truth and as to its implications, even assuming that we can draw a workable distinction between "internal" and "external" causes of wealth to begin with. In its absence, the concern about differential resource endowments might have been deployed to justify a distributive principle—like Charles Beitz's resource redistribution principle (Beitz 1999a, 136–43)—even in a hypothetical situation in which the production of goods and services in each country is "autarkic" (116).

My inclination is to grant Rawls's first presupposition. But even if it were incorrect, it is hardly obvious that a distributive principle without target and cut-off point would be justified. Resource inequalities might, instead, be redressed by a principle that did have a cut-off point, for example, one reached once a society had used up all of its excess resource endowment, having made the appropriate "tax" payments to relatively resource-poor societies for the privilege of doing so. Admittedly, some resource redistribution principles appear to lack a target and cut-off point. For example, Hillel Steiner contends that every individual is entitled to an equal share in the total value of natural resources (1994, chs. 3, 7, and 8). Presumably, this principle would necessitate indefinite redistribution in response to population changes. However, a principle of this sort faces insuperable problems of implementation, quite apart from the fact that its demands are insufficiently sensitive to the satisfaction of people's vital interests (see Beitz 1999b, 280–86).

The second background presupposition of Rawls's thought experiment is more troublesome. In both of his hypothetical scenarios, the societies are presented in abstraction from any ongoing structure of international interaction and cooperation. But it is only when the nature and effects of that structure are factored in, it might be thought, that the case for a global principle of distributive justice becomes convincing.

One version of this line of argument has been elaborated with great clarity and force by Thomas Pogge. He contends that the existing global economic order is one through which wealthy and powerful societies culpably damage the prospects of poorer and weaker societies. They do this by abusing their superiority to impose "a skewed global economic order" on them, one that fetters their economic development and further saps their bargaining power. The foreseeable and avoidable results of this skewed system include a world in which nearly half of all humankind lives in abject poverty and one-third of all human deaths are from poverty-related causes (Pogge 2001, 2004a, 2004b). Quite apart from any violation of *positive* duties to aid or redistribute, this state of affairs results from the violation of two crucially important negative duties of justice: the duty not to harm others and the duty to refrain from profiting from injustices perpetrated against them (2004a, 278). Moreover, as Pogge insists, these depredations cannot be adequately redressed by the simple precaution of ensuring that disadvantaged societies are not harmed to the extent that they fall below a previously specified minimum, such as Rawls's threshold of decency.

Although Pogge has explicitly advanced this argument in opposition to the Rawlsian duty of assistance (Pogge 2004a), I think it leaves the case for that duty undisturbed. Rawls could (and, perhaps, should) accept everything Pogge says here, yet still maintain both his hostility to principles of international distributive justice and his support for the duty of assistance. Two points bring this out.

To begin with, Rawls might argue that the kind of unfairly rigged economic order that Pogge invokes is not one that would prevail in the situation envisaged by ideal theory. For insofar as that situation is premised on a global environment in which the Law of Peoples is generally observed, the incidence of unfair advantage-taking would be severely restricted by such principles as those enjoining that the freedom and independence of peoples be respected, that human rights be honored, that peoples are equal and parties to the agreements that bind them, and that they observe a duty of nonintervention. So, for example, in a Society of Peoples there would be no oppressive regimes, hence they could not be, as they now are, afforded legal recognition by other societies along with the resource and borrowing privileges that are its concomitants and whose terrible effects Pogge rightly deplores. Moreover, it is arguable that the economic fate of decent and liberal peoples would not be dependent on international capital markets or international economic policies that express the interests of powerful states in the ways they do at present. For such relations of domination and exploitation would be subversive of their freedom and independence, thereby violating the first principle of the Law of Peoples.

Still, one might reply that these highly general principles leave considerable scope for some societies, even in a Society of Peoples, to take unfair advantage of their weaker consociates. But even if one concedes this residual moral hazard, it cannot be automatically inferred that the best response to it is a principle of international distributive justice. Any such principle would have to compete against a less radical alternative, one that is admittedly only broadly gestured at by Rawls (43, 115), that is, the development of rules and cooperative organizations to regulate such matters as tariffs, quotas, antidumping duties, subsidies, and global intellectual property regimes in ways that do not unfairly advance the interests of the powerful at the expense of the weak. Moreover, it would be vital to ensure that less well off peoples have the wherewithal, in the form of expert knowledge and other resources, to enforce these rules through the institutions charged with the regulation of the global economic order.[4]

Now, Pogge might reply that however things stand with respect to ideal theory, his argument at the very least grounds a principle of international distributive justice in nonideal theory. If so, this is enough to show that the duty of assistance is not, as Rawls thinks it is, the operative principle in nonideal theory. After all, it is a fantasy to suppose that even liberal and decent peoples (if any such exist) could insulate themselves from the moral obligations of repair that arise from their own tainted histories of colonialism and exploitation or from the gross unfairness of the global economic environment they perforce inhabit.

Here the second point I foreshadowed becomes relevant. I think that Rawls should concede that the duty of assistance does not exclude the applicability in nonideal theory of negative duties of the sort Pogge invokes: duties that prohibit the infliction of harm, or benefiting from wrongfully induced harm, together with rectificatory duties that are consequent upon their violation. To the extent that *The Law of Peoples*, largely through its silence on the matter, conveys the opposite impression, it stands in serious need of clarification and supplementation. But the important question is whether Pogge's argument validates any distributive principles without target or cut-off point, and it seems to me doubtful that it does. Instead, the negative duties invoked form the traditional subject matter of principles of corrective justice and retributive justice, which are not normally thought of as distributive principles that inherently lack a target and a cut-off point. For example, they often enjoin the payment of one-off compensation or the imposition of a specified amount of punishment.

Pogge has suggested, in response to this line of thought, that fair relations between societies may be, at least de facto, incompatible with certain levels of material inequality between them. Therefore, securing fair conditions of interaction will require compliance with principles lacking a target and cut-off point, since such principles will be sensitive to relative changes in global affluence. But even if the de facto significance of inequalities could be established in the way this argument assumes, we do not yet have a principle Rawls is committed to rejecting. The resulting egalitarian constraint will have been justified purely instrumentally, as a means of arriving at conditions of fair global interaction. But, as we noted earlier, Rawls's concern is to oppose according intrinsic significance to a principle without target and cut-off point, not the derivative significance contemplated by this argument.

---

[4] On the latter point, see Beitz (2001, 107–09), who stresses that this concern with procedural fairness need not reflect an antecedent commitment to the form of egalitarianism Rawls opposes.

We have not yet found any reason, therefore, to regard the duties that emerge from Pogge's argument as incompatible with the duty of assistance or any decisive reason to classify them as principles of distributive justice in Rawls's sense. Indeed, the specific rectificatory duty that Pogge himself has advocated—the Global Resource Dividend—is a principle that incorporates a target and cut-off point (2002, ch. 8; Rawls 1999, 118 n. 53). What is more, Rawls ultimately seems better placed than Pogge to accommodate the variety of duties of justice that do bear on well-ordered societies. For Rawls, they include both negative obligations to refrain from harming and positive obligations to assist irrespective of responsibility for harm. Whereas for Pogge positive duties could only be duties of international charity, which are less stringent than duties of justice, because positive duties are not correlative to rights (see Pogge 2002, ch. 2, and the criticism in Tasioulas forthcoming).

An alternative approach focuses not on the harms caused by the wrongful imposition of a discriminatory economic order but, instead, on the wider similarities between a domestic basic structure and the international basic structure. The aim is to out-Rawls Rawls by showing that there is an international analogue to the basic structure of a liberal democratic society in order to justify something like a global version of the difference principle. The relevant point of analogy might be the existence of a scheme of social cooperation for mutual advantage or, more minimally, of a network of institutions that has a profound, enduring, and fundamentally nonvoluntary impact on the life prospects of those enmeshed in it. Important arguments in this vein have been advanced by Beitz (1999a), Pogge (1994), Buchanan (2000, 2004), and Franck (1995), among others. It is impossible to address them properly here. I simply make one very obvious point about this strategy. In opposing a principle of international distributive justice one need not also endorse the difference principle, or indeed any principle of redistribution without a target and cut-off point, as regulating even the basic structure of a liberal democratic society. To the extent that one is justified in doing so, any argument from analogy loses its *ad hominem* sting.

Naturally, Rawls would dismiss this last suggestion, since he believes that the difference principle is the *most*—but not the only—reasonable way of guaranteeing to citizens of a liberal society the primary goods needed to make "intelligent and effective use of their freedom" (14). He would, therefore, be committed to showing that the analogical argument fails on its own terms. There is no doubt plenty of scope for pursuing this strategy. For instance, one might stress the absence of sufficiently extensive reciprocity (that is, cooperation for *mutual* benefit) in the global economic order. Or one might tie the difference principle to the legitimation of the state's monopoly of coercive power, a phenomenon that neither exists, nor would be desirable, at the global level (36). But better, in my view, would be to reject the difference principle even for a liberal democratic society (see Arneson 2000). One can do so while still cleaving domestically to a broadly liberal conception of political justice. This is because there are good reasons to suppose that the best way—or, as Rawls seemingly allows (14 n. 5), one of various eligible ways—to guarantee the requisite levels of primary goods, and so on, is through a principle with a target and cut-off point.[5]

Now, I do not pretend that anything so far constitutes a knock-down argument against principles of international distributive justice or even that such an argument exists. Unlike the preemptive forms of skepticism, Rawls's contention is not that such principles are nonstarters but rather that, when set against the duty of assistance, we should after due reflection prefer the latter to the former. So a lot turns on the appeal of his rival account, and it is this question that I address next.

3. The Inadequacy of Decency

In assessing Rawls's position, we need to disentangle two of its dimensions. The first is the formal claim that we should accept a principle with a target and cut-off point in nonideal theory, rather than any principle of distributive justice. The second is the substantive claim that the content of the principle is given by the duty of assistance as specified by Rawls. My reluctance to accept without qualification the Rawlsian position concerns this second, substantive component. For whereas I agree with him that the relevant principle ought to have a target and cut-off point, I contend that the duty of assistance sets an unduly modest target. Its target is disjunctive: burdened societies are to be assisted to become either liberal or decent. But a "decent society" is not one that can serve as an adequate minimum threshold for a society to be in good standing.[6] Nor can it, relatedly, set an acceptable cut-off point at which the duty of well-ordered societies to assist burdened societies is fully discharged. Now, Rawls himself anticipates controversy about the point at which "a people's basic needs ... are fulfilled and a people can stand on its own," yet he also insists that it is the existence of *some* such point that is "crucial to the Law of Peoples" (119). So, my line of criticism is in keeping with the prevailing spirit of the Rawlsian view, since it preserves what he took to be the "crucial" feature of the duty of assistance.

---

[5] For one example of this sort of view, see Crisp (2003), defending a "sufficiency principle" grounded in compassion for the badly off.

[6] A decent society satisfies two criteria (Rawls 1999, 64–67): (1) it has no aggressive aims in foreign policy and respects the political independence of other societies and (2) it satisfies a three-part criterion: (a) it has a "common good idea of justice" that secures the human rights of all its members, though not necessarily as extensively or as equally as they would be in a liberal society; (b) its legal system imposes bona fide moral duties, beyond those arising from human rights, on all persons within its territory; and (c) its judges and other officials have a sincere and not unreasonable belief that the law is guided by a common good idea of justice. Contrast the other sort of well-ordered people, liberal peoples (23–25).

I begin by granting Rawls three propositions. The first is that the target of the duty of assistance is set by the transnational standard of justice that has to be satisfied for a people to be well ordered, whatever that might be. The second is that a decent society is stably realizable. The latter proposition is open to two objections, both of which stem from the fact that a decent society does not honor a robust schedule of human rights, in particular, that it does not respect freedom of speech and rights of democratic participation. These features raise doubts as to whether a decent society really can be nonaggressive toward other well-ordered societies (given what Rawls calls "the Fact of Liberal Democratic Peace") and also whether it can secure the right to subsistence (given the empirical link Amartya Sen has established between democracy and famine prevention).[7] Finally, I grant that a decent hierarchical society, through the operation of its consultation hierarchy, affords its members a level of political participation that, although not democratic, suffices to underwrite meaningful collective political self-determination.

Even with these concessions, it can still be maintained that a decent society does not offer its members enough to constitute a well-ordered people, that is, one that enjoys good standing in ideal theory. Of course, this claim can be pressed in connection with the minimalist schedule of civil and political human rights that such a society respects, one that inter alia excludes rights to *equal* freedom of religion, to freedom of speech, and to democratic political participation (Rawls 1999, 65; see also Tasioulas 2002a, 381–82). Here Rawls's answer is that these are liberal rights, not authentic human rights, and that it would be grossly intolerant to require decent but nonliberal societies to secure them. Whatever one makes of this response, I want to focus instead on the exemption of decent societies from the requirement to guarantee certain social and economic (or "welfare") entitlements. Putative human rights of this kind are not traditionally synonymous with a liberal or Western perspective. On the contrary, leaders of communist and Asian states have invoked the urgent need to secure them as a justification for resisting democracy, free speech, and other values they regard as peculiarly "liberal" or "Western."

In order to see how a decent society affords inadequate welfare entitlements, we need to elucidate the content of Rawls's human right to physical subsistence. He follows Shue in interpreting this right as securing access to the means of subsistence—unpolluted air and water, adequate food, clothing and shelter, and a basic minimum of health care—thus enabling its holders to have what is needed for "a decent chance at a reasonably healthy and active life of more or less normal length, barring tragic interventions" (Shue 1996, 23).[8] My argument

---

[7] Sen 1981 and 1999, chs. 6–7. Rawls himself refers to this work (109), although he stresses the connection between famine prevention and his more limited set of human rights.

[8] Rawls endorses this interpretation (65 n. 1).

depends on contrasting this right, which secures the conditions for an austerely minimal standard of living, with more generous individual welfare entitlements. In particular, we can contrast it with a right to an *adequate* standard of living, one that justifies a claim to resources necessary for an *adequately good* life. Otherwise put, it is the difference between freedom from poverty that threatens one's continued existence and the fulfillment of one's basic needs and freedom from poverty that severely threatens one's ability to have a good life. The distinction here is rough and intuitive, and certainly in a fuller account one would have to spell out what determines the goodness of a life and the level at which the standard of adequacy is pitched.[9] But this does not, I think, detract from the widespread resonance of the distinction I am drawing.

That Rawls's theory is to be read in the light of this distinction is shown by the minimalist content of the human right to subsistence, the fact that it is interpreted as an implication of the right to life rather than a self-standing welfare right (Rawls 1999, 65), and by his attitude to Article 25 of the Universal Declaration of Human Rights. The latter refers to "the right to a standard of living adequate for the health and well-being" of a person and his or her family. International lawyers standardly construe this as an entitlement to more than the means of subsistence, that is, as a right to an adequate standard of living. Yet when Rawls contrasts his approved list of human rights with the lengthier schedule of entitlements in the Universal Declaration, Article 25 conspicuously does not figure among those he classifies as "human rights proper" (Articles 3–18), leaving the clear implication that he regards it as a "liberal aspiration" instead (80 n. 23).

With this background in place, we can begin to appreciate the inadequacy of a decent society on the score of welfare rights. Of course, nothing in its definition prevents a decent society making lavish provision for the welfare of its members. But the concept of "decency" is compatible with other, less attractive possibilities. A decent hierarchical society, it seems, could be one in which a class of people—owing perhaps to their religious affiliation—are systematically discriminated against by the law, basic institutions, and entrenched social attitudes, so that although they are entitled to the minimum resources necessary for subsistence, they are blocked from acquiring resources beyond that level. One way the society might do this is by restricting occupations with remuneration capable of sustaining levels of well-being significantly above subsistence to the adherents of the established religion. A decent hierarchical society, on Rawls's account, must protect its members from religious persecution, but

---

[9] The four living-standard levels distinguished by Andrew von Hirsch and Nils Jareborg (1991) are helpful here: (1) subsistence, (2) minimal well-being, (3) "adequate" well-being, and (4) "enhanced" well-being. Rawls's human right covers (1) and, possibly, aspects of (2), and I am contrasting it with a right to the requisites for (3).

it need not grant them "equal" freedom of religion. In particular, it is not prevented from establishing a state religion or excluding people from certain occupations on the grounds of their religious creed. Thus, the situation I have sketched would severely impair the ability of members of the minority to achieve an adequate living standard without unambiguously violating anything that Rawls would recognize as their human rights.

Admittedly, there is a nagging question whether this scenario could genuinely materialize in a decent society, that is, whether it would not contravene the requirement that such a society be animated by a common good idea of justice, including the minimalist schedule of human rights which that conception must honor. For example, this schedule includes a right to liberty, and an implication of that right according to Rawls is that people cannot be forced to hold certain occupations. In narrowing down the occupational prospects of members of the religious minority in the way described, it might be argued, a regime of forced occupation is imposed on them, since they are channeled willy-nilly into jobs with subsistence wages. Alternatively, a defender of Rawls might invoke the effects of a decent consultation hierarchy (71–72)—in registering dissent from official policy—as the reason for the unrealizability of my hypothetical example.

Still, the case I have described is not manifestly excluded by the idea of a decent society, and this alone impairs the claim of a decent society to count as well ordered within ideal theory.[10] Moreover, to dismiss the example on the grounds mentioned seems an unhappily roundabout way of proceeding. For this would be to attribute only derivative significance to whether people are guaranteed the conditions for an adequate standard of living. It is also a suspiciously arbitrary move, as one might naturally ask why freedom from forced occupation or entitlement to consultation are conditions of decency but a right to an adequate standard of living is not. Finally, one can object that both responses secure the intuitively desirable result on an unacceptably contingent basis. Certainly people can have good, even exceptional, lives in societies where a right to an adequate standard of living is not respected. But this no more undermines the case for such a right than does the fact that slaves have died of old age in societies that did not respect the human right to life undermines the case for the latter. Rawls was justifiably unmoved by empirical responses offered by utilitarians to his objection that they ignored the separateness of persons—responses along the lines that it is highly unlikely that utilitarian calculations would ever authorize hanging an innocent man in order to promote the general good. So he is notably ill placed to deploy a similar response here.

---

[10] Buchanan (2004, 211) also believes that scenarios of this kind are possible on Rawls's account, whether or not Rawls would have endorsed them.

In any case, we can avoid some of these complications by restating my criticism with the use of a different example. It might be that a formerly burdened society has graduated to the status of decency, but that because of meager natural resources and various other constraints on economic growth, a significant proportion of its population for the foreseeable future can be guaranteed a standard of living only at or slightly above subsistence level.[11] With assistance from other well-ordered societies, however, it could secure an adequate standard of living for its members within a few years. Is it plausible to suppose that societies able to offer this assistance are never under a duty of justice to do so, even if the cost to them were minimal? Of course, sometimes circumstances might dictate that the only way of discharging the duty of assistance is by helping the burdened society become liberal, for example, because decency is not a feasible goal for that particular community, given entrenched cultural and political traditions. But such a response is inadequate as a general answer to the problem, as it once again leaves the fulfillment of vital human interests hostage to circumstances, quite apart from any anxiety about liberal ethnocentrism.

Reflection on these two imaginary cases has a dual effect within Rawls's dialectic: it undermines the appeal of the duty of assistance and, in so doing, it strengthens the hand of the advocates of international distributive justice. I want to endorse the first of these effects while resisting its presumed corollary, the recoil to principles of international distributive justice. This will require dislodging the background assumption that we are faced with a choice between a global egalitarianism that seriously compromises self-determination and a duty of assistance that can be fully discharged by helping burdened societies become decent societies that need not secure any welfare rights beyond subsistence.

Let us accept that Rawls has set an excessively weak standard of transnational justice, that is, that in order to comply with the requirements of ideal theory a society must, inter alia, satisfy a more demanding internal requirement in connection with individual welfare entitlements than that of securing its members' rights to physical subsistence. Instead, a right to an adequate standard of living has to be secured for each member of a well-ordered society. But now the question arises of what it would take to secure such a right. One possibility is that it demands the implementation of the difference principle within every society in the world. Another is the utilitarian idea that maximizing overall utility requires more stringent limits on economic inequalities. Yet another is the "prioritarian" view according to which the interests of the worst off are accorded extra weight but need not be maximized. All such potential

---

[11] This example may require backtracking somewhat on Rawls's claim that the chief determinants of a people's economic condition are "internal."

principles of transnational justice would be principles of distributive justice in Rawls's sense, that is, they would lack a target and cut-off point.

In line with my general skepticism about such principles, I think there is a simpler and preferable way of understanding that right. This is as an independent ethical norm, one that has its source in the moral significance of the objective interests of the right-bearers, and that itself has a target and cut-off point. The latter consists in the provision of the conditions necessary for the right-holder to have an adequately good life. The details here would depend on explicating the notion of a good life, whether in terms of needs, objective goods, functioning, and so on, and in determining what counts as an "adequate" standard of living. Although such a right sets an absolute standard, the nature and level of resources to be provided would be sensitive to variations in circumstances. So, for example, subsistence may demand that one has access to clothing needed to stay reasonably healthy, but in order to have an adequately good life one needs something more, at the least access to clothing that will enable one to appear in public without shame, to take an example Sen derives from Adam Smith. In both cases, however, exactly what has to be provided for any particular individual will depend (within limits) upon general parametric factors that vary from one society to another, such as climatic conditions and cultural conventions. Whatever one thinks of this proposal for strengthening the requirements of transnational justice, the more general criticism I have made of Rawls's duty of assistance is independent of it.

If my argument so far is plausible, the diagnostic question arises: How did Rawls come to embrace this inadequate standard of transnational justice and, by implication, international justice? My suggestion is that his flawed position stems from the fact that Rawls's minimalist doctrine of human rights is made to play two markedly different roles. The first role is to set a standard for immunity from intervention (together with the requirement of nonaggression). Nonaggressive societies that comply with human rights are, in virtue of that compliance, immune from coercive intervention by other peoples (Rawls 1999, 80). The second role is that the doctrine of human rights helps determine the target and cut-off point for the duty of assistance in nonideal theory, since it partly defines what counts as a well-ordered society. Peoples have a duty to assist burdened societies to become well ordered, which includes, inter alia, helping them secure the human rights of their members. But once burdened societies have become well ordered, any further duty of assistance evaporates.

The question that obviously cries out for an answer here is this: Why should Rawls suppose that the selfsame minimal set of human rights, compliance with which confers immunity from coercive intervention on nonaggressive societies, also determines, together with various other factors, the cut-off point for assistance to burdened societies? More specifically, when it comes to the matter of individual welfare entitlements, why should it be the selfsame right, the human right to physical subsistence, that (a) provides a trigger for coercive intervention by one society into another if extensively violated and (b) defines the target and cut-off point for the duty of assistance?

Moreover, it is the first consideration, that relating to intervention, that is the real driving force in shaping Rawls's conception of human rights. For it would really take some quite egregious failing—something like the culpable failure to secure the subsistence of a significant proportion of its population—in order to justify one society forcefully intervening in another. Intervention, with its breach of a society's political independence and the grave risks often attendant upon it, is plausibly made to turn on the extensive violation of a very minimal set of requirements, for example, those in Rawls's truncated list of human rights (65).[12] But why need we think that a list of very basic human rights, the gross violation of which would, in principle, justify intervention, also helps define the target and cut-off point for a duty of assistance in the way Rawls supposes that it does? On the contrary, our ethical thought characteristically exhibits an asymmetry regarding the respective thresholds for forceful intervention and assistance given with the consent of its recipient.

Compare, by way of analogy, our attitude to the state's duties to the family. Typically, we hold that the state should abide by the principle that conditions of family life have to deteriorate rather drastically before any significant measure of forcible intervention is justified—for example, taking severely malnourished or physically abused children into the care of social services. But the cut-off point for the duty of assistance to families, if we can so describe it, is normally held to be well above the point at which things cease being bad enough to warrant state intervention. Thus, we acknowledge societal duties of justice to help families secure access to goods that are considerably beyond what is needed to render them safe from intervention—for example, by providing subsidized nursery places, cultural and recreational facilities, and the like. In short, in the domestic case, we endorse an asymmetry of intervention and assistance. The threshold below which the former is in principle justified is substantially lower than the threshold above which the latter ceases to be a duty.

Consider now the global context in the light of this asymmetry. Since what is being contemplated is *assistance* to another society, there is no apparent reason why the level of the assistance that better-off societies are obligated to provide should not likewise significantly exceed the threshold that renders a society safe from coercive *intervention*. Assistance involves the conferral of benefits on a society with its consent, so there is no issue

---

[12] Although even here, I think, the relationship between human rights and intervention is far looser and more complicated than Rawls allows; see my 2002a, 384–90, and forthcoming.

of violating its political autonomy or of incurring the serious costs attendant on high-risk activities, such as the use of military force. These latter considerations demand that the threshold at which a society is safe from coercive intervention should be set fairly low. But they are inapplicable in the case of assistance. Instead, when it comes to helping another society with its consent, it is natural to suppose that the level at which a duty to render further aid terminates should primarily be determined by the urgency of the interests of the disadvantaged society's members and the burdens that assistance would impose on donor societies. There is every reason to suppose that these considerations will underwrite a threshold of assistance significantly above the threshold below which intervention is in principle warranted.

Now, of course, Rawls is not totally insensitive to the asymmetry of intervention and assistance. He does not straightforwardly *identify* the threshold below which intervention is in principle justified with the lower of the two cut-off points for assistance (and well-orderedness). This is illustrated by his view of benevolent despotisms, which are not well-ordered peoples because of the insufficient level of political participation they allow their members, but whose respect for human rights renders them immune from forcible intervention (4–5, 65). Still, Rawls's theory does not adequately reflect the asymmetry. For when it comes to the *specific* matter of welfare entitlements as a basis for intervention or assistance, the very same standard—the human right to physical subsistence—is operative in both contexts. However sympathetic one might be to the idea that the extensive violation of the right to subsistence is an in-principle trigger for intervention, the reasons already given suggest that its fulfillment does not plausibly form part of the cut-off point for assistance.

There is, then, a bitter irony in Rawls's theory. The minimalist schedule of human rights that shields decent societies from legitimate sanctions and intervention also operates to disqualify them, and their members, from any entitlement to higher levels of assistance. To avoid the irony, we should break Rawls's nexus between intervention and assistance by rejecting the idea that the minimalist schedule of human rights helps to determine, in the way he supposes, both the grounds for intervention and the target and cut-off point of assistance. Another way of putting my suggestion is as follows. Rawls is right about the form of the relevant duty in nonideal theory: it is a duty of assistance with a target and cut-off point. But he is mistaken about the content of that duty, because he sets an insufficiently demanding target, allowing the attainment of a decent society to serve as a cut-off point. Well-ordered peoples should comply with a more exacting requirement of transnational justice. According to my suggestion, this requirement will incorporate a human right to an adequate—not merely subsistence—standard of living.

4. Objections and Replies

Consider now three objections to the more demanding duty of assistance: that it is impractical, unrealistic, and intolerant. The first objection starts from the fact that it is often very difficult to judge whether activities undertaken by one society in relation to another constitute intervention or assistance. In particular, it is often hard to determine whether consent has genuinely been given by the putative beneficiary (perhaps because it is a "weak" state that does not speak with a single, clear voice) or what is really motivating the putative duty-bearer. Moreover, it is arguable that a right to an adequate standard of living is a significantly less clear-cut standard than a right to subsistence. All these sources of indeterminacy make it difficult for societies to be guided by the duty of assistance and create scope for its abuse by powerful states acting to further their self-interest behind a smokescreen of humanitarian rhetoric. One way of addressing these problems is to insist that societies follow a more restrictive and determinate duty of assistance, one that incorporates only those basic human rights whose extensive violation would in principle justify intervention.

This objection can be construed in both moderate and radical versions. The former grants the existence of a more demanding duty of assistance at the level of principle but questions its practical relevance, at least in the foreseeable future. The latter rejects that duty even in principle. Either way, the objection is an important one, not least because considerations of practicality constitute an important argument, supplementing the argument from self-determination (in section 2), for favoring a principle with a target and cut-off point. For in spite of all the serious informational difficulties we face in seeking to comply with the duty of assistance (in either version), they are dwarfed by the difficulties involved in deciding whether the difference principle is satisfied globally.

Now, one immediate response is that Rawls conceives of the duty of assistance as applying to well-ordered societies, and they are not motivated in the self-serving way flagged by the objection. One could restrict the bearers of the revised duty of assistance in a similar manner. But this response is doubly unsatisfactory. First, it is a problematic feature of Rawls's duty of assistance that it appears to be borne exclusively by well-ordered peoples. Why should rich but non-well-ordered states, such as Saudi Arabia, not bear a duty to assist poorer societies to become well ordered in addition to a duty to become well ordered themselves? Indeed, why should non-statelike entities with the appropriate capabilities, such as transnational corporations and nongovernmental organizations, be exempted from the duty of assistance (see O'Neill 2004)? Second, the objection is motivated not only by the risk of bad-faith invocations of the duty of assistance but also more fundamentally by concerns about the very possibility of being determinately guided by the revised duty of assistance even when acting in good faith.

There is, of course, no neat solution to these problems. But it would be rather drastic to conclude that they entirely undermine the revised duty of assistance. Instead, one can take measures to ameliorate their impact, and here global institutions have an important role to play. Ideally, we should not regard the duty of assistance as one that societies, even well-ordered societies, typically comply with bilaterally or through ad hoc collaboration with other societies. This would place undue pressure on their capacities to act impartially and effectively. Instead, global institutions are needed to make authoritative determinations concerning which societies are burdened, whether they consent to assistance, what form it should take, and what contribution various societies should make toward bearing its costs. This means that societies will ideally discharge the duty of assistance through a process mediated by institutions that possess the expertise to make the requisite decisions without incurring quite the same risk of bad-faith manipulation. Of course, institutions charged with duties of this sort already exist, such as the International Monetary Fund and the World Bank, although their legitimacy and effectiveness are open to question.[13] Until an adequate institutional framework is established, it is advisable for states and existing institutions to leave a generous margin for error when complying with the revised duty of assistance. Indeed, it may be that they should concentrate mainly on securing the right to subsistence so far as welfare-based international assistance is concerned. For even in nonideal theory we need to distinguish between short-term and long-term goals. Only an attenuated version of the moderate form of the first objection, I conclude, is plausible.[14]

The second objection takes off from Rawls's own admission that of all the norms that make up the Law of Peoples, it is the duty of assistance and the norms concerned with just war that are most likely to be violated (Rawls 1999, 125). The reasons for this, in the case of the duty of assistance, center on the limited natural sympathies that exist between distinct political communities—a factor that can lead them to under-estimate "the great extent to which human rights are being violated in the foreign society" (126). In light of this situation, the objection goes, to press for an even more exacting duty of assistance transgresses the bounds

---

[13] For a judicious appraisal of the potentialities and "deformities" of international institutions, especially with regard to distributive justice (broadly construed), see Hurrell (2001).

[14] Allen Buchanan argues for this sort of conclusion on the grounds of current institutional incapacity: "[A]t present the nonideal moral theory of international law can include a basic role for human rights (other than rights of distributive justice that go beyond the right to resources for subsistence) but must assign a relatively minor or at least indirect role to more ambitious principles of distributive justice" (2004, 220).

of reasonable hope, tipping us over into a naive utopianism that courts a backlash of resignation, despair, and even violence.

Whether this objection can be refuted depends upon articulating the content of the alternative, more demanding duty of assistance and showing that the burdens it would likely impose are feasible. This is not something I can attempt here. But it is worth observing that the assistance required to achieve the higher cut-off point need not always take the form of large transfers of money or material resources from better-off societies. As Rawls himself insists, assistance can take different, and often less costly and more effective forms (108–09), such as the sharing of expertise, institution building, and the admission of disadvantaged societies into existing global networks of cooperation. In the long run, rendering assistance also serves the duty-bearer's legitimate interests by fostering a peaceful global environment and enhancing the possibilities for mutually advantageous cooperation.

What is more important, however, is that the considerations of feasibility registered by the objection can be taken to affect the content of the duty of assistance in particular cases without warranting the conclusion that a target higher than Rawls's is never obligatory. It is likely that Rawls would accept that the precise implications of the duty of assistance are variable, since some societies might be required to do more than others—or pursue different policies of assistance from others—to help a particular burdened society become well ordered. This may be because of differences in wealth, or in the societies' capacity to render certain forms of assistance effectively given their relative cultural affinity with the burdened society. In defending a stronger duty of assistance against the objection of unfeasibility, one can appeal to another sort of variability in its content, namely, in its target and cut-off point. In other words, the duty of assistance may *sometimes* impose a duty on some societies to assist particular burdened societies beyond the point at which Rawlsian decency is met, but not beyond the point of the more demanding requirement. Why should this possibility be excluded, if the higher target can be met at comparatively little cost?

Consider another response a Rawlsian might offer. The more exacting duty of assistance may be acceptable as an "imperfect" duty of *charity*, one that confers no correlative rights on burdened societies. But the Law of Peoples belongs to the doctrine of international *justice*, which is concerned with perfect duties that are correlative to rights. Only Rawls's more minimal duty of assistance qualifies as a duty of justice. But it is questionable that Rawls could advance this argument, since it is not at all obvious that he thinks of the duty of assistance as a perfect duty, with correlative rights on the part of burdened societies.[15] In any case, on my

---

[15] Pogge 2004a and Buchanan 2004, 209, 215ff., interpret Rawls's duty of assistance as an imperfect duty. This may be because Pogge (unlike Rawls) thinks that only negative

favored reading it *is* a duty of justice. It is not a duty correlative to the human rights of any individual right-holder, since no individual's interest taken in isolation justifies the imposition of such a far-reaching duty to assist in social transformation. But it can be construed as a duty correlative to a right to assistance on the part of the burdened society, the latter being a collective or group right that reflects the cumulative force of the rights of its individual members, including their rights to an adequate standard of living.

There is, however, a third objection that can be extracted from Rawls's text. I have argued that a stronger duty of assistance arises because of a more demanding standard of well-orderedness than Rawls allows. But this heftier standard—one incorporating a human right to an adequate standard of living—violates, it might be claimed, the principle of toleration between peoples. It would, in effect, impose upon decent societies a standard of intrasocietal justice that they have no good reason to accept, thereby unduly limiting their political self-determination. (Or, more precisely, one that they would not be "fully unreasonable" to reject, since decent peoples, by Rawls's lights, are well ordered without having a fully reasonable, that is, liberal democratic, constitution [74]). Instead, Rawls's minimalism about transnational justice reflects our intuitions that the distributional autonomy of a decent society ought to be respected. If, say, a decent society chooses to consign most of its people to a standard of living just above subsistence level in order to secure the virtues fostered by a frugal, pastoral lifestyle, one in keeping with their common good idea of justice, then it would be nothing but cultural imperialism on our part, Rawls might argue, to insist that they adopt a more exacting standard.

Everything here depends, of course, on whether it is "reasonable" for a decent society to deviate from the human right I have proposed. The thesis that the right to an adequate standard of living represents a peculiarly "Western" aspiration, symptomatic perhaps of a distinctively liberal or a consumerist mentality, borders on the absurd. Unfortunately, Rawls never really gets so far as advancing any argument for the parochial character of that right, perhaps because he assumes it would have to be underwritten by an egalitarian principle of transnational distributive justice that nonliberal societies could reasonably reject. More worryingly, he effectively avoids confronting the issue by interpreting the doctrine of human rights in such a way that two separate questions are conflated. The first is: What are the human rights we can reasonably accept, standards which if satisfied would help qualify a society as a member in good standing of the Society of Peoples? The other question is: What are human rights, nonfulfillment of which would in principle justify intervening in another society?

duties are duties of justice, while Buchanan overlooks the restricted meaning Rawls gives to distributive justice.

Rawls pitches the requirements of transnational justice with respect to individual welfare entitlements too low precisely because he thinks that the extensive violation of such a requirement, which would naturally be conceived as a human right, must trigger the in-principle justification of forceful intervention by other societies. This is the flip side of his taking it as definitive of the idea of human rights that "[t]heir fulfillment is sufficient to exclude justified and forceful intervention by other peoples" (80). But, as I have argued elsewhere, there is no compelling reason why human rights should be understood as conceptually bound up with the doctrine of intervention (Tasioulas 2002a and forthcoming). On the contrary, much is to be gained from resisting the assimilation of human rights, which are essentially concerned with the protection of fundamental interests, to the norms regulating coercive intervention between political communities. Which schedule of human rights should ideally be acknowledged is one question. Whether, and if so when, intersocietal intervention is in principle justified is another (indeed, it is many different questions, in line with the great variety of forms intervention can take). The answer to the first question is clearly *relevant* to answering the second question. However, we cannot simply assume that the answer to the first question automatically yields an answer, even a *pro tanto* answer, to the second question.

Once we have drawn this distinction, the path is clearer to affirming a human right to an adequate standard of living, while preserving Rawls's valuable insight that global justice is not liberal democracy writ large. Cultural variation would not, I conjecture, undermine the existence of a human right to an adequate standard of living; instead, it will bear on its interpretation and implementation in different societies. Among the many pertinent considerations here are the following. First, one can certainly have a good life that is focused on spiritual values and the renunciation of worldly goods. But such a life is not feasible for all individuals, or even a majority, within any given society. And even where it is feasible, the value of personal autonomy dictates that people are entitled to options for living a range of different kinds of good life, not all of which are of a narrowly spiritual kind. Second, even a frugal, spiritual existence has material conditions, such as sufficient leisure for contemplation and prayer, liberated from the necessity to procure the means of subsistence, and these are among the conditions that would be secured by a right to an adequate standard of living. Third, in asserting the existence of this right, there is no implication that the right-holders may be coerced by their governments into living an adequately good life.

5. Conclusion

I have sought to offer a sympathetic reading of Rawls's case against international distributive justice and in favor of a duty of assistance. The upshot of my discussion is that we should separate out at least three different standards: the threshold below which intervention is in principle justified, the threshold above which the duty of assistance terminates, and the threshold for a society to satisfy the requirements of ideal theory. Rawls believes that decent societies pass all three thresholds. I have argued that at least some decent societies pass the first without yet reaching the other two. This enables us to accept a more demanding duty of assistance to burdened societies than Rawls endorses, while still agreeing with him that we should reject any principle of international distributive justice. Nothing I have said, however, should obscure the fact that compliance with Rawls's duty of assistance by wealthier and relatively well-ordered societies would amount to a colossal improvement on the intolerable conditions that prevail in the world today.

Acknowledgments

Earlier versions of this essay were presented to seminars in Oxford and the European University Institute in Florence and to the international congress on Rawls held at the University of Lisbon in November 2003. More recent versions were delivered to audiences in Melbourne and Canberra, during my tenure of an Australian Bicentennial Fellowship at the Centre for Applied Philosophy and Public Ethics. I am especially indebted to Thomas Pogge and Christian Barry for their insightful written comments. My thanks are also owed to David Archard, Charles Beitz, Gillian Brock, Tony Coady, Roger Crisp, Patrick Emerton, James Griffin, Tim Lankester, Jeremy Moss, Michael Smith, Janna Thompson, and David Wood for valuable comments.

References

Arneson, R. J. 2000. "Rawls versus Utilitarianism in the Light of *Political Liberalism*." In *The Idea of a Political Liberalism: Essays on Rawls*, edited by Victoria Davion and Clark Wolf, 231–52. Lanham, Md.: Rowman and Littlefield.

Beitz, Charles R. 1999a. *Political Theory and International Relations*. Princeton: Princeton University Press.

———. 1999b. "International Liberalism and Distributive Justice: A Survey of Recent Thought." *World Politics* 51:269–96.

Buchanan, Allen. 2000. "Rawls's Law of Peoples: Rules for a Vanished Westphalian World." *Ethics* 110:697–721.

———. 2004. *Justice, Legitimacy, and Self-Determination: Moral Foundations for International Law*. Oxford: Oxford University Press.

Crisp, Roger. 2003. "Equality, Priority, and Compassion." *Ethics* 113: 745–63.

Franck, Thomas M. 1995. *Fairness in International Law and Institutions*. Oxford: Oxford University Press.

von Hirsch, Andrew, and Nils Jareborg. 1991. "Gauging Criminal Harm: A Living-Standard Analysis." *Oxford Journal of Legal Studies* 11: 1–38.

Hurrell, Andrew. 2001. "Global Inequality and International Institutions." *Metaphilosophy* 32:34–57.

Miller, David. 2000. *Citizenship and National Identity*. Oxford: Blackwell.

Nussbaum, Martha. 2000. *Women and Human Development*. Cambridge: Cambridge University Press.

O'Neill, Onora. 2004. "Global Justice: Whose Obligations?" In *The Ethics of Assistance: Morality and the Distant Needy*, edited by D. Chatterjee, 242–59. Cambridge: Cambridge University Press.

Pogge, Thomas. 1994. "An Egalitarian Law of Peoples." *Philosophy and Public Affairs* 23:195–224.

———. 2001. "Priorities of Global Justice." *Metaphilosophy* 32, nos. 1/2: 6–24.

———. 2002. *World Poverty and Human Rights: Cosmopolitan Responsibilities and Reforms*. Cambridge: Polity Press.

———. 2004. "'Assisting' the Global Poor." In *The Ethics of Assistance: Morality and the Distant Needy*, edited by D. Chatterjee, 260–88. Cambridge: Cambridge University Press.

———. 2004b. "The Incoherence between Rawls's Theories of Justice." *Fordham Law Review* 72:1739–60.

Rawls, John. 1999. *The Law of Peoples*. Cambridge, Mass.: Harvard University Press.

Sen, Amartya. 1981. *Poverty and Famines*. Oxford: Oxford University Press.

———. 1999. *Development as Freedom*. Oxford: Oxford University Press.

Shue, Henry. 1996. *Basic Rights: Subsistence, Affluence, and U.S. Foreign Policy*. 2nd edition. Princeton: Princeton University Press.

Steiner, Hillel. 1994. *An Essay on Rights*. Oxford: Blackwell.

Tasioulas, John. 2002a. "From Utopia to Kazanistan: John Rawls and the Law of Peoples." *Oxford Journal of Legal Studies* 22:367–96.

———. Forthcoming. "The Moral Reality of Human Rights." In *Freedom from Poverty as a Human Right: Who Owes What to the Very Poor*, edited by Thomas W. Pogge. Paris: UNESCO.

Walzer, Michael. 1993. *Spheres of Justice: A Defense of Pluralism and Equality*. Oxford: Blackwell.

———. 1995. "Replies." In *Pluralism, Justice, and Equality*. edited by Michael Walzer and David Miller, 281–97. Oxford: Oxford University Press.

3

ASSESSING GLOBAL POVERTY AND INEQUALITY: INCOME, RESOURCES, AND CAPABILITIES

INGRID ROBEYNS

1. Introduction

Are there fewer people living in poverty today than there were ten or twenty years ago? Is inequality between the poor and the rich countries decreasing? Do people in poor countries benefit from economic globalization? Have they become better off thanks to the policies of the International Monetary Fund (IMF) and the World Bank? Will their children face a better future and live happier lives, or does the available evidence suggest otherwise?

The answers that are typically given to these questions differ dramatically. Scholars, politicians, and social activists on the left of the political spectrum tend to answer the questions in the negative. Barbara Ehrenreich and Arlie Russell Hochschild, for example, write that "over the last thirty years, as the rich countries have grown much richer, the poor countries have become—in both absolute and relative terms—poorer" (2002, 8). The activists' collective Notes from Nowhere claims that "the central fact of our time is the upwards transfer of power and wealth—never have so many been governed by so few" (2003, 25). Similarly, Sarah Anderson, John Cavanagh, and Tea Lee assert that "wherever globalization impinges, inequality deepens. From Mexico to Japan, the rich are getting richer while the poor are becoming more desperate and numerous" (2000, x).

Most mainstream economists, scholars and politicians on the right, and spokespeople of the World Bank and the IMF answer these questions in the affirmative, giving much more upbeat assessments of current levels and trends in global poverty and inequality. Recently, the World Bank argued that between 1981 and 2001 the number of people below the poverty line of one dollar a day had halved (World Bank 2004a, b). According to David Dollar and Aart Kraay, "the best evidence available shows ... [that] the current wave of globalization, which started around 1980, has actually promoted economic equality and reduced poverty" (2002, 120). However, Branko Milanovic (2002), who was at the time working at the World Bank, calculated on the basis of improved data for the period 1988–1993 that world income inequality is not only very high but has also been rapidly increasing.

Those who claim that global capitalism is a force for good for the world's poorest people, and that inequality in the world is decreasing, often argue that those who think otherwise are ignorant at best and despite their good intentions may even damage the causes they defend. *The Economist* (2004), for example, writes that both global poverty and inequality are decreasing, and that social activists and global-justice scholars are doing "nothing but harm" to the world's most destitute people by opposing global capitalism.

In this essay I will discuss three evaluative approaches that can be used to assess well-being, poverty, and inequality in the context of globalization and global justice. By spelling out these three approaches, and by looking at their differences and their respective weaknesses and strengths, I will try to shed some light on the different languages and conflicting claims made by advocates and critics of global capitalism regarding the current levels and trends in global inequality and poverty. These three frameworks are income metrics, resourcism, and the capability approach. Sections 2 to 4 discuss each of the three evaluative frameworks in turn. Section 5 clarifies an obscurity in the debate between resourcism and the capability approach. Section 6 analyzes a core difference between Rawlsian resources and the capability approach: the question of whether conceptualizations of inequality and social justice should account for naturally caused inequalities. Section 7 then takes up the core question of this essay: What are the advantages and disadvantages of each of these evaluative frameworks for the assessment of global poverty and inequality? I will defend the claim that these frameworks can best be seen as complementary, rather than purely rival alternatives. Section 8 analyzes Thomas Pogge's claim that capability metrics, and the Human Development Index in particular, conceal global inequality.

2. Income Measures

Most statistics and assessments of world poverty and inequality are constructed using money metrics, that is, using income as the variable of comparison. In economic theory, it is standard knowledge that income can only serve as a proxy for individual welfare under specific assumptions (for example, the absence of negative externalities, such as environmental damage), and at the cost of neglecting production in the nonmarket economy. Income, despite its limitations in fully registering individual welfare, let alone well-being or the quality of life, is widely used because there is no consensus on a better alternative, and income is one-dimensional and thus allows for precise calculations and estimates.

Comparisons between countries, especially between poor countries and affluent ones, only complicate such calculations. As Robert Wade (2003) notes, these complications include the fact that these comparisons can be made using exchange rates, general-consumption purchasing-power parities, or purchasing-power parities that are based only on the goods typically consumed by the poor. The income data for some countries (including very large countries, such as China) is also unreliable. For the poverty statistics, there are problems caused by the fact that the income distribution is very flat at its lower end, implying that choosing a slightly higher poverty line could lead to a large increase in the number of officially poor. With respect to inequality statistics, it is generally acknowledged in welfare economics that they are sensitive to the measure chosen (Sen 1973).

What, then, are the results derived from the empirical studies of income trends? Some economists claim that the number of extremely poor people worldwide is declining and that the global gap between rich and poor is getting smaller (Chen and Ravallion 2004; Dollar and Kraay 2002; *The Economist* 2004; World Bank 2004b).[1] Other researchers have either used other data which suggest that income inequality is increasing rapidly (Milanovic 2002) or have criticized the World Bank poverty estimates, arguing that these conclusions are unwarranted and that the number of poor may even be increasing (Pogge and Reddy 2003; Reddy and Pogge 2003; Wade 2003).

At present the World Bank is the only producer of global poverty statistics. For the past few years, the World Bank has published annual estimates of global poverty, announcing any trends in the data with press releases that are then widely cited. In April 2004, the World Bank (2004a) announced in a press release that global poverty had halved since 1981. The number of poor people in developing countries, defined as those living on less than $1 a day, had dropped from 1.5 billion in 1981 to 1.1 billion in 2001. In percentages, this amounts to a reduction of extreme poverty from 40 percent to 21 percent of the total population in the developing countries.

We should note, first of all, that this press statement is inaccurate and misleading, as it tells us that the extremely poor people are those who have to live on less than a dollar a day. For many readers in affluent societies, this probably sounds like a plausible poverty line. Such readers are likely to believe that in Malawi or Bangladesh $1 must buy a local person quite a lot, as everything is assumed to be cheap. But this is not what these poverty statistics really measure: in fact, "a dollar a day" is shorthand for "the purchasing-power parity of $1.08 in the United States in 1993." In other words, a person is poor if he or she has to get by with fewer commodities than one could have bought with $1.08 in the United States in 1993. Such misleading press releases conceal the fact that the

---

[1] However, Chen and Ravallion's estimates (2004) also show that the 400 million fewer people living below the $1 a day line are almost entirely situated in China, and that the number of the poor under the $2 a day line increased between 1981 and 2001.

World Bank's poverty line is very low, which drastically reduces the poverty incidence, thereby downplaying the catastrophic nature of the current global poverty levels.[2] Indeed, according to the latest estimates by top economists of the poverty unit of the World Bank, the global poverty count went up over the same period if one uses the "two dollars a day" poverty line (Chen and Ravallion 2004). The fact that a global poverty estimate is so sensitive to its poverty line should make us cautious about the significance that can be attached to these estimates, and about how readily they are presented to the public as uncontested facts. After all, which newspaper reader has any comprehension of the difference between getting by on the purchasing-power equivalent of $2 rather than $2?

There are thus two problems with this debate: the wider public is not likely to comprehend fully the significance (or insignificance) of the 1$ a day poverty line, and the World Bank does not sufficiently highlight the contested nature of its poverty estimates, as this would jeopardize its own policy agenda.

In addition, Sanjay Reddy and Thomas Pogge have formulated a crushing critique of the World Bank's poverty statistics (Pogge and Reddy 2003; Reddy and Pogge 2003). They argue that the $1 a day poverty measure is arbitrary and lacks any conceptual foundations. The World Bank's poverty counts are not based on how we think of poverty, as people being undernourished or without shelter, or lacking other basic necessities. Instead, the global poverty line is chosen as the median of the lowest domestic poverty lines for the countries in the World Bank's data set (Reddy and Pogge 2003, 5–6; Ravallion 2003, 4). The World Bank's calculations also use purchasing-power parities that take into account the price levels of *all* goods and services in proportion to their share in the international consumption expenditure. In this calculation, the prices of basic necessities play a minor role, whereas they play a huge role in the consumption of the poor. Services in developing countries are relatively cheap in comparison with the consumption prices of basic necessities, which make up the consumption of the poor. Finally, Pogge and Reddy also show that the World Bank's method is internally inconsistent, and that a change of base year can have significant effects on the poverty estimates. They conclude that at this moment we do not know how many people in the world are poor, but that the biases in the current methodology most likely lead to an underestimation of the incidence of global poverty.

Reddy and Pogge do not suggest that we give up monitoring global poverty. Instead, they offer the outline of an alternative methodology,

[2] For a more profound critique of how the international discourse on global poverty tries to conceal the catastrophic situation of extreme poverty, in the context of the first U.N. Millennium Development Goal (which is based on the same World Bank poverty statistics), see Pogge forthcoming.

whereby an international poverty line would be developed starting from some basic capabilities or needs, which should be selected through an international deliberative process, and using the amount of money that would be needed to meet such needs to make international poverty comparisons:

> The serious flaws in the [World] Bank's method have a common root and are avoidable through a straightforward innovation: the definition of severe income poverty must be more appropriately focused on what being poor consists in: on what people generally need to achieve a set of elementary capabilities, rather than on arbitrary dollar amounts. (Reddy and Pogge 2003, 12)

It is remarkable that in his reply to Pogge and Reddy World Bank economist Martin Ravallion (2003) does not address this foundational critique. He argues that he would be surprised if consensus were possible on a fixed bundle of goods, as people consume different things in different countries, whereas there is consensus on the $1 a day concept. Angus Deaton (2003) uses the same argument that the $1 a day concept can rely on a consensus and has proven its value because it is widely used.

This strikes me as a poor argument in favor of the $1 a day concept. First, it is not clear that this supposed consensus actually exists. *All* simple statistics produced by international agencies are widely used (especially in the media), and this reflects less about their quality than about their availability and the authority of the institutions that produce and circulate them. Second, while the consensus on the $1 a day concept might be a consensus in Washington or among the supporters of World Bank methodologies and policies, it is certainly not a consensus among other people concerned with poverty and destitution. Social activists might well ask how on earth one should be able to survive on what $1 could have bought in the United States in the 1990s. But more important, applying Pogge's and Reddy's method would not, as Ravallion claims, require a consensus on specific commodities (such as rice or bread); rather, it would require a consensus on certain valuable states of being, such as being well nourished and minimally dressed and having access to some basic shelter. The poverty line would be defined as the money needed to buy the cheapest possible bundle of commodities that would deliver minimum levels of those crucial dimensions of well-being.

3. Classifying Resources

A second approach to global poverty and inequality assessments is resourcism. It is possible to identify at least five different accounts of resources that might be used in such assessments.

Type 1: GNP per capita. Gross national product (GNP) is the total income generated through market production in a particular country, after deduction of the cost for the inputs in this production. An increase in GNP per capita is economic growth, which is a crucial goal of macroeconomic policies. GNP per capita is a rough indicator of economic production, and its use as a proxy for well-being or the quality of life is dubious. Environmentalists have argued that GNP ignores whether economic production and the basic institutions in society are damaging or protecting our environmental resources. Feminists have argued that it ignores unpaid nonmarket production, like domestic production, and especially the vital activities of caring. More generally, GNP per capita values economic production in terms of its market value-added (that is, price minus the total costs), even if it concerns weapons production that will subsequently be used to oppress or kill people. Because it has been one of the few statistics available for each country, however, it has been widely used in research on global poverty and inequality.

Type 2: Individual disposable income. Welfare and development economists who work on the microeconomic aspects of development focus on individual disposable income, or in case one is looking at people who live partly in a subsistence economy, on consumption directly. These measures were discussed in the previous section.

Type 3: Individual entitlement of material goods. This notion extends individual disposable income by including an estimate for nonmarket production and the provision of public goods, and thus it gives us a more extended account of resources than does individual disposable income. This type of resource is used in more fine-grained micro studies in welfare economics but hardly ever in discussions about global poverty and inequality.

Type 4: Dworkinian resources. Dworkin's (1981) philosophical theory of equality distinguishes between two types of resources, impersonal resources and personal resources. Dworkin's impersonal resources are equivalent to individual entitlement to material goods. Personal resources in Dworkin's account are personal bodily and mental resources, like intelligence, physical and mental abilities and disabilities, and so forth.

Type 5: Rawlsian social primary goods. These resources are the goods that a rational person is presumed to want regardless of whatever else she may want. Social primary goods include income, wealth, liberties, opportunities, and the social basis of self-respect (Rawls 1999; 1982; 2001, 57–61). Thus, Rawlsian social primary goods are a combination of individual disposable income (type 2) and some civil and political human rights, opportunities, and the social basis of self-respect. Note that Rawls does not include the Dworkinian personal resources. I will discuss the implications of this in section 6.

4. Functionings and Capabilities

A third and final approach to assessing global inequality and poverty is the capability approach (Sen 1980; 1985; 1992; 1993; 1999).

As I pointed out earlier, welfare economics generally focuses on the means to achieve a good life, which are consumer goods and services, or the resources needed to generate them. Sen's core claim is that goods are important not in themselves but in what their characteristics enable people to do and to be, that is, in the capabilities that a person can generate from these goods and services. The extent to which a person can generate capabilities from goods and services depends on the factors that determine how smoothly this conversion can be made.

Three different types of conversion factors can be distinguished: social, environmental, and personal. The social conversion factors are determined by a number of societal aspects, such as social institutions (for example, the educational system, the political system, the family, and so on), social norms (including gender norms, religious norms, cultural norms, and moral norms), traditions, and the behavior of others in society (for example, stereotyping, prejudiced behavior, racism, sexism, homophobic behavior, and so forth). The environmental conversion factors are determined by the environment in which a person lives—for example, whether deforestation has caused erosion and flooding that threaten the stability of one's shelter. The personal conversion factors are determined by one's mental and physical aspects; these personal characteristics, such as disabilities or bodily vulnerabilities, affect the type and degree of capabilities one can generate with resources. Note that not all capabilities require some good or service as an input; for example, being respected by your peers often only requires respectful behavior from other people. A person's capability set, which comprises all the capabilities of a person, represents her freedom to achieve well-being and agency—and this is the dimension that Sen proposes as the informational basis for assessments of inequality, poverty, justice, and development. However, as a person's capabilities are her real and genuine opportunities to do what she wants to do and be the person she wants to be, these capabilities obviously are difficult to observe. Instead, what we can observe are those capabilities she has chosen to act upon, the capabilities she has chosen to realize. These realized capabilities are called her achieved functionings.

An important aspect of the capability approach, but one that is extremely hard to measure, is people's agency. The capability approach refuses to see people as patients, who can be helped by being given a handout or a cure that they can take or leave, but sees them rather as agents, who can and should be given the power and the necessary conditions to take their lives into their own hands. While agency may be relatively less important in the discussion of the capability approach as an approach to the *assessment* of inequality and poverty than it is in debates on policy design and public action, it has some bearing on the debate on global justice, as I will try to argue toward the end of the essay.

5. Capabilities versus Resources: A Clarification

Capability theorists and resourcists have formulated arguments for or against a particular type of resource for a specific purpose, such as the conceptualization of social justice or measurement of the quality of life. Sometimes the conclusion of these arguments have subsequently been used in another debate, without sufficiently acknowledging that some arguments in favor of (or against) one type of resource are convincing for some purposes but not for others.

For example, in his comparison of capability and Rawlsian resourcist accounts of social justice, Pogge argues that the feminist critique formulated by capability theorists is orthogonal to the comparison between resourcist and capability approaches (Pogge 2002a, 183–84). Capability theorists have criticized resourcist accounts of types 1, 2, and 3 by arguing that these resourcist accounts conceal inequalities between men and women. But Pogge reads this critique as if it were formulated as a comparison between the capability approach and resources of type 5—that is, social primary goods. While Pogge may perhaps be right that feminist arguments are orthogonal to the contrast between the capability approach and Rawlsian social primary goods, they are certainly not orthogonal to the contrast between the capability approach and resources as GNP per capita, individual disposable income, or individual entitlement to material goods. There are some structural reasons why income measures are unsuited to a nonreductionist account of gender inequality, including the fact that they cannot account for intrahousehold inequalities and also do not allow for the fact that while women may be worse off in most areas of life, men might be worse off in some other areas (Robeyns 2002; 2003).

Sen's writings have also sometimes failed to distinguish between different strands of resourcism. By discussing real income, Dworkinian resources, and Rawlsian social primary goods simultaneously, and by insufficiently explaining and stressing the differences between different types of resources, Sen has contributed to the belief that objections against one type of resourcist account can be generalized to others. For example, in *Development as Freedom,* in a section entitled "Incomes, Resources and Freedoms," Sen discusses real income, Rawlsian social primary goods, and the critique by Mahbub Ul Haq (1995) and the United Nations Development Program (UNDP) on the dominance of GDP. In that section, Sen also downplays the differences between social primary goods and resources understood as individual entitlement to goods when he writes:

> The broadening of the informational focus from incomes to primary goods is not, however, adequate to deal with all the relevant variations in the relationship between income and resources, on the one hand, and well-being and freedom, on the other. Indeed, primary goods themselves are mainly various

types of general resources, and the use of these resources to generate the ability to do valuable things is subject to as much the same list of variations ... in the context of reviewing the relationship between income and well-being: personal heterogeneities, environmental diversities, variations in social climate, differences in relational perspectives and distribution within the family. (1999, 72–73)

Sen is suggesting here that Rawlsian social primary goods boil down to material impersonal resources. This seems to me an unwarranted reduction of social primary goods, since liberties and opportunities and especially the social basis of self-respect go well beyond individual entitlements to material goods. Thus, Sen's capability critique of real income cannot automatically be extended to social primary goods. In conclusion, the debate between the capability theorists and resourcists can only be properly conducted if we distinguish more carefully between different types of resources.

6. Are Natural Endowments Morally Relevant?

Pogge (2002a) argues that the real difference between Rawlsian resourcists and capability theorists is whether they hold that natural endowments, such as disabilities, should give rise to compensatory claims of justice. I do not have the space here to make a full and detailed analysis of how the capability approach and Rawslian social primary goods deal with issues of disability and other natural endowments in theories of social justice, as this sort of analysis would require us to discuss other aspects of theories of justice as well, such as the Rawlsian social contract, the Rawlsian idea of the original position, and the underspecification of the capability approach (but see Brighouse 2001; 2004; Kittay 1999; Robeyns 2004). Instead, I will limit my analysis here to the question of whether *in the context of global inequalities and poverty* the evaluative metric should be sensitive to natural endowments.

Let us first take the case of international aggregate comparisons of poverty and inequality, that is, the comparison of countries. If the natural endowments that are negatively affecting the conversion of resources into functionings are randomly distributed among those countries, then the differences in poverty or average welfare levels between different countries will not be very much affected by whether we use a social primary goods or a functionings metric. To put it somewhat more precisely, the ranking of countries in terms of poverty count or average welfare level will not be affected. However, if the natural endowments are not randomly distributed in the world—that is, when some countries have many more disabled people than other countries—then international comparisons will be affected by the choice between a disability-sensitive versus a disability-insensitive metric. For example, income metrics, or social primary goods metrics, are unable to register the HIV/AIDS pandemic when making international comparisons, as these metrics are sensitive only to the indirect effects of HIV/AIDS on the distribution of primary goods and income, whereas the effects on functionings are much more devastating.

If we want to make microcomparisons of poverty and inequality, the case for moving beyond social primary goods and income to include deprivations in functioning because of handicaps is even stronger. If any of the resourcist approaches want to be able to make a claim that social institutions should be designed so as to limit the loss in quality of life caused by a disability, then they need to appeal implicitly or explicitly to a metric of well-being that must take into account how different resources affect functioning (Brighouse 2004). Pogge is concerned that acknowledging natural endowments in the capability approach leads to a stigma on the disabled. However, it is not at all clear that acknowledging a disability and providing the necessary financial compensation for additional medical and nonmedical expenditures would create any stigma. I submit that so long as a natural endowment significantly affects some core functionings, there is no inherent and unavoidable stigma in compensation for any additional costs needed to try to enhance these functionings. The difficulty for a government is how to demarcate those natural endowments and functionings that are a legitimate concern for government intervention, such as being paralyzed and unable to hold a job or move around, from those that are not, such as being sufficiently handsome to attract a sexual partner. The capability approach definitely needs to do more work in spelling out such distinctions, but I subscribe to its principle that we should not ignore all effects of natural endowments on people's functionings.

It seems to me that most people would—rightly—see the lack of compensation for the additional costs of trying to expand one's capabilities that are affected by a disability as an injustice, whereas Pogge holds that this falls outside the scope of justice:

> Even if there are some of us who have special needs and disabilities that the rest of us have no duties *of justice* to alleviate—because we did not contribute to their emergence and do not benefit from their existence—we may nonetheless have other quite stringent moral reasons individually or collectively to engage in such alleviation: duties of humanity towards all human beings, for example, or duties of solidarity towards those with whom we share a common political life. (2002a, 189–90, italics in original)

As Kittay (1999), Brighouse (2001), and others have pointed out, it is remarkable that the social primary goods approach sees our duties toward the disabled as lying outside the scope of justice—especially since Rawls regards justice as the first virtue of society. I fail to see how this disagreement about the scope of justice can be solved with rational arguments. However, it does make a difference for measurements of poverty and inequality: if these measurements are to correspond to a notion of justice, the social primary goods approach will be unable to pick up the negative effects of disabilities on a person's quality of life, in contrast to the capability approach.

7. Comparing Assessments Based on Income, Resources, and Functionings

Income metrics, resources metrics, and capability metrics are based on different theoretical conceptualizations of the quality of life. Income and resources metrics focus on the means of the quality of life, while capability metrics focus on the constitutive elements of the quality of life.

The consequence of the different conceptual foundations between income metrics, primary goods metrics, and functionings/capability metrics is that the last are able to process information that the former two cannot, information that may change the overall assessment of inequality or poverty. Let us look at two examples. First, take the case of Filipino women who leave their families to work as nannies in North America and Europe. Most of these Filipinas have children of their own, whom they leave in the care of their own mothers, their sisters, or a nanny back home. In financial terms, this "international care chain" is undoubtedly a positive process, as the Filipinas earn significantly more than they could in the Philippines, and they might create an income-generating opportunity for someone back home. An evaluation in terms of social primary goods would lead to the same conclusion. The remittances they send home feed, clothe, and shelter their own children and also provide an income for the women who are taking care of these children. Sometimes another family member, like the father, is able to start a small business, although sometimes the money sent home may also be spent on alcohol. According to Rhacel Salazar Parreñas (2002, 41), remittances constitute the largest source of foreign currency in the Philippines, totaling almost $7 billion in 1999. Such capital flows surely have a tempering effect on global poverty and inequality measurements of the type discussed in section 2.

However, if we do not assess this type of care worker's emigration in terms of income or resources but rather make assessments based on achieved functionings, the situation looks different. Several authors argue that while the financial evaluation may be positive, there are also nonfinancial effects that are negative (Ehrenreich and Hochschild 2002; Hochschild 2002; Parreñas 2002). It is estimated that 30 percent of Filipino children grow up in a household where at least one parent is working oversees (Hochschild 2002, 22), and that these children suffer "inevitable trauma" (Ehrenreich and Hochschild 2002, 13). The children endure emotional hardship, and older siblings are often forced to take on the role of substitute parents. Parreñas's (2002) study shows that these children suffer the loss of family intimacy and feel that they are denied time with their parents, and they all say that they would never leave their own children to take jobs as migrant workers. As one child in her study puts it, "Time together is something that money can neither buy nor replace" (Parreñas 2002, 51). The mothers, too, suffer emotional hardship, as they badly miss their children. While most mothers try to keep in touch with their children through letters, phone calls, and the odd visit back home, it is very doubtful that they can develop a profound emotional and social relationship with their children. As a result, some of these mothers are abandoned by their adult children later in life. In sum, the capability approach has the theoretical tools to pick up this morally relevant information that is overlooked by income metrics or resourcist approaches that are broader, such as social primary goods.

A second example illustrating this claim is Sabina Alkire's (2002) fieldwork in Pakistan, in which she evaluated three different poverty-reduction programs. Alkire (2002, 233–96) found that one project had a much greater positive effect on the inner peace of people and on their social relations. When these nontangible effects and the monetary effects go in opposite directions, the overall evaluation explicitly needs to address the trade-offs between monetary and nonmonetary effects. Suppose global poverty is decreasing, as the World Bank wants us to believe. If this comes at the expense of nonmonetary capabilities, such as democratic agency, respect, emotional well-being, and social cohesion, the overall evaluation is not automatically positive but would ultimately depend on what one values most. Mainstream economists tend to value only income, while social activists often value democratic agency and social relations very highly. A capability evaluation can make full theoretical sense of this. A social primary goods evaluation can make some theoretical sense of it, but not what concerns emotional and social-relation capabilities, except if one stretches the notion of social primary goods way beyond Rawls's original definition. An income evaluation is unable to capture these trade-offs at all.

The example of Filipino immigrant workers and their love-deprived children does, however, also indicate the main limitation of the capability approach: that it is difficult to operationalize and has structural limitations in measurement, because there are many morally relevant functionings and because many nonmaterial functionings, such as the quality of parental relationships, are very hard to measure. Economists generally hold that parsimony is a virtue; the capability approach obviously does not share that view. Achieved functioning levels can be measured, as the empirical survey in Kuklys and Robeyns (2004) shows. But often a capability assessment will be imprecise. Capability theorists are not bothered too much by this, since they hold that an ambiguous and complex phenomenon should not be assessed with measurement tools that are designed for precise phenomena. But obviously it will be hard to make inequality comparisons among more than 150 countries based on a multidimensional selection of fuzzy functionings. As the literature mentioned in section 2 makes abundantly clear, it is already hard enough to try to measure global poverty and inequality one-dimensionally. This would thus suggest that income, resources, and functionings based assessments should be seen as complementary to one another. However, Christian Barry (2003) has argued that these measurement problems will also be encountered by the more plausible resourcists views, such as Rawlsian social primary goods. In terms of measurability, there seems to be a continuum, with the most simple income metrics at one end and the most complex version of the capability approach at the other.

Apart from this complementarity, we could also ask whether income metrics, social primary goods, and capabilities correspond to a macro-micro continuum. A micro assessment allows for an abundance of data and a subtle weighting of all the different dimensions, but these often get lost in macro assessments. Of course, this is not to claim that income is unimportant at the microlevel, or that functioning achievements have no information to add at a macrolevel. Good counterexamples of the latter are the data on the numbers of girls and women "missing" from the aggregate population statistics, caused by female infanticide and sex-selective abortion (Sen 1990; Klasen and Wink 2003). These statistics, which could be understood both as a social primary good (the liberty to live) or as a capability (the capability to live) but which would never be captured by an income metric, do tell us something important about international differences in this dimension of gender inequality.

As we've seen from the discussion in this section, both capabilities and the different types of resources have strengths and weaknesses. I would therefore suggest that we start from the general assumption that both informational bases have advantages, and that either one of them, or both, might be appropriate to use, depending on the concrete kind of inequality or poverty analysis under consideration. Thus, I would suggest that the basic point of departure should be to consider *both* approaches, and to ask which one should be used for the assessment of local and global inequalities and poverty.

8. Does the Human Development Index Conceal Global Inequalities?

The Human Development Reports (HDRs) (UNDP 1990–2004) and in particular the widely used Human Development Index (HDI) are based on the capability approach, although it is fair to say that they are not the most refined applications of the capability approach. In his elaborate critique of the capability approach, Pogge also criticizes the HDI, arguing that it conceals global inequalities:

> Among economists, these issues—how global inequality is steadily increasing and how global institutional arrangements are exacerbating poverty and inequality—are taboo. In fact, the UNDP took heavy flak for printing [that inequality increased at a 3.04 average percentage during the 1990–97 post-cold-war globalization period]. By comparing countries in terms of their HDI

scores, the UNDP now avoids such unpleasantness. Its tables of countries and their HDI scores (ranging from Norway's 0.942 to Sierra Leone's 0.275) are of merely ordinal significance and thus provide no information about inequality or inequality trends. HDI scores convey no sense of what life is like for the majority of people in a poor country. And they encourage the thought that each country is solely responsible for its own development. (Pogge 2002a, 216)

And a few paragraphs further on, Pogge concludes:

[T]he large increase in global inequality and the consequent persistence of massive severe poverty in the developing world have contributed to the stunning success of the capability approach in international organizations as well as in popular and academic discourse. Capability metrics tend to conceal the enormous and still rising economic inequalities which resource metrics make quite blatant. (217)

There is some truth in this statement about the limited usefulness of the HDI if one wants to focus on global inequality. Indeed, Mahbub ul Haq (1995), who founded the Human Development Reports, has been quite clear in his writings that he believes that developing countries have primary responsibility for their own development, which clearly contrasts with Pogge's (2002b) focus on the responsibility of rich countries for the current state of affairs in the poor countries. Based on my present knowledge of the causal evidence, it seems to me that one needs both arguments, though I am sympathetic to Pogge's view that we must become more aware and analyze in more depth the degree to which the current international global structures create an injustice for which the rich countries are primarily responsible. If that is our goal, I agree that the HDI is not the appropriate assessment tool.

However, at least four arguments can be developed in defense of the HDI and the capability approach. First, the HDRs offer a much broader discussion of poverty and inequality in human development than the HDI only. Every HDR contains some narratives of best practice and failed strategies and adds much more detail and qualitative assessment than the HDI alone can capture. Thus, while the HDI might conceal the pervasiveness of poverty and inequality, the full reports do pay more attention to these issues.

Second, it is possible that the selection of capabilities in the HDI is so limited that it downplays global inequalities. If that is the case, then Pogge's critique of the UNDP is in fact a critique of the *selection* of the capabilities in the HDI, not of measuring inequality and development in capabilities per se. For example, advocates of the virtues of global capitalism often argue that the outsourcing of jobs to the South creates jobs for local people there, who accordingly improve their net disposable income, which will also be picked up by the income, poverty, and inequality measures of the World Bank. But these jobs vary enormously in their quality and thus can lead to drastically different effects on people's capabilities, such as being treated with dignity, having control over one's time-allocation, reproductive freedoms (as young women are often fired or not hired if they are pregnant), sexual safety and bodily integrity, occupational health, and so forth. These capabilities are obviously not captured by the HDI.

Third, insofar as the HDI conceals inequalities, we should ask to what extent this is due to its ordinal character, rather than the fact that it goes beyond GDP per capita to include some proxies of functionings. Pogge does not disentangle these two effects in his critique.

Fourth and finally, there is nothing that prevents us from using the HDI and income metrics simultaneously. To get a clear picture of trends and levels of inequalities, Pogge is right that global income inequality statistics remain vital. But they will not tell us the full story, perhaps not even half the story, of the current trends in local and global inequalities. I see no reasons why they could not be used simultaneously, given that they shed a different light on the subject matter.

It is somewhat ironic that Thomas Pogge himself, in two papers written with Sanjay Reddy, can be interpreted as providing a strong case for the capability approach as the basis of global poverty assessments. But while it is ironic, it need not be inconsistent. Pogge (2002a) *only* analyzes the capability approach as the basis of a theory of social justice, whereas the capability approach is also used in a range of areas that do rely on a capability-related notion of well-being without addressing issues of justice per se, such as poverty measurement, cost-benefit analysis, efficiency evaluations, and inequality evaluations. Pogge might thus hold the internally consistent view that the capability approach is useful for poverty measurement, but not as the foundation for a theory of social justice.

As explained in section 2, Reddy and Pogge advocate a capability-based global poverty assessment as an alternative for the $1 per day poverty line used by the World Bank to monitor trends and levels of severe poverty (Pogge and Reddy 2003; Reddy and Pogge 2003). In my view, their work provides a very good illustration of one way in which the complementariness between resources and capabilities could work. Recall that their proposal is that "the definition of severe income poverty must be more appropriately focused on what being poor consists in: on what people generally need to achieve a set of elementary capabilities, rather than on arbitrary dollar amounts." Pogge and Reddy's proposal shows that while the philosophical foundation of a poverty assessment could be in terms of achieved functioning levels, poverty could be translated into a monetary value so that the statistical comparison will be expressed in an income metric. Thus one is able to have a poverty measure that has a sound conceptual meaning and can be translated back to the income dimension in order not to compromise its measurability.

Pogge may not have conceived of his proposal in terms of capabilities, but in my understanding this is a capability metric (more precisely, an achieved-functionings metric), not a resource metric. It is a capability metric that defines the poverty line as the monetary value of the bundle of social primary goods needed to achieve the thresholds of the selected functionings. However, if Pogge and Reddy's conceptualization of poverty is interpreted as a functionings measure, then it should be noted that it does not account for each individual conversion factor. It will not, for example, account for differences in metabolic rates. As discussed in section 7, only measures at the microlevel allow for these fine-grained dimensions of the capability approach, whereas capability measures at the macrolevel, such as the global poverty statistic, will always have to make some simplifications.

9. Conclusion

In the past decade, issues of global poverty and inequality have regained renewed interest. In large part this is due to political activism of the global social movement (see, e.g., Fisher and Poniah 2003, Hertz 2002, Notes from Nowhere 2003, Roy 2001). These social activists are often reproached for ignoring the "fact" that inequality and poverty are decreasing, thereby doing more harm than good to the global poor through their anticapitalist activism.

My analysis of the literature suggests a different understanding. It suggests that so far as monetary assessments are concerned, there is substantial disagreement about the actual size and especially the trend of global income poverty and inequality. The confident rhetoric in the World Bank's press releases, along with the often insulting and arrogant tone in the articles by those who think that poverty and inequality are decreasing, may convince the broader public, but it does not get us any closer to the truth.

Moreover, another reason why social activists' views are so strongly at odds with those of their opponents might be that they use a very different evaluative framework. In this essay I have spelled out three main evaluative frameworks. Social activists are closer to a capability account (with particular attention to democratic capabilities) than to resourcist or income-based evaluations. I have provided arguments for why additional considerations should be taken into account when addressing whether the poorest people are better off and global inequality is less severe than before. If we endorse the conceptual arguments of the capability approach to well-being assessment, we would need to look at a wider range of issues, among them those that include people's agency. A person can live with a fixed amount of financial resources, but in one scenario she has relative economic security and control over her own labor, while in another she is vulnerable to the whims of the global capitalist markets and the bosses of the international corporations and their local subcontractors. Social activists would say that the purely income-based poverty and inequality measures cannot give us any information on people's democratic capabilities, that is, the extent to which they have a fair political decision-making power over things that matter to them. Activists generally have a comprehensive view of what poverty and inequality mean, not a view that first reduces poverty and inequality to economic poverty and economic inequality and then reduces them even further to income inequality.

People's agency to take their lives into their own hands and to make collective decisions about how to organize their communities and manage their commons can be as important for them as to secure minimal material or financial welfare. While the quantifiable functionings and capabilities may well be limited in capturing these dimensions, the overall framework of the capability approach gives a clear rationale for why we should pay due attention to nonmaterial dimensions, such as family time together, emotional well-being, and democratic agency. And it is precisely on those latter dimensions of agency and democracy that many of the social activists focus, dimensions that the purely income-based indicators of poverty and inequality are unable to capture.

Acknowledgments

An earlier version of this essay was written while I was a visiting scholar in the Department of Philosophy at Columbia University, New York, and was presented at the University of Maryland and Bryn Mawr College. For comments and discussions, I am grateful to Christian Barry, Harry Brighouse, David Crocker, Thomas Pogge, Roland Pierik, and Sanjay Reddy. The financial support of the Dutch Organization for Scientific Research, NWO, is also gratefully acknowledged.

Bibliography

Alkire, Sabina. 2002. *Valuing Freedoms: Sen's Capability Approach and Poverty Reduction*. New York: Oxford University Press.

Anderson, Sarah, John Cavanagh, and Thea Lea. 2000. *Field Guide to the Global Economy*. New York: New Press.

Barry, Christian. 2003. "Education and Standards of Living." In *A Companion to the Philosophy of Education*, edited by Curren Randall, 456–70. Oxford: Blackwell.

Brighouse, Harry. 2001. "Can Justice as Fairness Accommodate the Disabled?" *Social Theory and Practice* 27, no. 4:537–60.

———. 2004. "Primary Goods, Capabilities, and the Problem of the Public Criterion of Justice." Paper presented at the Annual Meetings of the American Political Science Association, Chicago, September 5–7.

Chen, Shaohua, and Martin Ravallion. 2004. "How Have the World's Poorest Fared since the Early 1980s?" *World Bank Research Observer* 19, no. 2:141–69.

Deaton, Angus 2003. "How to Monitor Poverty for the Millennium Development Goals." *Journal of Human Development* 4, no. 3:353–78.

Dollar, David, and Aart Kraay. 2002. "Spreading the Wealth." *Foreign Affairs* 81, no. 1:120–33.
Dworkin, Ronald. 1981. "What Is Equality? Part 2: Equality of Resources." *Philosophy and Public Affairs* 10:283–45.
Ehrenreich, Barbara, and Arlie Russell Hochschild. 2002. Introduction. In *Global Woman: Nannies, Maids and Sex Workers in the New Economy*, edited by Barbara Ehrenreich and Arlie Russell Hochschild, 1–13. London: Granta Books.
Fisher, William, and Thomas Ponniah, eds. 2003. *Another World Is Possible*. London: Zed Books.
Hertz, Noreena. 2002. *The Silent Takeover: Global Capitalism and the Death of Democracy*. London: Arrow. First published in 2001.
Hochschild, Arlie Russell. 2002. "Love and Gold." In *Global Woman: Nannies, Maids and Sex Workers in the New Economy*, edited by Barbara Ehrenreich and Arlie Russell Hochschild, 15–30. London: Granta Books.
Kittay, Eva Feder. 1999. *Love's Labor: Essays on Women, Equality, and Dependence*. New York: Routledge.
Klasen, Stephan, and Claudia Wink. 2003. "'Missing Women': Revisiting the Debate." *Feminist Economics* 9, nos. 2–3:263–99.
Kuklys, Wiebke, and Ingrid Robeyns. 2004. "Sen's Capability Approach to Welfare Economics." Cambridge Working Papers in Economics no. 0415. University of Cambridge. Available at http://www.econ.cam.ac.uk/dae/repec/cam/pdf/cwpe0415.pdf
Milanovic, Branko. 2002. "True World Income Distribution, 1988 and 1993: First Calculations Based on Household Surveys Alone." *Economic Journal* 112 (January):51–92.
Notes from Nowhere. 2003. "Emergence: An Irresistible Global Uprising." In *We Are Everywhere: The Irresistible Rise of Global Anticapitalism*, edited by Notes from Nowhere, 19–29. London: Verso.
Parreñas, Rhacel Salazar. 2002. "The Care Crisis in the Philippines: Children and Transnational Families in the New Global Economy." In *Global Woman: Nannies, Maids and Sex Workers in the New Economy*, edited by Barbara Ehrenreich and Arlie Russell Hochschild, 39–54. London: Granta Books.
Pogge, Thomas. 2002a. "Can the Capability Approach Be Justified?" *Philosophical Topics* 30, no. 2:167–228.
———. 2002b. *World Poverty and Human Rights*. Cambridge: Polity Press.
———. Forthcoming. "The First UN Millennium Development Goal: A Cause for Celebration?" *Journal of Human Development*.
Pogge, Thomas, and Sanjay Reddy. 2003. "Unkown: The Extent, Distribution, and Trend of Global Income Poverty." Mimeo, Columbia University, New York.
Ravallion, Martin. 2003. "How *Not* to Count the Poor? A Reply to Reddy and Pogge." Mimeo, World Bank, Washington, DC.

Rawls, John. 1999. *A Theory of Justice*. Revised edition. Oxford: Oxford University Press. Original published in 1971.

———. 1982. "Social Unity and Primary Goods." In *Utilitarianism and Beyond*, edited by Amartya Sen and Bernard Williams, 159–86. Cambridge: Cambridge University Press.

———. 2001. *Justice as Fairness: A Restatement*. Edited by Erin Kelly. Cambridge, Mass.: Harvard University Press.

Reddy, Sanjay, and Thomas Pogge. 2003. "How *Not* to Count the Poor." Version 4.5. Mimeo, Columbia University, New York.

Robeyns, Ingrid. 2002. "Gender Inequality: A Capability Perspective." Unpublished Ph.D. dissertation, University of Cambridge.

———. 2003. "Sen's Capability Approach and Gender Inequality: Selecting Relevant Capabilities." *Feminist Economics* 9, nos. 2–3:61–92.

———. 2004. "Justice as Fairness and the Capability Approach." Paper presented at the Annual Meetings of the American Political Science Association, Chicago, September 5–7.

Roy, Arundhati. 2001. *Power Politics*. Second edition. Cambridge, Mass.: South End Press.

Sen, Amartya. 1973. *On Economic Inequality*. Oxford: Clarendon Press.

———. 1980. "Equality of What?" In *The Tanner Lectures on Human Values*, edited by S. McMurrin, 195–220. Salt Lake City: University of Utah Press.

———. 1985. *Commodities and Capabilities*. Amsterdam: North Holland.

———. 1990. "More Than 100 Million Women Are Missing." *New York Review of Books*. December 20.

———. 1992. *Inequality Re-examined*. Oxford: Clarendon Press.

———. 1993. "Capability and Well-Being." In *The Quality of Life*, edited by Martha Nussbaum and Amartya Sen, 30–53. Oxford: Clarendon Press.

———. 1999. *Development as Freedom*. New York: Knopf.

The Economist. 2004. "Special Report: Global Economic Inequality." 13 March, 69–71.

Ul Haq, Mahbub. 1995. *Reflections on Human Development*. New York: Oxford University Press.

UNDP. 1990–2004. *Human Development Report*. New York: Oxford University Press.

Wade, Robert Hunter. 2003. "The Disturbing Rise in Poverty and Inequality: Is It All a 'Big Lie'?" In *Taming Globalization*, edited by D. Held and M. Koenig-Archibugi, 18–46. Cambridge: Polity Press.

World Bank. 2004a. "Global Poverty Down By Half Since 1981 But Progress Uneven As Economic Growth Eludes Many Countries." News Release 2004/309/S. 23 April.

World Bank. 2004b. *World Development Indicators*. New York: Oxford University Press.

4

BOUNDARY MAKING AND EQUAL CONCERN

KOK-CHOR TAN

The Problem

The fact of state boundaries is often said to be an "embarrassment" for liberals. On the one hand, on one understanding of liberal egalitarian justice the idea of equal opportunity applies globally to all individuals regardless of nationality or citizenship. On the other, taking political boundaries seriously seems to limit the ideal of equal opportunity to members within a state. While few commentators hold that foreigners count for nothing and that citizens of a society have no moral obligations whatsoever to foreigners, it is sometimes thought that the idea of equal opportunity—that individuals are entitled to the same background social and economic conditions under which to further their goals in life—is an ideal that applies among citizens but not globally. One reason for this is the belief that individuals are entitled (if not required) to show greater concern for their compatriots, and the basic institutions of their society could (or should) be designed to reflect this special patriotic concern; this patriotic concern seems to deny the ideal of global equal concern that an account of global equal opportunity must presuppose in some form.

This tension between global equal opportunity and patriotic concern is thought to be most pronounced for liberal nationalists. Liberal nationalists hold that all states, including liberal ones, ought to be in the business of nation building. According to liberal nationalists, as we will see in greater detail below, the liberal vision of a just political society in which the ideals of individual autonomy, democracy, and social justice flourish is best realized when citizens share a common nationality; hence it is important for a state actively to engender a common national culture and a sense of shared nationality among its citizens. Yet integral to any nationalist doctrine is the idea that members of a nationality may (indeed, are obliged to) show special concern for each other. As David Miller points out, "In acknowledging a national identity, I am also acknowledging that I owe a special obligation to fellow members which I do not owe to other human beings" (1995, 49). On this view, "there is no general obligation to help poorer states," in the sense that there is no place for a global distributive ideal, such as a global equal-opportunity principle (108). And this partial concern for fellow nationals, or conational partiality as I will call it, seems to contradict the ideal of global equal concern that *liberal* nationalists should support. This is one reason why Bhiku Parekh thought the doctrine of liberal nationalism to be "incoherent."[1]

Of course, the liberal nationalist may wish to escape this tension by renouncing the ideal of global equal concern.[2] Yet, other liberal nationalists openly affirm that they remain committed to global egalitarianism of some form. For example, Will Kymlicka has argued that as part of its nation-building project, the liberal state may regulate immigration into its society. Yet this will potentially run against the ideal of equal opportunity, Kymlicka concedes, unless the liberal state takes seriously its duties of global distributive justice. In short, for Kymlicka, liberal nation building, including the restriction of immigration, is permissible only if global equality of opportunity is not undermined (2001a, 270; also Tamir 1993, 161). The challenge for liberal nationalists who want to maintain the ideal of global equal concern is that they must be able to show how this global commitment is consistent with the idea of conational partiality, that "the existing use of boundaries to define and protect distinct national languages, cultures and identities is not inherently in conflict with liberal egalitarian values" (270).

I will suggest that the tension between global equal opportunity and conational partiality disappears once we clarify what it is that liberal nationalists are partial about. The relevant question for global egalitarianism is not whether liberal nationalism entails conational partiality but what kind of conational partiality it entails. Or, to put the question in a familiar form, what we need to ask is: "Conational partiality *with respect to what?*" My claim is that nothing in the theory of liberal nationalism presupposes an account of conational partiality that is antithetical to the ideal of global equal concern. To make this claim, I begin by recalling some of the basic features and goals of liberal nationalism. Then I consider these features and goals of liberal nationalism and examine whether each of these presupposes or requires an account of conational partiality that is at odds with global equal concern. I argue that while some kind of partiality is of course inevitable under liberal nationalism, it is not the kind of partiality that is troublesome for global equal concern.

---

[1] Parekh criticizes liberal nationalism, saying that the "nationalist privileges the moral claims of one's fellow nationals and assigns only a limited moral weight to those of outsiders" (1998, 316). To be sure, how strong Parekh's worry is depends upon how "limited" the weight given to outsiders is and how strong the "privileges" to conationals are. But, for Parekh, it is certain that the idea of global equal opportunity is ruled out for the nationalist, for even if outsiders do not count for nothing, they do *count for less* than one's fellow nationals.

[2] Without intending that he considers himself a liberal nationalist, see Richard Miller's "Cosmopolitan Respect and Patriotic Concern" (1998). Miller argues that global justice does not require global equal concern, and hence needs no commitment to global distributive equality in the forms that are familiar in discussions on domestic justice.

But before beginning my argument, let me make explicit the back-ground assumptions in this essay. I assume that there is a case for global equal opportunity and that this presupposes a form of global equal concern.[3] I also accept as given the doctrine of liberal nationalism. Thus, while some global egalitarians may say that it is so much the worse for nationalism if it allows for conational partiality, I will not proceed in this way.[4] I will not claim that there is nothing worth retaining in the idea of conational partiality as such. My intention is rather to show how one can be both a liberal nationalist and a committed global egalitarian. Further, I do not claim that all conceptions of liberal nationalism will be compatible with global egalitarianism. Indeed, some professed liberal nationalists openly reject the idea of global egalitarianism.[5] My present goal is not to show that all liberal nationalists must or should be global egalitarians but that the basic features and tenets of liberal nationalism need not necessarily be at odds with global egalitarian commitments. I will be focusing specifically on the problem posed by conational parti-ality, and will therefore allow that there may be other factors about national boundary making that can render it incompatible with global equality. Still, because the problem of conational partiality is one of the central challenges for global egalitarians, I believe it is important to dispel the misperception that the liberal idea of conational partiality is necessar-ily incompatible with liberal global equal concern. And to the extent that some liberal nationalists reject global egalitarianism on the ground that it contradicts the idea of conational partiality, my claims, if successful, will remove this particular source of resistance.

The Aims of Liberal Nation Building

In his defense of nationality, David Miller argues that democratic politics "are likely to function most effectively when they embrace just a single national community" (1995, 90). This is because the virtues of mutual trust and respect, moderation and self-restraint, to which one may add the ideal of public reason (Rawls 1993), are crucial for a functioning democratic political community; and common nationality provides the catalyst for engendering and nurturing these virtues. In addition, the ideals of distributive justice presuppose a community in which "members recognize such obligations of justice to one another" (Miller 1995, 93). In other words, "[w]here citizens of a state are also compatriots [i.e., conationals], the mutual trust that this engenders makes it more likely that they will be able to solve collective action problems, to support

---

[3] For one defense, see Caney 2001.

[4] See Parekh 1998; also Barry 1999.

[5] See David Miller (forthcoming) for some recent nationalist arguments against global egalitarianism. I discuss more fully the nationalist objections to global egalitarianism in Tan 2004, part 2, and Tan 2002.

redistributive principles of justice, and to practice deliberative forms of democracy" (98).

In much of contemporary political philosophy it has been thought that liberalism and nationalism are antithetical ideals and that, to the extent that liberal democracy and liberal egalitarianism must presuppose an underlying national community, liberalism is doomed to failure (MacIntyre 1984, Sandel 1992).[6] However, an increasing number of liberal theorists are coming to accept that some shared identity is required to sustain liberal democratic and welfare institutions, and that this may call for more than (pace Habermas) an allegiance to shared political values and principles (Kymlicka 1995, McMahan 1997, Yack 1999). They claim that the liberal democratic state must be undergirded by a common national community, and that to inculcate and foster this common nationality, the liberal state has to engage in some form of nation building (Kymlicka 2001b, chaps. 10, 11; Tamir 1993). Indeed, historically, liberals have been more attuned to the centrality of the nation. J. S. Mill famously thought that the success of liberal institutions in a given society depends on there being a common national culture.[7] The liberal state may, therefore, adopt and enforce certain policies to integrate all citizens into what Kymlicka has called a societal culture—that is, a set of public and social institutions operating with a common language (2001b, 1995)—to try to achieve this overlap between nation and state.

Liberal nationalists argue also that nationality, besides serving as the basis for democracy and social justice, provides the moral precondition for individual autonomy. This is because membership in a national community defines the cultural "context of choice" within which individuals form, pursue, and revise their conceptions of the good life and acquire their sense of identity and belonging (Kymlicka 1989, 1995; Margalit and Raz 1990; Tamir 1993).

Briefly put, then, liberal nation building serves the three core liberal ideals of (1) autonomy, (2) democracy, and (3) social justice (Kymlicka 2001b, 224–29). It is in the context of a national community that these liberal values can be best and most fully realized. For this reason, Tamir says that nationalism is a "hidden agenda" of liberalism and that "most liberals are liberal nationalists" (1993, 139).

Thus, the contrast between liberal states and nonliberal ones "is not *whether* states engage in nation-building, but rather what *kind* of nation-building" (Kymlicka 2001a, 262). Liberal nationalism is not predicated on what we may call the "Romantic-Collectivist" account of the nation (Canovan 1996, 6), whereby the nation is taken as a moral entity in itself,

---

[6] For instance, Sandel writes that Rawls's "difference principle ... is a principle of sharing. As such, it must presuppose some prior moral tie among those whose assets it would deploy and those whose efforts it would enlist in a common endeavour" (1992, 22).

[7] Mill, *Considerations on Representative Government* (1861), chap. 26.

with intrinsic worth and able to command individual sacrifices for its ends. Instead, for liberal nationalists, the moral standing of a nation depends on how it contributes to the well-being of its individual members. Also, liberal nationalism is an inclusive form of nationalism, based on a common societal culture that is in principle open to all, unlike exclusive forms of nationalism based, say, on the dubious yet selective notion of race.[8] Concerning immigration, for example, liberal nationalism would not permit restricting immigration on the basis of racial or ethnic criteria. The aim of liberal nationalism here would not be to protect a given racial or ethnic identity but would instead be to protect a national culture defined in terms of its political and public institutions and common language. The problem, then, is not that nonnationals cannot in principle be integrated into the national culture so defined (as they could not in the case of racially based nationalism) but that integration into a common societal culture takes time, and therefore too open an immigration policy might risk overwhelming a national culture at a given time. It is thus too quick, so argue liberal nationalists, to dismiss any form of immigration restriction as illiberal.[9] Some rationale for, and ways of, regulating immigration are more liberal than others; and a liberal conception of nationalism would strive to meet the requirements of the former.

Let me now examine whether liberal nationalists can be global egalitarians. Does liberal nationalism entail the kind of partial concern for conationals that is antithetical to egalitarian global justice? One way of answering this question is to see if the three stated goals and aims of liberal nationalism described above—individual autonomy, deliberative democracy, and social justice—rely on or entail a form of conational partiality that is contrary to the demands of global equal opportunity.

Nationality and Individual Autonomy

Consider first, then, the goal of securing the cultural context of choice for individual autonomy and the basis of individual identity. If it is correct that a person's national institutions, practices, and traditions serve as the cultural framework within which he or she meaningfully forms, pursues, and revises his or her conceptions of the good, then it follows quite plainly that liberal nationalism has to promote and foster a *particular* national or societal culture. Liberal nationalism is openly premised on the basic idea that individuals have certain predispositions or inclinations toward their own national culture: their own national culture, not another, gives their choices meaning; their nationality, not another, provides the basis of their identity.

---

[8] See Kymlicka 2001b for more discussion on liberal ways as opposed to nonliberal ways of nation building.

[9] But for one well-known liberal argument in favor of open borders, see Carens 1987. For an opposing liberal view, see Pogge 1997.

Thus liberal nation building is unavoidably biased in a real sense: it aims to engender and promote a given national culture for the benefit of its adherents. It helps secure for members of a nation access to *that* nation's cultural resources, without doing the same for nonnationals outside its borders.

But nothing about privileging conationals' access to their nation's cultural resources entails prejudicial attitudes or hostility toward other nations. A liberal nationalist can accept that the cultural institutions of other nations are as valuable to their respective members as her own institutions are to her, and that other states are as entitled to promote their own national cultures as her own state is.[10] More to the point, such partiality is not antithetical to the goals of global justice: nothing in the privileging of conationals' access to a cultural context is incompatible with the demands for global equality. As I mentioned, the idea of equal opportunity calls for a set of background conditions and allocation of goods and resources within which persons can all freely and fairly pursue their ends. But nothing in the idea of favoring the cultural life of one's nation necessarily interferes with this global egalitarian objective. The demands of cultural protection and global equal opportunity are two very different and distinct ones.

A more problematic form of conational partiality would be one that wants to privilege conationals' access to *material* resources as well. It is conational partiality in this sense—of privileging their access to the primary goods (if we like) of income and wealth—that would pose a serious obstacle to global equality, and it is conational partiality in this sense that is specifically at issue in debates about national partiality and global justice.[11] But even here one can say that a nation can privilege its members' access to material goods so long as it also supports the appropriate background global context required by the idea of equal opportunity. This will mean, in effect, that nations may privilege their members materially only within the rules of a just global distributive structure. Thus, conational partiality with respect to resource distribution presents a challenge for global egalitarians only if this partiality with respect to resources means that nations need not provide support for a just global distributive arrangement in the name of favoring their members' material interests.

The interesting question, then, is whether liberal nationalism requires or rests on this form of conational partiality—a partiality with respect to

[10] This is one crucial condition that sets *liberal* nationalism apart from *illiberal* forms of nationalism. Also, in this regard, liberal nationalists should accord minority nations within the state special rights to mitigate the effects of state nation building. See Kymlicka 2001b and 1995. But I will leave this important point of minority rights aside here and focus more on the implications of nation building for global justice.

[11] For an account of primary goods, see Rawls 1971, 93. For why cultural membership is also a primary good, see Kymlicka 1989.

resources and a partiality with respect to the design of the background global distributive framework. Let us examine the two parts of this question in turn. First, does the promotion of the national *cultural* context of choice require that the liberal state privilege conationals' over nonnationals' access to *material* resources? It is far from clear that it does. While the liberal nationalist's argument for autonomy necessarily favors the claim of conationals to their national culture, it says nothing, one way or the other, about privileging their claim to material resources. That the state ought to privilege the national cultural context of choice for its citizens alone does not entail that it should also privilege their access to material goods over that of strangers.

Another way of making the above point is in terms of the different values one can be cosmopolitan about. The cosmopolitan view, which is implicit in liberal accounts of global justice, holds that individuals are the ultimate units of moral concern and are entitled to equal consideration no matter where they reside. Here, Samuel Scheffler's distinction between "cosmopolitanism about culture" and "cosmopolitanism about justice" is illuminating. Cosmopolitanism about culture rejects the view that "individuals' well-being or their identity or their capacity for effective human agency normally depends on their membership in a determinate cultural group" (Scheffler 1999, 256). Instead, it believes that the truly free or autonomous individual is one who is not bounded within a particular cultural context but is culturally mobile, even culturally detached, and hence able to access and enjoy different cultural ways of life.[12] Cosmopolitanism about justice, in contrast, is not directly a view about culture. Rather, it is a conception of justice that "opposes any view which holds, as a matter of principle, that the norms of justice apply primarily within bounded groups comprising some subset of the global population" (256). Concerning distributive principles, for instance, cosmopolitan justice would say that how material goods and resources are to be distributed among individuals should be decided independently of the national boundaries within which individuals happen to be.

It should be evident that liberal nationalism, as I have described it, clearly rejects the cosmopolitan view about culture.[13] But it does not follow from this that it also has to reject cosmopolitanism about justice; nothing about liberal nationalism's denial of cultural cosmopolitanism rests on rejecting cosmopolitan justice. If anything, the liberal starting

---

[12] For a defense of cultural cosmopolitan, see Waldron 1992. See Kymlicka 1995 for one reply.

[13] Some liberal nationalists, of course, accept cosmopolitanism about culture. For them, liberal nationalism is a nationalism centered around certain political principles and ideals rather than culture (e.g., Ignatieff 1993, 6). But most liberal nationalists think that this culturally neutral account of nationalism is incoherent. I will not pursue this point here, my task being that of reconciling a culturally based liberal nationalism with the demands of global justice. But see, e.g., Kymlicka 1995 and Tamir 1993 for further discussion.

point of liberal nationalism would require that it endorse the cosmopol-itanism view of justice.[14]

Now it might be objected that if one is serious about rejecting cosmopolitanism about culture, one cannot also be fully committed to cosmopolitan justice. This is because, so the objection goes, if one takes the promotion and protection of one's national cultural identity to be a morally significant and legitimate goal, one is also likely to insist on greater resources for the purpose of such cultural protection, and may legitimately have them. After all, the more resources a given community has, the better able it is to promote and sustain its culture, all things being equal. Jeff McMahan makes a related point when he thinks that conational partiality is justifiable (to some extent) on the ground that materially "benefitting them [conationals] contributes to the flourishing of the nation" (1997, 130).[15]

This is a forceful objection, but I do not think that it is decisive. There is no doubt that if one takes cultural protection seriously, and if more resources means better cultural protection, then one would want to have more rather than fewer resources to this end. But the crucial issue here is whether it would be *legitimate* for one to acquire or retain more than one's fair share of resources for this purpose of protecting culture. That liberal nationalism takes it to be a legitimate (and indeed required) goal of states to promote and protect their own national cultures does not mean that it also accepts that this nationalistic end justifies any means. Among other things, it does not follow that a state may hang on to, or acquire, more than its *fair share* of resources and wealth in the name of nation building. The liberal starting point of liberal nationalism imposes typically liberal constraints on the pursuit of the nationalist agenda. And one typical liberal constraint is that of cosmopolitan justice. In short, liberal nation-alism operates within this larger question: "What resources and other means may a state legitimately employ to pursue its nationalist goals?" Liberal nationalism tells us how and why liberal states have to engage in national building, but cosmopolitan justice tells us what resources and methods are *rightly* at their disposal in the pursuit of this goal.

The discussion above thus provides a response to the second part of the question—whether conational partiality means that special concern for conationals is a legitimate consideration when determining the back-ground conditions of global distributive justice. Liberal nationalists can easily accept the cosmopolitan ideal of justice that holds that the principles of global distributive justice be determined independently of nationalist commitments. They can insist that the background social and economic institutions of the world, among other things, be impartially designed with respect to people's national membership and commitments, while permit-ting conational partiality within the rules of the just global structure. This

---

[14] Again, see Beitz 1979 and Pogge 1989.
[15] I thank Carol Gould for pointing out this possible objection to me.

does not show that all liberal nationalists must accept the priority of cosmopolitan justice.[16] It shows, rather, that there is nothing inherent in the idea of conational partiality *with regard to cultural belonging* that requires privileging the national standpoint when deliberating on the terms of global distributive justice. To take an example from a more familiar context, we accept that partiality among family members is reasonable and permissible within the bounds of justice for the domestic society, even though nothing in this account of familial partiality entails that such partiality may determine the terms of domestic justice.

Partiality and Liberal Democracy

Consider, next, the second objective of liberal nationalism—that of facilitating deliberative democracy. As I mentioned, the virtues of democratic citizenship, such as civility, mutual respect and trust, self-restraint, and public reasonableness presuppose a shared identity or solidarity among citizens. Moreover, as Kymlicka has argued, "democratic politics is politics in the vernacular": a common national language allows citizens to engage in political deliberation, to understand the symbols and customs of political deliberation, and is moreover itself an expression of democratic self-determination (2001a, 269–70).

But we have seen that there is no tension between promoting and participating in a particular societal culture while remaining a committed liberal universalist. That is, liberal nationalists can be actively partial toward conationals' access to their national language (or languages) without also having to be partial toward their living standards (that is, we may privilege the language but not the *material* interests of the users of that language). To repeat an earlier point, these are very distinct and separable categories of partiality. A "politics in the vernacular" can be secured without hindering global egalitarian commitments.

Does the realization of other ideals that are preconditions for democracy, such as mutual trust and respect, depend on some form of compatriot favoritism?[17] To answer this question, we must answer perhaps a more basic question: Why should deliberative democracy depend on mutual respect and trust?[18]

---

[16] I try to do this in Tan 2004.

[17] Another problem global justice might allegedly present for deliberative democracy is that the demands of global justice may appear to limit the domestic decisions of states. But my concern here is specifically with the ideals of mutual respect and trust that are integral to deliberative democracy, and the challenge is that mutual respect and trust between people requires some form of special concern among them. As for whether global justice can limit domestic decisions, let me just say that if these limitations are limitations as required by justice, then these will not be limitations against democratic decision making. We do not say that democratic decision making is compromised because a state may not collectively decide to engage in a war of aggression on the grounds that this would constitute a violation of international justice and law.

[18] I thank Will Kymlicka for helpful discussion here.

Deliberative democracy depends on certain mutual trust and respect because individuals are required to *respect* each other as autonomous agents capable of advancing and accepting reasonable and rational arguments in defense of each other's positions, and to respect the outcome of democratic procedures. And citizens can reasonably be expected to accept outcomes that they disfavor only if they can *trust* that, should the democratic process rule in their favor next time, the opposing side would honor that result.

If this is the function of mutual respect and trust with respect to deliberative democracy, it is not clear why conational partiality with respect to material distribution is required to support it. How does conational partiality motivate the respect of conationals as autonomous rational agents and instill the trust that they will honor democratic outcomes regardless of how their interests are affected? Merely assuming that solidarity, trust and respect, loyalty, fellow feelings, and conational partiality (the commonly cited list of national sentiments) must simply go together as a package begs the question. An argument is needed. And while some forms of nationalism may insist on conational partiality as inseparable from all these other national sentiments, liberal nationalism need not. Indeed, saying that conational partiality provides the necessary fuel for democracy would seem to reduce the democratic ideal to a form of bribery, or at best an association motivated entirely by self-interest.

If fostering the mutual trust and respect that are required for deliberative democracy is dependent on conational partiality, then this indicates a tension between global egalitarianism and deliberative democracy in general and is not peculiar to liberal nationalism. Further, it seems to involve a more general and controversial claim, which is that the very idea of the democratic state is antithetical to global egalitarianism. In any case, it remains to be shown that the fostering of mutual respect and trust *for the purpose of democratic deliberation* must rest on the practice of conational partiality.[19]

Furthermore, one could speculate in the opposite direction as well and say that conational partiality at the cost of injustices toward outsiders, rather than fostering mutual respect and trust within a nation, would breed mutual contempt and suspicion. It is just as likely that a nation that favors members' needs by ignoring the needs of strangers is unlikely to be a nation within which the ideals of trust and respect among individuals can flourish. Engels's observation that "a nation cannot become free and at the same time continue to oppress other nations" is quite apt here (cited in Cunningham 1995, 104).[20] This suggests that instead of enabling

---

[19] I am not suggesting that this problem thus disappears. Rather, this challenge has much wider (than intended) implications for the very idea of deliberative democracy.

[20] Or we may recall Plato's point that the ideals of cooperation, trust, and respect are likely to be absent within a band of thieves (*The Republic* 351d). On the contrary, generalizing from Plato again, it seems to me that mutual trust and respect are more conducively engendered in a nation that treats other nations justly.

deliberative democracy, neglecting the demands of global distributive justice in the name of conational partiality may in fact disenable it.

Shared Nationality and Social Justice

As I mentioned above, the liberal welfare state assumes that citizens are "mutually indebted and morally engaged to begin with" (Sandel 1992, 23), that they share a common moral world. Liberal citizens are thus expected to look beyond kin and neighbors and to include fellow citizens who are virtual strangers within their scope of moral concern. One way the moral horizons of individuals can be broadened beyond their parochial and traditional ties is by establishing a common nationality. Common nationality may thus provide the bond that transcends the physical and personal gulf between citizens of a modern state by drawing them into what David Miller calls a common "ethical community" (Miller 1995, 48).

But this creation of a moral community, it is said, inevitably leaves some people out, namely, noncitizens outside the country's borders. The worry is that insofar as liberal nationalism succeeds in expanding our moral world beyond our parochial ties, it does so only by limiting that world to the nation-state. Liberal nationalism risks championing a kind of moral isolationism in which an abiding sense of moral identity is enhanced nationally through excluding or weakening that identity globally.

If this is right, the project of liberal nation building is in trouble: the right of a state to maintain its culture by means of regulating its immigration policy, which is dependent on its fulfilling its obligations of global justice, has to be forfeited because the project of creating a national identity undercuts that very commitment. Of the three goals of nation building, the goal of promoting social justice within the state seems to pose the most serious obstacle to the liberal commitment to global justice.

But this worry may be exaggerated. If liberal nation building aims to extend the moral boundaries of individuals to include fellow citizens who are practically strangers and succeeds in doing so, then why should we think that such efforts cannot be sustained beyond the national boundaries? As Charles Jones asks, why not capitalize on this "expansionary momentum" to expand the scope of our moral concern beyond conationals to include also foreigners (1999, 160)? To assume that the construction of our moral world has suddenly to cease at our national borders seems arbitrary at best. To be sure, more arguments must be provided here to support this possibility (though there is evidence that this can be done—for example, the European Union), but one should not foreclose the discussion by assuming that national boundaries are morally impermeable, or that these boundaries fix once and for all the outermost limit of our moral sphere.

Parekh worries that "[i]f people are constantly told that they should care for each other because they belong together and if their educational, cultural, and other institutions are designed, as they must be, to reinforce this message, their moral imagination gets so emasculated and moral resources so depleted that outsiders will come to mean little to them" (1998, 316). But we can see now that this worry is too hastily voiced. That people are to be taught that they should "care for each other [i.e., conationals]" does not mean that they must be taught to care *exclusively* for each other; that our institutions must be designed to "reinforce this message" of national affinity does not mean that these institutions cannot also be designed to reinforce our cosmopolitan aspirations and commitments. If the original moral aim of nationalism is expansionary —to extend individuals' moral spheres to include not just kin, friends, and fellow tribesman but also their fellow citizens—there is no reason why nation-building aspirations cannot be supplemented by cosmopolitan aspirations. Both nationalism and cosmopolitanism push our moral horizons in the same direction—toward strangers—and hence provide complementary rather than conflicting aspirations.

Thus Amy Gutmann (responding to similar worries raised by Martha Nussbaum) argues that education for democratic *citizenship* and educating people to be moral *cosmopolitans* (in the sense that they are taught their duties to humanity at large) are not mutually exclusive projects (cf. Nussbaum 1996, 16; Gutmann 1996, 71). In fact, Gutmann goes on to argue that global justice might best be realized through democratic *citizenship* participation and education. She notes: "Democratic citizens have institutional means at their disposal that solitary individuals, or citizens of the world, do not. Some of those institutional means are international in scope..., but even those tend to depend on the cooperation of sovereign societies for effective action" (1996, 71).

If this is right, then instead of thwarting cosmopolitan aspirations, liberal nationalism may in fact be a vehicle for pursuing them. Take away national solidarity, and we take away democratic citizenship, and in doing so we risk surrendering an arena—the democratic state—within which liberal citizens can effectively fight for a better world. Moreover, it might be said that the weakening of national ties will have the opposite effect of driving people back into their subnational and parochial moral communities, instead of turning them into enlightened cosmopolitans. So, rather than expanding our moral horizons, disbanding national solidarity—*without a viable alternative basis of solidarity*—may in fact contract them (Kymlicka 1999; also Gutmann).

Here one might object that if the aim of nation building is to create a moral community, attempts to expand this moral community outward to include foreigners will thwart this very aim. "The idea of distributive justice presupposes a bounded world within which distribution takes place," as Walzer has put it (1983, 31). Yet, the objection continues, aspirations to global justice threaten that very world. Either we give preference to conationals (that is, maintain a limited but viable moral world) or we treat everyone equally but incapacitate ourselves morally. In other words, caring equally for all is incompatible with caring for our own—the demands of domestic justice and the demands of global justice pull us in opposite directions.[21]

If this is a comment about our moral attitudes, it is rather implausible. It assumes that individuals can consistently inhabit a morally split mental world, that one's intolerance of injustice at home is indirectly proportionate to one's intolerance of injustices abroad. There seems, however, to be more unity and consistency in moral attitudes; those who are indifferent about injustices abroad tend also to be indifferent about injustices domestically, and vice versa. The sorts of attitudes that would lead one to ignore foreign injustices are similar in kind to the sorts that would lead one to ignore domestic injustices (barring those directly affecting one and one's immediate circle). After all, we cannot say of conationals that they have a stronger pull on us because they are kin, more familiar, or intimate. Conationals are for the most part also strangers; thus to the morally indifferent, there is no significant difference between a local stranger and a foreign stranger. It seems to me that if we could not succeed in making people care for strangers *outside* their borders, we would not have succeeded in making them care for strangers *within* their borders; and that we do succeed in making people care for strangers within gives us hope that they too can be made to care for strangers without.[22] Indeed, the objection's assumption that there is an inverse relationship between national sentiments and the commitment to global equality needs more substantiation. It is interesting to note that the Scandinavian countries, whose stricter immigration policies are suggestive of strong national cultural sentiments, typically contribute more to foreign aid than do countries like Australia, Canada, and the United States, which are traditionally referred to as "immigrant" societies. This suggests that a strong nationalist need not be an indifferent internationalist.

Indeed, it seems to me that most arguments that nationalistic moral sentiments are in conflict with concerns for foreigners posit a condition of stark global scarcity such that concern for outsiders will be at the significant expense of one's commitments to conationals. Alasdair MacIntyre, for instance, famously discusses the tension between the nationalist particularist and universalist liberal viewpoints in terms of conflicts over resources seen as absolutely scarce (1984, 6). His point is that the liberal universalist will not be able to account for the patriotic sentiment

---

[21] One may refer to Rawls's comments on the "strains of commitment" here (1971, 145).

[22] In this regard, consider the dismal foreign-aid contributions (and isolationist policies) of Western governments that are also hostile to domestic welfare programs.

of going to war on behalf of one's nation against another over scarce resources (he uses the example of scarce fossil fuels). This illustrates for MacIntyre the tension between the nationalist and universalist moral viewpoints. I agree that under such extreme conditions of absolute scarcity there will indeed be a terrible tension between one's commitments. But while consideration of such cases has the advantage of testing the limits of our moral commitments and bringing to the fore potential contradictions within or between them, they may provide inadequate guidance in a world such as ours, which differs significantly from the imagined scenarios (see Pogge 2002, 7–8). In conditions of moderate scarcity rather than absolute scarcity (normally thought to be the conditions under which questions of justice become relevant), attitudes expressing a commitment to global justice and to nationalist commitments need not conflict in this way. To use a domestic analogy, while the care for one's family may be irreconcilable with any concern of justice for others in a Hobbesian state of nature or a Humean "society of ruffians," under conditions of moderate scarcity these two sets of concerns need not be irreconcilable. Indeed, most accounts of global equal opportunity will have to presuppose, plausibly, conditions of moderate rather than absolute global scarcity. This is just one of the circumstances of global justice.[23] Under current conditions at least, in educating individual citizens to be good liberal citizens who are committed to the well-being of their fellows we do not need to turn them into *illiberal* internationalists who must treat outsiders with less than equal concern.

Concluding Remarks

I have argued that there is no inherent conflict between liberal nation building and the purported liberal commitment to global equality. The goals of securing and protecting a cultural context of choice, and of enabling democracy through common language and mutual trust and respect, are achievable without yielding to conational partiality with respect to resource distribution. And while the fostering of a common moral community via common nationality may be thought, at first glance, to be antithetical to the cosmopolitan moral point of view, it need not be so. When we become clear on the question as to what it is that liberal nationalists are to be partial about—"Partiality for compatriots *with respect to what?*"—the alleged tension between liberal boundary making and global equal concern is alleviated.

If there is no tension within liberal nationalism, between its idea of conational partiality and its commitment to global egalitarianism, then liberal nationalists can meet Judith Lichtenberg's challenge that "first you equalize resources, then you can have your cultural belonging" (1998,

---

[23] See Rawls's discussion on Hume's circumstances of justice (1971, 126–30).

183). Liberal nationalists can have it both ways. This of course does not mean that no partial national interests can be satisfied until global equality of opportunity is realized—justice is an ongoing quest, not an end state that can be definitively achieved. Liberal nationalists can give special concern to cultural belonging only if they are also working toward creating the global background economic and social structure required by the ideal of equal opportunity. The point is not that liberals should abandon nationalism in the name of global egalitarian justice but that they can and should pursue their nationalist goals without neglecting their duties of global egalitarian justice. One way the ends of national boundary making and the ideal of global equal concern can be reconciled is for liberal nationalists to strive for a global basic structure whose rules and institutions treat all persons with equal concern. Within the rules and terms of such a global basic structure, national boundaries may be maintained and conational partiality may be exercised (e.g., Pogge 2002, 11–12 and 120–24). Indeed, only within such a world can nationalists *successfully* pursue their nationalistic agenda from the moral point of view. The critical success, one might say, of any nation-building enterprise is compromised otherwise.[24]

Acknowledgments

An early and much shorter draft of this essay was discussed at an Amintaphil conference in San Diego in March 2000 and is published in the conference proceedings, *Human Rights in Political Philosophy*, edited by Burton Leiser and Tom Campbell (Aldershot: Ashgate, 2002). I thank participants at the conference for their comments. Thanks are due also to Will Kymlicka and graduate students at Queen's University for helpful comments and discussions on the early drafts. In particular, I thank Christian Barry, whose detailed criticism, comments, and editorial advice on several drafts helped clarify certain important points for me.

References

Barry, Brian. 1999. "Statism and Nationalism: A Cosmopolitan Critique." In *Global Justice*, edited by Ian Shapiro and Lea Brilmayer, 12–66. New York: New York University Press.
Beiner, Ronald, ed. 1998. *Theorizing Nationalism*. Albany: SUNY Press.

[24] The passage here borrows from and adapts Ronald Dworkin: "If a just distribution has been secured, then the resources people control are morally as well as legally theirs; using them as they wish, and as special attachments and projects require, in no way derogates from their recognizing that all citizens are entitled to a just share. But when injustice is substantial, *people who are drawn to both the ideals*—of personal projects and attachments on the one hand and equality on the other—are placed in a kind of ethical dilemma. They must compromise on one of the two ideals, and each direction of compromise impairs the critical success of their lives" (1992, 222; my emphasis).

Beitz, Charles. 1979. *Political Theory and International Relations*. Princeton: Princeton University Press.

———. 1983. "Cosmopolitan Ideal and National Sentiment." *Journal of Philosophy* 80:591–600.

Caney, Simon. 2001. "Cosmopolitan Justice and Equalizing Opportunities." *Metaphilosophy* 32, nos. 1/2:113–34.

Canovan, Margaret. 1996. "Nationhood, Patriotism and Universalism." In *Nationhood and Political Theory*, 83–100. Cheltenham: Edward Elgar.

Carens, Joseph. 1987. "Aliens and Citizens: The Case for Open Border." *Review of Politics* 49, no. 3:251–73.

Cohen, J., ed. 1996. *For Love of Country*. Boston: Beacon Press.

Cunningham, Frank. 1995. *The Real World of Democracy Revisited*. Atlantic Highlands, N.J.: Humanities Press.

Dworkin, Ronald. 1992. "Liberal Community." In *Communitarianism and Individualism*, edited by Shlomo Avineri and Avner de-Shalit, 203–33. Oxford: Oxford University Press.

Goodin, Robert. 1988. "What's so Special about Our Fellow Countryman?" *Ethics* 98, no. 4:663–86.

Gutmann, Amy. 1996. "Democratic Citizenship." In Cohen 1996, 66–71.

Habermas, Jurgen. 1992. "Citizenship and National Identity: Some Reflections on the Future of Europe." *Praxis International* 12, no. 1:1–19.

Hume, David. 1991. *An Enquiry Concerning the Principles of Morals*. La Salle, Ill.: Open Court. Original published in 1777.

Ignatieff, Michael. 1993. *Blood and Belonging: Journeys into the New Nationalism*. Toronto: Penguin.

Jones, Charles. 1999. "Patriotism, Morality, and Global Justice." In *Global Justice*, edited by Ian Shapiro and Lea Brilmayer, 125–70. New York: New York University Press.

Kymlicka, Will. 1989. *Liberalism, Community and Culture*. Oxford: Oxford University Press.

———. 1995. *Multicultural Citizenship*. Oxford: Oxford University Press.

———. 1999. "Citizenship in an Era of Globalization: Commentary on Held." In *Democracy's Edges*, edited by Ian Shapiro and Casiano Hacker-Cordon, 112–26. Cambridge: Cambridge University Press.

———. 2001a. "Territorial Boundaries: A Liberal Egalitarian Perspective." In *Boundaries and Justice*, edited by David Miller and Sohail Hashmi, 249–75. Princeton: Princeton University Press.

———. 2001b. *Politics in the Vernacular*. Oxford: Oxford University Press.

Lichtenberg, Judith. 1998. "How Liberal Can Nationalism Be?" In Beiner 1998, 167–88.

Margalit, Avishai, and Joseph Raz. 1990. "National Self-Determination." *Journal of Philosophy* 89, no. 7:439–61.

MacIntyre, Alasdair. 1984. *Is Patriotism a Virtue?* The Lindley Lectures. Kansas City: University of Kansas Press.

McKim, Robert, and Jeff McMahan, eds. 1997. *The Morality of Nationalism.* Oxford: Oxford University Press.

McMahan, Jeff. 1997. "The Limits of National Partiality." In McKim and McMahan 1997, 107–38.

Miller, David. 1995. *On Nationality.* Oxford: Oxford University Press.

———. Forthcoming. "Against Global Egalitarianism." *Journal of Ethics.*

Miller, Richard. 1998. "Cosmopolitan Respect and Patriotic Concern." *Philosophy and Public Affairs* 27, no. 3:202–24.

Nussbaum, Martha. 1996. "Patriotism and Cosmopolitanism." In Cohen 1996, 2–20.

Parekh, Bhiku. 1998. "The Incoherence of Nationalism." In Beiner 1998, 295–325.

Pogge, Thomas. 1989. *Realizing Rawls.* Ithaca: Cornell University Press.

———. 1997. "Migration and Poverty." In *Citizenship and Exclusion,* edited by Veit Bader, 12–27. New York: St Martin's.

———. 2002. *World Poverty and Human Rights.* Cambridge: Polity.

Rawls, John. 1971. *A Theory of Justice.* Cambridge, Mass.: Harvard University Press.

———. 1993. *Political Liberalism.* New York: Columbia University Press.

Sandel, Michael. 1992. "The Procedural Republic and the Unencumbered Self." In *Communitarianism and Individualism,* edited by Shlomo Avineri and Avner de-Shalit, 12–28. Oxford: Oxford University Press.

———. 1996. *Democracy's Discontent.* Cambridge, Mass.: Harvard University Press.

Scheffler, Samuel. 1999. "Conceptions of Cosmopolitanism." *Utilitas* 11, no. 3:255–76.

Shue, Henry. 1980. *Basic Rights.* Princeton: Princeton University Press.

———. 1988. "Mediating Duties." *Ethics* 98, no. 4:687–704.

Tamir, Yael. 1993. *Liberal Nationalism.* Princeton: Princeton University Press.

Tan, Kok-Chor. 2002. "Liberal Nationalism and Cosmopolitan Justice." *Ethical Theory and Moral Practice* 5, no. 4:431–61.

———. 2004. *Justice Without Borders: Cosmopolitanism, Nationalism, and Patriotism.* Cambridge: Cambridge University Press.

Waldron, Jeremy. 1992. "Minority Rights and the Cosmopolitan Alternative." *University of Michigan Journal of Law Reform* 25, no. 3: 751–93.

Walzer, Michael. 1983. *Spheres of Justice.* New York: Basic Books.

Yack, Bernard. 1999. "Myth of the Civic Nation." In Beiner 1998, 103–18.

5

THEORIZING INTERNATIONAL FAIRNESS

NANCY KOKAZ

What constitutes fairness in international relations? Is free trade fair? Can intellectual property rights be fairly pursued in the face of public-health emergencies? What would a fair distribution of burdens look like in environmental preservation schemes? Is trading carbon credits fair? This essay strives to engage such questions by outlining the main elements of a conception of international fairness in the context of illustrative global economic debates over trade, health, and the environment.

Let me start by clarifying what I mean by a conception of fairness in light of Rawls's famous distinction between the concept of justice and conceptions of justice. People's conceptions of justice refer to "a characteristic set of principles for assigning basic rights and duties and for determining what they take to be the proper distribution of the benefits and burdens of social cooperation." By contrast, the concept of justice is "specified by the role which these different sets of principles, these different conceptions, have in common." Despite their many disagreements about justice, people can "still agree that institutions are just when no arbitrary distinctions are made between persons in the assigning of basic rights and duties and when the rules determine a proper balance between competing claims to the advantages of social life" (Rawls 1971, 5). The more precise meanings of the terms included in the concept of justice are filled in by the principles contained in conceptions of justice. Similarly, conceptions of fairness give content to the concept of fairness, which highlights what these different conceptions have in common.

Following Rawls, I understand the concept of fairness in relation to a moral idea of reciprocity that specifies obligations of compliance for participants in social cooperation (Rawls 2001, 6). Thus, when the terms of a cooperative practice are such that no participating party feels "taken advantage of or forced to give in to claims which they do not accept as legitimate," as assessed by the principles of a conception of fairness, the participants in the practice have a duty to comply with its rules (Rawls 1999a, 208). As Rawls puts it:

> Now if the participants in a practice acknowledge that it satisfies the principle of reciprocity, and so accept its rules as just or fair (as the case requires), then, from the standpoint of justice, they have no complaint to lodge against it.

> Moreover, their engaging in it gives rise to a prima facie duty (and a corresponding prima facie right) of the parties to each other to act in accordance with the practice when it falls upon them to comply. (1999a, 209)

Formulated in this way, the concept of fairness generates rights and obligations for participants in a cooperative practice. The rights refer, first, to the cooperating parties' entitlement to a practice that satisfies the general principle of reciprocity, as fleshed out in more detail by a conception of fairness, and, second, to their expectation of compliance from other participants in and beneficiaries of the practice. These obligations entail the duty of all participants to comply with the practice's rules when it is their turn.

> The main idea is that when a number of persons engage in a mutually advantageous cooperative venture according to rules, and thus restrict their liberty in ways necessary to yield advantages for all, those who have submitted to these restrictions have a right to a similar acquiescence on the part of those who have benefited from their submission. We are not to gain from the cooperative labor of others without doing our fair share. (Rawls 1971, 96)

Once again, the more precise meanings of the terms included in the concept of fairness, such as what it means for all to do their part as specified by the rules of the practice, are filled in by conceptions of fairness.

The central claim of this essay is that institutionalized practices of collective justification have to be taken seriously in theorizing international fairness. Institutions matter because they play a significant part in the construal of fairness claims through the provision of internal standards for moral assessment without reference to which specific invocations of fairness transpiring within particular settings become unintelligible. I take up the jurisprudential and institutional issues at stake in the specification of the moral grounds for compliance with international institutions, on the one hand, and international civil disobedience, on the other, to argue that conceptions of international fairness must spell out how collective justification works.

I attempt to do this in three parts. To concretize the types of questions that an adequate conception of international fairness needs to address, I start from examples of global policy debates pertinent to the regular operation of the world economy (as opposed to the use of force in extraordinary times) that bring fairness questions to the fore. I then outline a general framework for theorizing international fairness in relation to practices of collective justification that is informed by, and can in turn inform, moral problems we encounter in the policy debates. I contrast this normative account of international institutions with the dominant mode of theorizing institutions in the field of international relations, which is also occasionally used to provide moral assessments. The latter, I argue, is conceptually inadequate on fairness grounds because of its roots in a brand of exchange theory that is blind to the distribution of burdens and benefits from cooperation. I do not offer a complete conception of international fairness but rather present a framework for developing such a conception. I hope that by identifying the main elements of an agenda for collective justification I will have taken a first step toward closing the gap between theory and practice in the articulation of international responsibilities that can enhance the justice of global institutions.

Policy Debates

It is typical to theorize international relations in terms of interests and power, without much regard to justice and fairness, at least in mainstream scholarship in this field. The result is an incomplete theoretical understanding of the practice of world politics, since even the most cursory look at what important actors actually do in their international interactions reveals that they use normative language all the time. This has not gone unnoticed. Investigations of ethics in the international arena have multiplied in recent years. For the most part, however, such treatments remain less frequent than their counterparts in domestic political theory and largely emphasize the use of force.[1] The focus on overt force and direct violence in discussions of international ethics is problematic, since it can too easily lead to the unintentional neglect of realms of organized life that arguably pose even more pervasive ethical challenges for larger numbers of people around the globe. For this reason, I pay special attention in this essay to practical moral dilemmas arising from the ordinary daily workings of the world economy that can give rise to issues of life and death.

The language of fairness is prevalent in global economic interactions. Debates over trade, health, and the environment provide perfect examples, ushering in various interconnected ethical quandaries, of which I only give a sampling here as an illustration of the types of moral dilemma that the world economy presents us with in these three issue areas. Controversies about trade have been particularly visible since the WTO ministerial meeting in Seattle in 1999, with the increased intensity of antiglobalization protests that demand "fair trade" instead of "free trade." Paradoxically, some of the institutions that have been targeted in these protests as undermining fairness see themselves as committed to the promotion of fair trading practices, the WTO being a prominent example. Similarly, bilateral negotiations between countries often find both sides invoking the language of fairness, though on behalf of opposing positions, as the lumber dispute between Canada and the United States illustrates very well. The sheer number of incongruent appeals to fairness in the context of a

---

[1] There are notable exceptions, with among others the work of Thomas Pogge (e.g., 2002) and various contributors to *Ethics and International Affairs* providing perfect examples.

wide range of trade disagreements requires the development of a general framework for the assessment of such conflicting claims.

Trade is not the only area where fairness battles rage, as demonstrated by a recent issue of *Ethics and International Affairs* devoted to health and global justice. Recognizing the increasingly dense web of global interactions that shape the health prospects of all people everywhere, the contributors to this issue examine the obligation to provide relief from ill health on a global scale and articulate the limits of acceptable pluralism for domestic health regimes. Intellectual property rights offer a particularly vivid demonstration of the latter, since they involve a potential clash between domestic societal preferences and global guidelines espoused by the WHO concerning the fairness of different health systems. The questions raised by intellectual property rights go beyond the global health regime and have serious implications for other global institutions as well. The Doha declaration of the WTO endorsing the production of generic HIV medication forcefully brings this point home and reveals the difficult moral issues that lie at the intersection of health and trade.[2] The recent international agreement brokered by the WTO that further relaxes international rules on patent protection, allowing not only the production but even the export of generic medications to poor countries in need, highlights these connections even more boldly.[3]

The case of generic medicines is interesting for many reasons. It is significant that the WTO, of all international institutions, was persuaded to condone the production and export of these medications, despite the

---

[2] The WTO adopted the Declaration on the TRIPS Agreement and Public Health on 14 November 2001 in its ministerial meeting in Doha, Qatar. Recognizing the gravity of public-health problems confronting developing and least developed countries afflicted by the HIV epidemic, the declaration allowed for flexibility in the protection of intellectual property rights for pharmaceutical products, stating that the guarantees of the TRIPS agreement do "not and should not prevent members from taking measures to protect public health." Identifying the promotion of access to medicines for all as a key public-health concern in the context of HIV epidemics in the developing world, the declaration gave each member the right to grant compulsory licenses and establish its own regime regarding intellectual property protection, thus setting the stage for the production of generic medicines. The declaration also recognized that "WTO members with insufficient or no manufacturing capacities in the pharmaceutical sector could face difficulties in making effective use of compulsory licensing" and instructed "the Council for TRIPS to find an expeditious solution to this problem." Finally, the Declaration allowed the WTO's least developed members not to apply TRIPS until 2016. For the text of the declaration see http://www.wto.org/english/thewto_e/minist_e/min01_e/mindecl_trips_e.htm.

[3] The WTO adopted the Decision on the Implementation of Paragraph 6 of the Doha Declaration and Public Health on 30 August 2003. Recognizing "the difficulties that WTO Members with insufficient or no manufacturing capacities in the pharmaceutical sector could face in making effective use of compulsory licensing," the decision allows the trade of generic medications between eligible importing and exporting members under strictly defined conditions. The text of the decision can be found at http://www.wto.org/english/tratop_e/trips_e/implem_para6_e.htm.

central place that property rights occupy in the global trade regime.[4] Identifying the political process that led to these final decisions, as well as the ensuing pitfalls of application that have since accompanied their implementation, should be very informative for understanding how competing interests and principles are balanced in concrete institutional contexts. The episode also represents a striking instance of civil disobedience, where unilateral actions by a few affected countries successfully challenged a narrowly construed unjust rule that did not pay sufficient attention to shared public values regarding health emergencies.[5] Notice how framing this act in terms of civil disobedience recognizes the overall justness of the international trade regime insofar as it can be the vehicle for the actualization of the values that it was set up to promote. Emphasizing such public values further illustrates that even when the primary purpose of a particular regulatory regime is to facilitate international trade, its focus cannot be blindly and exclusively on trade alone if it is to remain just.

Another area closely intertwined with trade is the environment. Arresting global environmental degradation, which has dramatically accelerated with rising levels of planetary industrialization, is a worthy goal, albeit one that generates unequal burdens and benefits, not only between societies but also within them. Specific schemes for the allocation of these burdens and benefits engender fierce allegations of unfairness from those who would be adversely affected by them. For example, in light of the differential internal impact of compliance with the obligations it enacts, the Kyoto process gave rise to severe controversies within Canada, where the provinces that would bear the brunt of the cost for cutting emissions opposed ratification. Even though Canada eventually ratified the protocol, the implementation of the Kyoto commitments remains plagued by the distributive controversies that the ratification process made evident. Beyond producing distributive disputes, the Kyoto protocol also raises deep foundational questions about the fairness of the particular institutional devices it introduces to facilitate the achievement of aggregate global targets in practice, such as the option of purchasing carbon credits internationally, which effectively amounts to

---

[4] Perhaps not surprisingly, the WTO initially resisted the adoption of these public-health measures. The process toward eventual endorsement was not easy. What is significant for my purposes here, however, is that the WTO yielded in the end in the face of an effective political campaign involving various U.N. agencies as well as nongovernmental organizations. For a good example of a U.N. report that contributed to the global campaign for generic medicines, see http://www.unhchr.ch/Huridocda/Huridoca.nsf/0/c462b62cf8a07b13c1256 9700046704e?Opendocument. Thanks to Christian Barry for bringing this report to my attention.

[5] The policies of Brazil and India were critical in the global civil-disobedience effort on generic medicines. South Africa was also implicated in important ways, although in a more controversial manner, given its initial refusal to purchase and distribute generic medicines.

setting up a right to pollute that can be freely traded on the market. Given that most of us would have serious moral reservations about the introduction of such a right for the efficient implementation of the domestic politics of our own countries, it seems in order to at least raise similar questions internationally as part of a general assessment of whether there should be moral limits on the reach of the global market.[6]

As this brief overview illustrates, global debates surrounding trade, health, and the environment are rife with controversies about fairness. They reveal not only how common fairness claims are in contentious global economic interactions but also the many different forms that they take and the extent to which they cross established ideological divides. What is often at stake in disputes over fairness is not a contest between efficiency and fairness, as is often supposed, but rather a clash of rival conceptions of fairness that are not always fully articulated by the disputants. The disagreements take many different forms, ranging from conflicting claims made by rival sides in particular disputes, to potential and actual clashes between domestic and international regulatory regimes rooted in the institutional pluralism of our world, to misgivings about the problematic moral underpinnings of the institutional mechanisms that have been set up to respond to global problems. How these conflicts over fairness are resolved has serious philosophical and policy implications, but so far they have been taken up only in an ad hoc manner. Against this background, a systematic theoretical investigation of international fairness that can help to clarify the ethical challenges at stake in these concrete contexts becomes indispensable.

General Theoretical Framework

An effective theoretical response to the multitude of complicated ethical questions concerning the present world economy requires the integration of insights from all pertinent scholarly literatures. Accordingly, my preliminary attempt to identify the main elements of a general framework for conceptualizing international fairness draws upon debates in international ethics, international relations, political philosophy, and legal theory, with a primary focus on how relevant findings from each can advance our thinking about institutional fairness. In so doing, I do not

---

[6] It may be objected that the only politically feasible alternative to carbon credits is the status quo, where not even aggregate targets are achieved and all states seem to enjoy a de facto right to pollute without even paying compensation for doing so. While this is probably true, it does not establish the fairness of carbon credits, which in the final analysis must rest with the defensibility of their underlying institutional principles. As my subsequent discussion of Keohane's neoliberal institutionalist conception of fairness in this essay will show, the appropriate benchmark of comparison for analyzing underlying principles is not the absence of an institution but rather alternative arrangements for the institution. Many thanks to Christian Barry for pushing me on this point.

attempt to carry out an empirical assessment of the causal impact of normative discourse on outcomes. This is an important undertaking, but it is one that has already been embarked upon by a vast and now influential constructivist literature in international relations. Instead of investigating causal connections, I inquire into processes of justification and norm construction within institutional contexts. To that end, I draw upon seminal texts in political and legal theory to shed light on normative questions of enduring importance that pervade world politics. More specifically, I insist that the language of fairness is important in itself and that it deserves a serious philosophical study of what fairness demands in practice independently of its causal impact. This requires an examination of what respective parties mean when they make fairness claims in light of the plethora of theoretical and practical questions that such invocations entail.

Institutions are at the heart of my analysis for two reasons. First, it is important to subject institutions to moral scrutiny, because particular transactions in global economic interactions reflect the general justice or injustice of the social institutions within which they take place. Given the much discussed globalization of economic relations and the proliferation of regulatory institutions that has accompanied that process, tackling questions about the general fairness of global social institutions becomes particularly important. Second, institutions are implicated in the construal of fairness claims because they provide internal standards for moral evaluation. In other words, by invoking the language of fairness to assess global institutions, we are not simply importing an external moral framework but also drawing upon internal constructions. Simply put, international institutions constitute practices of collective justification, with significant repercussions for understanding what fairness entails.

Consider, for example, the foreign economic policies of states. When foreign policies are examined in the international ethics literature, they are evaluated in terms of either the characteristics of the policy act itself or the consequences that the policy act has given rise to, in line with the familiar debate between deontological and consequentialist normative theories.[7] Useful as this is as a starting point for ethical appraisal, it cannot shed light on instances where our judgments concerning fairness diverge, even when the relevant features of both the act under consideration and its consequences are roughly the same. To continue with our example, it is possible to assess two similar foreign economic policies differently even when they have similar consequences, calling one an act of "unfair" protectionism and the other a "fair" sanction, assuming here that the sanction in question is indeed generally regarded as fair. The rules of the international regimes of collective justification within which these

---

[7] For helpful overviews of the deontology-consequentialism debate in general and in the context of international ethics see Frankena 1973 and Mapel and Nardin 1992.

policies are undertaken are crucial for grasping the difference in our moral assessment. The relevant institutions here are the WTO and the U.N. Security Council, in their capacities as the central pillars of the global collective practices regulating trade and security. Even when they suffer from operational imperfections, these international institutions still perform a collective justification function, implying that our understanding of the fairness of particular policies formulated within their regulatory space are firmly tied to their internally generated rules.[8]

Once we recognize that institutional frameworks, understood as practices of collective justification, are important determinants of what fairness entails, an investigation of how justification actually works is called for. This in turn requires a clear specification of the jurisprudential underpinnings of collective justification in light of the complex relationship between law and morality. Justification occurs in institutional frameworks in part because these bodies are the makers of law. In most social systems, legalization is generally regarded as a source of collective justification. This is not to say, however, that legality automatically produces justification, since laws themselves can be unjust, thus turning disobedience into a moral duty. This potential tension between law and morality is ever present even in a generally just regime and invites a careful consideration of the sources of justification.

The case of the NATO intervention in Kosovo provides a vivid illustration of the jurisprudential issues at stake. In 2000, a specially appointed Independent International Commission on Kosovo concluded that "the NATO military intervention was illegal but legitimate. It was illegal because it did not receive prior approval from the UN Security Council. However, the Commission considers that the intervention was justified because all diplomatic avenues had been exhausted and because the intervention had the effect of liberating the majority population of Kosovo from a long period of oppression under Serbian rule" (Independent International Commission 2000).[9] Setting aside possible substantive

---

[8] The same can be said of most of the prominent international institutions of our time, which explicitly see themselves as performing a collective justification function and are widely acknowledged as doing so.

[9] Not the product of appointment by a government or nongovernmental organization, the Independent International Commission was created by the initiative of Göran Persson (prime minister of Sweden) in 1999 and brought together a number of international experts to undertake an independent analysis of the conflict in Kosovo. The commission was chaired by Richard Goldstone (South Africa) and Carl Tham (Sweden), and it included the following eleven members invited by the cochairs and selected "on the basis of known expertise and with due regard for the gender and geographical composition of the Commission": Hanan Ashwari (Palestine), Grace d'Almeida (Benin), Akiko Domoto (Japan), Richard Falk (U.S.A.), Oleg Grinevsky (Russia), Michael Ignatieff (Canada), Mary Kaldor (U.K.), Martha Minow (U.S.A.), Jacques Rupnik (France), Theo Sommer (Germany), and Jan Urban (Czech Republic). The project was endorsed by U.N. Secretary-General Kofi Annan.

disagreements about the legitimacy of this particular intervention,[10] it is worth noting that the commission's conclusion implicitly presupposed the jurisprudential view of H. L. A. Hart in positing law and morality as two separate domains (Hart 1963, 1983, 1994). When law and morality are strictly separated in this way, any single act can fall into one of four clusters in terms of how it fares on the legality and morality dimensions. An act may be both legal and moral; it may be illegal but moral (as the commission concluded for Kosovo); it may be legal but immoral; or it may be both illegal and immoral.[11] It is precisely this jurisprudential typology that the commission implicitly relied upon in delivering its verdict on Kosovo.

Interestingly, this was not a position shared by all, as was nicely captured in the statements of the U.N. secretary-general when in 1999 he declared both the "legal inaction" of the international community in the case of Rwanda and its "illegal action" in the case of Kosovo to be problematic on legitimacy grounds (Annan 1999b).[12] After affirming the moral tragedy that inaction in Rwanda represented, Kofi Annan also highlighted the dangers of undertaking military action outside established mechanisms for enforcing international law as in Kosovo.[13] This juxta-position between the *moral* costs of Rwanda and Kosovo set the terms of the dilemma of humanitarian intervention for the secretary-general.[14] The

---

[10] For divergent ethical and legal perspectives that take Kosovo as their point of departure, see Holzgrefe and Keohane 2003.

[11] For the sake of making the Kosovo example conceptually crisper, I temporarily use the terms *legitimacy* and *morality* interchangeably here.

[12] Thus, Annan asks: "To those for whom the greatest threat to the future of international order is the use of force in the absence of a Security Council mandate, one might say: leave Kosovo aside for a moment, and think about Rwanda. Imagine for one moment that, in those dark days and hours leading up to the genocide, there had been a coalition of states ready and willing to act in defense of the Tutsi population, but the council had refused or delayed giving the green light. Should such a coalition then have stood idly by while the horror unfolded? To those for whom the Kosovo action heralded a new era when states and groups of states can take military action outside the established mechanisms for enforcing international law, one might ask: Is there not a danger of such interventions undermining the security system created after World War II, and of setting dangerous precedents for future interventions without a clear criterion to decide who might invoke them and in what circumstances?" (Annan 1999b).

[13] Prior to his appointment as secretary-general, Annan, in his capacity as the head of the Department of Peacekeeping Operations, was directly implicated in preventing the U.N. peacekeeping force stationed in Rwanda from undertaking operations that could have halted the genocide. My point in bringing up Annan's characterizations of Rwanda and Kosovo is not to indicate agreement with them or to endorse his prior actions in Rwanda but rather to signal that, in his capacity as U.N. secretary-general, Annan recognized the moral tragedy of inaction in Rwanda in a way that implicitly hints at a complex connection between the domains of law and morality, regardless of this frayed history. My thanks go to Thomas Pogge for encouraging me to clarify this. For a more detailed overview of the secretary-general's role in the Rwandan tragedy, see Pogge forthcoming.

[14] As Annan sees it, the dilemma of humanitarian intervention concerns the tension between and reconciliation of two important principles: "While the genocide in Rwanda will

74 NANCY KOKAZ

former represents the moral costs of illegal action, whereas the latter represents the moral costs of illegal action. Given these dual pitfalls, Annan insisted on the importance of reaching consensus "not only on the principle that massive and systematic violations of human rights must be checked, wherever they take place, but also on ways of deciding what action is necessary, and when, and by whom" (1999a).[15] While the jurisprudential underpinnings of this position were not explicitly articulated, the secretary-general nevertheless seemed to hint at a more complex relation between law and morality when he suggested that illegality carries moral costs. In effect, this implied link challenges the strict separation of the two domains stipulated by Hartian jurisprudence.

Law and morality appear to be interrelated in intricate ways, but how? Is it law that drives morality? Or is it the other way around, with morality being the primary partner? Further, what is the character of the connection? Once the direction of the relationship has been specified, what exactly are the implications for the other partner? If law drives morality, is morality tantamount to what the lawgiver lays down, as Hobbes thought (1991)? Or is it that law sends subtle moral signals, without fully determining the content of morality, as Devlin proposed (1961, 1965)?[16] By contrast, if morality is the foundation of law, how is it to be used in

define for our generation the consequences of inaction in the face of mass murder, the more recent conflict in Kosovo has prompted important questions about the consequences of action in the absence of complete unity on the part of the international community. It has cast in stark relief the dilemma of what has been called 'humanitarian intervention': on the one side, the question of the legitimacy of action taken by a regional organization without a United Nations mandate; on the other, the universally recognized imperative of effectively halting gross and systematic violations of human rights with grave humanitarian consequences. The inability of the international community in the case of Kosovo to reconcile these two equally compelling interests was a tragedy. It has revealed the core challenge to the Security Council and the United Nations as a whole in the next century: to forge unity behind the principle that massive and systematic violations of human rights—wherever they may take place—should not be allowed to stand" (Annan 1999b).

[15] I do not aim to suggest that this is Annan's definitive position on the matter. Such a claim would require a detailed study of the secretary-general's official and nonofficial utterances and is beyond the scope of this essay. It is also not necessary for my purposes here, since my aim in invoking Annan's statements is simply to illustrate the range of jurisprudential possibilities that key figures in the international arena rely upon when subjecting various international actions to moral scrutiny. To reformulate Annan's dilemma of humanitarian intervention in light of the jurisprudential question at hand here, it can be said that the core challenge for the next century, as the secretary-general sees it, is to bring law and morality together in light of the intricate connections that exist between the two realms. While these are not exactly Annan's explicit words, I suggest that his observations on humanitarian intervention implicitly point in the direction of moving beyond Hart's strict separation view. Beyond this, I do not make any further claims about the final position of the secretary-general on the matter. Thanks to Thomas Pogge for pushing me to clarify this point.

[16] While not agreeing with Devlin's conservative conclusions concerning the substantive content of public morality, I find his analysis of the links between law and morality highly informative.

law making? Is a law that fails the test of morality no law at all, as natural law theorists, including Fuller, submitted (1949, 1967, 1968, 1969, 1981)?[17] Or is morality a resource to be drawn upon in law making in sophisticated ways as Dworkin argued (1977, 1985, 1986, 1996, 2000)? As in the Hartian typology, four alternatives are available in this new jurisprudential configuration, depending on how the connection between law and morality is formulated. Once the jurisprudential possibilities are thus expanded, the preferred basis for collective justification endeavors in international institutions can be spelled out.

Taking practices of collective justification seriously in theorizing fairness also raises several other questions about institutions. If international institutions, understood as practices of collective justification, play as fundamental a part in the configuration of fairness as I contend they do, it becomes absolutely essential to theorize fairness in relation to how institutions work. This can be done through a comparative assessment of the strengths and weaknesses of several distinct conceptions of international institutions in relation to their implications for international fairness. I sketch here three important conceptual avenues that can be pursued in this undertaking.

The natural starting point for the inquiry is the dominant mode of analyzing institutions in international relations associated with the work of Keohane (1984, 1986, 1989, 2002). As I show in more detail below, this approach may explain how international regimes emerge to make cooperation possible even among rational self-interested actors interacting in an anarchic international system, but it fails to advance our understanding of institutional fairness. This is because neoliberal institutionalist accounts of international regimes are rooted in a brand of exchange theory that is blind to the distribution of burdens and benefits from cooperation. As such, they yield the wrong benchmark of comparison for assessing fairness. This first conception of international institutions grounded in exchange theory can be contrasted with another one informed by the pioneering work of Franck on the subject in international law (1968, 1975, 1982a, 1982b, 1990, 1995, 2002). While the legal model represents a significant move forward from exchange theory in its explicit concern with fairness, it remains problematic because it rests upon a strict separation between procedural fairness (legitimacy) and substantive fairness (justice). This is untenable, because it leads to paralysis when procedure and substance pull in different directions, not to mention that it blinds agents to the links between procedure and substance. It would seem reasonable to suppose that procedure and substance must be connected in giving content to institutional fairness, both in general terms and in particular issue areas driven by the specific features of the activity

---

[17] For a classic historical statement of natural law, see Locke 1988, 2002, and 2003. For more contemporary overviews, see George 1992 and 1996 and George and Wolfe 2000.

subject to the regulatory framework. This can be accomplished in an interpretation of institutional fairness that appeals to an overarching notion of fair social cooperation characterized by moral reciprocity, with procedural and substantive implications. Such an account of fair cooperation can be found in political philosophy, most prominently in the work of Rawls (1971, 1996, 1999a, 1999b, 2001). This third conception can be expected to do a better job of systematizing our considered judgments about what fairness involves for institutions.

Finally, the jurisprudential exploration of the link between law and morality and the theoretical investigation of the operation of institutions in relation to fairness come together in an argument for civil disobedience that I consider essential to the justice of social practices. Preserving conceptual space for civil disobedience is crucial, especially in an account of fairness that places so much emphasis on collective justification. This is because all practices, even generally just ones, can at times become the perpetrators of injustice. When this happens, the moral foundations of the obligation to abide by the rules of the practice are eroded and it becomes a duty of justice to resist. Opening up the question of civil disobedience in this way revisits jurisprudential issues that were addressed earlier concerning the sources of justification. It also reiterates the limitations of conceptions of institutions rooted in exchange theory and procedural international law, since neither can allow for civil disobedience. Furthermore, affirming the place of civil disobedience in practices of collective justification raises new dilemmas about the possible moral grounds for unilateral as opposed to multilateral action. It is very important to distinguish between different forms of unilateral action here, especially given the new world order context of hegemony—or, as some have called it, empire—that currently turns American unilateralism into more than a thought experiment.[18] Thus, the Brazilian decision to produce and export generic HIV medications in defiance of intellectual property rights proved to be an instance of civil disobedience, whereas the American decision in March 2003 to go to war in Iraq did not. The difference lies in the public reasons given in support of these respective actions. It is no coincidence that in the end the Brazilian action was endorsed by the WTO, while the American action failed to receive Security Council approval. A further question concerns the reasons that can count as public reasons in a plural world. Once again the work of Rawls is instructive here for developing an account of civil disobedience as a political conception rather than a comprehensive one.[19]

---

[18] For examples of the recent revival of the academic discourse on empire, see Ignatieff 2003, Walzer 2003, and various authors in *Ethics and International Affairs* 2003. For earlier invocations of the notion of empire that received widespread attention, see Hardt and Negri 2000 and Johnson 2000.

[19] See especially Rawls 1996 and 1999a.

This short defense of civil disobedience concludes my preliminary overview of the main elements of a general framework for conceptualizing international fairness in relation to practices of collective justification. The goal of this theoretical discussion has not been to propose substantive principles of fairness but rather has been to identify the types of jurisprudential and institutional questions that need to be confronted in the articulation of such principles in concrete contexts. Ultimately, the success or failure of a theory of fairness must rest with the contributions it can make to the practice of fairness. What that involves can best be specified by embarking on a theoretically informed exploration of how debates about fairness are actually played out in specific cases. The jurisprudential and institutional issues identified by the theoretical framework can offer practical guidance for addressing the urgent ethical challenges the cases bring to the fore. The case studies, in turn, can enrich the theoretical apparatus through the uncovering of unanticipated problems of application. The global policy debates about trade, health, and the environment that provided the initial impetus for theorizing international fairness in a more systematic manner present excellent institutional settings for this undertaking. In the final analysis, it is only by bringing theory and practice together in this way that the quest to build just social practices for the global economy can progress.

The Normative Poverty of Neoliberal Institutionalism

I have argued that international institutions are key participants in the construal of international fairness in their capacities as practices of collective justification. The strong connection established between fairness and institutions in the process of justification calls for a deeper understanding of how international institutions actually function. Neoliberal institutionalist scholarship provides such an account in a vein that corresponds to the mainstream mode of analyzing cooperation in the discipline of international relations.[20] In this approach, institutions—or more broadly, regimes—are defined loosely as "sets of implicit or explicit principles, norms, rules, and decision-making procedures around which actors' expectations converge in a given area of international relations" (Krasner 1983, 2). The main purpose of institutions is seen to be the facilitation of cooperation between self-interested actors in an anarchic world through the alteration of patterns of costs and benefits. More specifically, institutions perform certain easing functions: they "reduce certain forms of uncertainty and alter transaction costs"; they "provide information" and "stabilize expectations"; they may even "make decentralized enforcement feasible" in a world characterized by the absence of

---

[20] Realism also makes up part of mainstream international relations theory, but it has been less influential in the study of international institutions.

hierarchical authority (Keohane 1989, 166). Neoliberal institutionalist accounts of cooperation in the global system explain how decentralized coordination can emerge and be maintained between rational self-interested actors driven by various considerations of mutual advantage (Keohane 1984).

I contend that this approach, notwithstanding the dominance it has achieved in the analysis of institutions in international relations, is ill equipped to advance our understanding of the notion of fairness. It may seem that this is not a particularly new point. It has long been pointed out that the positivist model of explanation underlying neoliberal institutionalist theory cannot make sense of the "normative structure" of international regimes; it cannot be "easily applied to cases in which norms, so defined [as standards of behavior that spell out rights and obligations], are a significant element in the phenomena to be explained" (Kratochwil and Ruggie 1986, 767). It has been suggested that an interpretive epistemology, rather than a positivist one, would emphasize legitimation much more prominently in its analysis of organizational design issues. Legitimation is important for an adequate explanation of cooperation because, as Kratochwil and Ruggie have put it,

> A regime can be perfectly rationally designed but erode because its legitimacy is undermined. Or a regime that is a logical non-starter can be the object of endless negotiations because a significant constituency views its aims to be legitimate. (1986, 773)

I agree. My concern at the moment, however, is different. I am interested neither in epistemological issues nor in explanation here. Instead, I am engaged in the exploration of what it means to make a fairness claim in institutional settings in controversies over various international transactions. Like Kratochwil and Ruggie, I find the dominant neoliberal institutionalist approaches to international institutions inadequate, but for my present purposes I do so for different reasons. Neoliberal institutionalism can explain the emergence and maintenance of cooperation among selfish actors with pregiven rational interests for instrumental reasons, but such synchronization need not be fair in either process or outcome, since it depends primarily on the convergence and stabilization of expectations in the face of various collective-action problems. A conception of institutions that strives to illuminate how they perform their collective justification function needs to be erected on the premise of fair social cooperation and legitimate expectations instead. It is precisely in this area that neoliberal institutionalism is doomed to silence, because of its roots in exchange theory that do not see any need for a normative assessment of the distribution of burdens and benefits from cooperation.[21]

---

[21] Alternative conceptions of institutionalism that are not grounded in exchange theory are also available and more promising from a normative point of view. These approaches

A closer look at Keohane's work, which represents the leading statement of neoliberal institutionalism in international theory, illustrates the point well. Keohane offers a functional analysis of the emergence and continued existence of cooperation among self-interested actors in an anarchic international system (1984, chap. 6). His analysis relies on what he calls an "inverted Coase theorem," inverted in the sense that Coase's seminal work in economic theory is deemed not to apply, given that its assumptions do not hold in international relations. Keohane summarizes what he sees to be the essence of Coase's contribution as follows:

> Ronald Coase (1960) argued that the presence of externalities alone does not necessarily prevent effective coordination among independent actors. *Under certain conditions*, declared Coase, bargaining among these actors could lead to solutions that are Pareto-optimal *regardless of the rules of legal liability*. (1984, 85)[22]

Keohane goes on to remark that the Coase theorem "has frequently been used to show the efficacy of bargaining without central authority, and it has occasionally been applied specifically to international relations" (1984, 86). As Keohane puts it:

> The Coase theorem could be interpreted, therefore, as predicting that problems of collective action could easily be overcome in international politics through bargaining and mutual adjustment—that is, through cooperation as we have defined it. The further inference could be drawn that the discord observed must be the result of fundamental conflicts of interest rather than problems of coordination. (1984, 86)

For Keohane, this particular application of the Coase theorem to international affairs and the conclusions drawn from it are mistaken, for the fundamental reason that the conditions given by the theorem's assumptions which make the conclusions of the Coase theorem hold in the domestic case are not satisfied in the international realm.[23] These

have not had similar levels of influence in the international-relations literature, however. For an excellent overview of different types of institutionalist theory, see Peters 1999.

[22] Emphasis added. I have added an emphasis to two segments of Keohane's summary of Coase that are important for my discussion. The first segment concerns the limited conditions under which Coase's conclusions hold and is essential for Keohane's inversion of the Coase theorem. The second segment highlights the irrelevance of the substantive content of the rules of legal liability and is crucial to my normative critique of the Coase theorem and, as a consequence, of neoliberal institutional accounts of international cooperation that rely on an inverted Coase theorem.

[23] The second reason Keohane gives in support of his position is that game-theoretical critiques of the Coase theorem have shown that "it cannot simply be applied to world politics," owing to complications that arise when, for example, more than two actors are introduced. I do not pursue this point any further because it does not play the crucial role that the first reason (concerning the underlying assumptions limiting the theorem's domain of applicability) does in Keohane's inversion of the Coase theorem in his effort to develop a functional account of international cooperation (Keohane 1984, 87).

assumptions concern the existence of a framework of legal liability, perfect information, and zero transaction costs. In assessing whether these conditions hold in the international realm, Keohane writes: "It is absolutely clear that none of these conditions are met in world politics" (1984, 87). It is at this point that Keohane inverts the Coase theorem to show how the dilemmas of collective action in international affairs can be overcome by the setting up of international institutions that can establish property rights, reduce uncertainty (so as to at least approach, if not attain, perfect information), and decrease transaction costs. Thus, Keohane's account of international cooperation rests on an argument about the mitigation of the logic of anarchy through the existence of regimes and institutions set up by rational self-interested actors for the performance of the three functions necessary to invert the Coase theorem (1984, 87–97).

It is important to note that while a framework of legal liability is necessary for the conclusions of the Coase theorem to be valid, the substantive content of this framework is irrelevant for the analysis. The most counterintuitive side of the Coase theorem concerns just this point: that Pareto-optimal outcomes can be reached regardless of the rules of legal liability. The famous case of the laundry that Keohane discusses in some length presents an excellent illustration. The example is meant to depict alternative possibilities for the Pareto-optimal resolution of a conflict that arises between a paint factory that pollutes the air as a byproduct of its operations, on the one hand, and a nearby old-fashioned laundry with no indoor drying equipment that ends up being harmed by the air pollution produced by the factory, on the other.

Given a cost matrix that yields a clear conception of social welfare, negative externalities can be eliminated equally well through either government enforcement or decentralized bargaining. In the case of the negative externality of air pollution, the first step is to identify the cost matrix. On the implicit assumption that no other harms exist outside the commercial consequences for the two parties, Keohane enumerates the following costs for dealing with the negative externality: the affected old-fashioned laundry would need to install indoor drying equipment at a cost of $20,000 in the event of the nonelimination of pollution, while it would cost the paint factory only $10,000 to install pollution-control devices. The second step is to identify the welfare-enhancing alternative in light of the cost matrix. Here, the welfare-enhancing alternative is understood to correspond to the actualization of the least costly alternative from a societal point of view. "Social welfare would clearly be enhanced," writes Keohane, "by eliminating the pollution rather than by installing indoor drying equipment" (1984, 86). Once the social-welfare-enhancing alternative is identified, the third step is to show that the governmental enforcement of antipollution rights, while representing one possible way for the actualization of this end result, is not necessary for it.

Drawing on Coase's analysis, Keohane suggests that a second possibility for the elimination of pollution is offered by mutually beneficial bargaining. Thus, even if the factory had a right to pollute rather than a duty not to pollute, the elimination of pollution could still be achieved if the laundry owner could pay the factory owner a sum between $10,000 and $20,000 for the installation of pollution-control devices. Such a bargain is very likely to materialize, as it is in the interest of both parties. At any given price in this range, if the laundry bought the right to pollute from the factory, it would incur less than the $20,000 necessary for the installation of indoor drying equipment, and the factory would make a profit by being paid more than the $10,000 necessary for the installation of pollution-control devices.

Mutually beneficial bargaining for the actualization of the societally least costly alternative constitutes the conceptual foundation for neoliberal institutionalist accounts of international cooperation and international regimes. These theoretical roots are deeply problematic from a normative point of view because they accord ultimate priority to the maximization of social welfare, regardless of how this is achieved. "In devising and choosing between social arrangements," writes Coase in the original article that provides the inspiration for Keohane's work, "we should have regard for the total effect. This, above all, is the change in approach which I am advocating" (1960, 44). As Keohane puts it in the context of assessing the respective merits of government enforcement and decentralized bargaining for the elimination of pollution in his laundry example,

> In either case, the externality of pollution would be eliminated. The key difference would not be one of economic efficiency, but of distribution of benefits between the factory and the laundry. (1984, 86)

In other words, the distribution of benefits is irrelevant from the point of view of neoliberal institutionalism if the outcome is efficient. This is why it does not matter what the substantive content of the liability rules are, so long as some legal framework of liability that would make bargaining possible is present. A neoliberal institutionalist cares about the existence of legal rules because in the absence of a framework that can stabilize expectations about enforcement, the bargain cannot be carried out. Legal frameworks are necessary for compliance with the terms of the bargain. The neoliberal institutionalist, however, could not care less about what the content of the legal rules in question might be and whether these rules are fair.

The point is illustrated well by Fried's deontological critique of the economic analysis of moral and legal rights that has been inspired by the Coase theorem (Fried 1978, chap. 4). In an exposition of the Coase theorem, Fried discusses four cases where Pareto optimality could be achieved regardless of the rules of legal liability. The first two cases are

examples that Coase himself analyzes in detail in support of his conclusions. These are the examples of factory pollution and straying cattle. The
main ideas of the factory example are already familiar from Keohane's
laundry narrative based on Coase's original formulation. The cattle
example concerns the case of a cattle rancher whose cattle wander onto
the neighboring farmer's land, leading to a destruction of crops.
The other two examples that Fried proposes to analyze in Coasean terms
are more sinister. These are the examples of the rapist and the driver. The
rapist example considers the case of a rapist's right to rape in opposition
to a victim's right to bodily integrity. The driver example is about a driver
who runs over an elderly man and thus opposes the driver's right to drive
as he pleases to the pedestrian's right to not be run over—in other words,
the pedestrian's right to life (Fried 1978, 87).

Unlike the examples of the factory and the cattle, the examples of the
rapist and murderous driver do not come from Coase's original article.
They are nevertheless reflective of general tendencies in the economic
analysis of rights, as a classic discussion of automobile safety devices
demonstrates well.[24] In the context of the examples of the factory, the
cattle, the rapist, and the driver, Fried insists that the conclusion is the
same in all four cases: assuming that factory pollution, wandering cattle,
rape, and being run over represent the socially more costly alternatives,
how legal liability is assigned is of no relevance to their prevention. It does
not matter that the victim will need to bargain with the rapist not to be
raped or that the old man will need to bargain with the driver not to be
run over, so long as bargaining can bring about the desired Pareto-
optimal outcome. The examples provide a powerful illustration of the

---

[24] Thus, Demsetz argues that levels of public investment in automobile safety devices
should depend on the price one would be willing to pay for additional expected years of life,
which could be estimated by a sophisticated economic model, if only the greater religiosity of
the poor did not interfere! Demsetz writes: "Suppose that we are interested in determining
how much the state should spend on automobile safety devices. To answer this question we
can calculate the cost of an additional safety device and compare it to the value of the lives
we expect it to save. If we are sophisticated, we can calculate this latter value by multiplying
the expected decrease in deaths by the value of a typical live person. The value of a typical
live person is frequently taken to depend on the discounted value of that portion of his
earnings that an accidental death will eliminate" (1966, 70). Demsetz continues: "The
difficulty with this analysis is that the correct solution will be to equate the marginal cost of
safety devices to the price that persons are willing to pay for expected reductions in their
accident rate. This price will be an individual matter. It will depend on a person's demand to
live longer, on his income, on the prices of other things, and on his taste for life. The latter
fact is knowable only to himself in principle, and although it will be revealed through
negotiation in the marketplace over the exchange of private property, it is only poorly
approximated by a sophisticated cost-benefit analysis. A poor man may be willing to pay a
higher price than a rich man for additional expected years of life, especially if he has a greater
fear of hell."

normative shortcomings of Keohane's Coase-inspired neoliberal institutionalism.[25]

When faced with these troubling illustrations, one may wonder how social welfare is to be defined. This worry is naturally compounded by the tendency of Keohane and Coase to equate welfare with efficiency and to measure efficiency in terms of monetary cost-benefit analysis whereby social welfare is identified with the least costly alternative from a societal point of view. The cost matrixes of the examples are constructed so that factory pollution, wandering cattle, rape, and pedestrian death are cast as negative externalities, as is evident in Keohane's adaptation for the case of the laundry as well. But what if the societal costs of letting the factory pollute, allowing the cattle to wander, raping the victim, and driving over the old man are lower than preventing these occurrences? This is a legitimate worry, one that has long haunted utilitarian theories that depend on such calculations.[26] I fully share the concern, especially in instances where those who disproportionately bear the costs of bargaining happen to be minority or relatively powerless groups. I want to stress, however, that significant fairness-related problems remain with an analysis of institutions rooted in the Coase theorem, regardless of how social welfare is defined. This is because for Coase

> *the problem* which we face in dealing with actions which have potentially harmful effects *is not simply one of restraining those responsible* for them. What has to be decided is whether the gain from preventing the harm is greater than the loss which would be suffered elsewhere as a result of stopping the action which produces the harm. (1960, 27)[27]

The allocation of costs and benefits is not of primary interest in this account; more important is the identification of the alternative that enhances social welfare. By contrast, from the point of view of fairness, *the problem IS simply one of restraining the perpetrator of the harm.* Accordingly, even on the most charitable understanding of social welfare and the normatively correct identification of the desired outcome, the substantive assignment of legal liability cannot be irrelevant.

It might be objected that I have been a little unfair to neoliberal institutionalism by reading Keohane out of context. After all, the functional theory of international regimes is developed to show how cooperation is possible even among self-interested actors in an anarchic international

---

[25] Keohane does not discuss any of these sinister examples. There are no references to Fried's earlier work (1978) in Keohane's book (1984). This is unfortunate, given that Fried offers a trenchant normative critique of the model that Keohane attempts to defend on normative grounds in his concluding chapter.

[26] Let me add that in the absence of a clearer specification, it is reasonable to suppose that Keohane's and Coase's conceptions of social welfare are rooted in a utilitarian moral theory.

[27] Emphasis added.

system. This is primarily a response to neorealist conceptualizations of the international system, rather than a normative account (Keohane 1986). In reversing the Coase theorem to provide the theoretical foundations of his functional view, Keohane is well aware that Coase himself made no claim to fairness when propounding the irrelevance of the substantive content of the rules of legal liability. In Keohane's words:

> Coase did not dispute that the rules of liability could be evaluated on grounds of fairness, but insisted that, given his assumptions, efficient arrangements could be consummated even where the rules of liability favored producers of externalities rather than their victims. (1984, 86).

Yet, despite having noted this in passing, Keohane goes on to conclude that the international regimes he theorizes and discusses are also justified from a variety of moral points of view, including cosmopolitanism.[28] Keohane's moral evaluation proceeds in terms of whether the effects of regimes are mutually beneficial for their participants above a certain threshold of voluntariness.[29] How demanding this threshold is depends on the particular features of the moral perspectives Keohane takes up in turn.[30] But even when the threshold is at its most demanding, as in cosmopolitan evaluation, the reference point for the moral assessment is given by the lack of international cooperation. Accordingly, the benefits reaped when regimes are present to facilitate international cooperation are contrasted with the benefits that would be reaped in their absence, in order to conclude that even "contemporary international economic regimes may be [morally] superior to politically feasible alternatives [such as the complete absence or collapse of such regimes], although the principles on which they are based are morally deficient" (Keohane 1984, 256, 252).

This is a highly problematic suggestion from a moral point of view, for two reasons. First, the comparison between presence and absence that Keohane relies on in making his case for moral justification is not fit for the task, since the proper reference point for evaluating regimes is not their

---

[28] In subjecting regimes to moral scrutiny, Keohane appeals to both a "morality of states" perspective and a "cosmopolitan" perspective. For Keohane's evaluation of international regimes on the basis of a "morality of states" perspective, see Keohane 1984, 248. For Keohane's evaluation of international regimes on the basis of a "cosmopolitan" perspective see Keohane 1984, 249–57. Keohane explicitly relies on Beitz's distinction between the "morality of states" and "cosmopolitan morality" here. See Beitz 1979, parts 2 and 3, respectively.

[29] Keohane does not specify in exact terms what the threshold of voluntariness would be and with respect to what it works but rather leaves it to different moral perspectives to fill in the details. The basic idea Keohane captures in emphasizing voluntary participation is to rule out coercion through the legitimation of regimes on the basis of consent.

[30] When considering different types of cosmopolitan morality, Keohane writes that the differences between utilitarianism and contractarianism are marginal, since "rights-based argument depends in practice on estimates of the consequences of action" (1984, 251). Needless to say, Keohane's reduction of rights-based contractarian moral theory into consequential analysis is inaccurate, but this is not a point I wish to pursue here.

absence or collapse but is rather their presence under alternative organizing principles. It does not pass the test of fairness to point out that things would be even worse if the regimes in question did not exist. It is not enough to suggest that a present or emerging regime is the only politically feasible alternative at any given time. Such arguments can establish particular regimes as temporarily desirable steps in the long road toward fairness but do not amount to a full collective justification. For the latter, alternative institutional structures that can be set up for the realization of collective goals need to be assessed in the light of their underlying principles. Second, it is erroneous to use a theoretical framework that is explicitly amoral, such as the Coase theorem for reaching moral conclusions. Together, these two points give me reason to read Keohane out of context in order to correct for faulty moral conclusions that can be drawn from exchange theory.

In response, I emphasize that institutional fairness is not merely about the beneficial outcomes that regimes bring about, or even the actual substantive principles that these regimes happen to institutionalize in practice, but concerns first and foremost the justification of these principles. It may be true that the presence of current international regimes is morally preferable to their absence, but that does not make these regimes justified. No account of coordination that is founded upon an inverted Coase theorem can be regarded as morally justified without asking whether the substantive principles that emerge from cooperation end up favoring the morally correct rules of legal liability. It may even be the case that Keohane has hit upon the correct substantive principles in his discussion of specific actual regimes, but, given his theoretical model, this would be a matter of sheer luck.[31] Yet fairness is too important a matter to be left to luck alone. Because it is impossible to ground the notion of fairness in an account of institutions that does not have the conceptual capabilities for specifying what fair procedures and fair substantive principles entail in the formation and regulation of cooperative practices, neoliberal institutionalism is doomed to remain normatively poor.

Conclusion

I have argued that international fairness must be theorized in relation to international institutions that serve as practices of collective justification. Taking the dimension of collective justification seriously in the construal of fairness claims requires being attentive to jurisprudential issues that involve the relationship between law and morality, as well as conceptual matters that concern the functioning of institutions. At a minimum, my theoretical sketch of the types of questions that emerge in these domains points in the direction of preserving space for civil disobedience in

---

[31] In various books, Keohane discusses at some length the actual international regimes regulating oceans, oil, and the environment, among others.

international institutions. I have also suggested that the dominant account of institutions in mainstream international relations scholarship is inadequate for the purpose of illuminating how collective justification works. While I have not proposed substantive principles of international fairness at this stage, I have identified the main ideas that need to be fleshed out more fully by a theory of fairness that has collective justification in institutional settings at its core. Ultimately, more specific principles can best be developed in light of these theoretical considerations in concrete case studies of practical dilemmas encountered in the various issue areas of world politics, such as those emanating from global policy debates over trade, health, and the environment. It is my hope that a conscious effort to complement theoretically informed case studies with a practice oriented theoretical framework in this way can not only induce a mutually enriching intellectual exercise but also open up creative new institutional possibilities for the advancement of global justice.

Acknowledgments

I would like to thank Christian Barry, Joe Carens, Stanley Hoffmann, Peter Katzenstein, Armen Marsoobian, Carla Norrlöf, Lou Pauly, Guy Peters, Thomas Pogge, and David Welch for their comments and encouragement. I also gratefully acknowledge the financial support of the Institute for Advanced Study, which provided me with the time to undertake this exploration.

References

Annan, Kofi. 1999a. "Secretary-General Presents His Annual Report to General Assembly." United Nations Press Release SG/SM/7136 GA/ 9596 (20 September 1999). Also available online at http://www.un.org/ News/Press/docs/1999/19990920.sgsm7136.html
———. 1999b. "Two Concepts of Sovereignty." *The Economist* 352, no. 8137 (18 September 1999): 49–50. Also available online at http:// www.un.org/News/ossg/sg/stories/kaecon.html
Beitz, Charles. 1979. *Political Theory and International Relations.* Princeton: Princeton University Press.
Coase, Ronald. 1960. "The Problem of Social Cost." *Journal of Law and Economics* 3 (October): 1–44.
Demsetz, Harold. 1966. "Some Aspects of Porperty Rights." *Journal of Law and Economics* 9 (October): 61–70.
Devlin, Patrick. 1961. *Law and Morals.* Birmingham: Holdsworth Club.
———. 1965. *The Enforcement of Morals.* Oxford: Oxford University Press.
Dworkin, Ronald, ed. 1977. *The Philosophy of Law.* Oxford: Oxford University Press.

Dworkin, Ronald. 1985. *A Matter of Principle.* Cambridge, Mass.: Harvard University Press.

———. 1986. *Law's Empire.* Cambridge, Mass.: Harvard University Press.

———. 1996. *Freedom's Law.* Oxford: Oxford University Press.

———. 2000. *Sovereign Virtue.* Cambridge, Mass.: Harvard University Press.

Franck, Thomas. 1968. *The Structure of Impartiality.* London: Macmillan.

———. 1975. "Constitutional Law of United Nations." Faculty of Law, Toronto: University of Toronto.

———. 1982a. *The New International Economic Order.* New York: United Nations Institute for Training and Research.

———. 1982b. *Human Rights in Third World Perspective.* Dobbs Ferry, N.Y.: Oceana Publications.

———. 1990. *The Power of Legitimacy Among Nations.* Oxford: Oxford University Press.

———. 1995. *Fairness in International Law and Institutions.* Oxford: Oxford University Press.

———. 2002. *Recourse to Force.* Cambridge: Cambridge University Press.

Frankena, William. 1973. *Ethics.* Englewood Cliffs, N.J.: Prentice-Hall.

Fried, Charles. 1978. *Right and Wrong.* Cambridge, Mass.: Harvard University Press.

Fuller, Lon. 1949. *The Problems of Jurisprudence.* Brooklyn: Foundation Press.

———. 1967. *Legal Fictions.* Stanford: Stanford University Press.

———. 1968. *Anatomy of the Law.* Westport, Conn.: Greenwood Press.

———. 1969. *The Morality of Law.* New Haven: Yale University Press.

———. 1981. *The Principles of Social Order.* Durham, N.C.: Duke University Press.

George, Robert, ed. 1992. *Natural Law Theory: Contemporary Essays.* Oxford: Oxford University Press.

———, ed. 1996. *Natural Law, Liberalism, and Morality: Contemporary Essays.* Oxford: Oxford University Press.

George, Robert, and Christopher Wolfe, eds. 2000. *Natural Law and Public Reason.* Washington, D.C.: Georgetown University Press.

Hardt, Michael, and Antonio Negri. 2000. *Empire.* Cambridge, Mass.: Harvard University Press.

Hart, H. L. A. 1963. *Law, Liberty, and Morality.* Oxford: Oxford University Press.

———. 1983. *Essays in Jurisprudence and Philosophy.* Oxford: Oxford University Press.

———. 1994. *The Concept of Law.* Oxford: Oxford University Press.

Hobbes, Thomas. 1991. *Leviathan.* Edited by Richard Tuck. Cambridge: Cambridge University Press.

Holzgrefe, J. L., and Robert Keohane, eds. 2003. *Humanitarian Intervention.* Cambridge: Cambridge University Press.

Ignatieff, Michael. 2003. *Empire Lite*. New York: Penguin.

Independent International Commission on Kosovo. 2000. *The Kosovo Report*. Oxford: Oxford University Press. Also available online at http://www.reliefweb.int/library/documents/thekosovoreport.htm

Johnson, Chalmers. 2000. *Blowback*. New York: Henry Holt.

Keohane, Robert. 1984. *After Hegemony*. Princeton: Princeton University Press.

———, ed. 1986. *Neorealism and Its Critics*. New York: Columbia University Press.

———. 1989. *International Institutions and State Power*. Boulder: Westview Press.

———. 2002. *Power and Governance in a Partially Globalized World*. New York: Routledge.

Krasner, Stephen. 1983. "Structural Causes and Regime Consequences: Regimes as Intervening Variables." In *International Regimes*, edited by Stephen Krasner, 1–21. Ithaca, N.Y.: Cornell University Press.

Kratochwil, Friedrich, and John Ruggie. 1986. "International Organization: A State of the Art on an Art of the State." *International Organization* 40, no. 4 (autumn): 753–75.

Locke, John. 1988. *Two Treatises of Government*. Edited by Peter Laslett. Cambridge: Cambridge University Press.

———. 2002. *Writings on Religion*. Edited by Victor Nuovo. Oxford: Oxford University Press.

———. 2003. *Political Writings*. Edited by David Wootton. Indianapolis: Hackett.

Mapel, David, and Terry Nardin, eds. 1992. *Traditions of International Ethics*. Cambridge: Cambridge University Press.

Peters, Guy. 1999. *Institutional Theory in Political Science: The "New Institutionalism."* New York: Printer.

Pogge, Thomas. 2002. *World Poverty and Human Rights: Cosmopolitan Responsibilities and Reforms*. Cambridge: Polity Press.

———. Forthcoming. "Power versus Truth: Greater Legal Flexibility for Military Interventions?" In *NOMOS: International Intervention*, edited by Terry Nardin and Melissa Williams. New York: New York University Press.

Rawls, John. 1971. *A Theory of Justice*. Cambridge, Mass.: Harvard University Press.

———. 1996. *Political Liberalism*. New York: Columbia University Press.

———. 1999a. *Collected Papers*. Cambridge, Mass.: Harvard University Press.

———. 1999b. *The Law of Peoples*. Cambridge, Mass.: Harvard University Press.

———. 2001. *Justice As Fairness: A Restatement*. Cambridge, Mass.: Harvard University Press.

United Nations High Commissioner for Human Rights. 2000. "Intellectual Property Rights and Human Rights" (17 August). http://www.unhchr.ch/Huridocda/Huridoca.nsf/0/c462b62cf8a07b13c12569 700046704e?Opendocument
Various authors. 2003. "The Revival of Empire." Special issue of *Ethics and International Affairs* 17, no. 2 (fall). http://www.carnegiecouncil.org/viewmedia.php/prm1D/1002?PHPSESSID = gf0e8f1f578e24dbeb e4edbe87bebaed
Walzer, Michael. 2003. "Is There an American Empire?" *Dissent* (fall) 50, no. 4. http://www.dissentmagazine.org/menutest/articles/fa03/walzer.htm
World Trade Organization. 2001. "Declaration on the TRIPS Agreement and Public Health" (14 November). http://www.wto.org/english/thewto_e/minist_e/min01_e/mindecl_trips_e.htm
———. 2003. "Decision on the Implementation of Paragraph 6 of the Doha Declaration and Public Health" (30 August). http://www.wto.org/english/tratop_e/trips_e/implem_para6_e.htm

6

THREE (POTENTIAL) PILLARS OF TRANSNATIONAL ECONOMIC JUSTICE: THE BRETTON WOODS INSTITUTIONS AS GUARANTORS OF GLOBAL EQUAL TREATMENT AND MARKET COMPLETION

ROBERT HOCKETT

1. Introduction

1.1.   The justice of the global economic order has received a healthy dose of renewed philosophic attention of late (e.g., Pogge 2002; Shue 1996; Steiner 1994, 1999; Unger 1996). Replace the word *philosophic* with *critical*, and the same may be said of three institutions widely viewed as lynchpins of that order—the International Monetary Fund (IMF, or "the Fund"), the World Bank (IBRD, or "the Bank"), and the General Agreement on Tariffs and Trade/World Trade Organization (GATT/WTO)—which, taking minimal license, I shall call collectively "the Bretton Woods Institutions" (e.g., Blustein 2001; Caufield 1996; Dunkley 2000; Stiglitz 2002).[1]

The recently renewed attention paid to global justice, however, has not as yet been notably rich in focus upon the constitutive roles originally envisaged for, or currently played by, the aforementioned institutions, or upon how those institutions act, or are designed to act, in concert. Nor has the widespread, and surely warranted, public controversy generated by the Bretton Woods institutions featured much in the way of any systematically articulated point of view from which to judge their performances.

I wish, therefore, in this contribution to bring two important lines of inquiry and criticism together—a task that now would seem to be both possible and pressing. For it is striking that on both a compelling,

---

[1] "License" because (a) the Bretton Woods conference actually brought us only the IMF and IBRD and (b) the WTO did not come into being until 1994. "Minimal" because, on the other hand, (a) the Bretton Woods framers explicitly viewed the financial institutions that they conceived as essential complements to the GATT (see, e.g., James 1996) and (b) the WTO, brought into being in 1994, in essence took on the role originally envisaged for an "International Trade Organization" (ITO) fifty years earlier (idem). It should also be noted here that the International Bank for Reconstruction and Development (IBRD) is but one of a small cluster of institutions collectively known as the "World Bank *Group*." I use the word *Bank* to refer to the collectivity rather than to the IBRD alone and use "IBRD" to refer specifically to one member of that collectivity.

institutionally informed conception of global justice and a plausible reading of the mandates of each of the Bretton Woods institutions, the three organizations together can be viewed, at least in potential, as a kind of "three-legged stool" upon which might rest a just global economic order. As the simile suggests, however, each leg must be adequately constructed before the founding might be considered secure. And each must bear its proper portion of the weight borne by the whole.

1.2.   In what follows, then, I first lay out what I take to be a compelling sketch of what a just world economic order will look like. That account prescribes what I shall label "three realms of equal treatment and market completion"—namely, the global products, services, and labor markets; the global investment/financial markets; and the global preparticipation opportunity allocation. I then note how, with minimal if indeed any departure from familiar canons of traditional international legal mandate interpretation, each of the Bretton Woods institutions can be viewed at least in part as charged with the task of fostering or guaranteeing equal treatment and market completion within one of those three realms. Thence I suggest that one of the Bretton Woods institutions in particular—the Bank—has, for reasons of negligent, reckless, or willful injustice on the part of influential state actors in the world community (*not* on the part of its *staff*), fallen farthest short in pursuit of its ideal mandate. And I suggest, only somewhat more tentatively, that many anxieties over the operations of the other two institutions—the GATT/WTO and the Fund—actually stem from dysfunctions visited upon the system as a whole by the Bank's falling short. I conclude accordingly that a fuller empowerment of the Bank to effect its mission will press the full system more nearly into balance—kicking the stool to its feet, so to speak—and thereby the world into justice. Short of that fuller empowerment, I suggest, the continued conferral of powers upon the other two Bretton Woods institutions should be conditioned upon those powers' likelihood of yielding or conducing to some "second best" that is substantially more just than the status quo.

2. Justice in Theory, Metatheory, and Mechanism

2.1.   I shall not here argue exhaustively for one, detailed conception of global justice (see Hockett 2004a, 2004b, 2004c). Nor shall I survey all candidates currently on offer or anticipate and address every objection that might be, or has been, raised to sundry components of the summary account that I shall set forth here (idem). I shall instead offer what I believe nearly anyone will recognize to be a presumptively persuasive conception. This conception bears critical resemblances to several quite influential accounts of justice (e.g., Arneson 1989; Cohen 1989; Dworkin 2000; Roemer 1998; Sen 1993), the realization of any of which would be preferable to the state in which we find the world at present.

2.2. Justice is concerned with appropriate distributions of benefit and burden over individuals.[2] That raises at least three constitutive concerns, as well as a trio of critical collateral concerns, that must occupy any complete theory of justice. Constitutively, we must give an account of what shall count for purposes of justice as relevant benefits or burdens. We must also give an account of the individuals whose benefits and burdens will concern justice. And we must say something about how we are to determine the propriety of the distribution. Collaterally, the fact that (a) we are concerned with distributions over plural individuals and that (b) plural benefits and burdens might be of various kinds requires that we also take account of three measurement concerns either in our constitutive account of justice, in our considerations of our justice account's practical instantiability, or both. Specifically, we must concern ourselves with measurement in an absolute, quantificational sense ("how much," simpliciter, "of benefit/burden B"); in an interpersonal comparability-in-the-holding sense ("how much B held by person P_1, in comparison to how much held by person P_2"); and in what, for reasons that will become clear in a moment, we might call an "interdistribuendanal" commensurability sense ("how much 'total benefit/burden' in case of this much B_1, that much B_2, and so on").

I call the relevant benefit/burden question the question of the proper *distribuendum* (plural, *-enda*). That of the proper characterization of justice's beneficiaries I call the question of the *distribuees*. And the question of a distribution's propriety I call the question of the appropriate *distribution rule*, or *formula*. I call the collateral measurement questions the quantificational, interpersonal comparability, and commensurability questions.[3]

---

[2] One could take the variable "individuals" to range over any number of sorts of entity—human persons, sentient beings, families, cities, "peoples" (linguistically or culturally identified groups), nation-states, and so on. I believe that any such selection that does not ultimately reduce consistently to justice over persons would be objectionably fetishistic, but I cannot argue for that proposition here. Please see Hockett 2004a and Hockett 2004b.

[3] I have argued elsewhere (Hockett 2004a) that we must answer each justice-constitutive and collateral question with a view to the others. Here I simply sketch that account of justice which it seems to me flows most "directly"—isomorphically, so to speak—from the most intuitively plausible fillings-in of each of the aforementioned variables. A further advantage

2.3.   The most plausible account of distribuees is that which construes them as boundedly responsible agents, capable of effecting or affecting their own well-being while constrained in so doing by features of the environments into which they are born. Their capacities—themselves features of those environments—only permit them limited latitude in altering or exiting from the same. To view a person as a responsible agent is to view her as, at least in part, self-regulating per a disposition to value outcomes and to choose from among alternative courses of action, as well as per a capacity to recognize and respect this same autonomy in others.

This view of distribuees suggests a view of justice-relevant distribuenda as anything which, consistent with respect for others' autonomy as just noted, distribuees themselves value or disvalue, anything which they would wish to obtain or attain or avoid.[4] If "benefits" are good and "burdens" ill, and if distribuees are environment-responsive, responsible agents whose autonomy in forming conceptions of the good and the ill is to be respected, then the distribuenda that are of concern to justice will be more or less whatever distributable items are of concern to justice's beneficiaries—its distribuees.[5]

These conceptions of distribuees and distribuenda appear to recommend the following formulation of the appropriate distribution rule, sometimes styled the "luck-egalitarian," but what I shall call the "endowment-egalitarian," principle: Allow distribuees' holdings of distribuenda or quantities thereof the holding of which tends to vary foreseeably in response to their responsible actions or attitudes to *vary* with those responsible actions or attitudes; and *equalize* holdings of all *other* distribuenda or quantities thereof. I call that first component of anyone's holdings the "ethically endogenous" component. It is that component for the holding of which the distribuee, conceived as a responsible agent, is appropriately held ethically accountable.

I call the second component of the agent's holdings the "ethically exogenous" component, or the "residuum." It is, as it were by definition, that portion for which she is not responsible—that portion over the holding of which there is good reason to suppose she bore no choice.

of my fillings-in, I believe—beyond their seeming more intuitively "direct" in their variable filling—is that they readily suggest a simple institutional embodiment.

[4] I trust that I need not tarry here over endogenous, "external" or otherwise objectionable preferences, about which of course any liberal theory of justice must ultimately speak. See, e.g., Stigler and Becker 1977; Dworkin 1977, 234f.; Sen 1979. The matter is too complex to dispose in this brief account, but I do not in passing over it intend to be taken for dismissing it.

[5] Again, with the caveat mentioned in the previous footnote.

2.4. These characterizations of the distribuee, distribuendum, and distribution formula variables operate in conjunction with both conceptual and operational measurement constraints in a number of complex and practically critical ways.

First, the matter of simple quantifiability has stood in the way of settlement upon mutually agreeable distribuenda and distribution formulae in the following way: On the one hand, luck, resource, opportunity, access, goods, and benefits are not intelligible *as* such—and thus are not appreciable as ethically significant—apart from some person's (actual or idealized) *preference* for or *valuation* of these items, hence, apart from their yielding some manner of "satisfaction," "value," "happiness," "utility," "welfare," or "well-being," conceived in some suitable manner.

On the other hand, these latter states—welfare, "utility," and so forth—do not lend themselves to cardinal measurement. Relatedly, they cannot be directly distributed to anyone. They are experienced only as "outputs" of utility functions the inputs to which must be some objective item or items, rather than some subjective state or states. And while these objective inputs are, by and large, cardinally quantifiable, so long as the outputs that render them ethically significant are not it is difficult to determine how much of any of them anyone ethically ought to have.

What is more, *bounded* agents are in part *responsible* for, and in part *not* responsible for, their own utility functions. One can be innately more difficult to satisfy than others, and one can in a manner *choose* to be more difficult—or expensive—to satisfy than others (see Arrow 1973; Dworkin 2000). And the difficulty of cardinally measuring happiness intractably afflicts the already difficult task of separately tracing the ethically endogenous (responsible) and the ethically exogenous (nonresponsible) grounds of one's utility function—of one's translating objective inputs into subjective outputs.

Second, even were welfare cardinally measurable as a state of any given person, it is unclear whether it would be *interpersonally comparable* as a state *type* enjoyed among *multiple* persons. For there can appear to be, intuitively, something radically distinct as between P_1's happiness and P_2's happiness, presumably owing in some manner to there seeming to be something radically unique about every sentient being's subjectivity, or consciousness, itself (see, e.g., Chalmers 1998; Nagel 1999, 1991).

Third, the fact that there are *multiple* inputs—benefits and burdens—that appear differentially to affect utility and disutility, coupled with the difficulty attending cardinally measuring the utility and disutility afforded by such benefits and burdens, would render it difficult, even were interpersonal comparability somehow unproblematic, to determine how much of benefit B_1 would compensate P_1 for a shortage of, say, B_2 relative to person P_2. Unless the appropriate distribution formula were to mandate a distinct distribution of each good and ill over all distribuees independent of the distribution of the other goods and ills—a seemingly implausible suggestion—we require "rates of exchange" between goods and ills themselves in order to derive a numéraire or index suitable to determining how much "good-or-ill-stuff in total" any distribuee holds. But since utility is the touchstone of some objective item's beneficial or burdensome status to an agent, and since said utility is problematic in the measurement, it is not clear how we are to commensurate disparate benefits and burdens in a manner pertinent to justice. Our would-be numéraire is itself cardinally nonquantifiable.

2.5.   Happily, there appears to be one mechanism, readily constructible in theory and seemingly approximable in practice, by which we might simultaneously *circumvent* all three *measurement* problems, *while* doing justice to the three values assigned the *constitutive* justice-theoretic variables (responsible agents, all benefits and burdens adjudged such by such agents, endowment-egalitarian distribution). The same mechanism enables us to address, at least in part, the problem posed by bounded agents' being responsible in part, while not in whole, for their own utility functions. To the degree that we can practically realize this mechanism, then, we can simultaneously render the world more practically just and resolve, or unobjectionably sidestep, the principal measure-theoretic problems.

Here, in schematic form, is the mechanism: Assume a "complete" market—a forum in which all and only desired voluntary trading occurs—in (a) all goods and services that can practically be made available and that anyone values (hence, that are cognizable in justice as ethically relevant distribuenda), and (b) contingent claims to compensation upon the occurrence of any eventuality that anyone disvalues, payable by anyone willing to take the opposite sides of these (what amount to) "bets," on the disvalued contingencies. Assume further that this market is "neutral" in the following sense: First, each participant enters it with an initial endowment of (in the nature of property rights to) desired assets equal to that with which everyone else enters it. And, second, regulatory norms effectively prevent such collusively, strategically, or expropriatively opportunistic behaviors as would effectively result in some participants' coming to possess greater or lesser holdings or "price-affecting effective demand powers" than would be traceable to their initial (ethically exogenous) endowments and independent (ethically endogenous) transaction histories alone.[6] This mechanism, I claim, straightforwardly instantiates the justice account sketched above.

2.6. Before turning to the ultimate realizability of the mechanism in its entirety or the question of a "second best" absent full realizability, let us note, first, how it satisfies the prescriptions entailed by the three above-offered fillings-in of the constitutive justice variables. Let us also note, second, how it addresses the critical measurement concerns. And let us note, third, how its realization both would seem to require and would seem to be straightforwardly brought about by equal treatment and market completion in the three Bretton Woods–associated realms noted at the very outset of this article.

2.6.1. The mechanism straightforwardly honors distribuees as respon-sible agents, who transact voluntarily pursuant to their own, autonomous relative valuations of items and contingencies that they prefer and disprefer. The mechanism straightforwardly treats as distribuenda what-ever goods and ills the distribuees themselves value or disvalue—what-ever goods and ills they seek to obtain, attain or avoid, from which goods and ills their "utilities" derive. And the mechanism, via the neutrality imposed upon it at the outset and retained throughout, equalizes all that is ethically exogenous—all that is not traceable in the holding directly to a choice—while allowing holdings over time none-theless to vary with ethically endogenous transactional decisions. All holdings at time T_n, that is to say, are traceable to equalized holdings at T_0 and voluntary choices.

2.6.2. The mechanism sidesteps, in an ethically satisfactory way, the problem of cardinal utility measurement by allowing distribuees, via their voluntary trading activity, presumptively—by dint of the "first funda-mental theorem of welfare economics" (see, e.g., Arrow 1951)—to "maximize" utility. And that maximization occurs in a manner that is consistent with (a) ethically exogenous endowment equality among all market participants, and (b) consequently equally shared scarcity of the resources from which distribuees "produce" their own utility. (In the jargon, the mechanism fosters regular tâttonement toward Equal Division Walrasian Equilibria, which, it is well established, are fair, envy free, and

---

[6] I shall here set aside the question of the means by which endowment equalization would be effected, and the "problem of future generations."

Pareto efficient (see Baumol 1986; Foley 1967; Hockett 2004a, 2004b, 2004c; Kolm 1972; Pazner and Schmeidler 1974; Varian 1974; Walras 1954). It doesn't matter for justice purposes, that is to say, what sort of number—cardinal *or* ordinal—that we might assign to distribuees' utilities, or how we manage to scale such numbers, so long as we know that the utilities are the "highest" possible consistent with the correct distribution rule and the (consequently equally shouldered) constraints posed by the environment.

Similarly, the mechanism—again unobjectionably—sidesteps the problem of interpersonal utility comparison. For we have stipulated that the resource "inputs" (that is, the ethically exogenous inputs, sometimes called "internal resources," e.g., Dworkin 2000) that go into "utility production" are themselves counted—in the form of drugs, supplements, or contingent claims to compensation—among the exogenous endowments that must be equalized over participants. And in such cases whatever the absolute or comparative "quanta" of "utility" enjoyed by distribuees, we shall know that these are the "highest" that they can be consistent with the appropriate distribution rule and the consequently equally shouldered constraints posed by the resource environment.

Finally, the mechanism "automatically," as it were, commensurates distribuenda in the only way that ethically matters, via the autonomous implicit comparative valuations of autonomously transacting distribuees (see Hockett 2004a; Hockett and Risse 2004.) We need not worry ourselves over how much of B_2 "would" or will compensate P_1 for a deficit of B_1, let alone construct a "perfectionist" index of all goods and ills (on which see Arneson 1990; idem). Our distribuees themselves will, in effect, autonomously and with equal voice construct the relevant index—a spontaneously emergent *price* index. That index amounts to an aggregated comparative "social" valuation of goods and ills, in the construction of which each participant has had an equal "vote" (idem). (Again, provided that there exist market completeness and neutrality in the senses explicated above.) And so yet again, in a manner that reflects the constraints both of relative environmental scarcities and of the appropriate distribution rule, we find the mechanism allowing the measurement question to "take care of itself" to precisely the degree that justice itself demands care be taken at all.

2.6.3.   Now recall that the two critical provisos to the mechanism's being capable of affording full justice were that the envisaged market be "complete" and "neutral." "Completeness" means, roughly, that all goods and ills that should count as ethically significant for justice purposes—namely, all items and contingencies that justice's distribuees themselves can acquire, provide or produce and that they value or disvalue—can be transferred from relatively less desiring holders to more desiring nonholders via voluntary transaction on that idealized market.[7] Familiar goods and services markets in "advanced" and even many barter economies are largely—or at any rate potentially—complete in this sense, at least within their jurisdictional walls. But gross disparities in ethically exogenous endowments, as well as certain artificial barriers found between jurisdictionally separated markets, tend to diminish the *fuller* completeness that those markets would enjoy were they both endowment egalitarian and unsegmented.

What is less immediately obvious is how very *in*complete the *"ills* markets"—that is, the contingent-claims markets—currently remain. We are only just beginning to appreciate—and take measures in light of— how much more in the way of risk could, even with current (largely new) technologies, be traded than currently are traded (see, e.g., Hockett 2004c; Shiller 2003; 1993; Allen and Gale 1994).[8] This is particularly so as we begin to remove barriers that segment the financial markets, in effect bringing changes that are greatly enriching the variety of risks that can be traded from less to more desiring bearers worldwide. Turning from

---

[7] This is my justice-theoretic modification of a concept more familiar to welfare and financial economists. See, e.g., Allais 1953; Arrow 1953; generally Magill and Quinzii 1996.

[8] An example or two might be helpful here: Financial derivatives, as has been widely observed, in recent decades have enabled relatively wealthy market participants—in particular, large financial institutions—to trade formerly untradable risks and thereby improve the aggregate efficiency of risk-bearing arrangements worldwide. See, e.g., Allen and Gale 1994. Hence, for example, two large lending institutions, one with its payments receivable denominated in terms of fixed interest rates and the other with receivables denominated in terms of variable interest rates, might enter into a "swap" contract pursuant to which each literally trades payment streams with the other for some term of time. They will do so, presumably, because they differentially assess or value the risk attendant upon the variable-denominated stream and the certainty attending the fixed-denominated stream. Options, warrants, futures, "swaptions," and a host of other derivative contracts similarly permit large market players to parcel out and trade classes of risk previously untradable. But no such contracts, as yet, permit smaller players to diversify away the risks that they bear. And the latter risks, when they eventuate, can be rather more devastating to their "small-player" bearers than are risks currently traded by large players. New data-gathering, -accounting, and -parceling technologies, however, accompanied by the "globalization" of the financial markets, hold promise for smaller players. Thus, for example, derivative securities whose values countervary with macroeconomic aggregates, which in turn vary with individuals' incomes—e.g., "GDP-consols," "local real-estate collars," and "average occupational income collars"—will enable individuals in effect to surrender some "upside" gains represented by rises above some stipulated average on the parts of aggregates with which their incomes are positively correlated, in return for compensation of "downside" losses represented by drops below the stipulated average on the parts of aggregates with which their incomes are positively correlated. Please see Hockett 2004c, 212–25.

completeness to neutrality, "neutrality" means, roughly, that each *participant* in the "complete" market should "count" for one and only one identically social-valuationally empowered, comparatively goods- and ills-valuing agent. Participants, that is to say, must enter and leave the market, no matter what the time, with holdings traceable only to equal exogenous endowments and whatever endogenous decisions they have made (such as gratuitously to transfer, trade, expend labor, waste, and so on). This is not only a straightforward requirement of the justice conception; it also, as suggested above, would appear to be required by the mechanism-requisite of "completeness" itself.

Now completeness and neutrality, in the senses just sketched, jointly require equal treatment of all market participants in the product and services (including labor) markets, in the investment/financial markets, and in the allocation of initial and continuing participation opportunity. What is more, equal treatment in these three realms appears to *suffice* to afford completeness and neutrality in the senses elaborated to the fullest extent practicable.

Begin with the necessity of equal treatment to the neutrality and completeness of the products and services markets: If the class of distribuees properly of concern to justice is the universe of *all* human agents, then the mechanism that is fully to *effect* justice must *reach* all human agents. *All* agents' valuations of the goods and ills potentially available to or threatening anyone, that is to say, which valuations are *carried out*—in trading behavior—relative to holdings traceable to equal endowments of all valuables and disvaluables, must *enter into* the aggregated transactional, and hence the aggregated implicit valuational, decisions that determine the uses, relative prices, and distributions of those goods and ills among all human agents. But to treat actual or would-be market participants *unequally*—that is, to prohibit their entry into the markets altogether or to tax their participation differentially according to their ethically irrelevant identities, attributes, or affiliations rather than simply to allow the circulation of their offerings and their desired goods and services to be determined by the distribution of wants over the full universe of agents—would in effect be both to disequalize their initial ethically exogenous endowments and partly to segment (render incomplete) the market. It would therefore be to fall short of both neutrality and completeness in the senses elaborated.

Let us turn next to the necessity of equal treatment, neutrality, and completeness of the investment/financial markets. The argument here is structurally identical to that offered in connection with the products and services markets. These markets are worth separate classification and consideration, however, for at least three reasons. First, these markets currently are radically—and now unnecessarily—less complete than are the goods and (other) services markets.[9] Second, they are the principal realm in which what I have called "ills trading" (via risk trading), as distinguished from "goods trading," is effected; and *both* goods and ills must be traded in order for justice to be effected via the mechanism that I have sketched. And, third, the investment/financial markets also are the means by which we trade *time*-indexed goods and services with others, in view of our differential valuations of goods and services according as they are consumed or provided at different times. They can be viewed as diachronic extensions of the synchronic goods and services markets, to some extent bridging the justice mechanism across time and generations.

Turn finally to the participation-opportunity allocation. By this I mean both the formal and the substantive capacity of every agent to participate in the "neutral" and "complete" markets schematically described above. Now an equal "formal" capacity to participate is, in essence, the legal right to take part on equal terms with others—that is, a right not to be excluded or taxed by dint of one's ethically irrelevant identity, attributes, or affiliations. Hence it already is guaranteed by the right to equal treatment in the products, services, and investment/financial markets. The "substantive" capacity to participate, however, is, in essence, the ethically exogenous endowment discussed previously. It is what each participant "brings to the market" at any given time in anticipation of participating. Market neutrality requires equal treatment with respect to this allocation, then, quite trivially: "Neutrality" has been *defined*, in part, *by reference* to equality of this sort. (The ethical significance and compellingness of the definition was, I trust, sufficiently elaborated above.)

But market *completeness also*, *less* trivially, requires equal treatment in respect of the participation-opportunity allocation. Here the reasoning again follows the lines of the reasoning offered in connection with the products and services markets: Practical completeness requires that total trading opportunity—the total number of transactions in which one might engage—be maximized within the constraints imposed (a) by others' wishes to trade or not to trade, (b) by technology, and (c) by the aggregate resource endowment. And that maximization is effected only when every agent capable and desirous of trading is a participant in the market on equal terms with everybody else.

---

[9] Please see the previous footnote.

Once it is established that each form of equal treatment is necessary to affording market completeness and neutrality, establishing at least a prima facie case that all three forms jointly *suffice* to affording such completeness and neutrality is straightforward. We simply note that affording every agent equal formal and substantive capacity to transact in the market and affect (that is, equally "vote" upon) the relative valuations and distributions of all things that are adjudged good or ill, and that are transferable, yields precisely that neutrality (traceability to equal ethically exogenous endowments supplemented or deducted from by ethically endogenous choices) and completeness (participation of all potential participants, on equal terms) defined above—the fullest forms of neutrality and completeness apparently possible. What has been left out? What practically satisfiable additional requirement will yield a greater or more satisfactory degree of neutrality or completeness? Affording global equal treatment to all human persons, that is, all responsible agents in the three realms noted, then, would appear to be extensionally equivalent to affording that market completeness and neutrality which jointly constitute the mechanism that is the most compelling justice conception's most straightforward embodiment.

3. Global Institutions, Best and "Second Best"

3.1. I turn now to what it would be institutionally to guarantee (a) equal treatment of all human agents and (b) practical market completeness in the three realms just elaborated. Remarkably, there is one global institution in each realm that can be viewed ideally yet plausibly as charged with guaranteeing, or at the very least furthering, equal treatment and market completion of precisely the kinds just elaborated for that realm. Were each fully to carry out its appointed or idealized task, it would provide a reasonable approximation of the mechanism schematized above.

3.2. Begin with the products and services (including labor) markets, where the case for the existence, already, of a global equal-treatment and market-completion norm policed by one of the Bretton Woods institutions is most easily laid out. Global equal treatment in and completion of these markets would entail, at a minimum, that goods and services trade for one another at rates of exchange determined solely by the untrammeled trading activities of those who trade them—hence by the relative valuations of the goods and services by agents implicit in the trades. What would be prohibited by an equal-treatment and market-completing norm in these markets would be any change to the relative exchange rates or valuations of goods and services worked by an organized imposition of a supply quota or surcharge, or by supply of a subsidy, to the availability, purchase, or provision of the goods or services in question on the basis of the ethically irrelevant (exogenous) identities, attributes, or affiliations of the purchasers or sellers. Yet such a prohibition is, in effect, precisely what is mandated—as an end state to which the governments of the world are expected gradually to move the global trading regime—by the GATT/WTO system.

Here is how: The GATT/WTO is commonly observed to operate via four foundational legal commitments, or "pillars" (see, e.g., Bhala and Kennedy 1998, 59–115; Das 1999, 11–45, 55–72; Jackson 1999, 139–73, 213–28; Krueger 2000). The first is the so-called unconditional most-favored-nation obligation. This norm prohibits any signatory or member from discriminating against or affording preferences to sellers of goods (or eventually services—see below) hailing from any other signatory or member (other than itself) relative to sellers hailing from the other signatories or members (see GATT Art. I; Bhala and Kennedy 1998, 60–78). The idea here is that citizens of all member states with whom citizens of a given member state trade should be treated identically.

The second foundational GATT/WTO commitment is the so-called national treatment obligation. This norm requires that all imports into a member country be treated identically to *domestically* supplied products (and eventually services, more on which, again, below) so far as "internal" taxes and regulations are concerned (see GATT Art. III; Bhala and Kennedy 1998, 90–105). The idea here is that, once goods (or eventually services) have entered a member country's borders and all entry duties (tariffs), if any, have been paid, those goods will circulate per the same terms as goods supplied domestically.

The third foundational GATT/WTO commitment is the so-called tariff-binding commitment. Pursuant to this obligation, member countries commit (a) to discriminate as between domestically supplied and nondomestically supplied products (and eventually services) in at most one way—namely, via the administration of customs duties (tariffs) laid upon entry into the member country's borders—and (b) over time, via negotiations among all member countries progressively to *reduce* those duties ultimately to the vanishing point (see GATT Art. II; Bhala and Kennedy 1998, 78–90). The idea here is to isolate unequal treatment by member states as between their own and other member states' citizens in one, particularly transparent, form and ultimately to minimize, then eliminate, that remaining form of unequal treatment itself.

The fourth foundational GATT/WTO commitment, rather like the second, actually amounts to a tautologous complement of the third: The so-called quantitative restrictions-elimination commitment (see GATT Art. XI; Bhala and Kennedy 1998, 105–14) is designed to end immediately—rather than merely gradually to phase out—the principal tariff substitute employed by member states to favor their own or some other members' suppliers over others through the imposition of import quotas.

Now, the GATT/WTO system remains, in more ways than are immediately apparent from the foregoing, incomplete and imperfect in its effectuation of equal treatment and market completion in the global products and services markets. There are numerous exceptions to the general rules that are the four foundational commitments related above— most of them exceptions invokable only temporarily and under conditions of acute domestic distress (so-called safeguard or Escape Clause provisions—see, e.g., GATT Art. XIX; Bhala and Kennedy 1998, 897–938), some invokable on behalf of the citizens of particularly poor member countries (see, e.g., GATT Arts. XVIII, XXXVI–XXXVIII; Bhala and Kennedy 1998, 399–488; Jackson 1999, 319–37). And member countries often prove quite clever, if in general only for brief periods, in evading GATT norms by, for example, exploiting the general health, public morals, and other exceptions to GATT obligations permitted under GATT Art. XX (see Jackson 1999, 229–45), or by maintaining that goods which consumers (our "distribuees") regard as substitutes nonetheless are not "like products" per GATT stipulation (see GATT Arts. II, III, VI, IX, XIII, XVI, XIX; Das 1999, 18–20). There also are markets— notably those in services (including financial services), intellectual property, telecommunications, trade-related investment measures, and government procurement—that have only recently—again, since 1994— gradually come to be reached by GATT norms (see GATS; TRIMS; TRIPS; Bhala and Kennedy 1998, 1241–333; Das 1999, 325–93; Jackson 1999, 305–17.) Finally, equal treatment in and completion of the *labor* markets as such—rather than via the goods and services markets—is not directly afforded by the GATT/WTO system at all—or, in any way effectively, by that international institution specifically charged with solicitude for labor, the International Labor Organization (ILO). (See, e.g., Basu et al. 2003, 271–325; Elliott and Freeman 2003, 93–110).[10]

But the ideal toward which the system is moving, and moving both more rapidly and effectively than ever before, should not be obscured by

---

[10] Rather remarkably, the most recent comprehensive treatise on international economic law and institutions—Lowenfeld 2002—does not even include so much as a citation of the ILO, let alone a discussion of its efficacy.

the afore-noted imperfections. We are headed toward a world in which there simply is no organized discrimination whatever among goods or services on the basis of the identities of their suppliers. In that world, suppliers of labor, too—a form of service—will be treated equally, at least insofar as treatment in the investment/financial markets and participation-opportunity endowments (discussed below) are also equalized. And, in light of the link between equality and completeness highlighted above, it will be a world in which products, services, and labor markets will be practically complete.

Now the *rationale* commonly proffered for the GATT/WTO system appeals to the comparative-advantage exploitation, hence the specialization, scale economies, and aggregate productivity gains, offered by global market integration. That rationale of course is fair enough in the proffering—the putative advantages would indeed tend to follow upon integration—insofar as we legitimately can be concerned with aggregate wealth apart from its distribution.[11] But what is seldom noted is that there is a *much—indeed, infinitely—more ethically compelling, justice-grounded* rationale for the equal treatment and ultimate market-completion norms promoted by the GATT/WTO system, at least when that system is complemented by the next two Bretton Woods sub-regimes that I shall discuss: It is that equal treatment in the products and services markets is necessary to effect that market completion and neutrality requisite to a just distribution of what responsible agents regard as benefits and burdens; and that, in conjunction with its two complements to which I next turn attention, it will *suffice* to effect that just distribution.

3.3. Turn now to the investment/financial markets. Here the case for equal treatment and market completion as jointly constitutive of a Bretton Woods institution's—in this case, the IMF's—raison d'être is only slightly more complicated in the making than was the case made in connection with the GATT/WTO. It is *somewhat* more complicated essentially because the Fund exists for rather *more* than equal-treatment and market-completion purposes.[12]

[11] Such concern is, of course, problematic, if not indeed ethically unintelligible. See, e.g., Dworkin 1980; Hockett 2004b.

[12] It is, for example, viewed both by its leading living legal commentator and by its most distinguished historian as above all else a forum for ongoing monetary cooperation between national authorities, the latter thought important owing to the dangers posed by global monetary instability (see Edwards 1985, 569, 655–57; James 1996, 586). However, this function itself can be viewed as providing a form of progressively financed global social insurance, the "premia" for which—in the form of member-country subscriptions—rise as

Let us consider the more transparently egalitarian aspects of the Fund's mandate.

First, as in the case of the products and services markets, global equal treatment and market completion in the investment/financial markets would require at a minimum (a) the elimination, in connection with financial flows, of obstacles predicated upon the ethically irrelevant ("exogenous") identities, attributes, or affiliations of the originators or recipients of such flows, rather as in the case of the GATT/WTO's "foundational commitments" in the products and services markets; and, perhaps more ambitiously, (b) the active facilitation of both (i) new financial markets in new forms of investment and risk trading and (ii) broader participation both in such new markets and in established financial markets.

Now note that precisely these desiderata are among the principal projects with which the Fund is engaged. Begin with the "constitutionally" easiest limb—the elimination of obstacles. The Fund's constitutive Articles of Agreement expressly prohibit member countries from slowing cross-border financial flows in one principal, "time-honored" manner in which such slowings have typically been imposed—namely, via discriminatory currency (exchange-rate) practices (see Fund Art. VIII, 3; Edwards 1985, 380–422). (It should be noted that this equal-treatment norm also complements those norms mandated by the GATT/WTO: One means, beyond tariffs and quotas, by which national governments traditionally have favored their own sellers is by manipulating the rates at which their currencies trade with other nations' currencies.)

The Fund also, in a rather more nuanced way, operates to lessen or eliminate member countries' slowings of capital flows in the *other* principal, "time-honored" manner commonly employed in the past—namely, via the imposition of capital-transfer controls.[13] The Fund's Articles of Agreement tend to be "dynamically" and "teleologically" interpreted (see Hockett 2002, 178–80). And while capital controls were seen among the institution's 1944 founders—Keynes in particular—as at that time necessary evils, the prevailing norm since the 1980s has been to view the necessity as having receded, and the evil now strictly to be avoided (idem; also Edwards 1985, 449–90). So the Fund tends, in its

---

the payer's wealth rises (see Fund Art. I (i); I (iii); I (v); I (vi); III, Schedule A (Quotas); Edwards 1985, 12–17, 167–298).

[13] Fund operations here are "more nuanced" in the following sense: On the one hand, the Fund's Articles expressly permit such controls (see Fund Art. VI, 3). On the other hand, the Fund exists in part to eliminate the need of, or the temptation to employ, such controls.

consultative, "surveillance," and conditional lending capacities strongly
and effectively to discourage the imposition of capital controls (see Fund
Arts. IV, 3; V, 3; Hockett 2002, 180–89; Hockett 2004b). The upshot is
that there truly does appear now to be quite nearly one, integrated global
financial market (see Hockett 2002, 170–77). That's one step in the direction of "completeness," via the imposition of an equal-treatment norm.

The next steps in the direction of "completeness" are recent and thus
far tentative. First, commencing with the breakup of the Soviet bloc in the
later 1980s, the Fund began to offer support to former bloc members in
the development of market-facilitative and market-expansive legal norms
and institutions (Hockett 2002, 154–57). Second, in the wake of the
"Asian Financial Crisis" (AFC), the Fund turned to the offering of expert
support in the way of bankruptcy law, corporate governance, and
financial regulation to actually and potentially affected member countries
(idem). Finally, the Fund has recently begun to show interest in proposals
for the creation of new markets in new forms of contingent-claims
contract (see Hockett 2004b).

All of these activities are geared toward broadening, hence rendering
more complete, investment and financial markets (indeed, in the case of
the former Soviet-bloc countries, product and services markets as well).
The case is clearest in the post-AFC period: The interest in bankruptcy
law, corporate governance, and financial regulation is prompted by an
interest in promoting the broadest possible participation in the markets
for ownership of and lending to value-productive firms (see Hockett 2002,
154–57, 174–77). Note also that the principal Fund corporate-governance
interest—insider trading—is *eo ipso* an interest in equal access to
information pertinent to securities prices. The interest in new risk markets
is, of course, by definition an interest in the greater completion of what I
have above called the "ills market"—a critical piece of the justice
mechanism.

The upshot of the fuller argument is, I believe, threefold: The Fund
began with a mission to complement the equal-treatment and market-
completion missions of the GATT/WTO in the products (and later
services) markets, essentially by facilitating, and to a half-degree requiring, equal treatment and market enhancement in the financial markets.
Over time, the Fund grew more robust and more comprehensive in its
treatment-equalizing and market-expanding roles vis-à-vis the global
investment and financial markets, as those markets themselves grew
markedly in extent (and partly, indeed, in response) (Hockett 2002,
154–57, 174–77). And the Fund both may and ought to *continue* its
development—again in keeping with its properly viewed mandate—

along these lines. Such is the best understanding of what the Fund is *for* (see Hockett 2004b).

3.4. Turn finally to the global preparticipation opportunity allocation. Here the case for full equal treatment and ultimate market completion as constitutive of a Bretton Woods institution's—now the Bank's—fundamental mandate is most difficult to make, in part because the Bank falls so far short of realizing any such ideal. I shall argue, nonetheless, that (perhaps gradual) realization of such an ideal is precisely what the Bank should be viewed as existing for; and that its falling short of that goal owes quite simply, to injustice on the part of certain influential state actors upon the Bank's founding and, indeed, ever since.

Consider first what would be required by equal treatment in the global preparticipation opportunity allocation. I take it that what would be ideally required is, at a minimum, precisely that "ethically exogenous endowment equality" discussed above. All persons—all human agents, who are justice's proper distribuees—would begin life with an equal claim upon the world's ethically exogenous resources and risk-trading opportunities, and all would retain an equal claim upon all new such resources and opportunities as might become available over time. The basic idea would be to ensure market neutrality and completion in the fullest practicable sense by ensuring that all persons enter the iterated market at any given time with equal ethically exogenous capacity to effect the ongoing relative social (now global) valuation and disposition of agent-adjudged benefits and burdens.

Now the Bank, on the one hand, cannot be said to have been instituted with so *fulsome* an egalitarian mission *clearly* in view. It was, after all, originally envisaged as an institution charged simply with facilitating the reconstruction of war-ravaged European infrastructures (Hockett 2002, 162–64). And it remains to this day a *lending* institution, charged with assisting member countries in the borrowing, not the outright acquiring, of funds to improve the capacities of their citizens to participate in the global economy (see Bank Art. I; Edwards 1985, 44–48). On the other hand, the Bank's very existence as an institution apart from the Fund is predicated upon the need for a publicly funded (via large-country subscriptions) supplement to—in the form either of facilitator of or guarantor to—lending markets insufficiently peopled by private parties willing to lend absent such supplementation (see, e.g., Kaul et al. 1998, 2000.) And the Bank's mission, like that of the Fund, has *evolved* since its inception—in the direction of greater compensation to the world's poor (or at least those who do not inhabit aggregately wealthy nation-states).

The evolution of the Bank into a more forthrightly compensatory institution has proceeded along two principal fronts. First, with the implementation of the U.S. Marshall Plan in the later 1940s and the rapid recovery of the European economies through the 1950s, the Bank's constituency came increasingly to be viewed as the more intractably "underdeveloped countries" (see, e.g., Pincus and Winters 2002, 1–15). This change can be seen in the Bank's recent shift of focus from traditional project investment in "big," material infrastructural projects—dams, roads, hydroelectric plants, and the like—to so-called human-capital investment projects—education, health care, population control, and so on (see, e.g., Fine 2002, 203–21; Lowenfeld 2002, 618).

Further, since 1960 the World Bank Group has included a subsidiary organization—the International Development Association (IDA)—specifically charged with the task of affording so-called soft loans to particularly impoverished nations. The loans are labeled "soft" in view of their long repayment terms (often up to fifty years) and low rates of interest (often as low as .75% per annum) (Lowenfeld 2002, 620). Unlike the IBRD proper, moreover, the IDA is financed by the revenues that IBRD investments throw off and by actual cash contributions—cheerfully termed "replenishments"—made by wealthier industrial countries every three years in proportion to their Bank subscriptions and voting power (idem). In that sense, the IDA is of course "progressively" financed. The ideal pursuant to which the Bank appears to be operating, then, is one according to which, at minimum, the least advantaged (in aggregately poor nation-states) are deserving of special solicitude.

3.5. Now it is clear that it is the Bank which is furthest—both in written mandate and, less fully, in its actual operations—from what I have argued would best be viewed as its actuating ideal. And it is not terribly mysterious why that should be: The mission that I have allotted to the Bank—equalization of the global preparticipation opportunity allocation—is that mission which would require that those persons holding unjustifiably large aggregations of ethically exogenous wealth compensate those holding unjustifiably meager portions of such wealth. And those persons who hold the unjustifiably large aggregations, of course, tend to populate and determine the active policies of the wealthiest, best armed, most influential state actors in the global polity. These states in turn largely constrain the design and conduct of international institutions. Quite simply, then, the principal beneficiaries of past and continuing injustice prevent the adoption of the principal measures that must yet be taken. What, then, is to be done?

I shall now propose two directions of policy and advocacy that I think all of those concerned with global justice ought to take.

3.6. First, we ought certainly to focus our attentions, and probably to concentrate our advocacy efforts, more with a view to the *failure* of the *Bank* to live up to *its* ideal mission than to the *successes* of the *GATT/WTO and IMF* in discharging *their* appointed missions. Specifically, we should push for the Bank to be empowered, presumably incrementally and first via the IDA, overtly to effect a gradual corrective channeling of ethically exogenous wealth, for the purpose of developing human market-participating capabilities, from those accidentally bearing greater access to the world's ethically exogenous stock of resources to those accidentally bearing less such access. An excellent start in this direction would be to advocate, for example, that the Bank be authorized to administer the collection and distribution of a Poggian global-resources dividend or its functional equivalent (see, e.g., Pogge 1994). One would hope, however, to see such an effort only *begin* "moderately" in the manner that Pogge suggests (1994, 204–08.) Over time, as it and its rationale grow more familiar, the effort should grow more ambitious. And its beneficiaries, of course, should be sought—as certainly they will be found—not merely in the aggregately "underdeveloped" countries but in *all* countries.

While at first, of course, such advocacy can be expected to be met with the familiar Reaganesque charge of "handouts to the Cadillac-driving [now global] welfare queens" from the unjustly overendowed, our expressly and specifically *tying* all proposals to the *market-preparing and market-facilitating* rationale offered above—and, thus, to the *responsibility*-tracing while exogenous *opportunity*-equalizing conception of *justice* offered above—should significantly undercut, if not indeed obliterate, the persuasiveness of such rhetorical stratagems. Those concerned with justice will be enabled to claim in response to the unjust, quite plausibly, "We simply call for a fuller, more extensive—more complete as well as more fair—global market even than you do. Why do you stand in the way of this extensive market? Why do you refuse to honor responsibility and equal opportunity worldwide?"

The reasons militating in favor of this first policy direction, I think, are plain: Attacks upon the GATT/WTO and the IMF, or upon global trade or global investment *as such*, are misdirected. Worse, they siphon off valuable advocative resources while offering little if any hope of any significant benefit. Keeping the "real" problem—that the Bank lacks the resources to fulfill its proper mandate—clearly in view is absolutely

critical even if, for strategic reasons, we nonetheless decide to call for
some restrictions—in the form of conditions—upon the operations of the
GATT/WTO and the IMF.

3.7. The second policy direction that critics of the Bretton Woods
system and others concerned with global justice ought to take is
strategically, and with a clear view of the end state ultimately sought,
to impose a sort of "conditionality" of their own in assenting to the
operations of the GATT/WTO and the IMF. (A fittingly ironical
demand!) It should be argued—with sophistication, not just slo-
gans—that "free trade" and "free finance" *are* to be tolerated and indeed
to be *sought,* but only insofar as they promote (or at any rate do not
retard) justice. And it should be explicitly *acknowledged* that they *can*
indeed promote full justice if and insofar as actual and would-be
participants in the global goods-trading and financial markets gradually
are rendered *equally* "free," that is, equally ethically exogenously endowed throughout their lives.

Insofar as such would-be global market participants are *not* equally
free in the requisite sense—that is, insofar as the Bank is not empowered
to effect the mission here envisaged for it—the global polity in general,
and those concerned with global justice in particular, must address a
thorny "problem of the second best" in evaluating the operations of
GATT/WTO and IMF regimes and in determining what precisely to
advocate. This problem cannot be dispatched by sloganeering. The
critical questions, which must be carefully addressed, become (a) to
what extent (if any) does a partial, rather than a full, movement in the
direction of filling justice's earlier-elaborated *requisites* result in some
actual justice improvement in the distribution of benefits and burdens and
(b) if the answer to the first question is "not at all," "it's ambiguous," "it's
indeterminate," or, worse, "it actually worsens things," what is to be
done? Those two questions are difficult to answer absent some specific
description of the particular "partial" movement in the direction of filling
justice's requisites that is contemplated. But it happens that we do have a
fairly specific, if necessarily rough, description of the requisite sort
available to us. And it looks as though we can fairly make some general
observations of the distributive outcomes that tend to be wrought in the
world so described. We can also, only somewhat more tentatively, fashion
recommendations in light of those likely outcomes. So we have at least
some rough, schematic answers to questions (a) and (b) as just formulated—answers that can be fleshed out with further empirical, including
econometric, work to be prescribed below.

3.7.1. First, note a familiarly observed effect likely to be wrought by equal treatment and market completion in the products and services markets absent equal treatment in the preparticipation opportunity allocation—that is, by success on the part of the GATT/WTO system absent success on the part of the Bank Group as I have idealized it: At time T_2, persons in some jurisdictions—for example, laborers in relatively wealthy countries—are unjustly underendowed but are less so than were many of their occupational (and, indeed, generally biologic) forebears at T_0. They are less unjustly underendowed than the aforementioned forebears in consequence of certain institutionalized justice concessions that intervening forebears during period T_1 were able to extract, in the forms of governmentally sanctioned collective bargaining and progressive taxation-financed social-insurance regimes, from earlier persons, such as holders of large landed estates or large equity stakes in productive enterprises—generally, indeed, the biologic forebears of our present holders of large land and equity shares—who were unjustly overendowed. Now at T_3, owing to the success of a global effort to equalize treatment and effect greater market completion in the products and services markets—an effort that has not as yet been matched by any global effort, analogous to earlier domestic efforts, to compensate for unjustly unequal endowments—these relatively better endowed but still unjustly underendowed persons find themselves "backsliding" in the direction of unjustly yet further underendowed status once again, as others who are unjustly even more underendowed than they are—generally the poor in lesser developed countries—suddenly are enabled to compete with them in selling, yet more cheaply, what labor—the underendowed's only legally protected asset—they can offer.

The backsliders, quite naturally, complain. They see, in effect, a rolling back of the underendowment-compensation provisions that their forebears were able to effect at T_1. The unjustly overendowed, for their part, predictably now posture as if they were ethically or progress minded, censoriously intoning (a) that the backsliders are unconcerned for the global poor struggling valiantly to work their way out of poverty, (b) that the backsliders stand in the way of progressive specialization and the consequent realization of fabulous economies of scale and ultimate aggregate growth that "benefits everybody," or both. That, of course, amounts to a "divide and conquer [the unjustly underendowed]" political-economic and rhetorical strategy taken by the unjustly overendowed, effected by means of a surprisingly successful, since not all that clever, sleight of hand: Attention is cynically diverted from the injustice of the endowment distribution as between the over- and the underendowed

generally, to a putatively self-serving, productivity-antagonistic, unchari-
table grousing on the part of the less underendowed over the marvelous
opportunities now being extended to consumers as a class and the more
desperately underendowed as potential producers. Any effort to redirect
attention to where it belongs is, again cynically—and now quite ironically—met with the pejorative charge of "class warfare." (As if the
protest, rather than the expropriation, were the "war.")

The backsliders and their supporters, regrettably, have in many cases
fallen into the trap to which the aforementioned strategy amounts. They
have protested often without proposing an end state, effectively lending
credence to the aggregationist and ad hominem attacks of free-trade
apologists. Their answers to those attacks, in turn, when offered at all,
often take the form, more or less, of a claim that "trade should be free,
but it also should be fair." That proposition is, of course, fair enough. But
what would *count* as "fair" too often is left obscure.

The obscurity appears to be a result of several factors. First, no
comprehensive conception of justice like that offered above is borne in
mind. Second, attention consequently is not fixed so much upon the
distribution between the unjustly overendowed and (all of) the unjustly
underendowed as upon that between the unjustly underendowed and the
unjustly yet more underendowed. And, third, as between two classes, each
of which is unjustly treated but one of which is yet more unjustly treated
than the other, it is not clear what distribution justice, even were one
possessed of a justice conception, could require—particularly when,
as a practical matter, effectively treating the two classes jointly as
exhausting the universe of appropriate distribuees diverts attention
from another class of persons who owe *both* of the unjustly treated
classes compensation.

In light of the discussion in part 2, however, it now should be clear what
global fairness would ideally entail, and what those concerned for both
the backsliders and the unjustly yet more underendowed should bear in
mind as a benchmark: Calculate at least the rough value of the aggregate
global ethically exogenous endowment—something like Steiner's "global
fund" (Steiner 1998, 99–100; 1994, 270–80)—and at least roughly
determine, on the basis of the global population, each person's rightful
share. Then calculate some functional equivalent of an ideal global
taxation and redistribution schedule that would determine appropriate
transfers from those possessed of more than their shares to those
possessed of less. In light of statistically well-documented disparities in
wealth within domestic economies and worldwide—small numbers with
huge aggregations, vast numbers with very little—chances are (a) that

those schedules would recommend transfers directly from the financial-capital-owning overendowed to *both* the backsliders *and* the currently yet more underendowed; and (b) that the backsliders, were they to act collectively—and particularly were they to cooperate with the yet more desperate—could successfully condition agreement to untrammeled trade upon some degree of conformity on the part of the overendowed to the schedules, or upon acceptance of some set of conditions that would amount to the functional equivalent of such a degree of conformity. (Were the form that compensation takes to include some manner of subsidized, market-facilitative "human-capital" development, [b] would be even more likely.) If that hypothesis is borne out, the question then becomes, in justice, *should* the backsliders so condition their assent to untrammeled trade? I believe that they should. Here is why, and more precisely how.

First, there would be a practical infinity of sets of conditions that would, if properly tailored, amount in their impositions to the imposition of rough "functional equivalents" of the ideal taxation and redistribution schedules in the aforementioned sense. One, for example, would be simply to condition the extension of the GATT/WTO most-favored-nation principle to any nation upon that nation's extending more or less the same compensatory collective bargaining and/or redistributive taxation benefits to its citizens as the backsliders' nations historically have done to them.[14] Another would be simply to calculate the additional profits gleaned by the overendowed in any given nation by dint of their effectively hiring cheaper, extranational labor, then guarantee that some appropriate portion of those profits be directed to consequently "backsliding" intranational labor, perhaps partly in the form of guaranteed "human-capital"-development rights. Still another rough functional equivalent would be to require that all persons disemployed or rendered less employed by firms in consequence of expanded global competition in the labor markets be compensated with dividend-yielding ownership shares in the firms that employ such cheaper laborers as do not avail themselves of collective-bargaining rights—a form of *financial* capital-development right extended to the backsliders (see Hockett 2005).

Second, note that any of these rough "functional equivalents" can be calibrated, such that gains realized through the hiring of desperate labor go not *entirely* to the less desperate labor but partly to the overendowed as well. Allowance for some portion of the latter sort presumably would

---

[14] The taxation benefits might be preferable, insofar—though only insofar—as the most underendowed among the divided and conquered might, as a practical matter, actually refrain from taking recourse to the collective-bargaining rights.

afford continued incentives to the overendowed to continue to hire—and presumptively to benefit—the desperately poor, even while compensating the less desperately poor sufficiently to prevent or substantially slow their backsliding. Why this manner of "incentivization" of the overendowed might be desirable is considered next.

Third, note that the historical tendency is for the desperately poor, as they are increasingly drawn into the industrial economy, to organize themselves and demand more in the way of compensation, at accelerating rates, from the unjustly overendowed (see, e.g., Beaud 2001, 144–50; Bernstein 2004, 333–34). A long-to-medium-term effect, then, of continued integration of the global labor market, provided that the no longer desperate are not thrown back into debilitating desperation, would appear likely to be a more consolidated effort on the part of the unjustly underendowed *as a whole* more effectually to bring about a gradual corrective global exogenous endowment redistribution from the unjustly overendowed.

Fourth, note again, as observed earlier, that it appears to be inherently problematic, if not indeed theoretically indeterminate, how we ought to regard the comparative distributions of two differentially unjustly under-endowed classes alone, with no view to the remainder of the universe of distribuees—the unjustly overendowed. This problem becomes particu-larly acute when the effort so to evaluate those distributions is apt to distract, as a practical matter, the would-be evaluator from attending to the unjustly overendowed class's endowment in a manner reasonably likely to entail redistributions of their endowment that would result *unambiguously*, because completely as regards the universe of distribuees, in an improvement in justice.

Fifth, in light of the fourth observation, it is not only the case that the "prize" upon which we should train our eyes is the overage held by the unjustly overendowed. It is also the case that (at least) *marginal* differences in such portions of an aggregate *gain* wrought by global market integration as would go to an unjustly underendowed class and an unjustly yet more underendowed class ought not to *concern* us overmuch. The unjustly underendowed *might* reasonably even tolerate a *minimal* degree of "*backsliding*" but *certainly* could reasonably tolerate a some-what *slowed* rate of *forward* movement in the short term, if there were good reason to suppose that *both* classes will be enabled to move forward *together* in the direction of receipt of *full compensation* from the unjustly overendowed fairly quickly in consequence of the toleration. (I appeal here to the third point raised above.)

I conclude, in light of these five observations, that advocates of global justice ought to condition assent to free trade upon "fair" trade in—and possibly only in—something like the sense elaborated above. They should require that a sizable share of such aggregate gains generated by the GATT/WTO regime as currently accrue to the unjustly overendowed be diverted to the "backsliders." But probably they should not demand so large a share as would remove the incentive of the unjustly overendowed to employ the currently unjustly yet more underendowed in the first instance. (Note that the dividend-yielding stock option proposed above would afford the backsliders themselves incentives in effect to do the desired hiring—through the management of the firms that they come partly to own, of course.)

This strategy can be summarized, I think, in the following maxim: Raise the condition of the most unjustly done by, in order to swell the ranks of the politically more influential next-most unjustly done by. Do so by capturing most of the aggregate gains wrought by free global trade and channeling them largely or principally to the most unjustly done by. But channel enough to the next-most unjustly done by to prevent their sinking back into desperation themselves, and allow enough to go to the unjustly *prospering* to "incentivize" their continuing to raise the material living standards (and thus eventual political influence) of the most unjustly done by. *Condition* assent to the *GATT/WTO* regime upon this distribution of the gains, since the unjustly prospering will be "incentivized" to *accept* the condition, and their accepting it will result, in the not-so-distant future, in sufficient strengthening of the unjustly done by as a whole to maximize the prospect ultimately of *full* compensation afforded them all—that is, of ongoing full justice's being institutionalized, for example, via the afore-envisaged strengthening of the Bank.

Framing the advice in this manner reduces our problem of the second best to a manner of at least theoretically tractable "accounting" problem. It becomes a matter of tracing the flows of benefits wrought by successful implementation of the GATT/WTO regime, calculating their amounts and rates of growth and estimating their effects upon the incentives of the unjustly overendowed. I have been assuming, of course, that implementation of the GATT/WTO regime does in fact result in sufficient aggregate gain to permit the channeling of benefits in significant measure in all three of the directions that I have advocated. The realism of that assumption, as well as of the assumption that there are institutional means of imposing and fulfilling the conditions, of course must be examined empirically and in adequate detail.

3.7.2.   The second general tendency likely to be wrought in a world shorn of any institution discharging the Bank's ideal function stems from the operations of the Fund, rather as the first such tendency stems from those of the GATT/WTO. Here the normative limb of the second-best analysis is somewhat more simply mapped than it was in the previous section.

Consider a class of unjustly underendowed persons, distributed throughout the world but found disproportionately in aggregately poorer nations lacking both in the finance-regulatory infrastructures and in the social insurance "safety nets" commonly found in most of the wealthier nations. This class of distribuees, precisely because its members are underendowed, comprises persons who are less able to diversify their assets and bear risks to their livelihoods than are better-endowed persons. These very same people, as a class, also tend to be *more frequently subject*, as a matter of actual occurrence, to those forms of economic volatility that place their livelihoods—which tend to accrue solely to their principal if not their only asset, their labor—at risk. For those forms of volatility are, above all else, *financial* in origin. They are consequent both upon the free mobility of investment capital, during market panic, out of the firms that employ the underendowed persons and upon the lack of such adequate finance- and firm-regulatory architectures as tend to inspire sufficient global investor *confidence* as is required to induce investors to *leave* their investments stably in place for uninterrupted durations. Moreover, the same instrumentality that has most authoritatively presided over the freeing of global financial flows as just described—the IMF—commonly counsels, and indeed often requires via its conditional lending, that affected nations both (a) scale back on whatever social insurance programs they have and (b) adopt restrictive, hence employment discouraging, monetary and fiscal policies more generally as a means of strengthening global investors' confidence in the prospects presented by investment in those countries. This of course tends, at least in the short term, to worsen the prospects of the disemployed destitute yet further.

On the other hand, these vulnerabilities in large measure constitute, in effect, the flipside of a free-finance-wrought *"advantage"* which our most underendowed persons have lately enjoyed relative to certain somewhat less underendowed persons more commonly found in wealthier nations: They have, precisely *because* less endowed, been attracting investment and consequent employment by the unjustly overendowed, as described above in connection with the success of the GATT/WTO regime in discharging its function. And the freeing of financial flows effected by the IMF regime has, of course, been instrumental in *bringing* this "advantage" to the unjustly desperate. The unjustly overendowed thus taketh away, so to speak, but they do so in considerable measure by the same means through which they giveth—the means of untrammeled global finance and investment.

The consequences for our normative second-best analysis of the free global finance and investment regime are twofold. First, with respect to the unjustly most underendowed, the justicial effects of the IMF's successful operations absent similar success on the part of the Bank in discharging its own ideal function as laid out above are *ambiguous*. The success results simultaneously in affording (at least a modicum of) greater opportunity to these distribuees, while also subjecting them to greater risk. It is not immediately clear, then, what precisely to propose by way of advocacy, at least in the form of an "all-or-nothing" admonition. One is tempted, first, to allow those who are simultaneously beneficiaries and victims of the regime to decide for themselves how comparatively to weigh the risks and rewards that it affords and thus whether they wish to continue with it or to terminate it. But one also is tempted, second, to seek means of retaining the benefits while lessening or mitigating the risks posed by continuation of the system, and perhaps to condition continuation in turn upon acceptance of such risk-reducing, mitigating measures.

As it happens, much useful thinking and advocating—by justice advocates and regulators alike—have begun to yield salutary results along the lines of that second "temptation." The IMF itself has begun both recommending, and assisting in the effectuation of, more effective market-facilitative finance-regulatory programs in less developed constituency nations since the time of the Asian Financial Crisis. By protecting investors and inspiring investor confidence, these programs can reasonably be expected in the long run to lessen financial volatility. Further, the IMF (along with the Bank) also has begun, in response to vigorous criticisms raised since the AFC and especially since the Argentine meltdown in the early twenty-first century, to recognize (or perhaps rediscover) the importance—for political and, indeed, economic stability if not forthrightly for reasons of justice—of effective social-insurance programs (see, e.g., Hockett 2004b; Fox 2003; Subbarao 2003). Finally, many influential (and not in all cases unorthodox) financial economists, and now policy makers as well, have begun to recognize the potential benefits of collectively imposing some degree of friction, in the form of transaction excises ("Tobin taxes"), upon financial flows themselves (see, e.g., ul Haq et al. 1996).

I provisionally conclude, then, that, at least so far as the worst off in the developing countries are concerned, advocacy along many lines already familiar has been successful and both ought to and will continue. There is not a strong justicial reason, then, so far as this constituency of distribuees is concerned, to condition continued tolerance of the IMF regime tout court upon a movement of the Bank more rapidly toward fulfillment of the ideal mission that I have designated for it—unless, of course, as an empirical matter it can be shown that imposing such a condition would render such movement of the Bank substantially more likely or more rapid, in which case there would of course be plausible *strategic* reasons fundamentally to change the discourse on the IMF.

The second consequence of the above-discussed IMF and free-finance empirics for our normative second-best analysis is a bit less cheery than that just laid out. But it also has, in effect, been laid out already: Recall that, in connection with the second-best discussion of the GATT/WTO's effects above in section 3.7.1, we observed that while the worst off among the unjustly done by appear, even notwithstanding the Bank's falling short of its ideal mission, to be rendered arguably better off, under the *same* circumstances the somewhat *less* badly off among the unjustly done by—the backsliders—tend to fare *worse*. Now this faring worse is not simply wrought by the success of the *GATT/WTO* regime. It is critically *facilitated* by the operation of the *IMF* regime, by dint of the critical linkages between the trade and investment regimes adumbrated above. The second-best question here accordingly becomes, Should the analysis offered above, from which we concluded that continued toleration of the GATT/WTO system ought to be conditioned, carry over to the IMF context?

Perhaps counterintuitively, I don't believe that there is an easy answer here. And I suspect that even a sensitive empirical assessment of likely tendencies is unlikely to prove capable of being sensitive *enough* to offer much help. Here, in essence, is why: In favor of conditionality here would be all of the arguments in favor of conditionality with respect to continued toleration of the GATT/WTO's operations, above. Against conditionality, on the other hand, might be the fact that conditionality in respect of the *GATT/WTO* system might well suffice to accomplish the stated end, while allowing the IMF system to chug ahead with the afore-noted reforms gradually being taken on will facilitate both a continued —and presumably now more continuous—lifting up of the living standards of the worst off and the continued development of a rapidly crystallizing global finance-regulatory *governance* system, which benefits everybody.

I provisionally conclude, then, that justice advocates ought definitely to pursue the conditions-imposing advocative posture recommended above in connection with the GATT/WTO regime, and perhaps—but only perhaps—ought to extend that posture to their treatment of the Bretton Woods system as a whole. They should first call forcefully for an enabling of the Bank as described above. They should, further, condition their continued acceptance of the GATT/WTO regime until the Bank is so empowered, in the manner described above. And they should, moreover, condition acceptance of the IMF regime upon continued progress of the sort observed above being under way (regulatory improvement, social-insurance acceptance, transaction taxation, and so forth). But they should table, for the moment, the question of whether also to condition acceptance of the IMF regime upon some specifically instituted aggre-gate-gain-apportionment system analogous to that required in connection with the GATT/WTO.

4. Conclusion

I have sketched what I take to be a metatheoretically and practically compelling theoretic and institutional ideal toward which those interested in global justice might coherently and realistically strive, as well as a plausible menu of advocative strategies, sensitive to institutional and power-distributional "facts on the ground," from which the same persons might choose in pressing ahead. There are of course many junctures along the argumentative path that I have followed at which I might be taken to task, and which therefore I should have to buttress more fully in a more complete argument. It nonetheless strikes me as both remarkable and encouraging that we have before us three institutions that stand so close, in theory and, indeed, in mandate, jointly to constituting a workable infrastructure of global justice. We stand so near to—and yet, until we get there, so agonizingly far from—where we now must go.

Acknowledgments

I would like to thank Dick Arneson, Jack Barceló, Christian Barry, Jerry Cohen, Jerry Mashaw, Richard Miller, Herbert Morais, John Roemer, Bob Shiller, and David Wippman for helpful conversation on the subjects of this essay.

References

Allais, Maurice. 1953. "Généralisation des théories de l'equilibre econo-mique général et du rendement social au cas du risque." *Econometrie, Colloques Internationaux du Centre National de la Recherche Scienti-fique* 11:81–120.
Allen, Franklin, and Douglas Gale. 1994. *Financial Innovation and Risk Sharing*. Cambridge, Mass.: MIT Press.

Arneson, Richard. 1989. "Equality of Opportunity for Welfare." *Philosophical Studies* 56:77–93.

———. 1990. "Primary Goods Reconsidered." *NOÛS* 24:429–54.

Arrow, Kenneth J. 1951. "An Extension of the Basic Theorems of Classical Welfare Economics." *Proceedings of the Second Berkeley Symposium*, edited by Jerzy Neyman, 507–32. Berkeley: University of California Press.

———. 1953. "Le rôle de valeurs boursières par la répartition la meilleure des risques." *Econometrie, Colloques Internationaux du Centre National de la Recherche Scientifique* 11:41–47.

———. 1973. "Some Ordinalist-Utilitarian Notes on Rawls's Theory of Justice." *Journal of Philosophy* 70:245–63.

Articles of Agreement of the International Bank for Reconstruction and Development, July 22, 1944, 60 Stat. 1440, 2 U.N.T.S. 134, amended Dec. 16, 1965, U.S.T. 1942, 606 U.N.T.S. 294. Available at http://www.ibrd.org (Last visited 12 October 2004.)

Articles of Agreement of the International Monetary Fund, July 22, 1945, 60 Stat. 1401, 2 U.N.T.S. 39. Available at http://www.imf.org. (Last visited 12 October 2004.)

Basu, Kaushik, et al. 2003. *International Labor Standards*. Oxford: Blackwell.

Baumol, William. 1986. *Superfairness: Applications and Theory*. Cambridge, Mass.: MIT Press.

Beaud, Michel. 2001. *A History of Capitalism: 1500–2000*. New York: Monthly Review Press.

Bernstein, William J. 2004. *The Birth of Plenty: How the Prosperity of the Modern World Was Created*. New York: McGraw-Hill.

Bhala, Raj, and David Kennedy. 1998. *World Trade Law*. Charlottesville, Va.: Lexis Law Publishing.

Blustein, Paul. 2002. *The Chastening: Inside the Crisis that Rocked the Global Financial System and Humbled the IMF*. New York: Public Affairs.

Caufield, Catherine. 1996. *Masters of Illusion: The World Bank and the Poverty of Nations*. New York: Henry Holt.

Chalmers, David J. 1997. *The Conscious Mind: In Search of a Fundamental Theory*. Oxford: Oxford University Press.

Cohen, G. E. 1989. "On the Currency of Egalitarian Justice." *Ethics* 99:906–44.

Das, Bhagirath Lal. 1999. *The World Trade Organisation: A Guide to the Framework for International Trade*. London: Zed Books.

Dunkley, Graham. 2000. *The Free Trade Adventure: The WTO, the Uruguay Round and Globalism—A Critique*. London: Zed Books.

Dworkin, Ronald. 1977. *Taking Rights Seriously*. Cambridge, Mass.: Harvard University Press.

———. 1980. "Is Wealth a Value?" *Journal of Legal Studies* 9: 191–226.

————. 2000. *Sovereign Virtue: The Theory and Practice of Equality.* Cambridge, Mass.: Harvard University Press.

Edwards, Richard W. 1985. *International Monetary Collaboration.* Dobbs Ferry, N.Y.: Transnational.

Elliott, Kimberly Ann, and Richard B. Freeman. 2003. *Can Labor Standards Improve Under Globalization?* Washington, D.C.: Institute for International Economics.

Fine, Ben. 2002. "The World Bank's Speculation on Social Capital." In *Reinventing the World Bank,* edited by Jonathan R. Pincus and Jeffrey A. Winters, 203–21. Ithaca, N.Y.: Cornell University Press.

Foley, Duncan. 1967. "Resource Allocation and the Public Sector." *Yale Economic Essays* 7:45–98.

Fox, Louise. 2003. *Safety Nets in Transition Economies: A Primer (World Bank Social Safety Net Series, April 30, 2003).* Washington, D.C.: International Bank for Reconstruction and Development.

General Agreement on Tariffs and Trade (GATT; also GATS, TRIMS, and TRIPS), Oct. 30, 1947, 61 Stat. pts. 5, 6, T.I.A.S. No. 1700, 55 U.N.T.S. 187. Available at http://www.wto.org (Last visited 12 October 2004.)

ul Haq, Mahbub, et al. 1996. *The Tobin Tax: Coping with Financial Volatility.* Oxford: Oxford University Press.

Hockett, Robert. 2002. "From Macro to Micro to 'Mission-Creep': Defending the IMF's Emerging Concern with the Infrastructural Prerequisites to Global Financial Stability." *Columbia Journal of Transnational Law* 41, no. 1:153–93.

————. 2004a. "The Deep Grammar of Distribution: A Meta-Theory of Justice." *Cardozo Law Review* 26.

————. 2004b. "From 'Mission-Creep' to Gestalt-Switch: Justice, Finance, the IFIs and Globalization's Intended Beneficiaries." *George Washington International Law Review* 37.

————. 2004c. "Just Insurance Through Global Macro-Hedging: Information, Distributive Equity, Efficiency and New Markets for Systemic-Income-Risk-Pricing and -Trading in a 'New Economy.'" *University of Pennsylvania Journal of International Economic Law* 25:107–257.

————. 2005. "A Jeffersonian Republic Through Hamiltonian Means: Asset-Diffusion Policies, Legal-cum-Financial Engineering, and the American Political Tradition." *Hofstra Law Review* 55.

Hockett, Robert, and Mathias Risse. 2004. "Primary Goods Revisited. A 'Political Problem' and Its Rawlsian Solution." Unpublished paper.

Jackson, John H. 1999. *The World Trading System: Law and Policy of International Economic Relations.* Cambridge, Mass. MIT Press.

James, Harold. 1996. *International Monetary Cooperation Since Bretton Woods.* Oxford: Oxford University Press.

Kaul, Inge, et al. 1998. *Global Public Goods: International Cooperation in the 21st Century.* Oxford: Oxford University Press.

————. 2000. *Providing Global Public Goods: Managing Globalization.* Oxford: Oxford University Press.

Kolm, Serge. 1972. *Justice et équité.* Paris: Centre National de la Recherche Scientifique.

Krueger, Anne O. 2000. *The WTO as an International Organization.* Chicago: University of Chicago Press.

Lowenfeld, Andreas. 2002. *International Economic Law.* Oxford: Oxford University Press.

Magill, Michael, and Martine Quinzii. 1996. *Theory of Incomplete Markets I.* Cambridge, Mass.: MIT Press.

Nagel, Thomas. 1991. *Mortal Questions.* Cambridge: Cambridge University Press.

————. 1999. *Other Minds: Critical Essays, 1969–1994.* Oxford: Oxford University Press.

Pazner, Elisha, and David Schmeidler. 1974. "A Difficulty in the Concept of Fairness." *Review of Economic Studies* 41:441–43.

Pincus, Jonathan R., and Jeffrey A. Winters. 2002. *Reinventing the World Bank.* Ithaca, N.Y.: Cornell University Press.

Pogge, Thomas. 1994. "An Egalitarian Law of Peoples." *Philosophy and Public Affairs* 23:195–224.

————. 1995. "Eine globale Rohstoffdividende." *Analyse und Kritik* 17:183–208.

————. 1998. "A Global Resources Dividend." In *Ethics of Consumption: The Good Life, Justice, and Global Stewardship*, edited by David A. Crocker and Toby Linden, 501–36. Lanham, Md.: Rowman and Littlefield.

————. 2002. *World Poverty and Human Rights.* Cambridge: Polity Press.

Rawls, John. 1971. *A Theory of Justice.* Cambridge, Mass.: Harvard University Press.

Roemer, John. 1998. *Equality of Opportunity.* Cambridge, Mass.: Harvard University Press.

Schleifer, Andrei. 2000. *Inefficient Markets: An Introduction to Behavioral Finance.* Oxford: Oxford University Press.

Sen, Amartya. 1979. "Utilitarianism and Welfarism." *Journal of Philosophy* 76:463–89.

————. 1992. *Inequality Reexamined.* Cambridge, Mass.: Harvard University Press.

Shiller, Robert. 1989. *Market Volatility.* Cambridge, Mass.: MIT Press.

————. 1993. *Macro Markets: Creating Institutions for Managing Society's Largest Economic Risks.* Oxford: Oxford University Press.

————. 2000. *Irrational Exuberance.* Princeton: Princeton University Press.

————. 2003. *The New Financial Order: Risk in the Twenty-First Century.* Princeton: Princeton University Press.

Shue, Henry. 1996. *Basic Rights: Subsistence, Affluence, and U.S. Foreign Policy.* Princeton: Princeton University Press.

Steiner, Hillel. 1994. *An Essay on Rights*. Oxford: Blackwell.

———. 1998. "Choice and Circumstance." In *Ideals of Equality*, edited by Andrew Mason, 95–111. Oxford: Blackwell.

———. 1999. "Just Taxation and International Redistribution." In *NOMOS XLI: Global Justice*, edited by Ian Shapiro and Lea Brillmayer, 171–91. New York: New York University Press.

Stigler, George J., and Gary S. Becker. 1977. "De Gustibus Non Est Disputandum." *American Economic Review* 67, no. 2:76–90.

Stiglitz, Joseph. 2002. *Globalization and Its Discontents*. New York: W. W. Norton.

Subbarao, Kalanidhi, and W. James Smith. 2003. *What Role for Safety Net Transfers in Very Low Income Countries? (World Bank Social Safety Net Primer Series, January 16, 2003)*. Washington, D.C.: International Bank for Reconstruction and Development.

Thaler, Richard. 1993. *Advances in Behavioral Finance*. New York: Russell Sage Foundation.

Unger, Peter. 1996. *Living High and Letting Die: Our Illusion of Innocence*. Oxford: Oxford University Press.

Varian, Hal. 1974. "Equity, Envy and Efficiency." *Journal of Economic Theory* 9:63–91.

Walras, Léon. 1954. *Elements of Pure Economics: Or the Theory of Social Wealth*. Translated by William Jaffé. London: Allen and Unwin. Original published in 1926.

NETWORK POWER AND GLOBAL STANDARDIZATION: THE CONTROVERSY OVER THE MULTILATERAL AGREEMENT ON INVESTMENT

DAVID SINGH GREWAL

For more than half a century, capital-exporting countries, particularly the United States, have attempted to achieve international protection for their investors abroad. They have proposed various treaties, all of which seek to establish a common international standard for managing overseas capital flows. The most dramatic effort to establish such a treaty collapsed in 1998, with the failure of the Multilateral Agreement on Investment (MAI).

Capitalists want protection from two main threats that foreign governments pose to their investments: outright expropriation of their property (nationalization), and government oversight that makes their investments less profitable (regulation). The protection against national-ization is represented in the principle of nonexpropriation, which dictates that a country cannot take property from a foreign national without due process of law and fair compensation. The protection against state interference with foreign investment is represented in the principle of national treatment, which asserts that foreign investors receive the same treatment as domestic investors. While these protections are routine in many bilateral trade arrangements, they have never been successfully implemented in a multilateral treaty except in North America through the North American Free Trade Agreement (NAFTA).[1] The MAI proposed to do precisely this.

Trade ministers launched negotiations for the MAI at an Organization for Economic Cooperation and Development (OECD) conference in 1995. Negotiations ended in 1998, for reasons relating both to external opposition and to internal conflict among the negotiating parties. The MAI would have established a neoliberal investment regime among these capital-exporting countries, inspired by the investor-protection provisions of NAFTA. There is great debate about how the MAI would have functioned and, indeed, whether it would have functioned at all, given the many national exceptions that participating countries were granted in the course of the negotiations. Of course, we will never know, because, in the first place, the MAI draft was never completed, despite running to two

[1] NAFTA was, of course, "multilateral" only in the narrowest sense, uniting Canada, the United States, and Mexico in a free-trade area.

hundred pages when negotiations were ended and, second, the MAI and its dispute-resolution system were never seen in practice. The purpose of the MAI, however, was clear: to liberalize capital flows between countries, and to provide protection for investment overseas. Like the investor protections in NAFTA, this agreement was aimed at restricting the ability of signatory nations to interfere with foreign investment flows, requiring them to refrain from governmental restrictions or controls on foreign investment. The OECD eventually failed to come to an agreement after two years, and the period of negotiations was extended for another year. That year passed without resolution, and in fall 1998 the French government withdrew from negotiations, under pressure from domestic anti-MAI opinion. The French pullout followed delays and extensions in what had become a difficult series of negotiations. In December 1998, the OECD deputy secretary-general announced an end to what had been an inconclusive process.

At least to some extent, the MAI negotiations failed because of loud public protests against them. These protests were among the first of the large-scale demonstrations against neoliberal economic policies, culminating in the global media spectacle in Seattle during the World Trade Organization (WTO) Ministerial Conference in 1999. (Interestingly, the Seattle City Council had declared the city an "MAI-free zone" in 1998.) Anti-MAI activists worried about various threats that they believed the MAI posed to labor unions, to the environment, to jobs in the developed world, to workers in the developing world, and so on. Whether the MAI would have actually had any of these impacts is unclear, and the protests were arguably less against the MAI in particular than against neoliberal economic globalization more generally—the MAI representing the latest, and allegedly the most potent, articulation of the neoliberal program.

Some commentators have argued that the anti-MAI protestors were confused in their charges and simply failed to understand the proposal adequately. In particular, they object to the activists' focus on problems that the agreement would allegedly cause in the developing world, since the agreement was being negotiated among OECD countries alone. I don't doubt that many protesters were indeed ignorant of the fact that the MAI was a construction of just the developed nations. I will argue in this essay, however, that many of the protestors seem to have intuited something about the potential effects of this agreement that their critics failed to recognize. Indeed, the MAI provides an illustrative example of the way that global interconnectedness gives rise to a new kind of power—and to new opportunities for its abuse.

Power in Globalization

Two different concerns mark the controversy over economic globalization. The first, and most familiar, is with the outcomes that neoliberal economic policies produce and the extent to which they achieve our moral ends.[2] The second relates not to whether different rules or regimes have beneficial or detrimental effects but to whether these rules and regimes are morally legitimate, that is, whether they have been implemented and sustained in ways that involve the morally objectionable use of power. This second concern is often articulated poorly, proceeding via accusations rather than reasoned argument, but this should not dissuade us from examining the claims of the many people who assert that the process of globalization subjects them to a kind of power and undermines their effective autonomy.

This second concern has emerged most sharply in the charge that contemporary globalization represents a kind of "empire" or an exercise in diffuse imperial control.[3] It appears less strikingly in the ordinary language that critics of globalization use to describe the contemporary world—for example, in allegations that countries are "forced" to adopt international regulations or that global standards are "imposed" upon weaker parties. Such criticism drove much of the anti-MAI activism, which was directed less at specific provisions of the draft than at the kind of globalization that it was designed to advance. Critics charged that the MAI would have subjected developing countries to a kind of power or oppression.

The power claimed to be at work in globalization seems at once commonsensical (to those critical of the process) and yet hard to identify or expose. How is it that the apparently voluntary and uncoerced actions that drive globalization, such as countries accepting new international commitments, are nevertheless experienced as unfree? Any plausible account of power in contemporary globalization needs to account for the fact that transnational rules and regimes are, for the most part, the result of formally free choices made against the backdrop of increasing, and voluntary, interconnectedness. In other words, we need to articulate how a collective choice can nevertheless be experienced as coercive.

In the following section I introduce the idea of "network power." I believe that this idea both characterizes the structural dynamic driving the adoption of transnational standards in trade, technology, governance, and communication and helps us to make sense of some the claims about the kind of power that is at work in globalization, at least in its present form.

---

[2] For example, consider the recent debates over the distribution and trend of global poverty. See Reddy and Pogge 2002.

[3] The accusation that globalization constitutes a form of empire is now widespread and comes from a variety of political and methodological commitments. See, for example, Bacevich 2003; Ferguson 2004; Hardt and Negri 2000; Purdy 2003; Wade 2003. My 2003 examines the claim that globalization represents an "informal" empire.

Network Power

My starting point is the role that standards play in the formation of transnational networks underlying international trade, regulation, governance, and other constituent aspects of what we call "globalization." A *network* is a group of people related in a way that makes them capable of beneficial cooperation, which can take various forms, including the exchange of goods and ideas. A *standard* defines the particular way in which a group of people is related in a network, a shared norm or practice that facilitates such cooperation among members. Standards can link members of a network in one of two ways, either by solving coordination problems, as in the case of a language, or by regulating membership to a particular in-group, by specifying criteria necessary for admission or belonging. Of course, these two broad categories are not mutually exclusive; indeed, the relation between them can be quite complex in any given instance. In either case, standards are valuable because they solve the problem of social cooperation, providing a common convention by which users can coordinate their activity. A general version of this dynamic underlies a great deal of ordinary social interaction, setting the terms on which people gain access to one another for the sake of cooperation.

This same dynamic, newly operative on a global scale, is also behind much of what we call globalization. Witness, for example, the increasingly global reach of the English language, which now constitutes an international standard in business, academia, and other important domains. Or consider the WTO, which now regulates almost all the world's trade according to a set of standards that govern many aspects of domestic and international economic policy.[4] The problem of international coordination is "solved" by the use of such common global standards that enable cooperation among diverse participants.

Studies of conventions or games offer insight into the way in which the solution to one coordination problem will prove enduring and attractive to others, constituting an established way of coordinating interdependent expectations (see Schelling 1960; Lewis 1969). The idea of network power begins with this work on coordination and considers the social structuration of standards as constituting a form of power. The argument of network power depends in particular on two characteristics of standards. First, that coordinating standards is more valuable when greater numbers of people use them. Second, that an effect of this coordination is to eliminate progressively the alternatives over which effectively free choice can be exercised. I describe this phenomenon as a form of power, but it need not be thought of as such. The general dynamic is operative in

---

[4] For a network-power analysis of the WTO, see my 2003.

globalization, regardless of how we choose to describe it conceptually and evaluate it normatively.

Consider any system of coordination, such as a language, or a trading regime, or the famous example of a rendezvous point like the clock in the middle of Grand Central Terminal. The more people who are accustomed to using that particular form of coordination—and who are expected to do so by others—the more valuable it will be for everyone else to use that same means of coordination to speak, or trade, or meet up with others in New York City. What are sometimes called "economies of scale" propel a standard to dominance because of a positive feedback dynamic that reinforces its desirability to people who do not yet use it. A system exhibits such positive feedback if a change in one variable leads to a further change in that same variable, and in the same direction. For example, an increase in the number of people who own telephones increases the value of the telephone network as a whole, which attracts new telephone users. (Economists sometimes speak of technologies or routines exhibiting "network effects," positive externalities to their adoption.)[5] Similarly, the more people who use a given standard, the more attractive it will be for others to use that same standard because of the positive feedback dynamic, the possibility of cooperating with greater numbers of people via the same convention. So the more people who adopt a given standard, the more valuable the standard becomes, inducing still more people to want to adopt it. And, as one standard becomes increasingly valuable for others to use, competing standards lose their attractiveness and become progressively less viable. The network power of a dominant standard diminishes the networks of lesser ones.

We should distinguish the *intrinsic* benefits of adopting a standard, the inherent advantages that it offers, from the *extrinsic* benefits, which depend upon on the number of others using it. Initially, people may be led to adopt a standard before it underlies a large network because of intrinsic benefits, or outright force, or even simple happenstance. But once a standard possesses great network power, none of these causes is as important as its extrinsic benefits, the ability to cooperate with so many others who already use it. In fact, a standard that may be intrinsically *less* beneficial may nevertheless be foisted on us—chosen by us—because of its extrinsic benefits, since the reason we use standards is to gain access to others.

To make the point clearer, consider in the abstract two standards, Standard A and Standard B, both of which govern access to some particular mode of cooperation. Suppose that Standard A supports a larger network of users than Standard B. Standard A will have more network power than B, exerting a pull on members of Network B who

---

[5] Famous contributions to the network effects literature in economics include Arthur 1994 and David 1985.

want to gain access to the greater number of members in Network A. Supposing incompatibility between these two standards—that one person cannot use both but must choose either one or the other—then the push to use Standard A will be clear. But as some people switch from using Standard B to Standard A, the increasing network power of A will mean the decreasing viability of B as an effective network. Because of the economies of scale in the adoption of a standard, members of Network B will face increasing costs rather than constant costs for staying put in Network B. As Network A expands and becomes more valuable, Network B will lose members and become progressively less attractive as an alternative.

We may assume that members of the smaller Network B face costs of different magnitudes in switching over to Standard A. The adoption of a new standard will prove varyingly difficult for different people, depending on a whole host of factors, including the ease of learning, the attachment to the original network, and so on. We might imagine the members of Network B distributed from one end of a cost curve to the other, from near zero, where we put those with smallest costs of switching over, to some large number at the other end, where we put those with the highest costs of adopting a new standard. Those with the least cost of switching will presumably do so first, since they face only the opportunity cost of losing access to Network B, and very few switching costs of any magnitude. Of course, given these first departures, the value of Network A will increase as its size increases. Thus the value of the lost opportunities—the opportunity cost—of remaining in Network B will not remain constant but will increase as each member of Network B switches to Network A. With each lost member, Network B becomes smaller in comparison to Network A, and hence less attractive, while Network A only grows in value. So each new defection from Network B to Network A will change the schedule of costs faced by remnant members of Network B, triggering the next wave of defections, drawn from the next set of members of B up the cost curve. The costs will mount on the remaining holdouts, increasing—perhaps even at an increasing rate—as the defections continue, and the disparity in network power is exacerbated. In the end, Standard A may replace Standard B altogether.

The loss of lesser networks does seem to operate according to such a dynamic. For example, in cases of gradual rather than sudden linguistic death, it is usually the elderly—those with the highest cost of switching from one language to another—who are left speaking a minority language, while the younger generations learn a more widespread national or regional one (Nettle and Romaine 2000, 126–49). Of course, members of a smaller network will not necessarily wait until mounting costs make switching to a dominant network necessary. Instead, they will anticipate this dynamic and prepare for it. These expectations become self-confirming and reinforce the network power of a dominant standard.

The Normative Evaluation of Network Power

Importantly, network power operates through formal consent or choice, not direct force. The choices to switch to a dominant network are formally free choices, even when the disparity in network size is so great that the alternative is effectively social isolation. A successful standard can rise to dominance by eclipsing others and compelling nonusers to *choose* to adopt it or else be faced with no viable choices at all. Thus, the member of a small network may be subject to the network power of a dominant one, even when there is no individual or group of individuals who wields this power directly. By acknowledging this dynamic we can maintain our view of people as more or less rational agents making choices based on good reasons and we can admit that they can still become trapped by structural conditions into making decisions they would not want to make if their collective arrangements were otherwise. The theory offers one way of understanding how structural conditions can be both the cause and the result of our individual choices.

Locating the power operative in an instance of social structuration is often difficult because our predominant ideas of power oppose consent and coercion, supposing that every exercise of power is an exercise in coercion, revealed by the absence of consent. Breaking that link is the first step in crafting an idea of power better able to illuminate the voluntary social processes underlying globalization.

The emergence of transnational standards governing globalization is at once enabling and entrapping. Such standards are enabling because they allow cooperation with other people, even geographically remote or culturally different people. They are entrapping because the demand for such cooperation generates the structural dynamic that pushes one among many standards to become the privileged mode of coordination. This dynamic of interdependent choice entails the progressive loss of alternatives over which effective choice can be exercised. And yet, the choice to switch to a dominant network remains a formally free choice, undertaken without direct compulsion.

I want to argue that the attraction a privileged standard exerts on nonusers—what I call its network power—constitutes a relation of power and is responsible for the subjective experience of globalization as coercive or entrapping. As one standard becomes increasingly valuable for others to use, competing standards lose their attractiveness and become progressively less viable. In this way, the free choice to switch from one standard to another leads eventually to circumstances in which effectively free choice among viable alternatives is gradually eliminated. The idea of network power captures the ways in which systematic features of our social world emerge from human action and remain intelligible in light of it, determining the choices that are effectively available to us and sometimes limiting them so severely that a structural dynamic proves as controlling of our fates as if an actual political superior had dictated them to us. This limitation occurs because, at the point at which a given standard is adopted by nearly everyone, the "choice" to adopt that standard becomes effectively unfree. It may be that there are good reasons to switch to a particular standard, but it is difficult to separate extrinsic benefits from external compulsion in the decision to adopt a dominant one.

The political economist Sanjay Reddy distinguishes the "freedom to choose," the freedom of choice without an acceptable alternative, from the "freedom to choose freely," by which he means the freedom of choice over viable alternatives, in order to reveal the poverty of simplistic doctrines that identify freedom with consent without examining the domain of choice.[6] According to this account, choice in the absence of acceptable alternatives is equivalent to coerced choice: the mere act of choosing the only option on offer counts for little. The network power of a dominant standard converts the freedom to choose freely into the freedom to choose by eliminating the viability of alternative standards. It is this dynamic of choice that makes the emergence of global networks a situation in which systematic power can lead to unfreedom rather than a large-scale act of international voluntarism or the free enactment of a worldwide social contract.

The idea of network power is meant to capture relatively widespread dynamics behind many processes in contemporary globalization. But whether the potential loss of autonomy or freedom by members of small networks represents an injustice will depend on the circumstances. It is worth noting the features often found in network power that can lead to serious injustice.

First, the extent to which countries and people benefit from network power dynamics is greatly uneven. Those that benefit most from the current global order economically and politically are, in general, those best positioned to take advantage of the network power of transnational standards. Beneficiaries of our present global order can leverage power in unrelated domains to exert influence over the creation or selection of particular standards that favor them. In this regard, network power is little different from other forms of power, which accord priority to the privileged in determining the rules of the game.

Second, the dynamic quality of network power means that earlier decisions have lasting repercussions. For example, many contemporary standards have a complicated history that may reflect or reinforce past relations of dominance. Once these are established, they have a staying power of their own as coordinating mechanisms. In fact, a standard that may have been formed with the participation of only a few parties can become the one by which many people must coordinate their activity for

---

[6] See Reddy 2000, which develops an idea from Cohen 1988.

the indefinite future. When designing new standards, then, we must be aware that, over time, they may lock in users to a single mode of coordination.

These two factors are clearly at work in the origins of many standards that are now globally dominant because they were promoted widely under colonialism. The English language is an obvious example. These standards are *currently* useful for coordinating an interdependent world, and their network power will draw new users, but they are *historically* associated with domination in international relations and may reinforce unequal relations inherited from the past.

Third, the loss of autonomy or authenticity concerns not only *how* the coordination on a transnational standard occurs but also *which* standards are chosen and which are eclipsed. We may rightly suspect that much less is at stake if the network power of the metric system obliges uniform global standardization in measurement systems than if the network power of neoliberal economic institutions unduly restricts the ability of poor countries to undertake domestic policy experiments. All standards affect the *interests* of their users, as they govern access to beneficial cooperation and determine, to some extent at least, the allocation of those benefits. But certain standards also impact the *identities* of their users.

Consider, for example, the loss of minority languages in circumstances of asymmetric bilingualism. To phrase this concern in the language of interests would focus on the costs and benefits and their distribution among the parties. But it is not simply that the "costs" are higher for members of minority communities required to speak another language or, in the extreme, faced with the loss of their language altogether. These losses cannot be compensated for in any clear way, since people's very identities may be at stake.

Finally, the dynamic of network power is generated because other countries want or need the positive benefits that coordination—even on relatively unfavorable terms—brings to their economies and ultimately their citizens. This means that a plausible alternative system of standards must enable cooperation at the same level of generality, ensuring the same possibilities of, but a different form for, the large-scale coordination that the dominant mode allows. Otherwise, we risk pitting a romantic but ineffectual localism against the benefits of global social coordination, rather than focusing on the possibilities of equally advantageous but more just globalisms.

Given widespread desire to achieve coordination with others in diverse areas of social life, the landscape of international relations will continue to be shaped by network power. Addressing these concerns and examining the form that transnational standards take must be part of any ethical assessment of globalization. Two points should be made about the role of network power in such an assessment. First, not all standards necessarily exhibit the same network power or the same degree of coercion. To the extent that some transnational standards are more compatible with diverse local standards, or allow more selective opting out of particular provisions, they will prove less entrapping. Second, where a standard possessing network power appears inevitable—that is, where we must face the loss of alternative standards—the debate about the form a universal standard should take must be as inclusive and transparent as possible, gaining legitimacy from a broadly democratic process.

Interpreting the Anti-MAI Activism

Anti-MAI protestors were anxious about the creation of a standard regulating international investment, though without clearly articulating why. In light of the discussion in the previous section, however, we can better understand the rationale that a relatively thoughtful person might have offered against it: When the rich nations of the world agree to something, they often find a way to "force" their agreement on poor countries. What the OECD was crafting was a standard that either was, or might have readily been transformed into, a universal standard through network power. The future of the developing world (and the environment) seemed threatened merely by the suggestion of a set of coordinating rules for rich countries, particularly given that the rest of the world had no say about them. Unlike the protestors against the MAI, who seem to have grasped this danger intuitively, many of its supporters seem ignorant of these dynamics, and perhaps even deliberately blind to them.

Consider, for example, the case for the MAI and against the activists laid out by Edward Graham in *Fighting the Wrong Enemy: Antiglobal Activists and Multinational Enterprises* (2000). Responding to the worry that most of the activists had that the MAI would affect the developing world, or the developed world in relation to the developing world (say, by job losses from offshoring), Graham argues (2000, 9):

> These criticisms of the MAI . . . can be dismissed with relative ease. The MAI was to have been, as noted at the outset, an agreement within the OECD, whose members are mostly industrial, not developing, countries. It would not have been binding on nonmembers. It therefore would have done little or nothing to foster the transfer of jobs or of polluting activities by foreign investors to most developing countries. Concerns about job loss in the industrial countries as a group, or about exploitation of workers in most developing countries, are therefore essentially a nonissue as far as the MAI was concerned.

Graham then continues: "Ironically in this light, the industrial countries seeking an MAI chose the OECD as the negotiating venue precisely in order to exclude the developing countries from the negotiating exercise" (9). Why were the developing countries left out? Graham writes, in what is almost certainly a correct assessment, that "the main reason for keeping these countries out of the MAI negotiations was the presumption that the OECD countries were 'like-minded' on the subject of investment policy and already had in place relatively liberal investment policy regimes." He explains (9):

> It was thought that these countries, because they shared similar views on investment policy and similar policies, could quickly conclude a 'high standards' agreement—that is, one in which relatively stringent rules would apply. In a negotiating forum such as the WTO, on the other hand, with its wider country representation, consensus would have been much more difficult to achieve, and any consensus would likely have been at a lower standard. In particular, the US and other OECD governments believed that a bloc of developing countries within the WTO would have prevented any high-standards agreement from ever coming into force.

Graham's indifference to concerns about developing-country participation is striking, given the explicit ambition to exclude them from negotiations. He asserts, against the imagined fears of environmental or social violations in the developing world, that "the agreement contained no provisions that would have significantly enhanced the ability of multinational firms to invest in developing countries" (10). This is true, but only insofar as developing countries were not party to the original agreement, which he explicitly recognizes would no longer have been the case had negotiations been successful. He notes, "To be sure, had the MAI come into force, some developing-world countries would have joined it. Indeed, the draft agreement made provisions for non-OECD countries to accede to the agreement, and some had expressed an interest in doing so" (10). In fact, five developing countries had "observer" status at the OECD negotiations: Argentina, Brazil, Chile, Hong Kong (China), and the Slovak Republic. As an OECD policy report on the MAI states, "OECD members hope that non-OECD countries will join the MAI as founding members, or soon after the agreement is put in place."[7]

The deeper reason that Graham does not acknowledge the concerns about the developing world is that he is firmly convinced that foreign investment is critical for poor countries, and that such investment should be shielded from government interference. He writes with regard to the developing world's stake in the MAI provisions, "In each of these areas, it seems in developing countries' interest to agree to currently accepted international standards, subject to specific exceptions, as would have been agreed to under the MAI" (175). Given this attitude, it follows that he would be unconcerned that developing countries could be coerced into an agreement that requires a hands-off approach to multinational investment. He is concerned with the desired outcomes of globalization, not the processes by which any such outcomes should come about.

A different approach can be seen in an article in *Le monde diplomatique*, which asked, "Why then is the MAI being discussed by 29 states at

---

[7] The policy report can be found online at http://www.oecd.org/publications/pol_brief/1997/9702_POL.HTM.

the OECD, and not at the WTO which, with 131 members states, is *a priori* the more legitimate forum?" (Cassen 1998).

> Using the language of diplomacy, Mr. Henri Chavranski [the French negotiator at the OECD] provides us with the answer: "The negotiations began and are continuing within the OECD exclusively, between member states that are providers of capital; those states are firmly convinced that this kind of internal procedure is the only way of producing a binding and therefore useful text that will subsequently be gradually extended to non-OECD countries wishing to attract foreign capital." He goes on to say that, at the WTO, "the presence of countries that have major reservations concerning or are actually hostile to the very principle of a binding agreement on investment mean that the negotiations would be unlikely to succeed."

Chavranski is admitting here that countries that do not want a particular agreement will be shut out of it until it has been drawn up, at which point it will be "gradually extended" to them based on the need to "attract foreign capital." What are we to make of this claim if the MAI is really supposed to remain merely an agreement among the rich countries? We should be wary of accepting Graham's assurance that concerns about the status of developing countries are nonissues in the MAI controversy.

The Network Power of the MAI

Considering the network power that the MAI would have possessed helps to clarify how it would have reshaped the global economy. It would have replaced the bilateral investment treaties (BITs) that are currently negotiated on a country-to-country basis by a single accord, with the potential to become fully globalized. And, like the move from bilateral trade agreements to the GATT and subsequently the WTO, the move from BITs to the MAI would have established an international standard for coordination capable of exerting network power (Grewal 2003). Whether the MAI would have been a beneficial part of the international economic order requires an empirical assessment that the theoretical framework of network power cannot provide. But a network-power analysis does indicate that such a standard, backed by the most powerful countries in the world, would have set up a structural dynamic by which small nations might be made either to join it or to face increasing costs of isolation from the network of international capital flows. In fact, as Chavranski admitted, this seems to have been the intended effect of using the OECD as the negotiating forum for the agreement.

Network power transforms the reasons that agents may have for adopting transnational standards. Without codification and a gatekeeping role, abstract principles, like those of national treatment and nonexpropriation have only the power to persuade, not the power to structure choice. Countries adopt them because they believe that national treatment, for example, will ultimately redound to the benefit of their own economy's investors. As these principles do not regulate desired access to economic cooperation with other countries, they are followed because of their intrinsic benefits, rather than because of network power.

How would these principles of international investment attain that power? First, they must become standardized in institutional forms and by explicit agreement. The principles then become standards with definite articulation. For example, the capital-exporting countries of the OECD have progressed the furthest in the standardization of investment principles. Seven OECD instruments form a framework for investment, and they were used in developing the draft MAI. The principles codified in these agreements include national treatment, protection from expropriation, and guidelines for corporate investment.

Second, these standards must then become part of country-to-country bargaining. In the absence of a multilateral agreement, many countries negotiate reciprocal protection for their investors in a BIT. There are more than thirteen hundred BITs today, so many of the investment standards are already instantiated concretely in international relations, perhaps easing the demand for a multilateral system. Such case-by-case protection does not generally have the same power as a centralized multilateral agreement. Further, it may also be more costly to negotiate separate BITs than a single centralized system, though this is a difficult assessment to make. Most important, perhaps, such standards do not necessarily possess network power. For a standard to gain network power, it needs to become a shared form of coordination among many countries, such that it becomes the main or only way to engage in cooperation that was, or might be, undertaken in a different manner. (Of course, a bilateral investment treaty negotiated between a powerful economy and an underdeveloped one will reflect other inequalities in power between the countries.)[8]

Had the MAI negotiations succeeded, the wealthy nations of the world would have become parties to an agreement articulating a set of rules they would have had to abide by. The MAI would then have operated as a gateway for membership, allowing relatively unencumbered access to foreign-investment markets. This benefit of further cooperation, however, would have come at the price of inhibiting innovation. And, like all standards that govern access to others, the MAI would have proved attractive to nonmembers, especially the capital poor. While the MAI negotiations failed and we can only suppose how it would have actually operated, it seems likely that the original MAI would have served as a

---

[8] Countries may face pressure to adopt a particular arrangement on a bilateral basis; however, that direct compulsion is not network power per se but a different form of what is sometimes called "soft power."

treaty organization to which new members might gain entry by coming into conformity with its terms, enabling its adoption beyond the OECD alone.

Hence, the MAI would have exerted network power on nonmembers, holding out the promise of access to needed foreign-investment markets in return for abidance by its rules and dispute settlement. Whether nonmembers would join the MAI in force depends on too many factors to be anything other than a matter for speculation. But the protestors' intuitions were plausible. By setting up an agreement to which the most powerful nations of the world are parties, the MAI probably would have become something more than a gentlemen's agreement within the OECD. Instead, we might view it as the "thin end of the wedge," with the potential to reshape the international economic order through its standardization of investment rules in an institutional configuration exhibiting network power. Even the mere existence of the MAI would have altered the bargaining position of nonmembers and would have significantly restricted the range of viable choices open to them.

Managing Network Power in Globalization

The failure of the MAI does not represent the end of efforts to establish transnational standards governing investment. Indeed, an investment treaty remains a controversial but important "Singapore issue" now under negotiation in the WTO. However, as the MAI negotiators foresaw, the success of an investment treaty protecting the capital-exporting countries remains highly uncertain if it must be agreed to in advance by the developing world, particularly in a forum like the WTO, in which developing countries can build negotiating alliances and pool resources strategically. No investment agreement emerged from the negotiations in the Doha or Cancun ministerial conferences of the WTO. Despite the frequent criticism of the WTO, it remains—at least in comparison to a purely OECD agreement negotiated in private—a more democratic forum for hashing out a world investment regime. And, as it is more democratic, it enables more actual choice, including the option of refusal. Democratic decision making engages politics rather than suppresses it. By contrast, neoliberal economic policies too often favor a hands-tied approach that keeps the demands of domestic politics away from the standards designed to ensure international economic compatibility.

Whether such a hands-tied approach will prove sustainable is radically unclear. As neoliberal principles are fashioned into standards wielding network power, they will be even more keenly resented than they are at present if they seem disproportionately to benefit the globally privileged or to deny effective choice to most others. How the politics of such an uneven globalization will impact international integration remains to be seen. In this sense, neoliberalism denies experimentation at the local level only to conduct it on the global, suppressing national interventions in the market but thereby jeopardizing international integration itself. If we need a world agreement on foreign investment, how should it be pursued? A strategy that takes advantage of network power would be to approach the matter as attempted with the MAI. The rich countries might bargain among themselves to achieve a solution they find satisfactory, and then—in what would no doubt be presented as an act of openness or inevitability—throw wide the doors of the new club for the rest of the world to join. Of course, in accepting these investment standards, new members would be admitted on previously settled terms they did not help to determine. Nevertheless, given the share of foreign investment represented in a bloc of the world's wealthy nations, network power would probably catapult the standards to global dominance.

A different approach, albeit a more difficult one, would be to see an agreement on global investment as necessarily a *global agreement,* requiring international negotiation about the costs and benefits of this new form of cooperation well in advance of the establishment of a multilateral regime possessing network power. It is obvious why this latter approach is not usually tried: it would cost currently powerful nations more of the gains they seek. Perhaps, in exchange for guarantees of protection from expropriation, the developing world would insist on receiving significant development assistance and expedited technology transfer far in excess of the relatively small sums currently spent (and often misspent) on foreign aid. Further, perhaps any agreement would need to accommodate environmental and social regulations that make industrial production less profitable, but also socially less costly, distinguishing between laws that legitimately reduce the profitability of foreign investment and those that illegitimately do so. Finally, it is not clear that any single, multilateral approach to investment is necessarily right for all countries in the world, particularly with regard to the difficult issue of capital mobility. Not merely the content but also the very existence of a multilateral agreement on investment is up for grabs, given democratic politics.

In fact, it is often unclear whether a transnational standard needs to be developed in a way that constrains the options available to countries seeking international cooperation. For example, we might prefer a piecemeal investment regime tailored to local circumstances, with specific opt-out provisions that exact less of a toll on participating countries. But where a transnational standard is desirable, and where we cannot make it compatible with existing practices, we have an obligation to develop it in a transparent and participatory fashion. In the case of the MAI, precisely the opposite strategy was pursued: a standard of dubious necessity was crafted in a nontransparent manner by an elite subset of countries with the intent that it be catapulted to global dominance through network power.

In an age of global interconnectedness—an age in which we require international standards to coordinate our activity—these network-power dynamics are a common feature, and they present complicated ethical problems. Since network power can be used strategically by the powerful, we need a different way of setting standards, enforcing a new regime for transnational standardization less dependent on the agency or influence of any particular country or bloc of countries. It is no longer enough for each country to pursue its own interests under the fiction that other countries can independently decide whether or not to participate in projects of transnational coordination. This "free market" in standards in which every country is offered the choice to join up with the powerful or face exclusion must be replaced by the functional equivalent of democratic oversight at the global level. To recognize this need is to acknowledge that the age of international voluntarism has passed and one of pervasive global interdependence has taken its place. It is to see foreshadowed in contemporary globalization a yet deeper and fairer globalization to come.

Acknowledgments

I am very grateful to Christian Barry for helping me to develop the main idea of this essay and for sharpening its articulation over several successive drafts.

References

Arthur, W. Brian. 1994. *Increasing Returns and Path Dependence in the Economy*. Ann Arbor: University of Michigan Press.

Bacevich, Andrew J. 2003. *The Imperial Tense: Prospects and Problems of American Empire*. Chicago: Ivan R. Dee.

Cassen, Bernard. 1998. "Wielding Power Behind the Scenes." *Le monde diplomatique* (March). http://mondediplo.com/1998/03/07ami

Cohen, G. A. 1988. "Are Disadvantaged Workers Who Take Hazardous Jobs Forced to Take Hazardous Jobs?" In *History, Labour, and Unfreedom: Themes from Marx*, edited by G. A. Cohen, 239–54. Oxford: Clarendon Press.

David, Paul A. 1985. "Clio and the Economics of QWERTY." *American Economic Review* 75, no. 2 (May): 332–37.

Ferguson, Niall. 2004. *Colossus: The Price of America's Empire*. New York: Penguin.

Graham, Edward M. 2000. *Fighting the Wrong Enemy: Antiglobal Activists and Multinational Enterprises*. Washington, D.C.: Institute for International Economics.

Grewal, David Singh. 2003. "Network Power and Globalization." *Ethics and International Affairs* 17, no. 2:89–98.

Hardt, Michael, and Antonio Negri. 2000. *Empire*. Cambridge, Mass.: Harvard University Press.

Lewis, David. 1969. *Convention*. Cambridge, Mass.: Harvard University Press.

Lukes, Stephen. 1974. *Power: A Radical View*. London: Macmillan.
Nettle, Daniel, and Suzanne Romaine. 2000. *Vanishing Voices: The Extinction of the World's Languages*. New York: Oxford University Press.
Purdy, Jedediah. 2003. "Liberal Empire: Assessing the Arguments." *Ethics and International Affairs* 17, no. 2:35–48.
Reddy, Sanjay. 2000. "The Freedom to Choose Freely." Unpublished manuscript on file with author.
Reddy, Sanjay, and Thomas Pogge. 2002. "How Not to Count the Poor." Mimeo. Barnard College, New York. www.socialanalysis.org
Schelling, Thomas. 1960. *The Strategy of Conflict*. Cambridge, Mass.: Harvard University Press.
Wade, Robert Hunter. 2003. "The Invisible Hand of the American Empire." *Ethics and International Affairs* 17, no. 2:77–88.

8

THE WORLD TRADE ORGANIZATION AND EGALITARIAN JUSTICE

DARREL MOELLENDORF

1

The rules and practices of the World Trade Organization (WTO) affect nearly all of the international trade conducted today. In principle, if not always in practice, the WTO is dedicated to global trade liberalization. As is well known, neither its guiding principles nor its practices are free from controversy. Both trade liberalization and a rules-based multilateral framework are defended by some as advancing the interests of under-developed countries. But massive street demonstrations around the world have been organized, in part at least, in rejection of this claim.[1] In this essay I attempt to consider the matter in a systematic way. After briefly surveying the charge of the WTO, I argue that international trade may be assessed from the perspective of justice, and that the correct account of justice for these purposes is egalitarian in fundamental principle. I then consider the merits of the WTO's basic commitment to liberalized trade in the light of egalitarian considerations. Finally, I discuss the justice of several WTO policies. While noting the complexity of the empirical issues relating to the effects of trade institutions and policies, I conclude that egalitarians have reasons to object to certain of the principles and policies of the WTO.

2

The WTO was founded in 1995 as a result of the Uruguay Round of meetings of the signatories to the General Agreement on Tariffs and Trade (GATT) (Marrakesh Agreement 1994). The purpose of the WTO is to administer multilateral trade treaties, especially GATT 1994, which includes the amended GATT 1947, the General Agreement of Trade in Services (GATS), and the Agreement on Trade-Related Intellectual Property Rights (TRIPS).

The WTO's functions include implementing multilateral trade agreements, providing forums for negotiations on trade issues, facilitating

---

[1] But often there seems also to have been a sizable component of these demonstrations making demands to protect producers in the developed world.

dispute settlements, and cooperating with the World Bank and the International Monetary Fund to achieve "greater coherence in global economic policy-making" (Hoekman and Kostecki 1995, 38). Decision making in the WTO is formally egalitarian; all members have a voice. For matters other than amendments to existing agreements and general principles, decision making is based upon negotiation and consensus. Consensus requires that no country represented in a meeting be "decisively against" an issue (Hoekman and Kostecki 1995, 40).

Members of the WTO must abide by negotiated trade rules that are guided by four basic principles: (1) nondiscrimination, (2) reciprocity, (3) market access, and (4) fair competition. The overarching goal of these rules is a uniform system of liberalized trade. Nondiscrimination has two aspects. First, members must treat all other members as most-favored nations (MFNs), which requires that a country treat the products originating in or destined for any other county no better than products originating in or destined for a member country (GATT 1994, Article I:1). Second, nondiscrimination requires conformity to the national treatment rule, which stipulates that, after importation, foreign goods must be treated no less favorably than domestic goods with respect to taxes and regulations (GATT 1994, Article III:1, 2, and 4).

Reciprocity requires that trade liberalization among members be accomplished on a mutual basis (Hoekman and Kostecki 1995, 27). Reciprocity also applies when countries join the WTO, which in practice means that countries that join the WTO are required to liberalize access to their markets. Market access requires that members agree to negotiate tariff reductions. This amounts to members being bound to schedules of tariff concessions agreed to at multilateral trade negotiations (Hoekman and Kostecki 1995, 31). Fair competition is meant to ensure competition on a level playing field. For example, if a government subsidizes export of an item, then that item may be subject to an antidumping duty by the importing country, thereby increasing the price of the item to compensate for the subsidy that lowered its price.

3

In this section I defend the claim that the trade relations maintained by WTO rules may properly be assessed in the light of the broad requirements of egalitarian social justice. I cannot defend particular principles of egalitarian social justice, for that is a larger project.[2] I take duties of social justice to be associative duties. They exist, when they do, because we owe persons equal respect and we are in a common association with some people.[3] Now, the category of association is somewhat vague. An

---

[2] For more on this see my 2002, 78–81; 2003, 225–40; and 2004, 203–25.
[3] For more on associations see my forthcoming.

association is an interaction of a special type. An association is strong to the extent that it is enduring, is comprehensively governed by institutional norms, regularly affects the highest-order moral interests of the persons associated, and is largely unavoidable. Weak associations blur into mere interactions. There is no bright line between associations and mere interactions. Nonetheless, certain uses of the term *association* are obviously correct or not. The modern state is an association. A group of friends in discussion is not. Determining where an association exists often requires careful attention to the facts of the matter.

The vagueness that results from limiting the duties of justice to the borders of associations could be avoided if the duties were limited instead to relationships in which persons interact directly, with the possibility of causing harm. For example, A has a duty of justice to B if and only if A has harmed B or A could harm B. This, however, would limit the persons obligated beyond what is plausible. For according to this account a person's duty of justice to the vast majority of her compatriots is negligible, since her causal relation to them is weak.

Another possibility would be to limit claims of justice to societies in which people actually cooperate for mutual advantage. This would eliminate considerable vagueness. A duty of justice would exist between two people only if their interaction produced mutual benefits. But this suffers from the same problem as the account that would limit duties of justice to persons who interact directly. It would rule out too many cases in which intuitively duties of justice exist. For example, if A were sufficiently oppressed by B, justice would not then govern the relationship between A and B.

The effects of the Asian economic crisis, felt far beyond Asia, in the late 1990s are evidence of a global economic association. The crisis did extensive damage to emerging markets around the globe. Eventually Russia defaulted on its debt, and Brazil narrowly avoided complete financial collapse. Private-capital flows to emerging market countries plunged, and commodity prices in underdeveloped countries declined, producing current-account crises in several cases.[4]

The extent and effects of globalization can be assessed in several ways, but consider foreign direct investment (FDI), trade, and international lending and currency transfers. In 1997 FDI was 64 percent of the world's gross fixed-capital formation (Sit 2001, 12). But this figure may considerably underestimate the full effects of foreign investment in domestic economies, since foreign investment is often a condition of domestic financing as well as financing from third-party countries. Total FDI-related investment after adjusting for these other sources could be as much as four times that normally measured in official statistics (Sit 2001, 13). Global competition for FDI has eroded working conditions among

---

[4] See World Bank 1999 and IMF 1999.

the most vulnerable workers around the world, especially women (Oxfam 2004).

Foreign trade as a percentage of the global domestic product is on the increase. The United Nations Development Programme reports that world exports averaged 21 percent of a state's gross domestic product (GDP) in the late 1990s, as compared to an average of 17 percent of a smaller GDP in the 1970s (UNDP 1999, 25). Moreover, the poorest countries are the most deeply integrated into world trade. For example, sub-Saharan Africa had an export-to-GDP ratio of 29 percent, as compared to 15 percent for Latin America (UNDP 1999, 31). Multilateral rules now govern trade relations among the overwhelming majority of countries. As of April 2004, the WTO consisted of 147 member countries (WTOa), accounting for more than 97 percent of world trade (WTOb).

International lending and currency transfers have also been steadily increasing. International bank lending grew from $265 billion in 1975 to $4.2 trillion in 1994. Meanwhile, the daily turnover in foreign-exchange markets increased from $10–20 billion in the 1970s to $1.5 trillion in 1998 (UNDP 1999, 25). Between 1980 and 1998 the International Monetary Fund (IMF) and the World Bank made at least 126 loans (Easterly 2000). Between 1987 and 1991 loans to the low-income, debt-distressed countries in Africa, most of which have relatively little FDI, amounted to 15.4 percent of the countries' real GDP and 75 percent of real imports (Sahn, Dorosh, and Younger 1997, 4). The conditionality associated with IMF and World Bank loans from the 1980s onward gave these financial institutions considerable voice in the policies of poor countries that in other ways were not greatly integrated into the global economy.

The life prospects of persons are dramatically unequal depending upon one's place within the institutional scheme of the global economy. The UNDP notes that the total income of the world's richest 1 percent of people is equal to that of the poorest 57 percent (UNDP 2002, 19). The assets of the three richest people in the world are more than the combined GNP of all the least-developed countries (UNDP 2002, 38). Nearly half of the world's population lives in abject poverty on $2 PPP per day.[5] Worse still, 1.15 billion people live on less than a $1 PPP a day (World Bank 2002, 30). Some 1.3 billion people lack access to clean water, and 840 million children are malnourished (UNDP 1999, 28).

These huge inequalities have dramatic effects on the life prospects of persons. One important index of this is longevity. According to the World Health Organization (WHO), "Over 60% of deaths in developed countries occur beyond age 70, compared to about 30% in developing countries" (Mathers et al. 2002, 54). The United Nations International Children's Emergency Fund (UNICEF) reports that 30,500 children

_____

[5] "PPP" stands for purchasing power parity. $2 PPP means the local currency equivalent of what one could purchase with $2 in the United States.

under the age of five die every day of mainly preventable causes (UNICEF 2000). Indeed, the condition of the world's poorest children provides evidence of growth in global inequality. In the 1990s children in sub-Saharan Africa were nineteen times more likely to die than children in the world's richest countries. By 2003 this figure had grown to twenty-six times (UNDP 2003, 39). According to the WHO, "In one hour over 500 African mothers lose a child; had they lived in a rich European country, nearly 490 of these mothers and their children would have been spared the ordeal" (Mathers et al. 2002, 44–45).

Regardless of whether persons are directly engaged with the global economy, their local economy is profoundly affected by FDI, international trade, and international lending and currency exchange. And although state leaders are formally free either to deepen engagement with the world market or not to do so, if they have no reasonable alternative path to development—as appears to be the case—then the moral significance of this area of choice is slight. Moreover, in many cases citizens of countries that choose such a development path effectively have no choice in the matter. The burdens of unequal life prospects and the constraints on domestic policy of the global market are not, therefore, in a morally relevant sense voluntarily assumed.

The immense disparity of life prospects among members of the global economy appears inconsistent with the requirements of equal respect. A commitment to equal respect places constraints on possible justifications for inequality. For example, respecting persons equally is inconsistent with expressing to some that they must endure lesser life prospects than others with whom they are associated merely so that the life prospects of these others may be enhanced.[6] The justificatory constraints of equal respect seem to have fundamentally egalitarian distributive implications. But libertarian critics of egalitarianism argue that an institutional arrangement that constrains the prospects of the most advantaged persons so that, for example, the prospects of the disadvantaged may be improved use advantaged persons merely as a means to benefit the disadvantaged.[7] The rhetorical power of this claim derives in large part from the assumption that deviations from the status quo of inequality require justification. I do not think that a commitment to equal respect requires this. Rather, a commitment to equal respect takes equality as the benchmark and limits the kinds of justifications that may be offered for deviations from that benchmark.

A full account of the justificatory demands of equal respect would require an account of which reasons for deviating from the benchmark of equality are arbitrary from the point of view of justice and therefore to be disqualified. A thought experiment that disqualifies these reasons from

---

[6] See also Rawls 1999, sec. 17.
[7] The classic presentation of this argument is in Nozick 1974, chap. 7.

entering the deliberative process would be of great use in determining what equal respect requires. This, I take it, is the promise of the Rawlsian original position.[8] But even without a full account of which reasons are arbitrary from the point of view of justice, and therefore without an account of the principles of distributive justice, we can discern an egalitarian tendency in the justificatory requirements of equal respect at the level of basic principle.

4

The basic commitment of the WTO is to a globally uniform system of liberalized trade. Does justice recommend this? According to neoclassical economic theory, trade liberalization should increase global economic efficiency and lead to increases in aggregate production and consumption. The basic idea is that international competition provides incentives for efficient production. The theory of comparative advantage holds that the most efficient strategy for a state to pursue in a free international market involves producing only those goods and services for which it has a comparative advantage and trading for the rest.[9] A standard critique of economic protectionism is that it frustrates the pursuit of comparative advantage, with the result that ultimately economic modernization suffers. "A high rate of economic interaction with the rest of the world speeds the absorption of frontier technologies and global management best practices, spurs innovation and cost-cutting, and competes away monopoly" (Frankel 2000, 60). Sometimes the efficiency argument in favor of liberalized trade is dismissed as merely an appeal to an economic good. But it cannot be so easily dismissed if what is at stake is the rate at which a country develops economically.

Karl Marx and V. I. Lenin were supporters of free trade in part at least on efficiency grounds.[10] Marx, as is well known, was impressed with the efficiency gains of capitalism achieved through the constant revolutionizing of the means of production.[11] He took these gains as a necessary precondition for socialism. "[T]his development of productive forces . . . is an absolutely necessary practical premise because without it want is merely made general, and with destitution the struggle for necessities and all the old filthy business would necessarily be reproduced" (Marx 1977c, 170–71). In addition to eschewing the national chauvinism that accompanies protectionism, a belief in the efficiency of free trade seems to have been a reason for Marxian support of free trade.

---

[8] This account of the original position is defended in Dworkin 1989.
[9] The classic statement is Ricardo 1973, chap. 7.
[10] For example, see Marx 1977a, Lenin 1960, and Lenin 1966.
[11] "The bourgeoisie cannot exist without constantly revolutionizing the instruments of production, and thereby the relations of production, and with them the whole relations of society." Marx 1977b, 224.

Appealing to the greater efficiency of a regime of free trade is not, however, as straightforward as one might assume. If efficiency is judged by the criteria of Pareto optimality and superiority, it may not be possible to determine that one social system is more efficient than another. The Pareto concepts of efficiency take welfare in terms of the satisfaction of preferences. To attempt to compare overall preference satisfaction in representative states of two different systems requires making problematic interpersonal utility comparisons. Because individual preferences differ, one cannot claim that a system that provides more of a certain good is more efficient than a system with another set of individuals that provides less; and therefore one cannot claim that individuals in a free-trade regime are more satisfied than others in a protectionist regime. The principle of Pareto superiority permits comparisons only of the well-being of the same set of individuals. But even comparing the satisfaction of interests of the same persons in two different social systems may not be possible, for their interests might be dependent on the larger social institutions.[12] The case for the greater efficiency of a regime of free trade, then, cannot be made merely by appealing to empirical comparisons; it inevitably involves ample economic theory.

If it is the case that free trade produces efficiency gains, this does not clinch the case for free trade on egalitarian grounds. For two equally optimal distributions may be appraised very differently with respect to distributive justice. Market distributions alone cannot realize the aims of egalitarian justice. One reason for this is that those who are lucky at birth will receive advantages deriving from their family circumstances and citizenship status, whereas others will not. Without institutions that remedy this, market advantage will result in inequalities for apparently morally arbitrary reasons.[13] Additionally, egalitarians criticize market inequality as productive of other severe social evils, such as exploitation and inequality of political influence.[14] So, even assuming the market liberalization serves the goal of efficiency, mere market liberalization is insufficient for realizing egalitarian goals.

Moreover, even if there were egalitarian grounds, on the basis of efficiency alone, to prefer a set of policies serving a particular goal, there may nonetheless be sufficient reasons for rejecting the policies, reasons associated with the effects of the policies rather than the goal they serve. For example, if (as is often argued) reducing agricultural protections in the underdeveloped world would undermine the ability of subsistence farmers to compete with agribusiness firms in the developed world, then any transition

[12] See Buchanan 1985, 37–39, for a more extensive discussion of the ideas presented in this paragraph.
[13] The claim must be qualified by "apparently" because, as noted in section 3, I cannot here give an account of what considerations are arbitrary from the perspective of justice.
[14] On exploitation see, for example, Pendlebury, Hudson, and Moellendorf 2001. On inequality of political influence see Daniels 1989.

to a free-trade regime would be objectionable on egalitarian grounds if it failed to provide compensation for those displaced in the transition (Cavanagh et al. 2002, 26–27). Pursuit of agricultural trade liberalization would require the WTO to provide income support for displaced subsistence farmers, and this would require institutions of taxation and transfer.

As a matter of nonideal theory, egalitarian considerations constrain the alternatives by which efficiency may be pursued. This is an instance of the following reasonable general constraint: The pursuit of egalitarian ideals by nonegalitarian means is justified only if (a) either more egalitarian means, or compensatory provisions, are not available or are themselves seriously unjust and (b) there are especially strong reasons to believe that the goal will be served by those policies within a reasonable time. I leave aside for present purposes a more precise account of the burden of proof and time frame. In order to appreciate the reason for the constraint, suppose its denial. Then in a world marked by deep and unjust inequalities, egalitarians would be justified in pursuing policies that exacerbate injustice, even if more egalitarian options would serve the same goal by appropriate means, on the grounds that these policies served the good of the distant egalitarian goal. This would have the untenable effect of rendering political egalitarianism the enemy of the disadvantaged.

A policy of trade liberalization that harms poor producers without compensation is objectionable on egalitarian grounds. But there may be even more at stake for developing economies. In the course of pursuing development, the countries of the developed world systematically protected their infant industries.[15] Indeed, infant-industry protection may be a necessary policy for successful economic development. If this is the case, then multilateral arrangements that hold underdeveloped countries to the same trade-liberalization requirements as developed countries consign the poor in the developing world to lesser life prospects than would well-crafted protectionist policies in the developing world. Assuming either the availability of the latter or the possibility of development compensation, there are egalitarian grounds for rejecting such arrangements. In this case the WTO's combined commitment to the principles of nondiscrimination and market access would be objectionable in the absence of compensation.

A similar argument, however, cannot be made with respect to the reduction of protectionism in the developed states. Consider agricultural tariffs and subsidies. One feature that distinguishes the WTO from the GATT is the former's commitment to liberalizing all trade in agriculture. Despite this commitment, developed-world protectionist agricultural

---

[15] The classic account of the infant industry protection argument is in List 1966, bk. 1. The argument has been revived in Chang 2002. On the basis of a theoretical model, Bardhan argues that the development benefits of protectionism are more mixed: "Protection of the more capital-intensive sector causes a fall in labor productivity in both sectors, while imposition of a tariff on the output of the more labor-intensive sector increases productivity in each sector" (2003, 110).

policies currently permitted by WTO rules have seriously restricted the possibilities for developing-world agricultural producers to find markets for their goods. The United Nations Conference on Trade and Development (UNCTAD) estimates that low-technology countries are losing out on $700 billion per year in export earnings due to developed-world protectionism (UNCTAD 1999). This amounts to more than four times the annual capital inflow into the developing world due to FDI (UN-CTAD 1999). But because of lack of resources, developing countries have been unable adequately to subsidize their smallholding farmers, while 70 percent of the world's poor live in rural areas (UNCTAD 1999). Currently, 827.5 million people in the world suffer from hunger (UNDP 2003, 54). A trade regime that allows developed countries to protect their agriculture to the disadvantage of agriculture from developing countries is objectionable on egalitarian grounds.

Hence, there are reasons to believe that the basic commitment of the WTO to trade liberalization might be fundamentally unjust. This is the case if tariff reduction in the developing world will impoverish the already poor for the foreseeable future, and if protecting infant industries is historically the most assured path to development. In any case, the WTO's policy of tolerating developed-world protectionism against underdeveloped countries is seriously unjust.

Even if there are significant injustices in WTO rules, underdeveloped countries that join the WTO are not necessarily implicated in those injustices. Consider an analogy to an exploitative employment contract. If the larger social circumstances leave a worker no reasonable alternative but to accept the terms of such a contract, she is hardly complicit in the injustice that she suffers. It may be perfectly rational for a weak developing country to support almost any rules-based system of trade over one that leaves it prey to the much larger market and military power of the developed countries, which are freer to exercise that power in bilateral negotiation with few, if any, background rules. Additionally, even if WTO rules are systematically prejudiced against underdeveloped countries, and I have not argued this, the stability of the multilateral trading system would require at least the appearance of impartiality in a sizable number of cases.[16] The imperative of maintaining appearances would provide reason to believe that appeals on the basis of legal principle would have some hope of success. Finally, the WTO's commitment to market access should eventually provide the leverage for appeals that would reduce protectionist policies directed against the underdeveloped world.[17]

---

[16] This idea is drawn from Thompson's discussion of class interests in the law in Thompson 1975, 263.

[17] Brazil's victorious case against U.S. protectionism of cotton evinces movement in this direction. See Associated Press 2004.

5

The WTO's toleration of trade tariffs in the developed world takes us away from a discussion of basic principle and into a discussion of practice. In this section I consider three criticisms of WTO practice.

First, there are serious concerns that poorer countries are marginalized in WTO decision-making procedures. This is in part due to inequalities in resources.

> Poor countries participate little in the formulation and implementation of the new rules that govern global markets. The 1994 Uruguay Round of GATT shows the difficulties facing small and poor countries. Of the 29 least developed countries in the WTO, only 12 had missions in Geneva, most staffed with a handful of people to cover the gamut of UN work. . . . Many small and poor countries had difficulty even ensuring representation at meetings. (UNDP 1999, 34–35)

A straightforward solution to this problem would be for the WTO to subsidize the participation of the least-developed countries (Shukla 2002, 281). The demand that participation of the least-developed countries be subsidized is fully consistent with the Marrakesh Agreement Establishing the WTO, which recognized "that there is need for positive efforts designed to ensure that developing countries, and especially the least developed amongst them, secure a share in the growth in international trade commensurate with the needs of their economic development" (Marrakesh Agreement 1994). The WTO procedural requirement of consensus has also been criticized as a means of ensuring that the interests of underdeveloped countries cannot be pursued if this involves burdening the developed world (Bello 2001, 28–29). Although the criticism has some force, it fails to appreciate that veto power can be wielded to protect the interests of the poor as well.

Another criticism of the WTO, raised by Peter Singer, among others, is that it tends in practice to prioritize economic efficiency over all other values. Singer's concern focuses on the WTO's application of the principle of nondiscrimination (Singer 2002, 57–70). Since determinations of whether products are discriminated against effects employment opportunities, the principle of nondiscrimination would seem to serve the purpose of reducing discrimination against persons on the basis of their national origin.

Singer charges, however, that the application of the principle of nondiscrimination by the WTO erodes the ability of states to legislate in accordance with environmental and other values. He cites as evidence the 1991 GATT *Dolphin-Tuna* dispute between the United States and Mexico.[18] The context of this dispute involves the U.S. Marine Mammal Protection Act, which sets standards for dolphin protection in the

---

[18] For the WTO's account of the dispute see WTOc.

harvesting of tuna. A country exporting tuna to the United States must meet the dolphin-protection standards set out in U.S. law, otherwise the U.S. government may embargo all imports of fish from that country. Mexico's exports of tuna to the United States were banned under the act. Mexico then complained in 1991 in accordance with the GATT dispute-settlement procedures. In its defense the United States cited GATT Article XX, which allows exceptions at (b) to protect animal or plant life or health and at (g) to conserve exhaustible natural resources (WTOd). In September 1991 a GATT panel found that the United States could not embargo Mexican tuna on the basis of the process through which it came to the market. In effect, the decision was that similar products must get equal treatment regardless of dissimilar production processes (WTOe). Singer observes that the requirement of nondiscrimination on the basis of processes erodes a state's ability to legislate to secure environmental and workplace safety goals. In 1994 a second GATT panel concurred with the earlier decision in a second dolphin dispute, *Son of Dolphin-Tuna*, this time between the European Union and the United States (WTOf).[19]

Singer's criticism, however, may not have as much basis in law as he suggests. Neither *Dolphin-Tuna* nor *Son of Dolphin-Tuna* is precedent setting, for in neither case was the decision adopted; rather, it was merely circulated. Moreover, in a subsequent similar case, *Shrimp-Turtle*, although the WTO found against the United States, it upheld the right of states to legislate in accordance with environmental values.[20] This would appear to be an evolving area of WTO jurisprudence, and it may be too early to tell how the law will eventually be decided.

The concern behind Singer's criticism is that the good of economic efficiency may be taken as trumping other values, which if taken seriously lead to production and workplace regulations. There are two routes for complementing trade rules to secure other values. One is to allow states to apply penalties in a nondiscriminatory fashion on products that were produced in manners that violate certain standards. If these penalties were applied to products without reference to their point of origin, no national discrimination could be claimed. Alternatively, international regulatory rules could be adopted that would be applicable in a non-discriminatory fashion. States may be able to press for environmental protection along the first lines within the constraints of existing WTO rules. But the prevention of competitive pressures to reduce costly regulation might recommend the second route.

Finally, the Agreement on Trade-Related Aspects of Intellectual Property Rights (TRIPS) has been met with considerable criticism. Consisting of seven major parts, TRIPS governs various kinds of intellectual property. Prior to its ratification there was significant dis-

---

[19] http://www.wto.org/english/tratop_e/envir_e/edis05_e.htm.
[20] See *United States—Import Prohibition of Certain Shrimp Products* 1999 and WTOg.

agreement about TRIPS among developed countries—major exporters of intellectual property—and underdeveloped countries—who are primarily importers of intellectual property (Hoekman and Kostecki 1995, 152). U.S. pharmaceutical, entertainment, and information industries were largely responsible for getting TRIPS on the negotiating agenda, and developing countries—many of which had little or no legal protection for intellectual property—were concerned that an intellectual-property-rights regime would make important goods, such as medicine, prohibitively expensive to their citizens in need (Hoekman and Kostecki 1995, 156).

Part I, Article 3, of TRIPS applies the national treatment principle to intellectual property (WTOh). Article 4 applies the most-favored-nation principle (WTOh). Part II, section 5, protects patent rights (WTOi). According to Article 28, patent protection shall prohibit the "making, using, offering for sale, selling, or importing" without consent of the patent-holder (WTOi). In effect, holding a patent gives the holder monopoly power in the market for the period of the patent. According to Article 33, this period shall last for twenty years (WTOi). Members have one year from the date of entry to implement the TRIPS requirements; developing countries have five years (but only one to implement the most-favored-nation principle); and least-developed countries have ten years, and may request extensions (Hoekman and Kostecki 1995, 155).

Consider the case of a country such as India, which previously provided patent protection for pharmaceutical processes for only seven years and provided no patent protection at all for pharmaceutical products (Hoekman and Kostecki 1995, 154). The lack of patent protection for products allowed firms to reverse engineer pharmaceutical products and produce them according to their own processes. Since typically this is done without investing as much in research and development as is required for invention, prices for pharmaceutical products are driven down, thereby allowing greater access to existing pharmaceutical products for the poor of India. With the advent of TRIPS, one can expect the price of pharmaceutical products to rise steadily in the developing world.

In 2000 the Sub-Commission on the Promotion and Protection of Human Rights under the auspices of the United Nations Commissioner for Human Rights declared:

> (S)ince the implementation of the TRIPS Agreement does not adequately reflect the fundamental nature and indivisibility of all human rights, including the right of everyone to enjoy the benefits of scientific progress and its applications, the right to health, the right to food and the right to self-determination, there are apparent conflicts between the intellectual property rights regime embodied in the TRIPS Agreement, on the one hand, and international human rights law, on the other. (UNHCHR 2000)

The subcommission cites the *Human Development Reports* of 1999 and 2000, by the United Nations Human Development Programme, as studies evidencing the deleterious effects of TRIPS on the stated rights (UNHCHR 2000).

The knowledge of the chemical structure of pharmaceutical products would appear to be public goods whose supply does not diminish with consumption. It would seem to be most efficient to have this knowledge held as widely as possible. What reasons, then, favor patent protection? Most often, the need to provide an incentive for the initial outlay of research and development is cited.[21] By granting monopoly-pricing power, a patent regime provides incentives for original, inventive, and innovative work. Without such an incentive, the most economical strategy would be to wait for others to make the initial outlay and then to reverse engineer their products.

TRIPS seeks to balance incentives to invention and innovation against the needs of consumers by providing a number of exceptions to patent protection. Article 27 allows leeway for exceptions in matters of public health:

> 2. Members may exclude from patentability inventions, the prevention within their territory of the commercial exploitation of which is necessary to protect *ordre public* or morality, including to protect human, animal or plant life or health or to avoid serious prejudice to the environment, provided that such exclusion is not made merely because the exploitation is prohibited by their law.
> 3. Members may also exclude from patentability:
> (a) diagnostic, therapeutic and surgical methods for the treatment of humans or animals. (WTOi)

Article 30 allows for exceptions provided that they "do not unreasonably conflict with a normal exploitation of the patent and do not unreasonably prejudice the legitimate interests of the patent owner" (WTOi). Article 31 requires that exceptions be for a limited time and only after failure to gain permission on satisfactory terms from the patent-holder (WTOi). It is impossible to know in advance of test cases and WTO dispute resolution whether part II, section 5, which protects patent rights, strikes a balance that will provide protection for the most important interests of consumers in the developing world.

It is doubtful, in any case, that the incentive argument for pharmaceutical patents provides a reason not to allow exceptions like those envisaged under Article 27 (2). In order for there to be a market-based incentive to produce a commodity, there must be effective demand for that commodity. Given the abject poverty of the developing world, it is extremely unlikely that under present conditions there can be effective demand for pharmaceutical inventions for many diseases. Indeed, according to one study, only fifteen of the new medicines patented between 1975

---

[21] See Hoekman and Kostecki 1995, 145–46. But Nozick 1974, 182, defends patents on natural-rights grounds. Sterckx 2004 criticizes various justifications of the TRIPS protection.

and 1997 were for tropical diseases (McNile 2000). Moreover, in the developing world access to existing pharmacological therapies is sometimes much more important than incentives for innovation. For example, of the six million people in the developing world currently in need of antiretroviral treatment, only four hundred thousand have access to it (WHO 2003, 5). Even if it is the case that a patent system provides necessary incentives for production that cannot be provided by any other means, lifting the production monopoly for a well-defined period of time to treat an epidemic need not disrupt the more entrenched system of incentives for future production.[22] So, there are good reasons for allowing exceptions to TRIPS along the lines of those envisaged in Article 27.

6

The WTO's failure to eliminate developed-world protectionism against underdeveloped countries is a clear case of injustice. Multilateral reduction of protectionist policies that do not allow provision for less-developed countries to protect vulnerable producers and infant industries are also unjust, if the harms that result are not compensated. At the level of policy, the failure of the WTO to subsidize the participation of underdeveloped countries casts serious doubts on its procedural fairness; and if the WTO does not allow for policies to protect the environment, workers, and public health, its practices will be further at fault. These criticisms do not, however, entail that an alternative without multilateral rules would be better. There is good reason to believe that the elimination of the multilateral trading system would be even worse for egalitarian justice, since it would leave weak countries even more vulnerable to the predatory trading practices of the rich and strong countries whose representatives invariably fail to take seriously the view that justice requires attention to the interests of the disadvantaged.

Acknowledgments

Many of the ideas in this essay were presented in a paper to the Political Theory Project and the Watson Institute at Brown University. I am grateful to the participants of that session for their helpful comments. I am especially indebted to Christian Barry for his probing comments and criticisms of an earlier draft. I would also like to thank the James Hervey Johnson Charitable Educational Trust for support.

---

[22] It is by no means clear that patents are required for there to be sufficient production incentives. Chang (2002, 2) reminds us that "Switzerland became one of the world's technological leaders in the nineteenth century without a patent law."

References

The Associated Press. 2004. "WTO Denounces U.S. Cotton Subsidies." MSNBC News (27 April). http://msnbc.msn.com/id/4844030/

Bardhan, Pranab. 2003. "Dynamic Effects of Protection on Productivity." In *International Trade, Growth, and Development*, 101–13. Oxford: Blackwell.

Bello, Walden. 2001. *The Future in the Balance: Essays on Globalization and Resistance*. Oakland: Food First Books.

Buchanan, Allen. 1985. *Ethics, Efficiency, and the Market*. Totowa: Rowan & Allanheld.

Cavanagh, John, et al. 2002. *Alternatives to Economic Globalization*. San Francisco: Berret Koehler.

Chang, Ha-Joon. 2002. *Kicking Away the Ladder*. London: Anthem Press.

Daniels, Norman. 1989. "Equal Liberty and Unequal Worth of Liberty." In *Reading Rawls*, edited by Norman Daniels, 253–81. Stanford: Stanford University Press.

Dworkin, Ronald. 1989. "The Original Position." In *Reading Rawls*, edited by Norman Daniels, 17–53. Stanford: Stanford University Press.

Easterly, William. 2000. "The Effects of IMF and World Bank Programs on Poverty." http://www.imf.org/external/pubs/ft/staffp/2000/00-00/e.pdf

Frankel, Jeffrey. 2000. "Globalization of the Economy." In *Governance in a Globalizing World*, edited by Joseph S. Nye Jr. and John D. Donahue, 45–71. Washington, D.C.: Brookings Institute Press.

GATT. 1994. http://www.wto.org/english/docs_e/legal_e/legal_e.htm#finalact

Hoekman, Bernard M., and Michel M. Kostecki. 1995. *The Political Economy of the World Trading System*. Oxford: Oxford University Press.

IMF. 1999. *Annual Report of the Executive Board for the Financial Year Ended April 30, 1999*. http://www.imf.org/external/pubs/ft/ar/1999/index.htm

Lenin, V. I. 1960. "The Economic Content of Narodism." In *Collected Works*, vol. 1. Moscow: Progress. Original published in 1895.

———. 1966. "Re the Monopoly of Foreign Trade." In *Collected Works*, vol. 33. Moscow: Progress. Original published in 1922.

List, Friederich. 1966. *The National System of Political Economy*. Translated by Sampson S. Lloyd, M.P. New York: Augustus M. Kelley.

Marx, Karl. 1977a. "Speech on Free Trade." In *Karl Marx Selected Writings*, edited by David McLellan. Oxford: Oxford University Press. Original published in 1848.

———. 1977b. *"The Communist Manifesto."* (1848) In *Karl Marx Selected Writings*, edited by David McLellan. Oxford: Oxford University Press. Original published in 1848.

———. 1977c. *"The German Ideology."* In *Karl Marx Selected Writings*. edited by David McLellan. Oxford: Oxford University Press. Original published in 1932.

Mather, Colin, et al. 2002. *Global Burden of Disease in 2002: Data Sources, Methods and Results*. World Health Organization Discussion Paper 54. http://www3.who.int/whosis/menu.cfm?path = whosis,burden,burden_estimates&laanguage = english

Marrakesh Agreement. 1994. http://www.wto.org/english/docs_e/legal_e/04-wto_e.htm

McNile, Donald G., Jr. 2000. "West's Drug Firms Play God in Africa." *Mail and Guardian* (May 26–June 1): 1.

Moellendorf, Darrel. 2002. *Cosmopolitan Justice*. Boulder: Westview Press.

———. 2003. "Reply to Miller and Satz." *International Journal of Politics and Ethics* 3, no. 2:253–68.

———. 2004. *"Cosmopolitan Justice* Reconsidered." *Theoria* 104: 203–25.

———. Forthcoming. "Persons' Interests, States' Duties, and Global Governance." In *The Political Philosophy of Cosmopolitanism*, edited by Harry Brighouse and Gillian Brock. Cambridge: Cambridge University Press.

Nozick, Robert. 1974. *Anarchy, State, and Utopia*. New York: Basic.

Oxfam International. 2004. "Trading Away Our Rights: Women Working in Global Supply Chains." http://www.oxfam.org/eng/policy_pape.htm

Pendlebury, Michael, Peter Hudson, and Darrel Moellendorf. 2001. "Capitalist Exploitation, Self-Ownership, and Equality." *Philosophical Forum* 32, no. 3 (fall): 207–20.

Rawls, John. 1999. *A Theory of Justice*. Revised edition. Cambridge, Mass.: Harvard University Press.

Ricardo, David. 1973. *The Principles of Political Economy and Taxation*. London: J. M. Dent.

Sahn, David E., Paul A. Dorosh, and Stephan D. Younger. 1997. *Structural Adjustment Reconsidered*. Cambridge: Cambridge University Press.

Shukla, S. P. 2002. "From the GATT to the WTO and Beyond." In *Governing Globalization*, edited by Deepak Nayyar, 254–86. Oxford: Oxford University Press.

Singer, Peter. 2002. *One World: The Ethics of Globalization*. New Haven: Yale University Press.

Sit, Victor S. F. 2001. "Globalization, Foreign Direct Investment, and Urbanization in Developing Countries." In *Facets of Globalization:*

International and Local Dimensions of Development, World Bank Discussion Paper No. 415, edited by Shahid Yusuf, Simon Evenett, and Weiping Wu, 11–54. Washington, D.C.: World Bank.

Sterckx, Sigrid. 2004. "Patents and Access to Drugs in Developing Countries: An Ethical Analysis." *Developing World Bioethics* 4, no. 1:58–75.

Thompson, E. P. 1975. *Whigs and Hunters: The Origins of the Black Act.* New York: Pantheon.

UNCTAD. 1999. "Industrial Countries Must Work Harder For Development If Globalization Is To Deliver On Its Promises." http://www.unctad.org/Templates/webflyer.asp?docid = 3082&intItemID = 2021&lang = 1

UNDP. 1999. *Human Development Report 1999.* http://hdr.undp.org/reports/global/1999/en/Ibid

UNDP. 2002. *Human Development Report 2002.* http://hdr.undp.org/reports/global/1999/en/pdf/chapterone.pdf

UNDP. 2003. *Human Development Report 2003.* http://www.undp.org/hdr2003/pdf/hdr03_chapter_2.pdf

UNHCHR. 2000. http://www.unhchr.ch/Huridocda/Huridoca.nsf/0/c462b62cf8a07b13c12569700046704e?Opendocument

UNICEF. 2000. *The State of the World's Children.* http://www.unicef.org/sowc00/

United States—Import Prohibition of Certain Shrimp Products. 1999. (38) *ILM* 118.

WHO. 2003. *Treating 3 Million by 2005.* Geneva. World Health Organization. http://www.who.int/3by5/publications/documents/isbn 9241591129/en/

World Bank. 1999. *Annual Report 1999.* http://www.worldbank.org/html/extpb/annrep99/over.htm

———. 2002. *Global Economic Prospects and the Developing Countries.* http://www.worldbank.org/prospects/gep2002/chap1.pdff

WTOa. "What Is the WTO?" http://www.wto.org/english/thewto_e/whatis_e/whatis_e.htm Accessed on 19 October 2004

WTOb. "The WTO In Brief." http://www.wto.org/english/thewto_e/whatis_e/inbrief_e/inbr02_e.htm Accessed on 19 October 2004

WTOc. "Mexico etc. Versus US: 'Tuna-Dolphin.'" http://www.wto.org/english/tratop_e/envir_e/edis04_e.htm Accessed on 19 October 2004

WTOd. "Relevant WTO Provisions: Descriptions." http://www.wto.org/english/tratop_e/envir_e/issu3_e.htm#gattart20 Accessed on 19 October 2004

WTOe. "CTE on: How Environmental Taxes and Other Requirements Fit In." http://www.wto.org/english/tratop_e/envir_e/cte03_e.htm#productvprocess Accessed on 19 October 2004

WTOf. "EU Versus US: 'Son of Dolphin-Tuna.'" http://www.wto.org/english/tratop_e/envir_e/edis05_e.htm Accessed on 19 October 2004

WTOg. "India etc. Versus US: 'Shrimp-Turtle.'" http://www.wto.org/
english/tratop_e/envir_e/edis08_e.htm Accessed on 19 October 2004
WTOh. "Part I—General Provisions and Basic Principles." http://
www.wto.org/english/docs_e/legal_e/27-TRIPS_03_e.htm Accessed on
19 October 2004
WTOi. "Part II—Standards Concerning the Availability, Scope and Use
of Intellectual Property Rights." http://www.wto.org/english/docs_e/
legal_e/27trips_04c_e.htm Accessed on 19 October 2004

9

WHOSE SOVEREIGNTY?:
EMPIRE VERSUS INTERNATIONAL LAW

JEAN L. COHEN

Let me begin by juxtaposing two facts: The world's sole superpower has invaded and occupied Iraq. Carl Schmitt's *Nomos der Erde* has just been translated into English, or I should say American (Schmitt 2003). Is this mere coincidence? Are not the questions Schmitt raised, if not his answers, once again on the agenda?

This essay focuses on the impact of globalization on international law and the discourse of sovereignty. We have been hearing for quite some time that state sovereignty is being undermined. The transnational character of "risks," from ecological problems to terrorism, including the commodification of weapons of mass destruction, highlights the apparent lack of control of the modern nation-state over its own territory, borders, and the dangers that its citizens face.

Moreover, key political and legal decisions are being made beyond the purview of national legislatures. A variety of supranational organizations, transnational "private global authorities," and transgovernmental networks engage in regulation and rule making, bypassing the state in the generation of hard and "soft law" (see Teubner 1997, 3–15 and passim; Teubner 2004; Abbott et al. 2002; Rosenau et al. 1997; Rosenau 1998). Indeed, the apparent decoupling of law from the territorial state suggests to many that the latter has lost legal as well as political sovereignty.

This conundrum has triggered the emergence of a set of claims about the transformation of international law. If law making is escaping the monopoly of states, then the standard view of international law as the law that states make through treaties, or consent to through long practice (custom), has to be revised. The emergence of human rights law based on consensus apparently implies that global cosmopolitan law trumps the will of states and their international treaties (consent).[1] Today the very category "international" appears outdated. The question thus becomes: What is to be the new "nomos" of the earth and how should we understand globalized law?[2]

---

[1] See Buchanan 2004, 301–13, for an argument that consensus should replace state consent as the principle of legitimacy in the international system.

[2] See Schmitt 2003, 336–51, for the concept of *nomos*. In short, a *nomos* is the concrete territorial and political organization of the world order, invested with symbolic meaning, that undergirds the formal rules of international law. For a critique of his essentialist understanding of this concept, see Koskenniemi 2004, 415–24.

Legal theorists have certainly risen to the challenge over the past decade. Talk of legal and constitutional pluralism, societal constitutionalism, transnational governmental networks, cosmopolitan human rights law enforced by "humanitarian intervention," and so on are all attempts to conceptualize the new global legal order that is allegedly emerging before our eyes (Teubner 1997; Walker 2002, 317). The general claim is that the world is witnessing a move to cosmopolitan law, which we will not perceive or be able to influence if we do not abandon the discourse of sovereignty (Goldstein et al. 2001). The debates from this perspective are around how to conceptualize the juridification of the new world order.[3] Despite their differences, what seems obvious to those seeking to foster legal cosmopolitanism is that sovereignty talk and the old forms of public international law based on the sovereignty paradigm have to go.

But there is another way of interpreting the changes occurring in the international system. If one shifts to a political perspective, the sovereignty-based model of international law appears to be ceding not to cosmopolitan justice but to a different bid to restructure the world order: the project of empire. The idea that we have already entered into the epoch of empire has taken hold in many circles, as the popularity of the Hardt and Negri volume, and the avalanche of writings and conferences on empire, witness (Hardt and Negri 2000; see also "The Revival of Empire" 2003; Ignatieff 2003a, 22). Like the theorists of cosmopolitan law, proponents of this view also insist that the discourses of state sovereignty and public international law have become irrelevant. But they claim that what is replacing the system of states is not a pluralistic, cooperative world political system under a new, impartial global *rule of law*, but rather a project of imperial world domination. From this perspective, governance, soft law, self-regulation, societal constitutionalism, transgovernmental networks, human rights talk, and the very concept of "humanitarian intervention" are simply the discourses and deformalized mechanisms by which empire aims to rule (and to legitimate its rule) rather than ways to limit and orient power by law.[4]

I agree that we are in the presence of something new. But I am not convinced that one should abandon the discourse of sovereignty in order to perceive and conceptualize these shifts. Nor am I convinced that the step from an international to a cosmopolitan legal world order *without* the sovereign state has been or should be taken. The two doubts are

---

[3] One battle is between traditional sovereigntists and cosmopolitans. Another debate exists within cosmopolitanism between centered versus decentered models. For more centered models of legal and political cosmopolitanism, see Held 1995 and Archibugi 2003.

[4] "The Revival of Empire" 2003 is more nuanced than this characterization. There is, of course, a debate over whether the United States is an empire, whether it can be a successful empire, when the empire began, and whether recent activities, including the invasions of Afghanistan and Iraq, are signs of its demise. See also Todd, Delogu, and Lind 2003. My interest is the fate of the discourse of state sovereignty in these claims and counterclaims.

connected: I argue that if we drop the concept of sovereignty and buy into the idea that the state has been disaggregated, and that international treaty organizations are upstaged by transnational governance, we will misconstrue the nature of contemporary international society and the political choices facing us. If we assume that a constitutional, cosmopolitan legal order already exists, which has replaced or should replace international law and its core principles of sovereign equality, territorial integrity, nonintervention, and domestic jurisdiction with cosmopolitan right, and if we construe the evolving doctrine of "humanitarian intervention" as the enforcement of that right, we risk becoming apologists for imperial projects. Under current conditions, this path leads to the political instrumentalization of "law" (cosmopolitan right) and the moralization of politics rather than to a global rule of law. I will argue that we face the following political choice today: We can either opt for strengthening international law by updating it, making explicit the particular conception of sovereignty on which it is now based and showing that this is compatible with cosmopolitan principles inherent in human rights norms; or we can abandon the principle of (equal) sovereignty and the present rules of international law for the sake of human rights, thus relinquishing an important barrier to the proliferation of imperial projects and regional attempts at *Grossraum* ordering (direct annexation or other forms of control of neighboring smaller polities by a local great power) by twenty-first-century great powers, who invoke (and instrumentalize) cosmopolitan right as they proceed.[5]

Clearly I opt for the former over the latter. The first project entails acknowledging the existence and value of a dualistic world order whose core remains the international society of states embedded within (suitably reformed) international institutions and international law, but that also has important cosmopolitan elements and cosmopolitan legal principles (human rights norms) upon which the discourse of transnationalism and governance relies, if inadequately. On this approach (my own), legal cosmopolitanism is potentially linked to a project radically distinct from empire and pure power politics—namely, the democratization of international relations and the updating of international law. *This requires the strengthening of supranational institutions, formal legal reform, and the creation of a global rule of law that protects both the sovereign equality of states based on a revised conception of sovereignty and human rights.* Much will depend on how the new, and its relation to what went before, is framed. Unlike the theorists of cosmopolitan law and justice without state

---

[5] Of course, international law can also be instrumentalized by the powerful. But the principle of sovereign equality and its correlate, nonintervention, provides a powerful normative presumption against unwarranted aggression. Abandoning it would be a mistake. I also provide noninstrumental, normative arguments in favor of the discourse of sovereignty and public international law below.

sovereignty, the paradox for which I want to argue is that today the rearticulation and democratization of sovereignty (internal and external), configured within a multilayered world order with effective international institutions and an updated international law, is the sine qua non for the emergence of a global "rule of law" and constitutes an important part of a counterproject to empire. Without a global rule of law that protects sovereignty as well as human rights, any talk of "cosmopolitan" right, especially and above all the alleged right to intervene militarily to enforce human rights, is inherently suspect. Cosmopolitan right can supplement—but not replace—sovereignty-based public international law.

I do not, however, mean to take a Schmittian or a "political realist" stance. For Schmitt and his contemporary followers, any version of international law articulating universalistic principles, and any conceivable form of cosmopolitanism, amount to empty formalism, irresponsible utopianism, and/or a set of moralistic platitudes cynically invoked to cover the power bids of a superpower or of a few great powers against the weaker ones.[6] To thinkers in this tradition, international law is either irrelevant or just another name for the policy of the powerful. This is especially true of international law purporting to criminalize aggression, protect human rights, and sanction violations through military or other means. For the Schmittian, "He who invokes humanity wants to cheat" (Schmitt 1996, 54). Accordingly, international tribunals applying international or cosmopolitan law and the "humanitarian interventions" allegedly legitimated by human rights discourse can never escape the charge of political justice (for this concept, see Kirchheimer 1961).

While the concepts of global law and global right can indeed turn into window dressing, it is not necessary to buy into Schmitt's theoretical assumptions regarding territory or spatial ordering in order to see this.[7] Against Schmitt, I will make a case for the importance and autonomy of formal international and cosmopolitan law. Yet neither do I want simply to affirm the arguments of moral cosmopolitans or, less kindly, contemporary human rights fundamentalists. If the political realist errs by overgeneralizing the perspective of strategic interaction (national or great power or imperial self-interest), the moral cosmopolitan errs in the opposite direction. The former is unable to account for the fact that today there is a great deal of effective international law that orients states

---

[6] On the influence of Schmitt on contemporary realism via his influence on Hans Morgenthau, see Koskenniemi 2004, 413–509. See also Kissinger 1994. Kissinger is also, in my view, clearly influenced by Schmitt. I include Hardt and Negri among the contemporary left followers of Schmitt.

[7] Nor do we have to accept his claim that legal limits on the right to go to war and sovereignty are incompatible. And we certainly should not embrace his wholesale rejection of legal formalism or adopt his substantive conception of "law" as merely the ratification of a concrete order.

and shapes their conception of state interest. The moral cosmopolitan focused on global justice and human rights, however, tends to fall prey to a parallel myopia. For reasoning exclusively from the perspective of human rights and what justice requires (overgeneralization of the moral perspective) also leads to contempt for existing international law and a disdain for legal reform through legal means. Like the political realist, the moral cosmopolitan sees sovereignty as a matter of power politics, involving the strategic calculation of national interest and pure *raison d'état*. Unlike the realists, however, the conclusion drawn by human rights fundamentalists is that international law and the discourse of state sovereignty it is based on must be abandoned in favor of the protection of human rights. In short, the demands of justice must trump both sovereignty and formal international law, equated with "legalism."[8] To the moral cosmopolitan, the legalistic discourse of sovereignty and power-oriented international organizations must not be permitted to block rescue operations in the face of gross human rights violations (see Walzer 2004a, 67–85; Tesón 1997). Accordingly, the default position of sovereignty in international law has to be given up: hence the rush to establish a new fundamental norm for the international order.[9] Among the candidates are a basic human right to security, a fundamental right to protection, a principle of civilian inviolability, and even a human right to popular sovereignty.[10] Indeed, violation of international law, we are told, may be the only means of updating it.[11]

While I cannot address the arguments of the moral cosmopolitans in the confines of this essay, I hope to redeem the discourse of sovereignty and international law against its attackers. In what follows, I concentrate on two recent attempts to theorize the new world order along the lines of decentered legal cosmopolitanism. I then present a critique of this construction on empirical and normative grounds. Next, I consider the claim that we have entered into the epoch of empire and show how this approach, despite its critical intentions, blocks crucial reforms in the international system. I conclude by presenting an alternative, dualistic conception of the "new" world order and offer some proposals for reform.

[8] The clearest statement of this position is that of Walzer 1977, esp. 51–117, and 2004a.

[9] See Ignatieff 2003b, 42, for the suggestion that the default position on sovereignty in the international order be abandoned. See also Tesón 2003; Beitz 1979 and 1994; Pogge 1992.

[10] On the human right to security, see ICISS 2001. On the human right to protection, see Walzer 2004b, 66–67; and my reply, Cohen 2004. On the principle of civilian inviolability, see Slaughter and Burke-White 2002. On popular sovereignty as a human right that trumps state sovereignty, see Reisman 1990.

[11] See Buchanan 2004 and 2003. I strongly disagree with his position. For a counterargument with which I do agree, see Byers and Chesterman 2003, 177–203.

From International Society to a Decentered World Order: Beyond Sovereignty?

There are two versions of the thesis that a decentered cosmopolitan world order has emerged that renders the discourse of sovereignty irrelevant: one focuses on political institutions and the other on legal developments. Both maintain that a transition has occurred away from the international society of states and international law to a decentered form of global governance and cosmopolitan law. And both cite the individualization of international law, the invocation of *jus cogens*, which signals the obligatory character of key human rights norms based on consensus, not state consent, and the emergence of transnational loci of decision and rule making as evidence for this shift.

The first approach focuses on the emergence of new forms of transnational governance that have allegedly replaced unitary states as the key actors in the global political system (see Slaughter, esp. 2004). This involves both an epistemological and an empirical claim. We must, first, stop imagining the international system as a system of states—unitary entities like billiard balls. In order to perceive its new structural features, we must open up the black box of the state and apply the idea of the separation of powers, thus far restricted to domestic governments, to the global political scene. This conceptual shift will allow the core components of the new world order to come into view: horizontal and vertical transgovernmental networks (Slaughter 2004, 15).

The empirical claim is that the state has been disaggregated into its component parts, each of which functions autonomously in the global political system. Intergovernmental relations now occur primarily through a multiplicity of horizontal networks linking government officials in distinct transnational judicial, regulatory, and legislative channels that operate independently of one another without any claim to represent "the state" as a unitary entity. Together with vertical governmental networks between national and supranational counterparts, these linkages comprise the main loci of global governance and law making, replacing diplomacy and interstate cooperation. The network structure of interaction is allegedly based on the disaggregation of the state and its sovereignty: it enables officials in each domain to solve common problems, share information, harmonize rules, generalize normative expectations, coordinate policy, and punish violators of global law without claiming to do so in the name of the state as a whole (Slaughter 2004, 63).

Transgovernmental networks involve collaborative work by the same officials who are judging, regulating, and legislating domestically. Examples of horizontal regulatory governmental networks are the G-7 and the G-20 organizations, the regular meetings of national finance ministers, as well as the IMF Board of Governors. These are only a small part of the myriad networks among such regulators as central bankers, securities commissioners, and so on, some of whom now even have their own international institutions: the Basel Committee, the International Organization of Securities Commissions, and the International Association of Insurance Supervisors (Slaughter 2004, 38). Such regulatory networks engage in information exchange, enforcement cooperation, and harmonization of practices. Indeed, Anne-Marie Slaughter refers to networked regulators as "the new diplomats" (Slaughter 2004, 36–64).

Examples of vertical networks include the relationship between the European Court of Justice (ECJ), the International Criminal Court (ICC), and the courts of their respective member states. In each case, primary responsibility for adjudication and enforcing decisions devolves upon the judges within the member states (of the European Union or the United Nations), thus differing from the traditional model of international law adjudication, which assumed that a tribunal such as the International Court of Justice (ICJ) would hand down a judgment applicable to "states," leaving it up to states to enforce or ignore (Slaughter 2004, 21). There are also vertical regulatory networks, in the EU, for example, which link antitrust authority of the European Commission and national antitrust regulators.[12]

This new world order is a world full of law, but to perceive the nature of the new global law, proponents of the disaggregated state argue that we need a concept of legalization that drops the idea that law is produced or enforced by a sovereign (see Abbott et al. 2002, 132–48). Accordingly, one must also finally relinquish the myth of formalism, accept the legal realist critique, shift to an external sociological perspective, and acknowledge a wide range of norms and regulations in the global system as law. Instead of a bright line between legalized and nonlegalized institutions in the global order, there is a continuum between legal and nonlegal obligations and a broad spectrum of norms that ranges from soft to hard law. The point is that as sovereignty breaks down, as the state becomes disaggregated transnationally, and as global transgovernmental (and nongovernmental) networks produce more and more norms to regulate their own interaction, "the dynamic of a politically oriented law will no longer tolerate formalism."[13] Indeed, compared with interstate cooperation and the slow collective action (and inaction) by formal international institutions such as the UN, coordinated action by networks of regulators, judges, and other government officials is fast, flexible, and effective.

This means that the discourse of sovereignty should be abandoned. Once a useful fiction for imagining international relations, the concept of the sovereign territorial state conceals more than it reveals today. For the networked global political system has allegedly moved beyond mere

---

[12] See Slaughter 2004, 36–127, for a full listing of such networks.

[13] See Koskenniemi 2004, 488, for a brilliant critique of the rejection of formalism in the combined work of Keohane and Slaughter.

interdependence to a situation of deep interrelationship and interconnect-edness. In short, the *background* conditions of the international system allegedly no longer involve a baseline of separation, autonomy, and defined territorial or jurisdictional boundaries, but rather entail connection, inter-action, and interpenetrating networks and institutions. Accordingly, "so-vereignty-as-autonomy" makes no sense today (Slaughter 2004, 267).

The claim is not only that there are new sources of global law today, but also that the "Westphalian" sovereignty paradigm of international relations, with its principles of sovereign immunity, domestic jurisdiction, and nonintervention that kept state-society relations opaque and imper-vious to international law (the "black box" problem), has already been displaced (de facto) by a new "principle of civilian inviolability," a corollary of human rights talk (Slaughter and Burke-White 2002, 8). Responding to the shift from war to armed conflict, the rise of transna-tional terrorism, and the proliferation of disastrous civil wars, the principle of civilian inviolability is allegedly the logical sequel to the progressive individualization of international law. In short, the dignity and integrity of the individual and her right to protection—the core principle of human rights law—is and should replace sovereignty as constitutive of global (rather than international) relations. Cosmopolitan law already protects individual citizens against abuses of power by their governments and imposes individual liability on soldiers and officials who commit grave human rights abuses. It renders the relations between citizen and the state transparent at last. Accordingly, we should acknowl-edge the principle of civilian inviolability as the new *Grundnorm* of the contemporary cosmopolitan legal and political order, replacing sover-eignty (Slaughter and Burke-White 2002, 8). Several theorists have not hesitated to take the next step, construing humanitarian intervention by coalitions of the willing as the enforcement of this principle against grave human rights violations.[14]

To parry qualms that this transformation of international relations amounts to global technocracy and governance by unaccountable reg-ulators and judges (given the paucity of legislative networks to date), this

---

[14] These theorists construe the Kosovo intervention (which was not authorized by the UN) as a "constitutional moment," which articulated a new "Grundnorm" for the new world order that has replaced the legal principle of sovereignty. It is worth pointing out that this use of Kelsen's term, "Grundnorm," goes against everything he stood for. Slaughter and Burke-White misconstrue the formal transcendental concept of a "Grundnorm," which in Kelsen's theory serves as the necessary presupposition for the validity and autonomy of the legal order, as a substantive material norm—"civilian inviolability"—which they derive and generalize from recent U.S. (NATO) policy in Kosovo. Here we have an example of "symbolic constitutionalism," the abuse of legal theory. The "principle of civilian inviol-ability" that now allegedly permits humanitarian intervention without UNSC authorization and is presented as a constitutional moment is really only the dressing up of policy as law. This is precisely what Kelsen fought against. No such constitutional moment has occurred in *opinio juris*.

analysis comes replete with a set of fundamental norms that should acquire "constitutional" status in the disaggregated world order (Slaughter 2004, 30, 216–60). I cannot go into detail here. Suffice it to say that since global governance exists, it must be oriented by moral principles and rendered accountable by appropriate mechanisms. Once these norms are in place, a fully disaggregated world order could dispense entirely with the anachronistic discourse and rules of sovereignty and replace the old international law and slow international institutions with decentered, efficient cosmopolitan governance and law making.

This brings me to the second version of the thesis that we have entered a postsovereign, decentered world order—namely, the claim that a cosmopolitan legal system regulating global politics actually exists and that it is *already* constitutionalized (Fischer-Lescano 2003 and 2005; Fassbender 1998). To the systems theorists who elaborate this approach, the key development is the emergence of a world society out of the old international order (see Teubner 1997). The idea is that international society has gone global, shifting from a segmental form of differentiation to a set of relations between many functionally differentiated global systems, of which the political subsystem is only one. Functional differentiation has also occurred within that subsystem, overlaying and undermining the previous order of "international society" composed of sovereign territorial states.

This analysis thus meshes with the image of the global political order presented above. Here too it is argued that this order is composed not of states but of components of states along with nongovernmental civil actors. From this perspective as well there is a proliferation of law making in world society independent of national governments' consent or control. But here the claim that a constitutional global legal system already exists (which regulates global politics) involves a shift from the external sociological to the internal legal perspective concerned above all with the production of legal validity. Accordingly, the focus is on hard, not soft, law—on the legal system, not on the mere proliferation of regulations. Nevertheless, on this approach too the discourse of sovereignty must be abandoned.

Indeed, from this perspective it is the legal system itself, and not external political, administrative, or corporate economic actors, that determines what the law is. A legal system cannot be understood in terms of the implementation of political programs or sovereign will; it must be seen as autonomous and in charge of the codification of the code: legal/illegal. Courts, in short, are at the core of any legal system, and they must decide whether the law has been violated in any particular instance and resolve any controversy over the legal status (validity) of norms. Accordingly, legality is not a matter of more or less, nor can legalization be understood in terms of a continuum. From the internal perspective concerned with validity, oriented by the code "legal/illegal," a legal order must be construed as a closed, gapless normative system.

However, under the conditions of globalization, the legal system and its courts escape the bounds of states and no longer require reference to the political or legal concept of sovereignty (Teubner 1997). Globalization undermines the traditional legal doctrine that traces the distinction between law and nonlaw back to the constitution (higher law) of the nation-state and to legislation ultimately by a constituent power (sovereignty). The global political constitution is produced not by legislation but through decentered legal self-reflection and through a global community of courts, which ascertain legal validity and legal violations. The emphasis here is on the emergence of a global political constitution and a global legal system through *polycentric*, plural, autological processes that produce valid legal norms that regulate actors connected through complex *networks* bounded not by territory but by function, communicative codes, and particular practices (see Teubner 2004).

Why does it matter that we perceive and help to further institutionalize decentered, cosmopolitan constitutional law? For the systems theorist, a constitution is a matter of "structural coupling" between subsystemic structures and legal norms. Its function is to guarantee the multiplicity of social differentiation and to liberate the internal dynamism of each subsystem while also institutionalizing mechanisms of self-restraint against their society-wide expansion. This problem emerged first for the political system within the nation-state: mechanisms that could block the political instrumentalization of civil society, of the economy, of law, and so forth, had to be found and legally institutionalized. The structural coupling of law and political power was the solution. Accordingly, constitutionalized rights in the form of negative civil liberties are mechanisms that preserve the autonomy of spheres of action in a countermovement to the expansionist logic of the state. Structural coupling reduces the harm that politics and law can cause each other. The theory of global constitutionalism generalizes this idea to the global political subsystem: human rights (negative and positive) are the functional equivalents of civil liberties.

Relying on H. L. A. Hart's criteria, this approach points to several indicia of global constitutionalism. The transnational judicial networks described above are construed as a "heterarchical" organization of courts, which provide *global remedies* and are at the center of global political constitutionalism. These involve various levels of communication, ranging from the citation of decisions of foreign courts by national courts, to organized meetings of supreme court justices, such as those held triennially (since 1995) by the Organization of Supreme Courts of the Americas, to the most advanced forms of judicial cooperation involving partnership between national courts and a supranational tribunal, such as the ECJ and more recently the ICC (see Slaughter 2003). The proliferation of supranational courts must be seen as providing *global* remedies for violations of *cosmopolitan law* despite the fact that they originate in treaty organizations. Even national courts can double as elements of this cosmopolitan legal system, insofar as they participate in the interpretation and judgment of violations of global law. Thus, despite the fact that states are the primary agents responsible for delivering on individual rights, what they enforce are cosmopolitan legal norms, and their failure to do so may expose them to "cosmopolitan justice."

The treatment of human rights law as *jus cogens* in the Vienna Convention on the Law of Treaties means that *formal constitutional law* exists and functions as higher law vis-à-vis the will of states. No treaty will be considered valid that violates human rights norms, for these are now based on "consensus." Included in this category are such preemptory norms as the prohibitions against torture, genocide, extralegal killing and disappearances, crimes against humanity, and so on. The proliferation of *erga omnes* rules (which obligate all states whether they signed a treaty) is another sign of constitutional cosmopolitanism indicating transcendence of the old international legal order. The fact that the individual is now a key subject at international law, as evidenced by human rights law, also confirms the cosmopolitan character of the global legal system.

Finally, courts decide what amounts to violations of *jus cogens* norms, and they settle disputes about legal validity in the global legal system. There are now norms in that system designating the sources by which norms become law. This ultimate indication of a global political constitution means that there is legal law making (a rule of recognition, higher law regulating lower law). Whenever a question arises about the source of law, it immediately becomes a question about whether a law invoked really is law—a question that only the legal system (courts) can resolve. Thus, there exists a closed, autopoietic (self-creating) global legal system.

These developments are indeed impressive and certainly transcend traditional international law principles. However, to claim that they *already* amount to a cosmopolitan political constitution that should be or is in the process of replacing the international society of sovereign states and international law is premature and dangerous. The risk is that of "symbolic constitutionalism"—that is, the invocation of the core values and legal discourse of the international community to dress up strategic power plays, self-interested regulations, and interventions in universalistic garb. The Bush administration's justification of its invasion of Iraq as an enforcement of human rights law and Security Council resolutions, despite the failure to win Security Council authorization for this action, is a case in point. The invocation of cosmopolitan principles to classify a state as "rogue" (criminal), and to justify military intervention as the "enforcement" of global right, allows the violator of international law to appear as the upholder of global constitutional legal norms. Some systems theorists are aware of this risk, but they attribute it to the incompleteness of the transition from international to cosmopolitan law, insisting nonetheless on the constitutional and systemic character of the global legal system (Fischer-Lescano 2003). The problem from their perspective is the restricted reach of global remedies: the ICJ lacks compulsory jurisdiction, the ICC lacks a definition for the crime of aggression, the Security Council is legally unrestrained and escapes subjection to separation of powers principles, and so on. When these restrictions are overcome, law will be able to control politics.

These are serious problems and I will return to them. But I argue that there is a basic flaw in this overall approach, which renders it defenseless against political instrumentalization despite its intentions. In short, articulating what a decentered cosmopolitan legal system must involve conceptually by reasoning from the standpoint of legal validity is not enough to demonstrate the sociological claim that it in fact exists. The problem lies in a specific kind of legalism: generalizing from a purely internal juridical perspective focused on validity, coupled with an overly narrow concept of constitutionalism and an indefensible evolutionary bias. Constitutional elements and some structural coupling do not amount to constitutionalism, and the presence of some global remedies, preemptory human rights norms, and so forth does not mean that a full-fledged autonomous cosmopolitan legal system already exists (see Petersmann 1999, 753).

Moreover, to claim that the concept of sovereignty is irrelevant because it is not needed for internal legal validity or for the narrow concept of constitution that is deployed in this approach is myopic. Unfortunately, this undermines a key principle of international law—the sovereign equality of states—and blocks needed reflection on how to reconcile it with the new importance ascribed to human rights law and other cosmopolitan principles with which it may conflict. In the current context, in which there is a powerful imperial project afoot seeking to develop a useful version of "global right" that can be invoked to justify quick, unilateral military reactions to alleged human rights abuses, undermining the principle of equal state sovereignty in the name of legal cosmopolitanism plays into the wrong hands.

Critical Reflections on the New Legal Cosmopolitanism

Empirical Complexity

There are several problems on the empirical level. First, the existence of a global, networked, constitutionalized political order, even an incomplete one, is vastly overstated. States have yielded some powers to supra- and transnational organizations, transgovernmental networking is an important new phenomenon, there is a good deal of nonstate governance and rule making, and certainly there are trends in a cosmopolitan direction, especially regarding human rights. The most important is indeed the striking move toward accepting individuals as legal subjects endowed with fundamental rights under international law. A person in violation of this law can be brought before an international tribunal without going through the medium of the respective national legal system, and claims to sovereignty or domestic jurisdiction do not shield state actors when they violate the human rights of their own citizens.

But it is not clear that these constitutional elements are the sign of a cosmopolitan legal order that has *replaced* instead of *supplementing* international law based on the consent of states, which remain sovereign, albeit in an altered way. To legal cosmopolitans, these developments indicate that we are in a transitional phase away from internationalism toward a cosmopolitan world society and legal system. But it is not the case that all of the constitutive principles of the new international order can be so characterized—several of them point in the opposite direction. Indeed, it is unclear just which version of international society and which model of sovereignty is being replaced. The legal cosmopolitans speak as if the move is from Westphalian sovereignty to a cosmopolitan legal order, but this is a conceptual sleight of hand: the former, if it ever existed, disappeared long ago. Certainly one would be hard pressed to construe the principle of the sovereign equality of states or the strictures of nonintervention and nonaggression, articulated in the UN Charter, as either Westphalian or as indicating the disaggregation and irrelevance of sovereignty.

Moreover, it is important to acknowledge that such principles as sovereign equality, nonaggression, nonintervention, and self-determination are, in key respects, *new*: they are not remnants of the traditional Westphalian international order or of the conception of sovereignty that prevailed within it. The latter involved a legal arrangement, *jus publicum europaeum*, that attributed Westphalian sovereignty and equal recognition only to European states, and gave these states the right to acquire colonies and the right to go to war for any reason (see Schmitt 2003, 140–210). The principles of nonintervention and domestic jurisdiction applied only to European member states, not to the rest of the world—there no such norm of nonintervention applied, for no equal sovereignty was ascribed to non-European polities.

The new version of sovereign equality articulated by the UN Charter is ascribed to *all member states*, and since the 1960 General Assembly Resolution (1514 and 1541), *colonialism* has been explicitly rejected. This shift allowed for the emergence in principle of an egalitarian international system with a single norm of nonintervention applying to all states (see Brown 2002, 145). Inherent in this conception of *sovereign equality*, the newly generalized principle of nonintervention, together with strictures regarding the peaceful settlement of disputes and the principle of nonaggression in the UN Charter, is meant to protect state sovereignty while also limiting it.[15] To be sure, the Charter also articulates the principle of

---

[15] Chapter I, Article 2, of the UN Charter states, "The Organization is based on the principle of sovereign equality of all its Members."

collective security, eliminating the *jus ad bellum*, and it gives the Security Council wide authority to decide when to use force to parry threats to peace and security. Today this discretion is taken to apply to domestic as well as international conflicts if they pose such threats. This is the cosmopolitan dimension of the Charter. Nevertheless, sovereign equality, reconstituted and revised, remains the default position in the Charter, the collective enforcement provisions and the recent *jus cogens* status of human rights norms notwithstanding.

These principles should thus be seen as part of a project to "democratize," not to "abolish sovereignty." Of course, the conception of what are the prerogatives of sovereignty has changed. Today the "sovereign equality" of states is deemed compatible with limits on what were once considered their sovereign privileges. These limits, imposed by international institutions, articulate a new form of international society, based on increased cooperation among states and an altered conception of sovereignty, not a wholesale shift to a different principle of international order. Indeed, the growth of international cooperation, the increased emphasis on human rights since the 1990s, the expansion of intergovernmental organizations and their increased capacity to meddle should drive the international community to define more clearly where states are entitled to remain immune form outside interference. In the current hybrid global political order, with its international and cosmopolitan elements, the answers are no longer self-evident. But we are certainly not in a world where functional differentiation and transnational networks have replaced states and rendered sovereignty irrelevant. There has, to be sure, been a *partial* disaggregation of sovereignty in the sense that some functions once considered the prerogatives of the sovereign state are now placed in the hands (authority) of supranational bodies: courts, the Security Council, and some transnational regulatory bodies. But the overly strong and misleading disaggregation thesis described above is not helpful: representative government (internal and external) has not been replaced by governance, and the unity and sovereignty of the state remain intact, as does the importance of public international law and institutions despite the emergence of transnational governmental networks.

I argue that the core of the world political system remains the "international society of states," although it has undergone important transformations.[16] The global political system is *dualistic*, composed of sovereign states and international law along with nonstate actors, new legal subjects, and consensual, cosmopolitan elements. Segmental differentiation persists alongside the new functional differentiation. There can be collisions between the principles expressed in each aspect of the global political order. It is hardly news that the principles of human rights can clash with the principles of nonintervention and "domestic jurisdiction."

---

[16] For the concept of international society, see Bull, Hurrell, and Hoffman 2002, 1–94.

What is needed today is the articulation of new legal rules that anticipate and regulate these clashes. Whether one should construe this multifaceted order as inherently contradictory, unstable, and therefore transitory —that is, as disorder for which the remedy is a wholesale shift from international to cosmopolitan society and law—or as a new phase of international society, internally dynamic with important new heterogeneous elements that need to be coordinated with the existing principles of international law via legal reform, cannot be decided empirically. Normative and political issues are involved.

Normative Ambiguities

Cosmopolitan moral and legal theorists, along with many human rights advocates, are eager to abandon the concept of sovereignty because it signifies to them a claim to power unrestrained by law and a bulwark against legal, political, and military action necessary to enforce human rights.

I contend that this view is profoundly mistaken and that the discourse of sovereignty involves normative principles and symbolic meanings worth preserving. Even if one particular sovereignty regime has waned, another can take its place with continuity on this level. Indeed, the absolutist conception of sovereignty that corresponds to the negative assessment cited above has long since been abandoned, Schmitt's attempted revival of a decisionistic, existentialist model notwithstanding (see Schmitt 1986). Indeed, the Hobbesian claim that internal sovereignty must be located in one single institutional center whose will is *legibus solutus* has been belied ever since the first modern constitutional democracy emerged in the United States in the eighteenth century, based on the separation of powers, checks and balances, and popular sovereignty, not to mention the division of powers entailed by federalism. The theory and practice of modern constitutionalism demonstrates that limited sovereignty is not an oxymoron, and that sovereignty, constitutionalism, and the rule of law are not incompatible. It also shows that functions or prerogatives once ascribed to the unitary sovereign can be divided and/or ascribed to other bodies (such as the EU or the UN) without the abolition of sovereignty or the disaggregation of the state.

I make an even stronger claim. Situated at the boundary between politics and law, sovereignty evokes both the public power that enacts law and the public law that restrains power (see Laughlin 2004). The concept of sovereignty is a reminder not only of the political context of law but also of the ultimate dependence of political power and political regimes on a valid, public, normative legal order for their authority. Sovereignty is thus a dynamic principle of the mutual constitution and mutual containment of law and politics (Laughlin 2004). From a purely juridical perspective, sovereignty refers to a valid, *public* legal order that allocates authority and jurisdictional competence.

From a political perspective, sovereignty evokes the *autonomy of the political* and, in the form of popular sovereignty, a *distinctive political relationship* between a citizenry and its government within a defined territory (Laughlin 2004). Today, sovereignty means that political power is public and impersonal, as it is lodged in a set of offices, or government. Indeed, the discourse of sovereignty articulates the political as a distinct realm of public activity within which power is supposed to serve public purposes, to be exercised through law, and which involves consensus building, deliberation, and compromise. The citizen is the referent of public power and of the constitutional principles and design regulating the exercise of sovereign power. The discourse of popular sovereignty implies that government is representative government. Precisely because sovereignty is a relational concept, it cannot be located in any political body—neither in the hands of rulers nor in a particular institution such as a parliament or the presidency, nor in a particular group of citizens. Internal sovereignty is thus, in the final analysis, based on the consent of the governed; government is to serve the interests of the citizenry and public purposes generally. It involves a claim to ultimate *authority* within a political community, but it is also a contingent claim, which requires recognition, domestically and internationally. Today, external sovereignty has to be understood against this background of meanings.

The discourse of external sovereignty arises within a plural political universe, one in which neither a single global authority nor an unchallenged world empire exists. In such a context, sovereignty becomes the constitutive frame of reference for international relations and serves an epistemic function: allowing one to think of the multiplicity of autonomous political communities and their interrelationship (see Walker 2004 and 2002). State sovereignty and international law are coconstitutive: international law accords the recognition, standing, and rules of behavior for sovereign states; sovereign states are a key source of international law. Nevertheless, international law orients and delimits state sovereignty. International institutions are also the products of treaties among sovereign states but, similarly, develop their own autonomous logic and become an additional source of law and power without thereby undermining the core principle of contemporary international society: sovereign equality.

From the external perspective, sovereignty entails the normative principle of autonomy, ascribed by the community of sovereign states to one another. To be sure, the claim to *autonomy* was tightly coupled, in the Westphalian model, to *exclusivity*: the territorial sovereign state in the system of states would brook no interference in its "internal affairs." The system of sovereign states was construed as one of discrete, mutually exclusive, comprehensive territorial jurisdictions. This implied that a nonexclusive authority is typically a dependent one. There could be no overlapping jurisdictions within a sovereign state.

In the contemporary post-Westphalian order, these two dimensions of sovereignty can and have become decoupled. It is possible, in other words, to conceive of autonomy without comprehensive territorial exclusivity and to imagine jurisdictional overlap without subsumption (see Walker 2004). This means that the integrity and autonomy of a polity qua polity need not be impugned by the coexistence of other jurisdictional claims, some of which may even assert supremacy within the same territorial space. The mere fact that there are rules obligating states or rules that ascribe competence over what were once considered internal matters to supranational bodies does not mean that states are no longer sovereign, for it is the rules of international law that tell us in what sovereignty consists. Thus, the new *jus cogens* status of certain human rights norms are now part of the rules that constitute and limit sovereignty, but they are not proof that it is irrelevant. Similarly, the development of functionally delimited supranational and transnational jurisdictional claims in the global political system can supplement and overlap without abolishing the autonomy of segmentally differentiated territorial sovereign states.

International and cosmopolitan law can have their own integrity and jurisdictional scope without threatening the autonomy of the polities to which they are applied. Such law can reach right through the state, without destroying the latter's internal legal or political coherence, its legal status in the society of states, its identity as a polity, or its ultimate authority and supremacy in its respective jurisdictional domain. The state can be sovereign so long as the political relationship between the government and the citizenry remains intact and autonomous, and provided that new institutional arrangements or jurisdictions promote more efficacious external action by the state.[17] Accordingly, the normative plus that the discourse of sovereignty entails—namely, the autonomy and equality of polities, including their nonsubordination and nondomination by others, and the presumption against unwarranted intervention—can be had without the downside of the black box problem, without comprehensive territorial exclusivity, without insisting on the untrammeled will of the state, once we give up the Westphalian conception. The principle of sovereign equality should be understood in these terms. I submit that especially in the epoch of "humanitarian intervention," it must remain the default position of the international order. Accordingly, the principle of nonintervention (the correlative of sovereignty) retains its primacy even though it may have to be reinterpreted in light of whatever formal legal rules are developed to regulate humanitarian actions authorized by the UN. In short, keeping the principle of

---

[17] The example of the EU is most instructive. Strong claims to state sovereignty coexist with strong claims to supremacy of European Union Law over union matters. This is a productive paradox involving division and the increase of power.

sovereign equality front and center keeps the burden of proof where it should be: on the shoulders of would-be interveners.[18]

The paradox of a multilayered global political order that enunciates sovereign equality and human rights can be a productive one. It should spur jurists and political theorists to make new distinctions that develop formal international law in ways adequate to the shifts in values and to the complexities of the contemporary world order.[19] Indeed, that is how the recurrent tension between rights and sovereignty has been handled in domestic political systems—the assertion of new rights or new claims regarding the scope and design of democracy has triggered innovative legal and political distinctions in order to resolve conflicts. The core intuition that makes the paradox productive rather than destructive is the idea that rights and democracy (popular sovereignty) are coequivalent—democracy without constitutionalism is as unacceptable today as is constitutionalism without democracy (see Habermas 1996, 84–118). The parallel intuition regarding external sovereignty is that we must sever political autonomy from the idea of comprehensive jurisdiction and realize that the apparent antinomy between sovereignty and human rights or between state sovereignty and multiple sources of international law is based on an anachronistic conception of the former as absolute.

Sovereign equality and human rights are *both* new and indispensable principles; in international relations, both are based on what Jürgen Habermas has called egalitarian universalism, and they can become complementary if the attempt is made in good faith to make new distinctions and update the rules of the international legal order accordingly (Habermas 2003). As opposed to imperial universalism, which perceives the world from the centralizing perspective of its own worldview (hoping to impose its version of global right), egalitarian universalism demands that even superpowers relativize their particular interpretations of general principles vis-à-vis the interpretive perspectives of equally situated and equally entitled agents. The universalistic core of the principles of sovereign equality and human rights requires the rejection of the hierarchal, ethnocentric, and racist assumptions that informed the Westphalian sovereignty order. It implies that political autonomy, democratic self-determination, and human rights are the legitimate aspirations of citizens in every polity.

Let me be very clear here. I am most certainly *not* arguing that external sovereignty be made contingent upon a particular internal political arrangement, such as constitutional democracy, or that a "human right to popular sovereignty" renders unilateral military intervention to protect

---

[18] See the debate in Holzgrefe and Keohane, eds., 2003, over whether a new norm of unilateral humanitarian intervention has in fact emerged and whether legal reform should occur to make it hard law.

[19] On the productivity of legal paradoxes, see Fletcher 1985; Luhmann 1988.

this right acceptable. To construe popular sovereignty or democracy as a human right is to make a category mistake: it collapses political into moral categories, reducing the citizen to "person" and confusing collective political action of a citizenry with the citizen's legal standing. Yes, citizenship involves basic individual rights, such as the right to vote, but it also has a political meaning and an identity component that cannot be reduced to the dimension of individual rights (see Cohen 1999). To argue for making the international legal principle of sovereignty contingent on the "human right" of popular sovereignty as an individual right is sophistry. Popular sovereignty is a regulative principle, not an individual right. The relation between internal sovereignty, citizenship, constitutional democracy, and external sovereignty I outlined above must be understood differently—namely, as constituting a regulative principle, a normative set of meanings to which we should aspire, not a recipe to justify abolishing the principle of sovereign equality.

Global Law without the State—the Ideology of Empire?

Of course for Schmitt and contemporary Schmittians, sovereign equality is always predicated on inequality. Only equals are equal. Equality means identity—homogeneity along a substantive dimension. And indeed, the system of sovereignty he analyzed (*jus publicum europaeum*) restricted sovereign equality to "friends"—members of the European community. There was no equality, no sovereignty, no "bracketing of war" for non-European polities.

Although this system was already undermined by the end of the nineteenth century after its Eurocentric character was abandoned, it took two world wars and the emergence of non-European superpowers to give it its final deathblow. Writing in 1950, Schmitt argued that the passing of the Westphalian sovereignty order expressed in *jus publicum europaeum* leaves us with three alternatives: (1) The new "nomos" of the earth could retain the old structure in ways consistent with contemporary technical means. America would step into England's shoes and guarantee the balance of the rest of the world; (2) A plurality of regional groupings, or *Grossräume*, could emerge and balance one another, while dominating the smaller polities; (3) The victor in the global antithesis between West and East (the Cold War) would be the world's sole sovereign and appropriate the whole earth—land, sea, and air—dividing and managing it in accord with its plans and ideas (Schmitt 2003, 354–55).

From the perspective of the twenty-first century it certainly looks like the third option is well under way. The current U.S. administration seems bent on undermining the international order it helped establish with the signing of the UN Charter and later important international agreements. It is also determined to prevent the development of clear, coherent legal principles (and hard procedural law) that could help regulate the enforcement of human rights in ways consistent with the sovereign equality of states and existing international law and institutions. The United States' failure to pay its full UN dues, its rejection of the ICC, its refusal to sign the Kyoto Protocol on global warming, are only a few examples indicating that it disdains international institutions. The recent invasion and occupation of Iraq became the occasion for making the move against international law explicit. Far from accepting the role of responsible hegemon participating in international structures, backing up international law and helping to codify the new, the United States has resuscitated the discourse of "old versus new" in order to split Europe, undermine international institutions, and reorder basic relationships unilaterally.

Open hostility to international law and to the UN is coupled with the use of moralistic discourses of humanitarian intervention to "enforce" human rights, including the newly alleged human right to democracy, and justifications for "preventive wars." Hand in hand with these discourses goes the insistence on maintaining unrivaled military power. This indicates more than the empirical fact that the United States happens at the moment to be the world's sole superpower. For it appears to be trying to position itself as the only power able to secure world peace and justice, police and punish violators, guarantee human rights, and protect democracy and "civilization" in the name of global right. It sees itself as engaging in "just wars" at the periphery, and combating terrorism everywhere. But it often wants to do this without subjecting itself to international law or participating in international institutions or in the international community. The name of such an "order and orientation" is empire.

The imperial project is certainly on the agenda today. As indicated above, Hardt and Negri assume that the project has already succeeded, although they propound a rather vague concept of empire, which, most importantly and least convincingly, lacks a center. They explicitly deny that its center is the United States, arguing instead for an imperial network with multiple centers (Hardt and Negri 2000, xii, xiv). They are wrong on both counts: the project has not yet triumphed, and it does have a center and a carrier. Given their position, it is odd and deeply contradictory to insist as they do that sovereignty has not faded away but rather has become imperial. For their decentered "imperial sovereignty" is based on the loss of the autonomy of the political, on the elimination of the distinction between public and private, on the erosion of "hard" international law in favor of "soft" deformalized rulings, and on the disintegration of a distinctive political relationship between a polity or government and its citizenry (see Laughlin 2004). Accordingly, decentered imperial "sovereignty" replaces government with governance, public law with the rules of self-regulating systems and networks, relational sovereignty between equal cooperating units in a community of states with globalized and unitary imperial right. The conceptual confusion here is staggering, for the kind of rule they describe is the antithesis of the theoretical concept of sovereignty, which perforce has as its referent public power and public law.

Be that as it may, Hardt and Negri construe the discourse of decentered cosmopolitan constitutionalism (along with the concepts of soft law, self-regulation, human rights, humanitarian intervention, and revived just war doctrine) as an obvious candidate for the job of legitimating empire by dressing up its mode of exercising domination as law. They are right to warn that this discourse can be instrumentalized by the imperial project. Talk of global constitutionalism and the death of sovereignty *avant la lettre* helps marginalize international law and to legitimize interventions. It invites the claim that even a unilateral military intrusion into a weaker state is not a violation of international law but rather an enforcement of global right and cosmopolitan justice. Indeed, some international lawyers and human rights theorists have explicitly embraced the task of justifying the imperial project in the name of global right (see, for example, Slaughter and Burke-White 2002; Ignatieff 2003a). Even if this role is refused, in a context in which a world republic is not on the agenda, and in which a strong, centered imperial project bent on undermining international institutions and law does exist, it is dangerous to make unwarranted claims about global constitutional law and the irrelevance of sovereignty. Indeed, Hardt and Negri's conception of a decentered empire, coupled with their rejection of the concepts of state and popular sovereignty, public power and public international law, and government in favor of governance, entails some complicity with the imperial project. Such claims deflect attention away from the only viable political alternative to empire: a strengthened international society and law informed by the culture of rights but based on the principle of sovereign equality.

Maintaining Sovereign Equality

There is an alternative to the project of empire and to the restricted set of choices Schmitt described. I believe that it is possible to strengthen international institutions and develop international law in a way that protects state sovereignty and human rights, supports popular sovereignty, and helps regulate the self-regulation of the new nonstate transnational powers while fostering a global rule of law. This requires certain theoretical and practical steps.

The disassociation of the tight link between autonomy and exclusivity is the *first theoretical step* toward such a project. The *second* is the abandonment of the absolutist and decisionistic concept of sovereignty in favor of the relational model described above. If these two ideas are linked together, then it is perfectly conceivable that international law could penetrate the black box of the state without undermining its sovereign autonomy or integrity. When states agree to certain restrictions, when they "delegate" jurisdiction to supranational entities, when they establish frameworks for cooperation that create binding rules, they do not thereby lose or divide their sovereignty—indeed, they may even enhance it.

Despite its polemical character, Schmitt's analysis of the Westphalian understanding of sovereignty in *Nomos of the Earth* is helpful in this regard. In describing the system of sovereign states that was the basis for the *jus publicum europaeum*, Schmitt states the obvious: European international law was grounded in a balanced relationship of a plurality of sovereign territorial states. The balance of power was crucial to maintaining plurality. It was also the precondition for effective international law: if one power was stronger than all the others put together, it might think it had no need for international law. However, he goes on to insist,

> Such an order was not a lawless chaos of egoistic wills to power . . . these egoistic power structures existed side-by-side in the same space of one European order, wherein they mutually recognized each other as sovereigns. *Each was the equal of the other*, because each constituted a component of the system of equilibrium. (Schmitt 2003, 167)

Accordingly, the articulation of sovereignty within a community of states *that decide to consider one another as equals* is the political precondition for feasible and effective international law. In other words, international law has to be based on a set of political relationships between states to which sovereignty is ascribed within a common framework, based on shared political norms, involving mutual recognition, balance, and institutionalized cooperation.

Moreover, formal equality has to be linked to some degree of material equality among the states. In an institutionalized structure of power and counterpowers, no single sovereign state should be able to prevail over all the others and impose its will as law. This does not exclude a guarantor of international right and international law—that is, a state powerful enough to ensure that others play by the rules to which it also subscribes. The ascription of sovereignty to states by an international "community" by virtue of which they become members and equals is thus a way of limiting as well as empowering those states. Without this, an opponent becomes nothing more than an object of violent measures, while law becomes mere window dressing.

I see no reason why this conception cannot be generalized to all states construed as equal members of the international community along the lines of the UN Charter. Equality need not be construed as a substantive principle of homogeneity based on a friend/enemy conception of the political. It is enough that the general principles of the international order—sovereign equality and human rights—are accepted in principle (as they are by any state that has joined the UN), and allowed to develop into a shared culture of mutual respect of rights and accountability. The "democratization" of external sovereignty backed up by international law is thus the *third* step in the project. Certainly this is the idea behind the principle of "sovereign equality." It informs the key "transformative" developments in international relations since World War II: sovereign states gave up their "sovereign" right to go to war and aggressive war became illegal; colonialism was dismantled and deemed a violation of the principle of self-determination; sovereign states began actively to pursue cooperation in a multiplicity of international institutions; and they accepted being limited by human rights principles, renouncing impermeability to international law in this domain. These are the new rules of sovereignty in the society of states, not indications of its abolition. Pace Schmitt, participation in supranational institutions and further development of international law, spurred in part by the efforts of nongovernmental organizations of international civil society, can thicken commonalities and consensus.

The *fourth step* involves fostering the internal democratization of all states, large and small. With the disintegration of formal colonialism and the Cold War–era blocs, the autonomy of countries once subordinated to the great powers has the potential to take on real meaning, especially if they become involved in regional associations based on the principles of sovereign equality and constitutionalism, like the EU. But what makes the sovereignty of states valuable in the long run is that autonomy is a precondition for popular sovereignty and democracy within a polity. Today, the idea of self-determination is not only a principle of national identity and liberation but also a principle of popular sovereignty involving democratic self-government under law. The dimension of political autonomy at issue here has nothing to do with defining an external enemy and everything to do with the internal construction and articulation (constitutional design and articulation of rights) of the "friend" component of Schmitt's infamous distinction.

The spread of the discourse of popular sovereignty (and the rule of law) and the emergence of representative constitutional governments in more and more states throughout the world fosters the tide of democratization (equal autonomous voice) in international relations. We got an inkling of what this could mean when governments of countries large and small, having to worry about their citizens' views, refused to cave in to the most intense pressure by the world's sole superpower and insisted on weapons inspections rather than voting for the war in Iraq. Instead of being able to bask in the global legitimacy of a widely accepted "peace action" that a positive vote in the Security Council would have afforded, the United States confronted one of the most multipolar moments in history and to this date has not been able to muster the support for its Iraq venture that a well-established empire would expect.

Support for internal democratization, however, must not be taken as a green light for violent interventions by powerful outsiders purporting to *impose* democracy, liberating the locals against their will and thus forcing them to be free. As I already indicated, there is no such thing as a human right to popular sovereignty, and any attempt to justify interventions by invoking such a right is pure ideology. In short, the principle of sovereign equality and nonintervention is and must remain the default position of the international order. The problem of what to do in the case of dictatorial authoritarian regimes that overthrow democratic institutions or block their emergence is of course a troubling one. So is the issue of how to deal with regimes that violate the most basic rights of their own citizens. The decision taken in 1997 by the Organization of American States (OAS) to amend its charter to permit suspension of a member whose democratic government is overthrown by force is a fascinating example of a set of rules agreed upon by sovereign states aimed at linking recognition of state sovereignty to the protection of internal popular sovereignty (see the OAS Charter). One thing is sure, however: the claim of a superpower to be defending democracy while engaging in unilateral military intervention is bound to appear as, and usually is a fig leaf for, parochial ends. In light of today's imperial project and the recent experience in Iraq, the world community rightly condemns such actions.

This does not preclude regional associations like the EU or the OAS from agreeing not to tolerate the forcible overthrow of a constitutional democracy by a would-be dictator or to insist on the observance of certain democratic and legal principles of would-be members. In such cases, military intervention can be avoided precisely because sovereign states have accepted these rules ensuring a link between popular sovereignty, political representation, and external sovereignty. Such agreements do not undermine the principle of sovereign equality, they strengthen it.

A *fifth step* must be taken if the project of empire is to be defeated—namely, the emergence of effective counterpowers within the world community, able to balance the superpower of the United States as well as the "infra-power" of "private" transnational networks involved in governance. This is the "truth content" of political realism—neither law nor morality can conjure away political power or strategic calculations. Unless viable counterpowers emerge *willing to strengthen international law and institutions and draw the United States back into their framework*, cosmopolitan right will be nothing other than what Schmitt always said it is: utopian and ideological. It would be disastrous if the emerging superpowers of the twenty-first century emulated the disdain for international law and the imperial gesturing of the United States. It would be far better if effective state alliances emerged that were articulated in regional associations, along the lines of the EU, and that were committed to shouldering the responsibilities of their combined power, strengthening international law, fostering a global rule of law, and, with UN authorization, helping to enforce international law. Membership in regional associations could protect the sovereign equality of small polities and make their voices matter more on the world scene. It would also help enormously if the regional association stood for democratic principles and human rights and encouraged its members to foster and maintain them. This is the level on which plurality, in the sense of effective political power (counterpower), will matter, as Schmitt rightly foresaw. But it can exist in conjunction with the legal principle of sovereign equality for all states within regional associations (thus blocking *Grossraum* projects) and with international and cosmopolitan law on the global level (thus blocking imperial projects).

The *sixth and final step* is to stop the trend toward the deformalization of international law that began in the 1990s with the invasion of Kosovo and that has been fostered by every subsequent "humanitarian intervention." These interventions are usually justified in moral terms of an obligation of the powerful to act in dire emergencies, to rescue people (the powerless) from disastrous human rights violations (genocide, ethnic cleansing, and so on), regardless of legal niceties. For there is at present no "law of humanitarian intervention," and, strictly speaking, the Security Council is authorized to approve military interventions only when international peace and security are threatened. There is no customary rule that construes military intervention as the way to "enforce" human rights law. There is only the imprecise and ad hoc expansion of the definition of threats to peace and security from interstate to internal civil disturbances, and the generalized moral discourse of human rights, which enable the Security Council and others to justify violations of state sovereignty in the name of humanitarianism. The point is, pace human rights fundamentalists, that one cannot simply postulate a human right to protection, to rescue, to security, or to civilian inviolability and then assert that any state or collective body able to do so has the moral duty to enforce such rights through military intervention. Indeed the argument, via analogy with civil disobedience, that it is necessary to update international law by such illegal military means is deeply unconvincing and counterintuitive.[20]

The proliferation of "exceptional" rescue operations, which violate international law in the name of cosmopolitan right, undermines rather than fosters respect for the rule of law. Several authors have traced the ways in which such a deformalized moral-humanitarian discourse has undermined existing international law, and how it is being used (especially by the United States) to block the creation of new, coherent legal rules that could and should regulate humanitarian intervention in ways that respect the principle of sovereign equality (see Koskenniemi 2002; Teitel 2002, 355). These include: the formal international legal articulation of the relevant rights; clearly articulated and agreed upon substantive standards identifying what kind and level of violation would be sufficient

---

[20] I am referring to Buchanan and Keohane 2004.

to warrant intervention (thresholds); formalization of the rules, including procedural rules, indicating how claims can be made; determination of who (which public body) is authorized to make the judgment that a violation has occurred, and what to do about it, including who is authorized to act to stop the violation. Without such rules, one cannot speak of updating international law or enforcing cosmopolitan right. Indeed, moral cosmopolitans disagree about minimal and maximal interpretations of the human right to security or protection and about what constitutes a violation.[21] Only international law can mediate between the moral and the political so as to establish clear limits and rules while affording legality and legitimacy to appropriate action.

We do not have a global rule of law today or a constitutionalized international order, but we do have hard international law that can be developed in the right direction. The Security Council and Chapter VII of the UN Charter is the place to start. Security Council authorization is indispensable, in my view, for any military intervention, but it is not enough: one needs the articulation of coherent and consistent rules to regulate the new powers that the Council has arrogated to itself by extending those granted to it under Chapter VII to apply to domestic conflicts and grave rights violations that do not cross borders. The principle of sovereign equality can remain intact under these circumstances only if the rules are formalized after public deliberation and if they are consistently applied. Otherwise, a two-tiered system will emerge that leaves the weak (developing countries) defenseless against the powerful (developed, industrialized countries). Such a system would have a familiar ring—and stands little chance of being accepted today. There are many suggestions for reform of the UN, and this is not the place to discuss them in any detail (see Muller, ed., 1997). Yet there clearly is a need to find a way to bring the Security Council itself (a political body, after all) under the principle of the separation of powers and to render it accountable. Global remedies and compulsory jurisdiction for international courts should apply to this body as well as to states. Among the most frequent reform proposals are the expansion of the permanent membership of the Security Council to include twenty-first-century great powers (maybe even the EU), a voluntary renunciation of the veto in favor of a two-thirds vote when "humanitarian" intervention is at issue,

---

[21] In Buchanan and Keohane 2004, the authors offer a very long list that includes not genocide, ethnic cleansing, and torture but the "more damaging forms of discrimination" and the "right to the means of subsistence." They support interventions by "coalitions of democratic states" without the detour of the UNSC. Others, like Reisman, support intervention in favor of a right to popular sovereignty that "trumps state sovereignty." While still other lists, like that of Walzer, are more minimal. Moral philosophy cannot adjudicate among these different lists of "fundamental" human rights. See Cohen 2004.

and some expanded, deliberative, advisory role for the General Assembly in these matters. The idea is to make international institutions more effective, so that it becomes more likely that necessary interventions take place and less likely that purely self-interested ones do. All interventions will be based on mixed motives. Only if one is forced to give reasons not only to one's domestic public or the informal world publics of international civil society but also in institutionalized, decisional, political public spheres (like the Security Council and those in regional bodies) in order to garner support and convince others to share responsibility for authorizing an action will it be possible to make a plausible claim that there are genuine, universally acceptable reasons for an intervention. Without further development of hard international law along these lines, predicated on the default position of sovereign equality yet oriented toward "norming the exception," without legality complementing alleged moral legitimacy, interventions justified by the discourse of human rights will threaten the autonomy not only of failed or rogue states but of every political community.

Constitutionalization of the global political system is a work in progress, not a fait accompli. The dualistic model I have in mind would involve the articulation of public power and public law on multiple levels of the world political system. It would seek to harmonize the core principles of international relations today—sovereign equality and human rights—not abandon one in favor of the other. At issue is a shift of the culture of sovereignty from one of impunity to one of accountability and responsibility of states in light of their obligation to protect (see, for example, ICISS 2001). This entails reformulating, not abandoning, the default position of sovereignty and its correlate, the principle of non-intervention, in the international system.

We really face only two choices today: strengthened international law or imperial projects by existing and future superpowers. We know that though strong states are the most effective guarantors of human rights, states also violate these rights. The old rules don't suffice, but the time has certainly not come for abandoning the discourse of sovereignty as human rights fundamentalists and empire enthusiasts propose. Instead, the current rules of international legal sovereignty have to be rethought. For it is the revised discourse of sovereignty, backed up by international institutions, that can situate global regulation and cosmopolitan law on the side of the first project and help prevent their instrumentalization by the second. This is the only answer to Schmitt's charge that "he who invokes humanity wants to cheat."

References

Abbott, Kenneth W., Robert O. Keohane, Andrew Moravcsik, Anne-Marie Slaughter, and Duncan Snidal. 2002. "The Concept of Legalization." In *Power and Governance in a Partially Globalized World*, edited by Robert O. Keohane, 132–51. New York: Routledge.

Archibugi, Daniele. 2003. "Cosmopolitan Democracy." In *Debating Cosmopolitics*, edited by Daniele Archibugi, 1–16. New York: Verso.

Beitz, Charles R. 1979. *Political Theory and International Relations*. Princeton: Princeton University Press.

———. 1994. "Cosmopolitan Liberalism and the States System." In *Political Restructuring in Europe: Ethical Perspectives*, first edition, edited by Chris Brown. New York: Routledge.

Brown, Chris. 2002. *Sovereignty, Rights and Justice: International Political Theory Today*. Cambridge: Polity Press.

Buchanan, Allen. 2003. "Reforming the International Law of Humanitarian Intervention." In *Humanitarian Intervention: Ethical, Legal, and Political Dilemmas*, edited by J. L. Holzgrefe and Robert O. Keohane, 177–203. Cambridge: Cambridge University Press.

———. 2004. *Justice, Legitimacy, and Self-Determination: Moral Foundations for International Law*. New York: Oxford University Press.

Buchanan, Allen, and Robert O. Keohane. 2004. "The Preventive Use of Force: A Cosmopolitan Institutional Proposal." *Ethics & International Affairs* 18, no. 1 (winter): 1–22. Included in this collection.

Bull, Hedley, Andrew Hurrell, and Stanley Hoffman. 2002. *The Anarchical Society*. New York: Columbia University Press.

Byers, Michael, and Simon Chesterman. 2003. "Changing the Rules about Rules? Unilateral Humanitarian Intervention and the Future of International Law." In *Humanitarian Intervention: Ethical, Legal, and Political Dilemmas*, edited by J. L. Holzgrefe and Robert O. Keohane. Cambridge: Cambridge University Press.

Cohen, Jean L. 1999. "Changing Paradigms of Citizenship and the Exclusiveness of the Demos." *International Sociology* 14, no. 3: 245–68.

———. 2004. "Loi internationale ou intervention unilatérale?" *Esprit* 9, (August–September): 80–88.

Fassbender, Bardo. 1998. "The United Nations Charter as Constitution of the International Community." *Columbia Journal of Transnational Law* 36:529–615.

Fischer-Lescano, Andreas. 2003. "Die Emergenz der Globalverasung." *Zeitschrift für ausländisches öffentliches Recht und Völkerrecht— Heidelberg Journal of International Law, ZaöRV* 63, no. 3:717–60.

———. 2005. "Redefining Sovereignty via International Constitutional Moments?" In *Redefining Sovereignty: The Use of Force after the Cold War*, edited by Michael Bothe, Mary Ellen O'Connell, and Natalino Ronzitti, 335–64. Ardsley: Transnational.

Fletcher, G. P. 1985. "Paradoxes in Legal Thought." *Columbia Law Review* 85:1263–92.

Goldstein, Judith, Miles Kahler, Robert O. Keohane, and Anne-Marie Slaughter. 2001. "Introduction." In *Legalization and World Politics*, edited by Judith Goldstein et al., 1–15. Cambridge, Mass.: MIT Press.

Habermas, Jürgen. 1996. *Between Facts and Norms: Contributions to a Discourse Theory of Law and Democracy*. Translated by William Rehg. Cambridge, Mass.: MIT Press.

———. 2003. "Interpreting the Fall of a Monument." Translated by Max Pensky. *German Law Journal* 4, no. 7 (July 1).

Hardt, Michael, and Antonio Negri. 2000. *Empire*. Cambridge, Mass.: Harvard University Press.

Held, David. 1995. *Democracy and the Global Order*. Stanford: Stanford University Press.

Ignatieff, Michael. 2003a. "The Burden." *New York Times Magazine* (January 5): 22.

———. 2003b. "Human Rights as Politics." In *Human Rights as Politics and Idolatry*, edited by Amy Gutmann. Princeton: Princeton University Press.

International Commission on Intervention and State Sovereignty (ICISS). 2001. *The Responsibility to Protect*. Ottawa: International Development Research Centre.

Kirchheimer, Otto. 1961. *Political Justice: The Use of Legal Procedure for Political Ends*. Princeton: Princeton University Press.

Kissinger, Henry. 1994. *Diplomacy*. New York: Simon & Schuster.

Koskenniemi, Martti. 2002. "The Lady Doth Protest Too Much: Kosovo and the Turn to Ethics in International Law." *Modern Law Review* 65, no. 2.

———. 2004. *The Gentle Civilizer of Nations: The Rise and Fall of International Law, 1870–1960*. New York: Cambridge University Press.

Laughlin, Martin. 2004. "Ten Tenets of Sovereignty." In *Sovereignty in Transition*, edited by Neil Walker, 55–87. Oxford: Hart.

Luhmann, Niklas. 1988. "The Third Question: The Creative Use of Paradoxes in Law and Legal History." *Journal of Law and Society* 15, no. 2 (summer): 153–65.

Muller, Joachim, ed. 1997. *Reforming the United Nations: New Initiatives and Past Efforts*. Three volumes. The Hague: Martinus Nijhoff.

Organization of the American States (OAS) Charter. Available at www.oas.org/juridico/english/charter.html

Petersmann, Ernst-Ulrich. 1999. "Constitutionalism and International Adjudication: How to Constitutionalize the U.N. Dispute Settlement System?" *New York University Journal of International Law & Politics* 31.

Pogge, Thomas W. 1992. "Cosmopolitanism and Sovereignty." *Ethics* 103:48–75.

Reisman, W. Michael. 1990. "Sovereignty and Human Rights in Contemporary International Law." *American Journal of International Law* 84, no. 4:866–76.

"The Revival of Empire." 2003. Special section of *Ethics & International Affairs* 17, no. 2:34–98.

Rosenau, James N. 1998. "Governance and Democracy in a Globalizing World." In *Re-Imagining Political Community: Studies in Cosmopolitan Democracy*, edited by Daniele Archibugi, David Held, and Martin Kohler, 28–58. Palo Alto: Stanford University Press.

Rosenau, James N., et al. 1997. *Along the Domestic-Foreign Frontier: Exploring Governance in a Turbulent World.* New York: Cambridge University Press.

Schmitt, Carl. 1996. *The Concept of the Political.* Translated by George Schwab. Chicago: University of Chicago Press.

———. 2003. *The Nomos of the Earth in the International Law of the "Jus Publicum Europaeum."* Translated by G. L. Ulmen. New York: Telos Press.

———. 1986. *Political Theology: Four Chapters on the Concept of Sovereignty.* Translated by George Schwab. Cambridge, Mass.: MIT Press.

Slaughter, Anne-Marie. 2003. "A Global Community of Courts." *Harvard International Law Journal* 44 (winter): 191–219.

———. 2004. *A New World Order.* Princeton: Princeton University Press.

Slaughter, Anne-Marie, and William Burke-White. 2002. "An International Constitutional Moment." *Harvard International Law Journal* 43, no. 1 (winter).

Teitel, Ruti G. 2002. "Humanity's Law: Rule of Law for the New Global Politics." *Cornell International Law Journal* 35.

Tesón, Fernando R. 1997. *Humanitarian Intervention: An Inquiry into Law and Morality.* Second edition. Dobbs Ferry, N.Y.: Transnational.

———. 2003. "The Liberal Case for Humanitarian Intervention." In *Humanitarian Intervention: Ethical, Legal, and Political Dilemmas*, edited by J. L. Holzgrefe and Robert O. Keohane, 93–129. Cambridge: Cambridge University Press.

Teubner, Günther. 1997. "'Global Bukowina': Legal Pluralism in the World Society." In *Global Law Without a State*, edited by Günther Teubner. Brookfield, Vt.: Dartmouth Publishing Group.

———. 2004. "Societal Constitutionalism: Alternatives to State-Centered Constitutional Theory?" In *Transnational Governance and Constitutionalism*, edited by Christian Joerges, Inger-Johanne Sand, and Günther Teubner, 3–29. Portland, Ore.: Hart.

Todd, Emmanuel, C. Jon Delogu, and Michael Lind. 2003. *After the Empire: The Breakdown of the American Order.* New York: Columbia University Press.

UN Charter. Available at www.un.org/aboutun/charter

Vienna Convention on the Law of Treaties. Available at www.un.org/law/ilc/texts/treaties.htm

Walker, Neil. 2002. "The Idea of Constitutional Pluralism." *Modern Law Review* 65, no. 3:317–59.

———. 2004. "Late Sovereignty in the European Union." In *Sovereignty in Transition*, edited by Neil Walker, 3–32. Oxford: Hart Books.

Walzer, Michael. 1997. *Just and Unjust Wars*. New York: Basic Books.

———. 2004a. *Arguing about War*. New Haven: Yale University Press.

———. 2004b. "Au-delà de l'intervention humanitaire: Les droits de l'homme dans la société globale." *Esprit* 9 (August–September): 66–67.

10

HUMAN RIGHTS AND GLOBAL HEALTH:
A RESEARCH PROGRAM

THOMAS W. POGGE

1

Some eighteen million human beings die prematurely each year from medical conditions we can cure—this is equivalent to fifty thousand avoidable deaths per day, or one-third of all human deaths.[1] Hundreds of millions more suffer grievously from these conditions.[2] The lives of additional hundreds of millions are shattered by severe illnesses or premature deaths in their family. And these medical problems also put a great strain on the economies of many poor countries, thereby perpetuating their poverty, which in turn contributes to the ill health of their populations.

This huge incidence of mortality and morbidity is not randomly distributed. For a variety of social reasons, females are significantly overrepresented among those suffering severe ill health (UNDP 2003, 310–30; www.unifem.org). Being especially vulnerable and helpless, children under the age of five are also overrepresented, accounting for about two-thirds of the death toll (USDA 1999, iii). But the most significant causal determinant is poverty: Nearly all the avoidable mortality and morbidity occurs in the poor countries (WHO 2004b, annex table 2), particularly among their poorer inhabitants.

There are different ways of attacking this problem. One approach, exemplified in much of my previous work, focuses on the eradication of severe poverty. In the world as it is, consumption by the poorest 44 percent of humankind, those living below the World Bank's "US$2/day"

---

[1] In 2002, there were fifty-seven million human deaths. Among the main avoidable causes of death were (with death tolls in thousands): respiratory infections (3,963—mainly pneumonia), HIV/AIDS (2,777), perinatal conditions (2,462), diarrhea (1,798), tuberculosis (1,566), malaria (1,272), childhood diseases (1,124—mainly measles), maternal conditions (510), malnutrition (485), sexually transmitted diseases (180), menengitis (173), hepatitis (157), and tropical diseases (129). See WHO 2004b, annex table 2; cf. also FAO 1999 and UNICEF 2002.

[2] Such morbidity is due to the conditions listed in the preceding footnote as well as to a variety of other communicable diseases, including dengue fever, leprosy, trypanosomiasis (sleeping sickness and Chagas disease), onchocerciasis (river blindness), leishmaniasis, Buruli ulcer, lymphatic filariasis, and schistosomiasis (bilharzia). See Gwatkin and Guillot 1999.

benchmark (1993 purchasing power), accounts for approximately 1.3 percent of the global social product. If all 2,736 million currently below it were instead living right at the US$2/day threshold, their consumption would still amount to only 2.2 percent of the global social product.[3] But they would then be much better able to gain access to things that help the rest of us ward off ill health, such as adequate nutrition, safe drinking water, adequate clothing and shelter, basic sanitation, mosquito nets in malaria-infested regions, and so on.[4]

Another way of addressing the huge mortality and morbidity rates is through ensuring improved access to medical treatments—preventive (like vaccines) or remedial. This way is exemplified in the research to be sketched here. The two ways of addressing the problem are complementary: Just as the eradication of severe poverty would greatly reduce the global disease burden, so improved access to essential medicines would greatly reduce severe poverty by enhancing the ability of the poor to work, and to organize themselves, for their own economic advancement.

Exemplifying the latter approach, this essay outlines how one crucial obstacle to a dramatic reduction in the global disease burden can be removed by giving medical innovators stable and reliable financial incentives to address the medical conditions of the poor. My aim is to develop a concrete, feasible, and politically realistic plan for reforming current national and global rules for incentivizing the search for new essential drugs. If adopted, this plan would not add much to the overall cost of global health-care spending. In fact, on any plausible accounting, which would take note of the huge economic losses caused by the present global disease burden, the reform would actually save money. Moreover, it would distribute the cost of global health-care spending more fairly across countries, across generations, and between those lucky enough to enjoy good health and the unlucky ones suffering from serious medical conditions.

The decision about whether and how to implement such a plan obviously rests with national parliaments and international organizations, such as the World Trade Organization (WTO) and the World

---

[3] According to the World Bank's (flawed) estimate, there are 2,736 million people worldwide living below the "$2/day" international poverty line, which means that their daily consumption falls below the purchasing power of US$2.15 in the United States in 1993 (Chen and Ravallion 2004, 153). This threshold is today equivalent to the purchasing power of about US$1,000 per person per year and, at current exchange rates, amounts to somewhere between US$120 and US$480 (depending on the poor-country currency in question). According to the World Bank's researchers, these global poor live, on average, 42 percent below the $2/day poverty line (Chen and Ravallion 2004 tables 3 and 6, dividing the poverty-gap index by the headcount index). See Pogge 2004, 395 nn. 15–16, for additional references and detailed calculations supporting my estimates.

[4] Among the global poor, some 831 million are undernourished, 1197 million lack access to safe water, 2742 million lack access to basic sanitation (UNDP 2004, 129–130); more than 880 million lack access to basic health services (UNDP 1999, 22); approximately 1,000 million have no adequate shelter and 2,000 million no electricity (UNDP 1998, 49).

Health Organization (WHO). But these decision makers could benefit from an exploration of the more promising reform options together with a full assessment of their comparative advantages and disadvantages, resulting in a specific reform recommendation.

2

The existing rules for incentivizing pharmaceutical research are morally deeply problematic. This fact, long understood among international health experts, has come to be more widely recognized in the wake of the AIDS crisis, especially in Africa, where the vital needs of poor patients are pitted against the need of pharmaceutical companies to recoup their research-and-development investments (Barnard 2002). Still, this wider recognition does not easily translate into political reform. Some believe (like Churchill about democracy) that the present regime is the lesser evil in comparison to its alternatives that have any chance of implementation. And others, more friendly to reform, disagree about what the flaws of the present system are exactly and have put forward a wide range of alternative reform ideas. What is needed now is a careful comparative exploration of the various reforms that have been proposed by academics, nongovernmental organizations (NGOs), and politicians as well as in the media, with the aim of formulating and justifying a specific alternative that is clearly superior to the present regime.

Filling this gap requires economic expertise. But it also, and centrally, requires moral reflection. From an economist standpoint, health care is a commodity like many others in the service sector (for example, haircuts and car repairs) and, from that standpoint, the creation of effective new medical treatments is an intellectual achievement like many others (for example, the creation of new music or software). From a moral standpoint, however, there is a world of difference between poor people lacking access to haircuts and poor people avoidably lacking access to treatment for serious medical conditions—and also a world of difference in importance between the aim of encouraging the creation of new music and the aim of encouraging the creation of new essential drugs.

We need to develop and defend a moral standard that can ground the assessment of the current patent regime (trade-related aspects of intellectual property rights, or TRIPS, as supplemented by a growing number of bilateral agreements that the United States has been pressing upon its trading partners) against the various ideas for reforming it and can guide the formulation of a specific reform plan as well as organize the argument in its favor. To be useful as a policy option for decision makers, and as a clear focal point for advocacy, media discussions, and the general public, this must be a detailed and specific reform plan fully informed by the relevant facts and insights from science, statistics, medicine, economics, law, and (moral and political) philosophy.

In addition, this plan must be politically feasible and realistic. To be *feasible* it must, once implemented, generate its own support from governments, pharmaceutical companies, and the general public (taking these three key constituencies as they would be under the reformed regime). To be *realistic*, the plan must possess moral and prudential appeal for governments, pharmaceutical companies, and the general public (taking these three constituencies as they are now, under the existing regime). A reform plan that is not incentive compatible in these two ways is destined to remain a philosopher's pipe dream.

3

Bringing new, safe and effective life-saving medications to market is hugely expensive, as inventor firms must pay for the research and development of new drugs as well as for elaborate testing and the subsequent approval process.[5] In addition, newly developed medical treatments often turn out to be unsafe or not effective enough, to have bad side effects, or to fail getting government approval for some other reason, which may lead to the loss of the entire investment.

Given such large investment costs and risks, very little innovative pharmaceutical research would take place in a free-market system. The reason is that an innovator would bear the full cost of its failures but would be unable to profit from its successes because competitors would copy or retro-engineer its invention (effectively free riding on its effort) and then drive down the price close to the marginal cost of production. This is a classic instance of market failure leading to a collectively irrational (Pareto-suboptimal) outcome in which medical innovation is undersupplied by the market.

The classic solution, also enshrined in the TRIPS regime (adopted under WTO auspices in the Uruguay Round), corrects this market failure through patent rules that grant inventor firms a temporary monopoly on their inventions, typically for twenty years from the time of filing a patent application. With competitors barred from copying and selling any newly invented drug during this period, the inventor firm can sell it at the profit-maximizing monopoly price well above, and often very far above, its marginal cost of production.[6] In this way, the inventor firm can recoup its

---

[5] This point may be controversial to some extent (e.g., Angell 2004). It has been asserted that pharmaceutical companies wildly overstate their financial and intellectual contributions to drug development and that most basic research is funded by governments and universities and then made available to the pharmaceutical industry for free. See Consumer Project on Technology (www.cptech.org/ip/health/econ/rndcosts.html) and UNDP 2001, ch. 5.

[6] The inventor firm can also sell permissions to produce its invention. Paying a hefty licensing fee to the inventor firm, the producer must charge a price well above, often very far above, its marginal cost of production. In this case, too, the second market failure I go on to discuss in the text arises, though it does so somewhat differently.

research and overhead expenses plus some of the cost of its other research efforts that failed to bear fruit.

This solution corrects the market failure (undersupply of medical innovation), but its monopoly feature creates another. During the patent's duration, the profit-maximizing sale price of the invented medicine will be far above its marginal cost of production. This large differential is collectively irrational by impeding many mutually beneficial transactions between the inventor firm and potential buyers who are unwilling or unable to pay the monopoly price but are willing and able to pay substantially more than the marginal cost of production. If modified rules could facilitate these potential transactions, then many patients would benefit—and so would the drug companies, as they would book additional profitable sales and typically also, through economies of scale, reduce their marginal cost of production. Such a reform would not merely avoid a sizable economic loss for the national and global economies. It would also avoid countless premature deaths and much severe suffering worldwide that the present patent regime engenders by blocking mutually advantageous sales of essential medicines.

There are two basic reform strategies for avoiding this second market failure associated with monopoly pricing powers. I will refer to these as the differential-pricing and public-good strategies, respectively. The *differential-pricing strategy* comes in different variants. One would have inventor firms themselves offer their proprietary drugs to different customers at different prices, thereby realizing a large profit margin from sales to the more affluent without renouncing sales to poorer buyers at a lower margin. Another variant is the right of governments, recognized under TRIPS rules, to issue compulsory licenses for inventions that are urgently needed in a public emergency. Exercising this right, a government can force down the price of a patented invention by compelling the patent holder to license it to other producers for a set percentage (typically below 10 percent) of the latter's sales revenues. The United States claims this right under 28 USC 1498, particularly for cases where the licensed producer is an agency of, or contractor for, the government,[7] but has been reluctant to invoke the right in the case of pharmaceuticals, presumably to avoid setting an international precedent detrimental to its pharmaceutical industry. Thus, during the anthrax scare of 2001, the United States preferred to pressure Bayer into supplying its patented drug CIPRO for US$0.90 per pill (versus a wholesale price of US$4.67) over purchasing generic versions from Polish or Indian suppliers. Canada invoked compulsory licensing in this case but backed down under pressure four days later (www.cptech.org/

---

[7] See www4.law.cornell.edu/uscode/28/1498.html. This right has been litigated in various important cases, producing licensing fees as low as 1 percent in the case of the Williams patent held by Hughes Aircraft Corporation (for details, see www.cptech.org/ip/health/cl/us-1498.html).

ip/health/cl/cipro/). It has often been suggested that poor countries should assert their compulsory licensing rights to cope with their public-health crises, particularly the AIDS pandemic.

Differential-pricing solutions are generally unworkable unless the different categories of buyers can be prevented from knowing about, or from trading with, one another. In the real world, if the drug were sold at a lower price to some, then many buyers who would otherwise be willing and able to pay the higher price would find a way to buy at the lower price. Selling expensive drugs more cheaply in poor developing countries, for example, would create strong incentives to divert (for example, smuggle) this drug back into the more affluent countries, leading to relative losses in the latter markets that outweigh the gains in the former. Anticipating such net losses through diversion, inventor firms typically do not themselves try to overcome the second market failure through differential pricing, resist pressures to do so, and fight attempts to impose compulsory licensing upon them. As a result, differential pricing has not gained much of a foothold, and many poor patients who would be willing and able to purchase the drug at a price well above the marginal cost of production are excluded from this drug because they cannot afford the much higher monopoly price (Kanavos et al. 2004). While such exclusion is acceptable for other categories of intellectual property (for example, software, films, and music), it is morally highly problematic in the case of essential medicines.

To be sure, insofar as a government does succeed, against heavy pressure from pharmaceutical companies and often their home governments, in exercising its right to issue compulsory licenses, any net losses due to diversion are simply forced upon the patent holders. But such compulsory licensing, especially if it were to become more common, brings back the first market failure of undersupply: Pharmaceutical companies will tend to spend less on the quest for essential drugs when the uncertainty of success is compounded by the additional unpredictability of whether and to what extent they will be allowed to recoup their investments through undisturbed use of their monopoly pricing powers.

4

In light of these serious problems, I doubt that the differential-pricing strategy can yield a plan for reform that would constitute a substantial improvement over the present regime. So I am proceeding, for now, on the assumption that an exploration of the *public-good strategy* is more promising, that is, more likely to lead to the formulation of a reform plan that would avoid the main defects of the present monopoly-patent regime while preserving most of its important benefits. The great difficulty to be overcome lies in devising the best possible reform plan within this much larger domain of the public-good strategy.

We may think of such a reform plan as consisting of three components. First, the results of any successful effort to develop (research, test, and obtain regulatory approval for) a new essential drug are to be provided as a public good that all pharmaceutical companies may use free of charge. This reform would eliminate the second market failure (associated with monopoly pricing powers) by allowing competition to bring the prices of new essential drugs down close to their marginal cost of production. Implemented in only one country or a few countries, this reform would engender problems like those we have found to attend differential-pricing solutions: Cheaper drugs produced in countries where drug development is treated as a public good would seep back into countries adhering to the monopoly-patent regime, undermining research incentives in the latter countries. The reform should therefore be global in scope, just as the rules of the current TRIPS regime are. The first reform component, then, is that results of successful efforts to develop new essential drugs are to be provided as public goods that all pharmaceutical companies anywhere may use free of charge.

Implemented in isolation, this first reform component would destroy incentives for pharmaceutical research. This effect is avoided by the second component, which is that, similar to the current regime, inventor firms should be entitled to take out a multiyear patent on any essential medicines they invent but, during the life of the patent, should be rewarded, out of public funds, in proportion to the impact of their invention on the global disease burden. This reform component would reorient the incentives of such firms in highly desirable ways: Any inventor firm would have incentives to sell its innovative treatments cheaply (often even below their marginal cost of production) in order to help get its drugs to even very poor people who need them. Such a firm would have incentives also to see to it that patients are fully instructed in the proper use of its drugs (dosage, compliance, and so on), in order to ensure that, through wide and effective deployment, they have as great an impact on the global disease burden as possible.[8] Rather than ignore poor countries as unlucrative markets, inventor firms would moreover have incentives to work together toward improving the heath systems of these countries in order to enhance the impact of their inventions there. In addition, any inventor firm would have reason to encourage and support efforts by cheap generic producers (already well established in India, Brazil, and South Africa, for example) to copy its drugs, because such

---

[8] The absence of such incentives under the present rules gravely undermines the effectiveness of drugs delivered into poor regions, even when these drugs are donated (cf. UNDP 2001, 101).

copying would further increase the number of users and hence the invention's favorable impact on the global disease burden. In all these ways, the reform would align and harmonize the interests of inventor firms with those of patients and the generic drug producers—interests that, under the current regime, are diametrically opposed.[9] The reform would also align the moral and prudential interests of the inventor firms who, under the present regime, are forced to choose between recouping their investments in the search for essential drugs and preventing avoidable suffering and deaths.

This second component of a plausible public-good strategy realizes yet one further tremendous advantage over the status quo: Under the current regime, inventor firms have incentives to try to develop a new medical treatment only if the expected value of the temporary monopoly pricing power they might gain, discounted by the probability of failure, is greater than the full development and patenting costs. They have no incentives, then, to try to develop treatments that few people have a need for and treatments needed by people who are unable to afford them at a price far above the marginal cost of production. The former category contains treatments for many so-called orphan diseases that affect only small numbers of patients. The latter category contains many diseases mainly affecting the poor, for which treatments priced far above the marginal cost of production could be sold only in small quantities. It may be acceptable that no one is developing software demanded only by a few and that no one is producing music valued only by the very poor. But it is morally problematic that no treatments are developed for rare diseases, and it is extremely problematic, morally, that so few treatments are developed for medical conditions that cause most of the premature deaths and suffering in the world today.

Even if common talk of the 10/90 gap[10] is now an overstatement, the problem is certainly real: Malaria, pneumonia, diarrhea, and tuberculosis, which together account for 21 percent of the global disease burden, receive 0.31 percent of all public and private funds devoted to health research (GFHR 2004, 122). And diseases confined to the tropics tend to be the most neglected: Of the 1,393 new drugs approved between 1975 and 1999, only thirteen were specifically indicated for tropical diseases and five out of these thirteen actually emerged from veterinary research

[9] This opposition was displayed most dramatically when a coalition of thirty-one pharmaceutical companies went to court in South Africa in order to prevent their inventions from being reproduced by local generic producers and sold cheaply to desperate patients whose life depended on such affordable access to these retroviral drugs. In April 2001, the attempted lawsuit collapsed under a barrage of worldwide public criticism (see Barnard 2002).

[10] "Only 10 percent of global health research is devoted to conditions that account for 90 percent of the global disease burden" (Drugs for Neglected Diseases Working Group 2001, 10; cf. GFHR 2000, 2002, 2004).

(Trouiller et al. 2001; Drugs for Neglected Diseases Working Group 2001, 11).

Rewarding pharmaceutical research on the basis of its impact on the global disease burden would attract inventor firms toward medical conditions whose adverse effects on humankind can be reduced most cost effectively. This reorientation would greatly mitigate the problem of neglected diseases that overwhelmingly affect the poor. And it would open new profitable research opportunities for pharmaceutical companies.

One might worry that the second component of the reform would also *reduce* incentives to develop treatments for medical conditions that, though they add little to the global disease burden (on any plausible conception thereof), affluent patients are willing to pay a lot to avoid. But this worry can be addressed, at least in part, by limiting the application of the reform plan to *essential* drugs, that is, to medicines for diseases that destroy human lives. Drugs for other medical conditions, such as hair loss, acne, and impotence, for example, can remain under the existing regime with no loss in incentives or rewards.

Incorporating this distinction between essential and nonessential drugs into the reform plan raises the specter of political battles over how this distinction is to be defined and of legal battles over how some particular invention should be classified. These dangers could be averted by allowing inventor firms to classify their inventions as they wish and then designing the rewards in such a way that these firms will themselves choose to register under the reform rules any inventions that stand to make a real difference to the global disease burden. Such freedom of choice would also greatly facilitate a smooth and rapid phasing in of the new rules, as there would be no disappointment of the legitimate expectations of firms that have undertaken research for the sake of gaining a conventional patent. The reform plan should be *attractive* for pharmaceutical companies by winning them new lucrative opportunities for research into currently neglected diseases without significant losses in the lucrative research opportunities they now enjoy—and by restoring their moral stature as benefactors of humankind.

This second reform component requires a way of funding the planned incentives for developing new essential medicines, which might cost some US$45–90 billion annually on a global scale.[11] The third component of

---

[11] The precise amount each year would depend on how successful innovative treatments would be in decimating the global disease burden. My estimate in the text is thus necessarily tentative and speculative, meant to provide a rough orientation and thus to illustrate the order of magnitude and hence the degree of realism of the reform. My estimate derives from current corporate spending on pharmaceutical research, which is reckoned to have been US$30.5 billion in 1998, the latest year for which I have found a credible figure (GFHR 2004, 112). This suggests that the current figure is around US$40 billion. Only part of this money is spent toward developing *essential* drugs. But the reformed rules would stimulate substan-

the reform plan is then to develop a fair, feasible, and politically realistic allocation of these costs, as well as compelling arguments in support of this allocation.

5

While the general approach as outlined may seem plausible enough, the great intellectual challenge is to specify it concretely in a way that shows it to be both feasible and politically realistic. This is an extremely complex undertaking that involves a formidable array of multiply interdependent tasks and subtasks. Here one main task, associated with the second component, concerns the design of the planned incentives. This requires a suitable measure of the global disease burden and ways of assessing the contributions that various new medical treatments are making to its reduction. When two or more different medicines are alternative treatments for the same disease, then the reward corresponding to their aggregate impact must be allocated among their respective inventors on the basis of each medicine's market share and effectiveness.

More complex is the case (exemplified in the fight against HIV, tuberculosis, and malaria) of "drug cocktails" that combine various drugs that frequently have been developed by different companies. Here the reform plan must formulate clear and transparent rules for distributing the overall reward, based on the impact of the drug cocktail, among the inventors of the drugs it contains. And it must also include specific rules for the phase-in period so as not to discourage ongoing research efforts motivated by the existing patent rules. It is of crucial importance that all these rules be clear and transparent, lest they add to the inevitable risks and uncertainties that complicate the work of inventor firms and sometimes discourage them from important research efforts. This task requires expertise in medicine, statistics, economics, and legal regulation.

Another main task, associated with the third component, concerns the design of rules for allocating the cost of the incentives as well as the formulation of good arguments in favor of this allocation. Effective implementation of the reform requires that much of its cost be borne by the developed countries, which, with 16 percent of the world's population, control about 81 percent of the global social product (World Bank 2004, 253). This is feasible even if these countries, after retargeting existing subsidies to the pharmaceutical industry in accordance with the reformed

tially greater spending on pharmaceutical research toward developing new essential drugs (especially for heretofore neglected diseases). Such outlays might well exceed corporate expenditures on *all* pharmaceutical research under the existing rules. The rewards offered under the reformed rules must not merely match but also substantially exceed these outlays, because pharmaceutical companies will brave the risks and uncertainties of an expensive and protracted research effort only if its expected return substantially exceeds its cost.

rules, still had to shoulder around US$70 billion in new expenditures.[12] This amount, after all, is only 0.27 percent of the aggregate gross national income of the high-income countries, or US$70 for each of their residents.[13] To make this planned spending increase realistic, the taxpayers and politicians of the high-income countries need to be given compelling reasons for supporting it.

The plan can be supported by prudential considerations. For one thing, the taxpayers of the more affluent countries gain a substantial benefit for themselves in the form of lower drug prices. Under the current regime, affluent persons in need of essential drugs pay high prices for them, either directly or through their contributions to commercial insurance companies. Under the projected scheme, the prices of such drugs would be much lower, and their consumers, even the richest, would thus save money on drugs and/or insurance premiums. To be sure, such a shifting of costs, within affluent countries, from patients to taxpayers would benefit less-healthy citizens at the expense of the healthier ones. But such a mild mitigation of the effects of luck is actually morally appealing—not least because even those fortunate persons who never or rarely need to take advantage of recent medical advances still benefit from pharmaceutical research that affords them the peace of mind derived from knowing that, should they ever become seriously ill, they would have access to cutting-edge medical knowledge and treatments.

A second prudential argument is that, by giving poor populations a free ride on the pharmaceutical research conducted for the benefit of citizens in the affluent countries, we are building goodwill toward ourselves in the developing world by demonstrating in a tangible way our concern for the horrendous public-health problems these populations are facing. This argument has a moral twin: In light of the extent of avoidable mortality and morbidity in the developing world, the case for giving the poor a free ride is morally compelling.

These last twin arguments have wider application. The reform plan would not merely encourage the same sort of pharmaceutical research differently but would also expand the range of medical conditions for which inventor firms would seek solutions. Under the current regime, these firms understandably show little interest in tropical diseases, for example, because, even if they could develop successful treatments, they would not be able to make much money from selling or licensing them. Under the alternative regime I suggest we design, inventor firms could make lots of money by developing such treatments, whose potential

[12] This figure is in line with the estimates made by the WHO Commission on Macroeconomics and Health (chaired by Jeffrey Sachs), according to which some eight million deaths could be prevented each year in the developing world through providing real access to medical care at a cost of about US$60 billion annually (WHO 2001).

[13] See World Bank 2004, 253, for the aggregate gross national income and the aggregate population of the high-income countries.

impact on the global disease burden is enormous. Measles, malaria, and tuberculosis each kill well over a million people per year, mostly children, and pneumonia kills more than these three combined. New drugs could dramatically reduce the impact of these diseases.

But, it may be asked, why should we citizens of the high-income countries support a rule change that benefits *others* (poor people in the developing world) at our expense? Viewed narrowly, underwriting such incentives for research into widespread but currently neglected diseases might seem to be a dead loss for the affluent countries.

Taking a larger view, however, important gains are readily apparent: The reform would create top-flight medical-research jobs in the developed countries. It would enable us to respond more effectively to public-health emergencies and problems in the future by earning us more rapidly increasing medical knowledge combined with a stronger and more diversified arsenal of medical interventions. In addition, better human health around the world would reduce the threat we face from invasive diseases. The recent SARS outbreak illustrates the last two points: Dangerous diseases can rapidly transit from poor-country settings into cities in the industrialized world (as happened in Toronto); and the current neglect of the medical needs of poor populations leaves us unprepared to deal with such problems when we are suddenly confronted with them. Slowing population growth and bringing enormous reductions in avoidable suffering and deaths worldwide, the reform would further-more be vastly more cost effective and also be vastly better received by people in the poor countries than similarly expensive humanitarian interventions we have undertaken in recent years and the huge, unrepay-able loans our governments and their international financial institutions tend to extended to (often corrupt and oppressive) rulers and elites in the developing countries. Last, but not least, there is the important moral and social benefit of working with others, nationally and internationally, toward overcoming the morally preeminent problem of our age, which is the horrendous, poverty-induced and largely avoidable morbidity and mortality in the developing world.

6

In the remainder of this essay, I will further underscore the moral urgency of the task of dramatically lessening the global burden of disease by formulating it in human-rights terms. We are used to relating human rights to the conduct of individual and collective agents—such as prison guards, generals, corporations, and governments, whose conduct may be criticized for failing to safeguard the human rights of persons falling within their domain of responsibility. And their conduct may also be criticized (typically more severely) for actively violating the human rights of persons. In the former case, such agents stand accused of failing to fulfill positive responsibilities they have toward specific persons by not taking reasonable steps toward ensuring these persons have secure access to the objects of their human rights.[14] In the latter case, such agents stand accused of violating negative responsibilities they have toward all human beings by actively depriving some persons of secure access to the objects of some of their human rights.

Social (paradigmatically: legal) rules, too, can be criticized in human-rights terms. This is clearest when such rules explicitly mandate or authorize conduct that violates human rights, as with laws authorizing the enslavement of blacks and mandating the forcible return of fugitive slaves. Such laws violated the human rights of blacks. And those who participated in imposing such laws, even if they did not themselves own slaves, violated their negative responsibilities by helping to deprive blacks of secure access to the objects of their human rights.

Even social rules that do not explicitly mandate or authorize conduct that violates human rights may still violate human rights. This is most clearly the case with economic rules that avoidably produce massive extreme poverty or even famine, as exemplified by the economic regimes of feudal France and Russia, the economic rules Britain imposed on Ireland and India (causing the Irish potato famine of 1846 to 1850 and the great Bengal famines of 1770 and 1942 to 1945), and the economic regimes temporarily imposed in the Soviet Union and China (the "Great Leap Forward"), which led to massive famines from 1930 to 1933 and 1959 to 1962, respectively.

The assertion that the mentioned economic regimes violated human rights crucially presupposes the claim that the horrendous deprivations and famines in question were in part *due to* those regimes and would have been—partly or wholly—avoided if a suitably modified regime had been in place instead. If this presupposition holds, the economic regimes mentioned were indeed in violation of human rights.

Here it may be objected that a just economic order should be immune from criticism on human-rights grounds: If a laissez-faire libertarian or communist or feudal economic order is what justice requires, then it is right that such an order should be upheld, even if doing so avoidably leads to deprivations on a massive scale.

The flaw in this objection is obvious. The objection assumes that the justice of an economic order is independent of how this order affects the fulfillment of human rights. But human rights are the core values of our moral and political discourse, central to how justice is conceived in the

---

[14] Here the *object* of a human right is whatever this human right is a right to—adequate nutrition, for example, or physical integrity. And what matters is *secure access* to such objects, rather than these objects themselves, because an institutional order is not morally problematic merely because some of its participants are choosing to fast or to compete in boxing matches. For a more elaborate statement of my understanding of human rights, see Pogge 2002a, 2002b.

modern world. Social rules that avoidably deprive large numbers of persons of secure access to the objects of their human rights are, for this reason alone, unjust (assuming again that these deprivations are avoidable, wholly or in part, through suitably modified rules). In the era of human rights, then, social rules are in good part judged by their effects on the fulfillment of human rights. To be just, such rules must not violate human rights, that is, they must afford human beings secure access to the objects of their human rights insofar as this is reasonably possible.

When social rules violate human rights without explicitly mandating or authorizing conduct that violates human rights, then those who participate in upholding these rules may not be human-rights violators. They are not violators of human rights when they are sincerely and on the basis of the best available evidence convinced that the social rules they are upholding do not violate human rights (that is, that these rules contribute to the realization of human rights insofar as this is reasonably possible). Participation in the imposition of social rules constitutes a human-rights violation only when these rules *foreseeably* and avoidably deprive human beings of secure access to the objects of their human rights—when the imposers of the rule could and should have known that these rules fail to realize human rights insofar as this is reasonably possible, could and should have known that there are feasible and practicable reforms of these rules through which a substantial portion of existing deprivations could be avoided.

Much of the account I have just given is suggested by Article 28 of the 1948 *Universal Declaration of Human Rights*:

> Everyone is entitled to a social and international order in which the rights and freedoms set forth in this Declaration can be fully realized. (*UDHR*, Article 28; cf. also Article 22)

Three points are worth noting about this article. First, its peculiar status. As its reference to "the rights and freedoms set forth in this Declaration" indicates, Article 28 does not add a further right to the list but rather addresses the concept of a human right, says something about what a human right is. It is then consistent with any substantive account of what human rights there are—even while it significantly affects the meaning of any human rights postulated in the other articles of this *Universal Declaration*: They all are to be understood as claims on the institutional order of any comprehensive social system.

Second, this idea about how the human rights postulated in the *Universal Declaration* are to be understood fits well with what I have just outlined—with how human rights can figure centrally in the critical examination of social rules. In fact, we can achieve perfect congruence through four plausible interpretive conjectures:

(1) Alternative institutional orders that do not satisfy the requirement of Article 28 can be ranked by how close they come to
enabling the full realization of human rights: Social systems
ought to be structured so that human rights can be realized in
them as fully as possible.

(2) How fully human rights *can* be realized under some institutional
order is measured by how fully these human rights generally are,
or (in the case of a hypothetical institutional order) generally
would be, realized in it.

(3) An institutional order *realizes* a human right insofar as (and
fully if and only if) this human right is *fulfilled* for the persons
upon whom this order is imposed.

(4) A human right is fulfilled for some person if and only if this
person enjoys *secure access to the object of this human right*.

Taking these four conjectures together, Article 28 should be read as
holding that the moral quality, or justice, of any institutional order
depends primarily on its success in affording all its participants secure
access to the objects of their human rights: Any institutional order is to be
assessed and reformed principally by reference to its relative impact on
the realization of the human rights of those on whom it is imposed.[15]

The third noteworthy feature of Article 28 is its explicit reference to the
international order. When we reflect on social rules, we tend to think of
the institutional (and more specifically legal) rules of a territorial state
first and foremost. Less familiar, but no less important in the modern
world, are the rules of the international institutional order, whose design
profoundly affects the fulfillment of human rights, especially in the poorer
and weaker countries. Recognizing this point, Article 28 requires that the
rules of the international order be shaped, insofar as this is reasonably
possible, so as to afford human beings everywhere secure access to the
objects of their human rights.

In the world as it is, some eighteen million human beings die each year
from poverty-related causes, mostly from communicable diseases that
could easily be averted or cured. Insofar as these deaths and the immense
suffering of those still surviving these diseases are avoidable, their victims
are deprived of some of the objects of their human rights—for example,
of their "right to a standard of living adequate for the health and well-
being of himself and of his family, including food, clothing, housing and
medical care and necessary social services" (*UDHR*, Article 25; cf.
ICESCR, Articles 11–12).

---

[15] "*Relative* impact," because a comparative judgment is needed about how much more
or less fully human rights are realized in this institutional order than they would be realized
in its feasible alternatives.

If these victims are so deprived, then who or what is depriving them, violating their human rights? Several factors, national and global, substantially contribute to the deprivations they suffer. As I have been arguing, one important such factor is the way pharmaceutical research into drugs and vaccines is incentivized under the current rules of the TRIPS Agreement as supplemented by various bilateral agreements the United States has been pursuing.

With this background, we can look once more at the question of why we citizens of the high-income countries should support a reform of the global health system that benefits others (poor people in the developing world) at our expense. The landholders of feudal France or Russia could have asked likewise. And the answers are closely analogous: We ought to support such a reform, even if it involves significant opportunity costs for us, because it is necessary for rendering minimally just (in the explicated sense of "realizing human rights insofar as this is reasonably possible") the rules of the world economy considered as one scheme. Minimal justice in this sense is compatible with these rules being designed by, and with their greatly and disproportionately benefiting, the governments and corporations of the developed countries. However, minimal justice is not compatible with these rules being designed so that they result in a much higher incidence of extreme poverty and in much higher mortality and morbidity from curable diseases than would be reasonably avoidable.

7

Against this line of argument, it may be objected that accession to the TRIPS Agreement (and the whole WTO Treaty) is voluntary. Since the poor countries have themselves signed on to the rules as they are, the imposition of these rules cannot be a violation of their human rights. *Volenti non fit iniuria* (to the willing, no wrong is done).

There are at least four distinct responses to this objection, each of which seems sufficient to refute it.

First, appeal to consent can defeat the charge of rights violation only if the rights in question are alienable and, more specifically, can be waived by consent. Yet, on the usual understanding of human rights, they cannot be so waived: Persons cannot waive their human rights to personal freedom, political participation, freedom of expression, or freedom from torture. (Persons can promise, through a religious vow perhaps, to serve another, to refrain from voting, or to keep quiet. But, wherever human rights are respected, such promises are legally unenforceable and thus do not succeed in waiving the right in question.) There are various reasons for conceiving human rights in this way: A person changes over time, and her later self has a vital interest in being able to avoid truly horrific burdens her earlier self had risked or incurred. Moreover, the option of placing such burdens on one's future self is likely to be disadvantageous even to the earlier self by encouraging predators seeking to elicit a waiver from this earlier self through manipulation of her or of her circumstances (for example, by getting her into a life-threatening situation from which one then offers to rescue her at the price of her permanent enslavement). Finally, waivers of human rights impose considerable burdens on third parties who will be (more or less directly) confronted with the resulting suffering of people enslaved or tortured or starving.

Second, an appeal to consent blocks the complaint of those now lacking secure access to the objects of (some of) their human rights only insofar as they have *themselves* consented to the regime that perpetuates their deprivation. Yet, most of those who are endangered by diseases or are severely impoverished live in countries that are not meaningfully democratic, and consent to the present global economic order by their rulers thus cannot be counted as consent by their subjects. For example, in 1995 Nigeria's accession to the WTO was effected by its brutal military dictator Sani Abacha, Myanmar's by the notorious SLORC junta (the State Law and Order Restoration Council), Indonesia's by the kleptocrat Suharto, and Zimbabwe's by Robert Mugabe and, two years later, Zaire's (since renamed the Congo) by Mobutu Sese Seko.

Third, consent to a very burdensome global regime can have justificatory force only if it was not impelled by the threat of even greater burdens. Thus, your consent cannot justify your enslavement when your consent was your only escape from continued torture or, indeed, from an accidental drowning. An appeal to consent thus blocks a complaint by the poor against the present global economic order only if, at the time of consenting, they had an alternative option that would have given them secure access to the objects of their human rights. Yet, the populations of most poor WTO member states would have suffered even more if they had remained outside the regime. These people would still have been subject to coercively enforced global rules preventing them from offering their products in the more affluent countries or from migrating there. Thus, even the unreal case of a poor country's population voting with full information and unanimously for WTO accession does not exemplify appropriate consent if the severely deprived within this population were only given a choice between the deprivations they now endure and the even greater deprivations they would have had to endure outside the WTO.[16]

---

[16] I am not disputing that joining the WTO was better for most poor states, and even for their poor citizens, than staying out. But this claim cannot defend the WTO regime (though it is often so used): Analogously, one could defend the fascist order briefly established in Europe by pointing out that countries cooperating with Hitler and Mussolini did better than countries opposing that order.

Fourth, an appeal to consent cannot justify the severe impoverishment of children who are greatly overrepresented among those suffering severe poverty and account for about two-thirds of all deaths from poverty-related causes (thirty-four thousand daily).[17] The claim that the present global economic order foreseeably and avoidably violates the human rights of *children* cannot be blocked by any conceivable appeal to consent.

8

Participation in the imposition of social rules constitutes a human-rights violation only when these rules *foreseeably* and avoidably deprive human beings of secure access to the object of their human rights—only when the imposers of the rules could and should have known that these rules fail to realize human rights insofar as this is reasonably possible, could and should have known that there are feasible and practicable reforms of these rules through which a substantial portion of existing deprivations can be avoided. I think this condition is fulfilled in the world today. The governments and citizens of the high-income countries could and should know that most of the current premature mortality and morbidity is avoidable through feasible and modest reforms, such as the global health-system reform outlined here. Still, with the suffering of the poor far away and invisible, powerful psychological tendencies and economic incentives suppress such knowledge through a constant barrage of rationalizations and deceptions. It may be possible to break through this barrage with a concrete plan for a feasible and realistic institutional reform that would help extend the benefits of the enormous technological and economic gains of the previous century to that other half of humankind currently still largely excluded from them.

Bibliography

Anand, S. 2002. "The Concern for Equity in Health." *Journal of Epidemiology and Community Health* 56, no. 7:485–87.

Angell, M. 2004. *The Truth about the Drug Companies: How They Deceive Us and What to Do About It*. New York: Random House.

Attaran, A., K. I. Barnes, C. Curtis, U. d'Alessandro, C. I. Fanello, M. R. Galinski, et al. 2004. "WHO, the Global Fund, and Medical Malpractice in Malaria Treatment." *Lancet* 363, no. 9404:237–40.

Attaran, A., and L. Gillespie-White. 2001. "Do Patents for Antiretroviral Drugs Constrain Access to AIDS Treatment in Africa?" *Journal of the American Medical Association* 286, no. 15:1886–92.

[17] USDA 1999, iii. The U.S. government mentions this fact while arguing that the developed countries should *not* follow the U.N. Food and Agriculture Organization's proposal to increase development assistance for agriculture by $6 billion annually, that $2.6 billion is ample. See ibid., appendix A.

Balasubramaniam, K. 2001. "Equitable Pricing, Affordability and Access to Essential Drugs in Developing Countries: Consumers Perspective." WHO/WTO Secretariat Workshop on Differential Pricing and Financing of Essential Drugs. www.wto.org/english/tratop_e/trips_e/ hosbjor_presentations_e/35balasubramaniam_e.pdf
Banta, H. D. 2001. "Worldwide Interest in Global Access to Drugs." *Journal of the American Medical Association* 285, no. 22:2844–46.
Barnard, D. 2002. "In the High Court of South Africa, Case No. 4138/98: The Global Politics of Access to Low-Cost AIDS Drugs in Poor Countries." *Kennedy Institute of Ethics Journal* 12, no 2:159–74.
Barry, C., and K. Raworth. 2002. "Access to Medicines and the Rhetoric of Responsibility." *Ethics and International Affairs* 16, no. 2:57–70.
Barton, J. H. 2001. Differentiated Pricing of Patented Products." Commission on Macroeconomics and Health Working Paper Series, Work Group 4, Paper 2. www.cmhealth.org/docs/wg4_paper2.pdf
Beitz, C. R. 1979. *Political Theory and International Relations.* Princeton: Princeton University Press.
———. 1981. "Economic Rights and Distributive Justice in Developing Societies." *World Politics* 33, no. 3:321–46.
Beitz, C. R. et al., eds. 1985. *International Ethics.* Princeton: Princeton University Press.
Black, R. E., S. S. Morris, and J. Bryce. 2003. "Where and Why Are 10 Million Children Dying Every Year?" *Lancet* 361, no. 9376:2226–34.
Boelaert, M., L. Lynen, W. van Damme, R. Colebunders, E. Goemaere, A. V. Kaninda, et al. 2000. "Do Patents Prevent Access to Drugs for HIV in Developing Countries?" *Journal of the American Medical Association* 287, no. 7:840–43. Also available at www.accessmed-msf.org/prod/ publications.asp?scntid = 21520031747452&contenttype = PARA&
Canadian Medical Association Journal. 2003. "Patently Necessary: Improving Global Access to Essential Medicines" (editorial). *Canadian Medical Association Journal* 169, no. 12:1257.
Chatterjee, D. K., ed. 2004. *The Ethics of Assistance: Morality and the Distant Needy.* Cambridge: Cambridge University Press.
Chen, S., and M. Ravallion. 2001. "How Did the World's Poorest Fare in the 1990s?" *Review of Income and Wealth* 47:283–300.
———. 2004. "How Have the World's Poorest Fared since the Early 1980s?" *World Bank Research Observer* 19, no. 2: 141–69.
Claeson, M., J. De Beyer, P. Jha, and R. Feachem. 1996. "The World Bank's Perspective on Global Health." *Current Issues in Public Health* 2, nos. 5–6:264–69.
Cohen, J. C., and P. Illingworth. 2004. "The Dilemma of Intellectual Property Rights for Pharmaceuticals: The Tension Between Ensuring Access of the Poor to Medicines and Committing to International Agreements." *Developing World Bioethics* 3, no. 1:27–48.

Corbett, E. L., C. J. Watt, N. Walker, D. Maher, B. G. Williams, M. C. Raviglione, et al. 2003. "The Growing Burden of Tuberculosis: Global Trends and Interactions with the HIV Epidemic." *Archive of Internal Medicine* 163, no. 9:1009–21.

Cornia, G. A., R. Jolly, and F. Stewart, eds. 1987. *Adjustment with a Human Face: Protecting the Vulnerable and Promoting Growth*. 2 volumes. Oxford: Clarendon Press.

Correa, C. 2000. *Intellectual Property Rights, the WTO and Developing Countries: The TRIPs Agreement and Policy Options*. London: Zed Books.

Crocker, D. A., and T. Linden, eds. 1998. *Ethics of Consumption: The Good Life, Justice, and Global Stewardship*. Lanham, Md.: Rowman and Littlefield.

Daniels, N. 1985. *Just Health Care*. Cambridge: Cambridge University Press.

Danzon, P. M. 2003. "Differential Pricing for Pharmaceuticals: Reconciling Access, R&D, and Patents." *International Journal of Health Care Finance and Economics* 3:183–205.

Dasgupta, P. 1993. *An Inquiry into Well-Being and Destitution*. Oxford: Oxford University Press.

De Greiff, P., and C. Cronin, eds. 2002. *Global Justice and Transnational Politics*. Cambridge, Mass.: MIT Press.

Deaton, A. 2003. "How to Monitor Poverty for the Millennium Development Goals." *Journal of Human Development* 4:353–78.

Denicolo, V., and L. A. Franzoni. 2003. "The Contract Theory of Patents." *International Review of Law and Economics* 23, no. 4:365–80.

Diamond, J. 1999. *Guns, Germs, and Steel: The Fates of Human Societies*. New York: Norton.

Dreze, J., and A. K. Sen. 1995. *India: Economic Development and Social Opportunity*. Delhi: Oxford University Press.

Drugs for Neglected Diseases Working Group. 2001. *Fatal Imbalance: The Crisis in Research and Development for Drugs for Neglected Diseases*. Geneva: Médecins Sans Frontières Access to Essential Medicines Campaign and the Drugs for Neglected Diseases Working Group. Also available at www.msf.org/source/access/2001/fatal/fatal.pdf

Dworkin, R. 1993. "Justice in the Distribution of Health Care." *McGill Law Journal* 38, no. 4:883–98.

Eichengreen, B., J. Tobin, and C. Wyplosz. 1995. "Two Cases for Sand in the Wheels of International Finance." *Economic Journal* 105, no. 127:162–72.

Elster, J., and J. Roemer, eds. 1991. *Interpersonal Comparisons of Well-Being*. Cambridge: Cambridge University Press.

Evans, R. G., M. L. Barer, and T. R. Marmor. 1994. *Why Are Some People Healthy and Others Not?: The Determinants of Health of Populations*. Hawthorne, N.Y.: Aldine de Gruyter.

Evans, T., M. Whitehead, F. Diderichsen, A. Bhuiya, and M. Wirth. 2001. *Challenging Inequities in Health: From Ethics to Action.* New York: Oxford University Press.

FAO (Food and Agriculture Organization of the United Nations). 1999. *The State of Food Insecurity in the World 1999.* www.fao.org/news/1999/img/sofi99-e.pdf

Farmer, P. 1999. *Infections and Inequalities: The Modern Plagues.* Berkeley: University of California Press.

———. 2003. *Pathologies of Power: Health, Human Rights, and the New War on the Poor.* Berkeley: University of California Press.

Finger, J. M., and P. Schuler. 1999. "Implementation of Uruguay Round Commitments: The Development Challenge." World Bank Research Working Paper 2215. http://wdsbeta.worldbank.org/external/default/WDSContentServer/IW3P/IB/2001/02/10/000094946_01013005324822/Rendered/PDF/multi_page.pdf

Friedman, M. A., H. den Besten, and A. Attaran. 2003. "Out-Licensing: A Practical Approach for Improvement of Access to Medicines in Poor Countries." *Lancet* 361, no. 9354:341–44.

Fukuda Parr, S., and A. K. Shiva Kumar, eds. 2003. *Readings in Human Development: Concepts, Measures, and Policies for a Development Paradigm.* New Delhi: Oxford University Press.

GFHR (Global Forum for Health Research). 2000. *The 10/90 Report on Health Research 2000.* Geneva: Global Forum for Health Research. Also available at http://www.globalforumhealth.org/Site/002__What%20we%20do/005__Publications/001__10%2090%20reports.php

———. 2002. *The 10/90 Report on Health Research 2001–2002.* Geneva: Global Forum for Health Research. http://www.globalforumhealth.org/Site/002__What%20we%20do/005__Publications/001__10%2090%20reports.php

———. 2004. *The 10/90 Report on Health Research 2003–2004.* Geneva: Global Forum for Health Research. Also available at http://www.globalforumhealth.org/Site/002__What%20we%20do/005__Publications/001__10%2090%20reports.php

Goodin, R. E. 1988. "What Is So Special about Our Fellow Countrymen?" *Ethics* 98:663–86.

———, ed. 1996. *The Theory of Institutional Design.* Cambridge: Cambridge University Press.

Gupta, R., J. Y. Kim, M. A. Espinal, J. M. Caudron, B. Pecoul, P. E. Farmer, et al. 2001. "Public Health: Responding to Market Failures in Tuberculosis Control." *Science* 293, no. 5532:1049–51.

Gwatkin, D. R., and M. Guillot. 1999. *The Burden of Disease among the Global Poor: Current Situation, Future Trends, and Implications for Strategy.* Washington, D.C., and Geneva: The World Bank and the Global Forum for Health Research.

Gwatkin, D. R. 2000. "Health Inequalities and the Health of the Poor: What Do We Know? What Can We Do?" *Bulletin of the World Health Organization* 78:3–15. Also available at http://www.who.int/docstore/ bulletin/pdf/2000/issue1/bu0287.pdf

Hurrell, A., and N. Woods, eds., 1999. *Inequality, Globalisation and World Politics*. Oxford: Oxford University Press.

ICESCR (*International Covenant on Economic, Social, and Cultural Rights*). 1966. Available at www.unhchr.ch/html/menu3/b/a_cescr. htm

ILO (International Labour Organisation). 2002. *A Future without Child Labour*. Geneva: International Labour Office. Also available at www.ilo.org/public/english/standards/decl/publ/reports/report3. htm

Jha, P., A. Mills, K. Hanson, L. Kumaranayake, L. Conteh, C. Kurowski, et al. 2002. "Improving the Health of the Global Poor." *Science* 295, no. 5562:2036–39.

Juma, C. 1999. "Intellectual Property Rights and Globalization: Implications for Developing Countries." Science, Technology and Innovation Discussion Paper No. 4, Harvard Center for International Development, www2.cid.harvard.edu/cidbiotech/dp/discuss4.pdf

Kagan, S. 1989. *The Limits of Morality*. Oxford: Oxford University Press.

Kamm, F. M. 1993, 1996. *Morality, Mortality*. 2 volumes. Oxford: Oxford University Press.

Kanavos, P., J. Costa-i-Font, S. Merkur, and M. Gemmill. 2004. "The Economic Impact of Pharmaceutical Parallel Trade in European Union Member States: A Stakeholders Analysis." London School of Economics and Political Science Working Paper. www.lse.ac.uk/col lections/LSEHealthAndSocialCare/pdf/Workingpapers/Paper.pdf

Kaul, I., P. Conceicao, K. Coulven, and K. Mendoza. 1999. *Providing Global Public Goods: Managing Globalization*. Oxford: Oxford University Press.

Kaul, I., I. Grunberg, M. Stern, and M. A. Stern. 2003. *Global Public Goods: International Cooperation in the 21st Century*. Oxford: Oxford University Press.

Kawachi, I., B. P. Kennedy, and R. G. Wilkinson. 1999. *The Society and Population Health Reader: Income Inequality and Health*. New York: New Press.

Kessel, E., S. Chattopadhyay, and B. Pecoul. 1999. "Access to Essential Drugs in Poor Countries." *Journal of the American Medical Association* 282, no. 7:630–31.

Keusch, G. T., and R. A. Nugent. 2002. "The Role of Intellectual Property and Licensing in Promoting Research in International Health: Perspectives from a Public Sector Biomedical Research Agency." Commission on Macroeconomics and Health Working Paper Series, Work Group 2, Paper 7. www3.who.int/whosis/cmh/ cmh_papers/e/pdf/wg2_paper06.pdf

Kim, J. Y., J. V. Millen, A. Irwin, and J. Gershman. 2000. *Dying for Growth: Global Inequality and the Health of the Poor*. Monroe, Me.: Common Courage Press.

Kindermans, J., and F. Matthys. 2001. "Introductory Note: The Access to Essential Medicines Campaign." *Tropical Medicine and International Health* 6, 11:955–56.

Kremer, M. 2001. "Public Policies to Stimulate the Development of Vaccines and Drugs for Neglected Diseases." Commission on Macroeconomics and Health Working Paper Series, Work Group 2, Paper 8. www.cmhealth.org/docs/wg2_paper8.pdf

Kremer, M., and R. Glennerster. 2004. *Strong Medicine: Creating Incentives for Pharmaceutical Research on Neglected Diseases*. Princeton: Princeton University Press.

Landes, D. 1998. *The Wealth and Poverty of Nations: Why Some Are So Rich and Some So Poor*. New York: Norton.

Lanjouw, J. O. 2001. "A Proposal to Use Patent Law to Lower Drug Prices in Developing Countries." Commission on Macroeconomics and Health Working Paper Series, Work Group 2, Paper 11. www.cmhealth.org/docs/wg2_paper11.pdf

———. 2002a. "A New Global Patent Regime for Diseases: U.S. and International Legal Issues." *Harvard Journal of Law and Technology* 16, no. 1:85–124.

———. 2002b. "Beyond TRIPS: A New Global Patent Regime." *Policy Brief No. 3*. Washington, D.C.: Center for Global Development.

———. 2003a. "A Proposed Solution to the TRIPS Debate over Pharmaceuticals." *Technological Innovation and Intellectual Property Newsletter* 2003, no. 3. Also available at http://www.researchoninnovation.org/tiip/index.htm

———. 2003b. "Intellectual Property and the Availability of Pharmaceuticals in Poor Countries. In *National Bureau of Economic Research Innovation Policy and the Economy*, vol. 3. Cambridge, Mass.: MIT Press.

Loff, B. 2002. "World Trade Organization Wrestles with Access to Cheap Drugs Solution." *Lancet* 360, no. 9346:1670.

Milanovic, B. 2002. "True World Income Distribution, 1988 and 1993: First Calculation Based on Household Surveys Alone." *Economic Journal* 112:51–92. Also available at www.blackwellpublishers.co.uk/specialarticles/ecoj50673.pdf

Miller, D. 2001. "Distributing Responsibilities." *Journal of Political Philosophy* 9, no. 4:453–71.

MSF (Médecins Sans Frontières). 2001. *Fatal Imbalance: The Crisis in Research and Development for Drugs for Neglected Diseases*. Geneva: Médecins Sans Frontières.

Murphy, L. 2000. *Moral Demands in Non-Ideal Theory*. Oxford: Oxford University Press.

Musgrave, R. A., and A. T. Peacock, eds. 1958. *Classics in the Theory of Public Finance*. London: Macmillan.

Nagel, T. 1977. "Poverty and Food: Why Charity Is Not Enough." In *Food Policy: The Responsibility of the United States in Life and Death Choices*, edited by P. Brown and H. Shue, 54–62. New York: The Free Press.

———. 1991. *Equality and Partiality*. Oxford: Oxford University Press.

Nussbaum, M. C. (with respondents). 1996. *For Love of Country: Debating the Limits of Patriotism*. Boston: Beacon Press.

———. 2000. *Women and Human Development: The Capabilities Approach*. Cambridge: Cambridge University Press.

———. 2001. *Women and Human Development*. Cambridge: Cambridge University Press.

Nussbaum, M. C., and J. Glover, eds. 1995. *Women, Culture, and Development: A Study of Human Capabilities*. Oxford: Oxford University Press.

Nussbaum, M. C., and A. K. Sen, eds. 1993. *The Quality of Life*. Oxford: Oxford University Press.

Okin, S. 1989. *Justice, Gender, and the Family*. New York: Basic Books.

———. 1986. *Faces of Hunger*. London: Allen and Unwin.

———. 1974. "Lifeboat Earth." *Philosophy and Public Affairs* 4: 273–92.

Orbinski, J. 2001. "Health, Equity and Trade: A Failure in Global Governance." In *The Role of the World Trade Organization in Global Governance*, edited by G. Sampson, 223–41. Tokyo: United Nations University Press.

Parfit, D. 1984. *Reasons and Persons*. Oxford: Oxford University Press.

Pecoul, B. 1999. "Access to Essential Drugs in Poor Countries—Reply." *Journal of the American Medical Association* 282, no. 7:631.

Pecoul, B., P. Chirac, P. Trouiller, and J. Pinel. 1999. "Access to Essential Drugs in Poor Countries—A Lost Battle?" *Journal of the American Medical Association* 281, no. 4:361–67.

Pennock, J. R., and J. W. Chapman, eds. 1981. *Human Rights*. New York: New York University Press.

———. 1982. *Ethics, Economics, and the Law*. New York: New York University Press.

Pogge, T. W. 1989. *Realizing Rawls*. Ithaca: Cornell University Press.

———, ed. 2001. *Global Justice*. Oxford: Blackwell.

———. 2002a. *World Poverty and Human Rights: Cosmopolitan Responsibilities and Reforms*. Cambridge: Polity Press.

———. 2002b. "Human Rights and Human Responsibilities." In *Global Justice and Transnational Politics*, edited by P. de Greiff and C. Cronin, 151–95. Cambridge, Mass.: MIT Press.

———. 2004. "The First U.N. Millennium Development Goal." *Journal of Human Development* 5, no. 3:377–97.

———. Forthcoming. "Relational Conceptions of Justice: Responsibilities for Health Outcomes." In *Public Health, Ethics, and Equity*, edited by S. Anand, F. Peter, and A. K. Sen, 135–62. Oxford: Oxford University Press.

Pogge, T. W., and S. G. Reddy. 2003. "Unknown: The Extent, Distribution, and Trend of Global Income Poverty." Available at www.social analysis.org.

Ramsey, S. 2001. "No Closure in Sight for the 10/90 Health-Research Gap." *Lancet* 358:1348.

Rawls, J. 1996. *Political Liberalism*. New York: Columbia University Press. Original published in 1993.

———. 1999a. *A Theory of Justice*. Cambridge, Mass.: Harvard University Press. Original published in 1971.

———. 1999b. *The Law of Peoples*. Cambridge, Mass.: Harvard University Press.

———. 2001. *Justice as Fairness: A Brief Restatement*. Cambridge, Mass.: Harvard University Press.

Reddy, S. G., and T. W. Pogge. Forthcoming. "How *Not* to Count the Poor." Forthcoming in an anthology edited by S. Anand and J. Stiglitz. Also available at www.socialanalysis.org

Roemer, J. 1996. *Theories of Distributive Justice*. Cambridge, Mass.: Harvard University Press.

Rome Declaration on World Food Security. 1996, www.fao.org/wfs/

Rorty, R. 1996. "Who Are We?: Moral Universalism and Economic Triage." *Diogenes* 173:5–15.

Ruggie, J. G. 1998. *Constructing the World Polity*. London: Routledge.

Sachs, J., and P. Malaney. 2002. "The Economic and Social Burden of Malaria." *Nature* 415, no. 6872:680–85.

Scanlon, T. M. 1998. *What We Owe to Each Other*. Cambridge, Mass.: Harvard University Press.

Scheffler, S. 2001. *Boundaries and Allegiances*. Oxford: Oxford University Press.

Scherer, F. M., and J. Watal. 2001. "Post-TRIPS Options for Access to Patented Medicines in Developing Countries." Commission on Macroeconomics and Health Working Paper Series, Work Group 4, Paper 1. www.cmhealth.org/docs/wg4_paper1.pdf

Schüklenk, U. 2001. "Affordable Access to Essential Medication in Developing Countries: Conflicts Between Ethical and Economic Imperatives." *Journal of Medicine and Philosophy* 27, no. 2:179–95.

Sen, A. K. 1981. *Poverty and Famines*. Oxford: Oxford University Press.

———. 1982. *Choice, Welfare and Measurement*. Cambridge: Cambridge University Press.

————. 1984. *Resources, Values, and Development*. Cambridge, Mass.: Harvard University Press.

————. 1987. *The Standard of Living*. Cambridge: Cambridge University Press.

————. 1992. *Inequality Reexamined*. Cambridge, Mass.: Harvard University Press.

————. 1999. *Commodities and Capabilities*. Delhi: Oxford University Press. Original published in 1985.

————. 2000. *Development as Freedom*. New York: Anchor Books.

Sen, A. K., and B. Williams, eds. 1982. *Utilitarianism and Beyond*. Cambridge: Cambridge University Press.

Shue, H. 1996. *Basic Rights: Subsistence, Affluence, and U.S. Foreign Policy*. Princeton: Princeton University Press. Original published in 1980.

Singer, P. 1972. "Famine, Affluence and Morality." *Philosophy and Public Affairs* 1, no. 3:229–43.

————. 1993. *Practical Ethics*. 2nd edition. Cambridge: Cambridge University Press.

————. 2002. *One World: The Ethics of Globalization*. New Haven: Yale University Press.

Smith, A. 1976. *The Wealth of Nations*. Oxford: Clarendon Press. Original published in 1776.

————. 1982. *A Theory of the Moral Sentiments*. Indianapolis: Liberty Classics. Original published in 1759.

Smith, R., R. Beaglehole, D. Woodward, and N. Drager. 2003. *Global Public Goods for Health: Health, Economic, and Public Health Perspectives*. Oxford: Oxford University Press.

Stansfield, S. K., M. Harper, G. Lamb, and J. Lob-Levyt. 2002. "Innovative Financing of International Public Goods for Health." Commission on Macroeconomics and Health Working Paper Series, Work Group 2, Paper 22. http://www.cmhealth.org/docs/wg2_paper22.pdf

Stiglitz, J. 2002. *Globalization and Its Discontents*. Harmondsworth: Penguin.

Townsend, P., N. Davidson, and M. Whitehead. 1990. *Inequalities in Health: The Black Report and the Health Divide*. London: Penguin.

Trouiller, P., P. Olliaro, E. Torreele, J. Orbinski, R. Laing, and N. Ford. 2002. "Drug Development for Neglected Diseases: A Deficient Market and a Public-Health Policy Failure." *Lancet* 359, no. 9324:2188–94. Also available at www.accessmed-msf.org/prod/publications.asp?scntid = 2592002174315&contenttype = PARA&

Trouiller, P., E. Torreele, P. Olliaro, N. White, S. Foster, D. Wirth, et al. 2001. "Drugs for Neglected Diseases: A Failure of the Market and a Public Health Failure?" *Tropical Medicine and International Health* 6, no. 11:945–51.

UDHR (Universal Declaration of Human Rights), approved and proclaimed by the General Assembly of the United Nations on December 10, 1948, as Resolution 217 A (III).

U.N. Millennium Declaration, General Assembly Resolution 55/2, 2000, www.un.org/millennium/declaration/ares552e.htm

UNCTAD (United Nations Conference on Trade and Development). 1999. *Trade and Development Report 1999*. New York: U.N. Publications. Also available at http://www.unctad.org/en/docs/tdr99ove.en.pdf

UNDP (United Nations Development Programme). 1998. *Human Development Report 1998*. New York: Oxford University Press. http://hdr.undp.org/reports/global/1998/en/

———. 1999. *Human Development Report 1999*. New York: Oxford University Press. http://hdr.undp.org/reports/global/1999/en/

———. 2001. *Human Development Report 2001*. New York: Oxford University Press. Also available at http://hdr.undp.org/reports/global/2001/en/

———. 2003. *Human Development Report 2003*. New York: Oxford University Press. Also available at http://hdr.undp.org/reports/global/2003/

———. 2004. *Human Development Report 2004*. New York: UNDP. Also available at http://hdr.undp.org/reports/global/2004/

UNICEF (United Nations Children's Fund). 2002. *The State of the World's Children 2002*. New York: UNICEF. Also available at www.unicef.org/sowc02/pdf/sowc2002-eng-full.pdf

USDA (United States Department of Agriculture). 1999. *U.S. Action Plan on Food Security*. Washington, D.C.: USDA. Also available at www.fas.usda.gov/icd/summit/usactplan.pdf

Velasquez, G., and P. Boulet. 1999. "Essential Drugs in the New International Economic Environment." *Bulletin of the World Health Organization* 77, no. 3:288–92.

Wallerstein, I. 1984. *The Politics of the World Economy*. Cambridge: Cambridge University Press.

Watal, J. 2000. "Access to Essential Medicines in Developing Countries: Does the WTO TRIPS Agreement Hinder It?" Science, Technology, and Innovation Discussion Paper No. 8, Harvard Center for Interna tional Development. www2.cid.harvard.edu/cidbiotech/dp/discussion8.pdf

WHO (World Health Organisation). 2000. *WHO Medicines Strategy: Framework for Action in Essential Drugs and Medicines Policy 2000–2003*. Geneva: WHO Publications.

———. 2001. *Macroeconomics and Health: Investing in Health for Economic Development: Report of the Commission on Macroeconomics and Health*. Geneva: WHO Publications. Also available at http://www3.who.int/whosis/cmh/cmh_report/report.cfm?path = whosis,cmh,cmh_report& language = english#

————. 2003. *World Health Report 2003: Shaping the Future*. Geneva: WHO Publications.

————. 2004a. *Medicines and the Idea of Essential Drugs (EDM)*. Geneva: WHO Publications. Also available at www.who.int/medicines/rationale.shtml

————. 2004b. *The World Health Report 2004*. Geneva: WHO Publications. Also available at www.who.int/whr/2004

WHO and WTO (World Trade Organisation). 2002. *WTO Agreements and Public Health: A Joint Report of the World Health Organisation (WHO) and the Secretariat of the World Trade Organisation (WTO)*. Geneva: Secretariat of the WTO.

Wilkinson, R. G., ed. 1986. *Class and Health: Research and Longitudinal Data*. London: Tavistock.

Wilkinson, R. G. 1996. *Unhealthy Societies: The Afflictions of Inequality*. London: Routledge.

WIPO (World Intellectual Property Organization). 2000. *Patent Protection and Access to HIV/AIDS Pharmaceuticals in Sub-Saharan Africa*. Washington, D.C.: International Intellectual Property Institute.

Woodward, D. 2001. "Trade Barriers and Prices of Essential Health-Sector Inputs." Commission on Macroeconomics and Health Working Paper Series, Work Group 4, Paper 9. www.cmhealth.org/docs/wg4_paper9.pdf

World Bank. 1993. *World Development Report 1993: Investing in Health*. New York: Oxford University Press.

————. 2004. *World Development Report 2004*. New York: Oxford University Press.

WTO (World Trade Organization). "TRIPs and Pharmaceutical Patents, Fact Sheet." www.wto.org/english/tratop_e/trips_e/factsheet_phar m00_e.htm

————. "Pharmaceutical Patents and the TRIPs Agreement." www.wto.org/english/tratop_e/trips_e/pharma_ato186_e.htm

11

JUST INTERNATIONAL MONETARY ARRANGEMENTS

SANJAY G. REDDY

The existence of money and credit is an integral and probably unavoidable feature of complex, modern societies. How money and credit are supplied, how much, to whom, and when has significant implications for the nature, quantity, and distribution of goods and services produced and consumed. This fact has made money and credit subjects of enduring and central interest for economists. The frequent occurrence of currency crises—recently (in the late 1990s) in East Asia, Latin America, and Russia—and their dramatic social consequences have also made money and monetary institutions focal points for activists and policy-makers. Yet despite the acknowledged centrality of monetary arrangements in modern economies, they have received surprisingly little attention from philosophers concerned with distributive justice, whether in the national or the global context. I define monetary arrangements here broadly as the accustomed practices and rules governing the creation, distribution, and management of money and credit. Rather, monetary decisions can have real effects on the level and distribution of advantages. There is therefore a need to integrate considerations related to money and credit into a fully adequate and practically relevant account of international distributive justice.

The lack of attention of philosophers to monetary arrangements reflects the preference of recent philosophical discourse to focus on the normative justifications for specific distributions of advantage (resources, freedom, or well-being) rather than on the details of the institutional arrangements that produce these distributions (see, e.g., Dworkin 1981, 185–243; Sen 1992). It also reflects the need to possess a degree of specialized knowledge of economic facts and reasoning, which can appear difficult to gain.

Since monetary arrangements can play a role in the "basic structure" that determines distributions of advantage, it may be important to assess how they should be designed in identifying the form of just international institutions. Any discussion of the requirements of international distributive justice other than the most abstract must address such institutional questions. Lack of attention to the specificities of economic institutions can have severe consequences in terms of the realism and applicability of theories of distributive justice.

An adequate account of how international monetary institutions should be structured would depend on the conception of international distributive justice that governs the assessment of institutions. I will not defend a highly specific conception of international distributive justice here but instead will assume the acceptance of some form of global egalitarianism—a doctrine that, broadly put, improvement in the level of advantage of less-advantaged individuals is to be pursued as an important goal (possibly one among many), regardless of where these individuals live. The advantage of individuals may be understood in terms of resources, well-being, or freedoms. Global egalitarianism, as employed here, is a weak doctrine, as it does not require a commitment to strict equality, or even a concern for *relative* inequalities as such. Moreover, it does not demand that improving the circumstances of the less advantaged should take a specific degree of precedence over improving the circumstances of the more advantaged. The doctrine as defined here demands merely that the former goal should be held to be "important," a criterion that is chosen to be deliberately vague. Global egalitarianism can be consistent with, but is different from, both prioritarian views (which stress the importance of improving the condition of the worst off without being committed to diminishing relative inequalities) and sufficientarian views (which stress the importance of ensuring that persons achieve an adequate minimum level of advantages). I adopt this broad position in order to show that even weak normative positions which give some weight to the interests of the globally less advantaged may plausibly require significant reforms in the international monetary system. The empirical arguments that I will examine might also be used to show that doctrines outside the global egalitarian family of views, such as those that stress the importance of purely procedural values, like avoiding injury to others, also carry strong implications for the reform of current institutional arrangements. However, my focus will not primarily be on implications of this kind.

I will explore below the kinds of reasoning that global egalitarians should undertake when assessing monetary arrangements. It may, of course, be easier to agree that existing monetary arrangements fail to satisfy fully the requirements of justice than to agree upon the institutions that should be adopted in their place. Judgments concerning how the justice of institutions may be enhanced are likely to be influenced by practical assessments of what institutions are feasible as well as by the specificities of the conception of justice adopted as a guide to moral judgment.[1] Although I will not advocate any specific reform proposal, I will attempt to show that global egalitarians should be critical of

---

[1] Proponents of alternative conceptions of justice may differ on the shape of fully just institutions and yet form an overlapping consensus as to specific ways in which existing institutions may be incrementally more just.

existing international monetary arrangements, and be vigorous and imaginative in their pursuit of alternatives that enhance international distributive justice.

My focus here is on the "middle range" of normative arguments regarding international distributive justice which lies between abstract considerations about the nature and extent of the claims that we may make upon one another, on the one hand, and the concrete ethical dilemmas faced by individuals in everyday life that arise when existing institutions are taken as given, on the other. This is therefore an exercise in realistically utopian reasoning. Existing monetary arrangements are extremely diverse and complex. To add to the challenge of taking adequate note of this diversity and complexity, normative reasoning must consider possible alternatives to existing institutions. Therefore such reasoning is necessarily partially speculative, in the sense that it must extend beyond empirical observations and be informed by imaginative reasoning.

Monetary Arrangements in the World Economy

The world is divided into multiple currency zones, frequently coextensive with nation-states. Monies are typically issued by states, which also often regulate private and public financial transactions and commitments involving the exchange of money and the creation and discharge of credit obligations. Markets for money and credit have an international as well as a national dimension: flows of money and credit take place across borders. These flows have significant implications of interest to global egalitarians.

There are at least three categories of questions concerning money and credit that can be raised in the international context. These questions, relating respectively to money supply, exchange rates, and debts, exemplify rather than exhaust the dilemmas that arise with regard to international monetary arrangements. First, who should have control over key monetary decisions, such as how much, and on what terms, money and credit are being supplied within each monetary zone? Should this control belong to the citizens of a given monetary zone or their representatives alone? How should the benefits arising from the ability to create money be distributed internationally? Second, should the stability of exchange rates be a goal and, if so, how should the responsibility for maintaining stability be apportioned? When adjustment of exchange rates is required, who should bear the burdens associated with such adjustment? Third, what arrangements should govern the accumulation and discharge of debts in the international setting? In what respects should debts contracted by states be governed by different rules than debts contracted by private agents? What forms of conditionality may be imposed by creditors, such as international institutions, governments, or private lenders, as part of a just framework of international borrowing and repayment?

Control over Monetary Decisions

Decisions taken by the government or, often, the central bank of a state can have significant external effects that are felt by populations beyond that state's borders. These can operate through various channels, from their impact on the exchange rate between countries, and thereby on relative prices, affecting the pattern of trade and capital flows, to their effect on the cost of borrowing in the world at large.

The substantial external effects of monetary decisions can generate obligations to take into account the concerns of non-citizens or justify claims on the part of non-citizens that they be consulted about, or included in the making of, the decisions. These obligations and claims are likely to be especially strong when the globally disadvantaged are adversely affected by these monetary decisions.

A significant case of the international externalities associated with national monetary policy is that of the developing country debt crisis that emerged dramatically in the early 1980s and that has continued for a number of countries in chronic form to this day. It is widely agreed that one of the main reasons for the emergence of the debt crisis was the sharp rise in world real interest rates that occurred in that period primarily as a result of the simultaneous tightening of U.S. monetary policy, itself a response to the domestic inflationary circumstances of the late 1970s, and expansion in U.S. government expenditures as a response to the domestic recession of the early 1980s (see, e.g., James 1996). Since the major world markets for loanable funds are closely linked, the rise in U.S. real interest rates influenced the cost of borrowing in the world as a whole. This rise in world real interest rates made it difficult for many countries with large debt stocks to maintain solvency. The social and economic costs that arose from the decrease in public and private investment and social expenditure that resulted from monetary contraction, fiscal retrenchment, and policy reorientation in these countries are by now well known (see, famously, Cornia, Jolly, and Stewart 1987). It is difficult to establish that the rise in world real interest rates was the decisive factor in the debt crisis. It is possible that in the absence of the crisis many of the countries concerned would have eventually faced problems of insolvency. However, it is clear at the very least that the timing and scale of the debt crisis were linked to the rise in world real interest rates. The developing country debt crisis was an unintended consequence of U.S. monetary policy. When it was confronted at a late stage as an independently important policy issue, it was primarily because of the threat that the debt crisis posed to the stability of the world economic system as a whole (James 1996).

The causal mechanism underlying the debt crisis was a special case of a more general one, which is that the supply of the main global currencies significantly determines the global supply of loanable funds, or liquidity, and thereby the cost of borrowing in the world market, which has an impact on individual countries in more than one way. First, as countries typically possess a stock of debt that is continuously rolled over, increases in the cost of borrowing influence the cost of repayment, and thereby the resources remaining to countries after their debt service obligations have been met, as well as countries' capacity for debt repayment. Second, the cost of borrowing influences the level of domestic income. For instance, an increase in the cost of borrowing in the global market can discourage investment and consumption, which can lower domestic income and diminish growth. This can happen because the cost of borrowing in domestic capital markets is linked to the cost of borrowing in global capital markets, as foreign borrowing and domestic borrowing act as partial substitutes from the point of view of the government or private agents permitted to borrow abroad, or because the cost of borrowing in global capital markets influences the level of economic activity outside a country, and thereby the demand for goods from as well as the supply of investment funds to it. Of course, these linkages may be of diverse kinds. It is certainly possible that investment inflows to a country may increase as a result of the slowing of economic activity elsewhere. However, insofar as the foreign investors' animal spirits—Keynes's famous description of the psychological dispositions that influence investment—to any given country are determined primarily by the global level of economic activity, that is unlikely to be true. The cost of borrowing may also have an impact on the level of economic activity through the indirect influence that it exerts on the balance of payments of a country and thereby its exchange rate, which in turn has effects on the level and distribution of incomes within a country.

These forms of dependence on the world credit market, and thereby on other countries' monetary policy decisions, are faced to some extent by all countries. However, developing countries experience them in the most acute way, due to their often heavy indebtedness, their dependence on imported capital to finance investment, their vulnerability to fluctuations in export earnings and import costs, which is related to their dependence on primary commodity exports and weak manufacturing capabilities, and their insignificant role in determining world real interest rates because of the small size of their economies.

Capital-scarce developing countries can suffer great costs to their development programs as a result of high costs of capital. For this reason a recurrent feature of North–South debates over the last three decades has been the call by developing countries for fresh infusions of loanable funds to the global system, and for increases in the quantity of loanable funds to which developing countries have access. In particular, developing countries have regularly called for increases in the quantity of funds available to be borrowed at lower rates through the International Development Agency—the concessionary lending facility of the World Bank—and other official lenders as well as for new issues of Special Drawing Rights, the hard currency line of credit available to member countries of the International Monetary Fund (see, e.g., James 1996; Ezekiel 1998; Soros 2002). Developing countries typically have a bias toward liquidity in the world system as a result of their developmental needs for capital and the structural constraints which make it difficult to meet these needs for capital purely from internal sources. In contrast, developed countries may have a bias against liquidity which derives from the desire to combat inflation.

Decisions that affect world real interest rates and credit availability are unlikely to be those that are in the best interests of developing countries, or even that are efficient from a global point of view, simply because they are not made with those goals in mind. As one author has noted:

> That a monetary system in which a substantial part of world liquidity is met by the accumulation of the short-term obligations of one or a few reserve-currency countries cannot be considered efficient has been pointed out by Robert Triffin in several of his writings. Such a monetary system is . . . highly dependent on the decisions of a few individual countries. Unfortunately, excessive concern with the liquidity requirements of the world monetary system has led many economists to ignore . . . 'the highly erratic and unpredictable factor' arising from the dependence on a few individual countries for the creation and acceptance of world liquidity. (Gulati 1980, 15)

There is a strong case to be made from the standpoint of global distributive justice that southern interests should be considered when monetary policy decisions that significantly influence global costs of capital and global levels of economic activity are made. Global egalitarians will agree that this is so to the extent that the external effects of key monetary policy decisions can worsen the life chances of disadvantaged individuals in the world. Even those who do not focus on the consequentialist considerations of interest to global egalitarians but subscribe to other moral principles, such as that of refraining from causing significant harms, may also see the merit of this view.

One way to ensure that southern interests are adequately considered is to provide for some form of joint consultation, or even joint decision-making. There are currently a number of groupings of countries, such as the G-20, and, within the Bretton Woods structure, the Development Committee and the International Monetary and Financial Committee, drawn jointly from the North and South, that take the role of monitoring global economic developments and making policy recommendations. However, their influence over the world economy is minor in comparison with that of groupings such as the G-8 that represent the rich countries alone. The calls for a Global Economic Security Council that would have a more substantive role reflect a somewhat more significant step in this direction (see, e.g., Commission on Global Governance 1995). Nevertheless, as long as monetary authorities in the rich countries act with substantial independence even of their own governments and are mandated to further the economic self-interest of their own citizens alone, these measures are unlikely to have any discernible impact.

Another important monetary externality with which developing countries are faced occurs because the main reserve currencies in the world belong to rich countries. All countries must attempt to accumulate and maintain some amount of internationally accepted means of payment in order to facilitate external trade and payments and to defend the value of their own currency. In addition to gold, the main internationally accepted means of payment are the currencies of a select number of countries, which, due to their economic prosperity and political stability, are trusted to maintain their value and viability as means of payment. In the postwar era, the currency that has had unquestioned predominance as a reserve unit has been the U.S. dollar.

An important issue of international distributive justice that arises in relation to the role of the U.S. dollar and other currencies of rich countries as reserves is that the benefits arising from their creation accrue largely to the countries that produce them. These benefits are of diverse kinds. Reserve-issuing countries gain seignorage, or the revenue that emerges from the creation of money. In addition, they face less stringent balance-of-payments constraints than countries that rely on others to issue reserves. When running a balance-of-payments deficit, reserve-issuing countries can rely on foreign demand to absorb the net injections of their currencies abroad. The elastic foreign demand for reserve currencies permits the countries that produce them—at present most notably the United States—to generate balance-of-payments deficits representing a net transfer of resources from other countries without facing disciplines in the form of depreciating currency and rising costs of borrowing comparable to those faced by others.

An important distributional consequence of the world demand for a reserve currency is that it leads to the ability of the reserve-producing country to command current goods and services from abroad or assets that represent claims on future goods and services, in return for the issuance of the reserve currency. This leads to a regressive transfer of resources from the developing countries to the developed ones, insofar as the former are forced to hold the currencies of the latter as internationally acceptable reserves: "By allowing the national currencies of one or two countries to perform the reserve-currency role, the world monetary system is clearly allowing the reserve-currency countries to become net recipients of current resources or to gain command over future resources from the rest of the world" (Gulati 1980, 15). The amounts involved are sizable. At the end of 2001, $1.25 trillion worth of official foreign exchange reserves alone were held by major nonindustrial countries. Moreover, on average more than 75 percent of official foreign exchange reserves were held in the form of U.S. dollars.[2] In addition, specific reserve currencies are used outside the reserve-issuing country, as the U.S. dollar is in relation to a range of international markets such as the oil market, and within countries that have undertaken dollarization, such as Ecuador and El Salvador. This expands the zone within which the reserve currency is required to facilitate transactions and the ability of the reserve-producing country to issue new currency, gain seignorage, perhaps at the expense of other countries, and issue debt without incurring exchange rate depreciation or increases in the cost of borrowing comparable to those that would be otherwise experienced.

A possible response to the regressive transfer implicit in the uneven possession of the reserve-creating privilege is to provide compensatory transfers of resources that implicitly or explicitly share the advantages resulting from this privilege. A more imaginative alternative may be, as advocated by Gulati, to create new reserve assets backed by goods such as primary commodities that are in the possession of developing countries.

The Stability of Exchange Rates

The stability and, at least, the orderly adjustment of exchange rates have long been considered important goals for the international monetary system. A major reason for upholding these goals has been the belief that a stable monetary system is likely to lead to greater predictability of the business environment and, consequently, a more rapid expansion of trade and investment with a resulting increase in national and world income growth. Stability of exchange rates is also associated with stability of prices at the national level, which is perceived to have analogous benefits.

Under the postwar Bretton Woods system, which lasted through the early 1970s, the stability of exchange rates was maintained through countries' commitment to maintain agreed par values, or fixed exchange rates with respect to the U.S. dollar, except in special circumstances, as determined by the International Monetary Fund (IMF). The maintenance of par values was pursued as a goal partially in response to the perception that in the interwar period competitive devaluations had been a major destabilizing factor that had led to the collapse of open trade and contributed to the Great Depression. The Bretton Woods system in contrast sought to create the stable institutional conditions within which trade could expand without this threat.

[2] For these figures, see Bank for International Settlements 2002, 82. Gulati 1980 shows that the amounts involved in the 1970s were very substantial.

However, the Bretton Woods system gave the entire responsibility for adjustment of payments imbalances to countries running deficits. This meant that a country experiencing persistent deficits as a result of an overvalued exchange rate would be required to reduce them through devaluation, restrictions on capital outflows and imports, and other, possibly painful, changes to its policy regime. Surplus countries, in particular the United States, bore no responsibility for modifying their policies. This detail was of special concern to the United Kingdom, which foresaw during the negotiations that led to the Bretton Woods system that it would run persistent balance-of-payments deficits as a result of its weak industrial position, its substantial foreign liabilities, and the demands of reconstruction in the aftermath of the war. It fought hard to have included in the Articles of Agreement of the IMF a clause requiring surplus countries to bear some of the burden of adjustment. This clause has never been invoked in practice, however. Under the more flexible exchange rate system—more accurately described as a "non-system" since each country is free to manage exchange rates in its own way—that has followed the collapse of the Bretton Woods fixed exchange rate regime in the early 1970s, the governing principle has been that deficit countries must bear the burden of adjustment. Only a few cases are exceptions, such as the bilateral relationship between Japan and the United States, in which the former has taken substantial de facto responsibility for reducing its surplus.

The principle that deficit countries should bear the burden of adjustment is of substantial interest from the standpoint of distributive justice. In one view, persistent deficits result from irresponsible overspending of resources by countries, and as a result primary responsibility for remedying deficits must rest with them. There is also a contrary view, however. The principle that deficit countries ought to bear the burden of adjustment may be questioned on the grounds that some deficits are the consequence of factors that are in the control of countries only to a limited extent. Many poorer countries may be at greater risk of recurrent and unsustainable balance-of-payments deficits than richer countries regardless of how responsibly they manage their macroeconomic policies. This is partly because they are more likely to be dependent on a small range of commodity exports, the values of which are fluctuating, making a bad run that causes depletion of foreign exchange reserves more likely. Moreover, structural deficits can be generated by the progress of development itself, which can require net importation and borrowing. For instance, imports of capital goods are required in order to invest in facilities and initiate production. As a result of their already weak balance-of-payments position, many developing countries are exceptionally vulnerable to increases in their import bill, as evidenced by the experience of the oil-importing developing countries during various oil price shocks. Finally, the fiscal discipline required to maintain a balance-of-payments equilibrium may be much more costly in human terms at low levels of income than at high levels. One can think here, for example, of the large bills for importation of staple foods of some poor countries that have specialized in nonstaple food crops or that have weak or variable agricultural capabilities. In these cases, fiscal "indiscipline" might arise from the necessity to fulfill human needs. This is not an argument for overlooking irresponsibility, but rather for taking note that balance-of-payments deficits often do not result from it.

Poorer countries disproportionately suffer from balance-of-payments deficits caused by factors beyond their control. Moreover, the human costs of balance-of-payments adjustment in poor countries can be severe. Egalitarians ought therefore to favor principles by which some of the burden of adjustment is taken up by surplus countries, at least under some circumstances. The Oil Facility created at the IMF in the 1970s to enable poor countries to meet the rapidly rising cost of oil imports is an instance of the acceptance of a shared responsibility for balance-of-payments adjustment, which emerged from the recognition that oil-importing poor countries' balance-of-payments deficits in this period were caused by factors beyond their control. A more general example is the IMF's Compensatory and Contingency Financing Facility, which exists to provide emergency finance to help countries cope with certain unanticipated external shocks, such as changes in export prices or increases in the cost of cereal imports. However, although these facilities provide a partial cushion for the effect of exogenous shocks by allowing the distribution of their burden over time through permitting countries to borrow, they do little to share this burden across countries. Global egalitarians should favor both an approach to the management of the international economy that diminishes the adverse external shocks to which poor countries are subject and a fuller sharing of the burden.

In the post–Bretton Woods regime, as often volatile private capital flows have become increasingly sizable and have begun to dwarf public resources, a new issue has arisen of how to manage exchange rates in the presence of these flows (Bordo, Eichengreen, and Irwin 1999). Significant issues of distributive justice arise in this regard that have been discussed relatively little. In particular, exchange rates may vary substantially over time as a result of changes in private agents' expectations and sentiments even when the underlying features of the real economy do not change. In such circumstances it may be difficult to maintain exchange rates within a given range, even if there is an extensive commitment of governmental resources to intervene in the market. There is the possibility that there is a fundamental indeterminacy in market-determined exchange rates—that is, under the same circumstances, there are different possible exchange rate values that depend only on investors' sentiments (Furman and Stiglitz 1999; Stiglitz 1998). Exchange rates have substantial implications for rates of return to business activities, the allocation of resources across sectors of an economy, and the cost of essential commodities. Fluctuations in exchange rates that correspond to changes in investors' sentiments rather than changes in underlying market fundamentals raise issues of distributive justice because the prime beneficiaries of the ability to undertake large and speculative international capital flows may be different from those who bear most of the cost of market volatility and adverse outcomes, notably including the global poor.

Instructive examples in this regard are provided by the East Asian financial crises of the late 1990s. In a number of these crises, exchange rates proved unsustainable as private market agents sought to liquidate the domestic assets they held. These crises may have had an element of self-fulfilling expectations (see, e.g., Stiglitz 2002). Prior to these crises, high levels of domestic and foreign investor and creditor confidence led to a robust inflow of funds that supported the value of domestic assets. Highly priced domestic assets were often used as collateral to back debts, which were sometimes denominated in foreign currencies. The asset values were high enough to offer creditors the confidence to hold the debt. Conversely, diminished asset values led to diminished investor and creditor confidence that brought about a diminished flow of funds to asset markets and reinforced the lower values for the assets. Because many of these assets had been used as collateral, their collapse led in turn to a weakened banking system and diminished credit availability that harmed the productive, as well as the speculative, economy. Although this process, typical of scenarios in which asset bubbles arise, may not have been entirely driven by the expectations of foreign capital holders, its rapidity and size were undoubtedly accentuated by them because of the impact of their large inflows and withdrawals of capital on exchange rates and asset values.

The movement from high to low levels of creditor and investor confidence had a significant social as well as economic cost. In particular, the sharp deterioration of asset values, depreciation of exchange rates, and diminished availability of credit in the countries affected by financial crises caused bankruptcies of domestic firms and sharply higher prices for a variety of essential commodities such as imported foodstuffs and pharmaceuticals, which had significant consequent effects on consumers. Dramatic scenes of massive reverse migration from cities to rural areas in countries such as Indonesia testified to the depth of the crisis. The possibility that an arbitrary shift in international private agents' sentiments led to massive adverse social consequences in poor countries offers cause for concern.[3] If it is also true that free capital mobility offered its benefits primarily to private agents in rich and poor countries who were

---

[3] For instance, Das and Mohapatra 2002 report evidence that stock market liberalization in developing countries typically resulted in income share growth for the top quintile of the income distribution and income share reduction for the middle three quintiles.

well insulated from the human costs of the crises, then the system's distribution of risks and rewards may appear to global egalitarians to be unjust.

There are substantial demands upon empirical inference involved here. If something like this empirical account is the right one, then in a regime of free capital mobility, egalitarians may wish to argue for some international resource transfers that would reduce the social costs of these fluctuations. Egalitarians may also wish to argue for modifications to the rules that govern global capital flows, such as the Tobin Tax on cross-border transactions, which is meant to reduce primarily speculative movements of capital by throwing sand in the wheels of global finance. In the absence of such modifications to the system of rules of global capital movements, global egalitarians may wish to argue at least for the right of countries to pursue national policies that better protect them from the vicissitudes of the system. In particular, global egalitarians might wish to be skeptical of the call for full convertibility on the capital account—the free flow of capital regardless of purpose—to become a goal that international institutions encourage countries to pursue in all circumstances. Recently, the demand made in the mid-1990s to make full capital mobility a formal objective of the IMF has subsided, perhaps due to the embarrassment associated with the financial crises that occurred subsequently (see, e.g., Wade and Veneroso 1998; Bhagwati 1998).

The Accumulation and Discharge of Debt

The international monetary system is not a war of all against all but a system of social cooperation, embodied in the rules of its formal institutions, and reflected in the norms of mutual support that exist between its members.

These rules and norms have often been controversial. For instance, historically, the IMF has established "conditionalities" that require that specific policies be adopted in return for the provision of emergency finance to countries availing of its assistance as a result of their balance-of-payments difficulties. IMF conditionalities have, however, been widely criticized, primarily for reflecting a narrow doctrine concerning what is required to restore a balance-of-payments equilibrium and for applying this doctrine in a manner that has been inattentive to social concerns (Cornia, Jolly, and Stewart 1987).

A possible defense of such conditionalities might lie in an appeal to the "role morality" of international institutions, that is the obligations or permissions that direct or allow them to act in ways they would not be obliged or permitted to follow were it not for the specific role assigned to them within a just scheme of social cooperation. The Articles of Agreement of both the IMF and the World Bank require that they restrict their activities to those that help to promote stated economic objectives. Over time, these objectives have expanded to focus to a greater extent on social criteria, such as poverty reduction, but have never been confined to these goals. Can the pursuit of a mandate that shows limited direct concern with explicit obligations of justice (such as furthering the interests of the globally less advantaged) be defended on grounds that an institution can best further the interests of justice by acting single-mindedly in its assigned role? A justification for international institutions to focus narrowly upon economic goals, such as restoring the balance-of-payments equilibrium, rather than upon broader considerations of justice depends on the truth of empirical postulates, such as, for instance, that in order to obtain the cooperation of sovereign governments, international institutions must restrict themselves to this narrow role, or that the longer-term interests of the poor are best served by the single-minded pursuit of macroeconomic stability. If these propositions are untrue, the case for a role morality of international institutions that requires them to adhere to rules that show little direct attention to principles of justice is diminished. Moreover, the justifiability of a specific role morality for any individual actor will depend on the nature of the overall institutional scheme in which it is placed, and on whether it can be demonstrated that the pursuit of the role that is assigned to a specific institution is that which will best serve desired and justified ends. For instance, the narrow-minded pursuit of macroeconomic goals by some institutions may be easier to justify if there existed complementary institutions that effectively furthered the social goals that other institutions failed to further or even undermined.

A second issue that arises concerns the limits of a voluntarist justification for policy conditionalities. The voluntarist justification holds that conditionalities contained in a voluntary agreement between states or between a state and an international organization are consequently legitimate and cannot be criticized from the standpoint of justice. A reason that this principle may not be fulfilled in the context of international monetary affairs is that difficult background conditions over which agents have no control may cause individual parties to have no acceptable alternative to acquiring funds from international organizations or other governments that are offered in return for the acceptance of policy conditionalities. The issues involved in assessing the degree to which such contracts create binding obligations and confer legitimacy upon the resulting outcomes are similar to those involved in assessing such choices in the case of individuals.[4] Balance-of-payments crises are by their nature circumstances in which few alternatives to seeking external assistance remain. Often, assistance can be gained only at the cost of drastic internal

---

[4] On the distinction between being free to choose and choosing freely, see Cohen 1988.

reorganization and retrenchment that entails significant social costs and is accepted because the failure to acquire external assistance entails even more severe social costs. In this case the circumstances certainly involve difficult background conditions, and it may be argued that the choice being made is fundamentally unfree, although the country is certainly free to have chosen not to enter into the agreement (Cohen 1988).

In such cases, the nature of the conditionalities involved is worthy of careful scrutiny. Conditionalities that are designed to offer advantages to certain parties as a result of the weak bargaining position of others may be deemed exploitative. Justice therefore requires that international actors do not take undue advantage of adverse background conditions to enforce choices that are predominantly in their own interest. The suspicion that the conditionalities imposed by the Bretton Woods institutions are in fact of this type—for instance, because these institutions demand changes in policies that permit access to national economies by foreign capital on more favorable terms—shadows them. The view that the conditionalities put forward are in the ultimate interest of poor nations does not command universal agreement. The existing international financial institutions are the sole providers of emergency finance with a worldwide reach and, moreover, are often the only providers of any kind, and therefore are to a degree monopolistic. They are also viewed as proponents of the interests of private capital rather than those of distributive justice.[5] These considerations compound the widespread perception that currently observed conditionalities have a coercive character. Institutional transformation that diminishes the degree of monopoly of such institutions and that shifts the focus of their objectives should therefore likely be favored by global egalitarians, on both procedural and consequentialist grounds.[6]

A third issue of interest concerns the distribution of risks and rewards between debtors and creditors in the international credit market. Until recently, an unquestioned international norm had been that sovereign borrowers' debts should be repaid in full, irrespective of circumstances. Although ad hoc adjustments in the debt repayment schedules of particular countries were frequently made, to permit an uninterrupted stream of repayments, especially in the case of larger countries, the adjustments made were just that—ad hoc. Creditors fiercely resisted the idea that protection from repayment obligations under specific circumstances should be accepted as a regular principle of international commercial law. Recently, the debate on this issue has opened more widely. Reformers have called for debtor protection concepts derived from domestic bankruptcy law to be recognized in the domain of

[5] On the relationship between the IMF and creditors' interests, see Stiglitz 2002, ch. 8.
[6] See in this regard the important proposal to eliminate this monopoly in Unger 1996.

sovereign debt. The IMF has tentatively advocated an international Chapter 11 and others have called for an international Chapter 9, which refer to the parts of the U.S. bankruptcy code that offer temporary protection from creditors to, respectively, firms and municipalities. The goal is to permit orderly workouts of unmanageable debt obligations, necessary for the maintenance of fundamentally viable economic assets of the debtor and the fulfillment of the debtor country population's basic human requirements. The principle common to these proposals is that the debtor is offered temporary protection from creditors during the course of the reorganization of assets and the restoration of creditworthiness. There are efficiency arguments for reforms of this kind, which center on the need to protect creditors from themselves by diminishing the collective action problems that exist among them. For instance, creditors may be more likely to be repaid if the debtor is permitted to suspend payments temporarily and reorganize assets so as to increase income. However, each creditor may find such a scheme attractive only if they can be assured that other creditors will also agree to it. There are also often overlooked arguments for such reforms from the standpoint of distributive justice, however. Global egalitarians should favor arrangements that distribute risks more evenly between creditors and borrowers and that seek to ensure adequate minimum conditions of life for the populations of highly indebted poor countries, irrespective of their historically incurred debt obligations. These normative considerations should of course be pursued in a manner that takes note of the existence of moral hazard and other incentive problems.

A fourth and overlapping issue of interest is that debtor countries are quite unlike individual debtors in that they represent large collectivities with shifting memberships. Typically, the decision to contract debts is made by a small group of persons who may or may not act as legitimate representatives of a larger group. Even when they do, they may not especially represent the interests of the least advantaged within a society. Moreover, debt obligations can continue over long periods of time and can ultimately be attached to individuals who were not even alive at the time that the debts were contracted. The enormous difficulties that are encountered in attempting to justify the interpersonal and intergenerational transmission of debt obligations, especially for countries where institutions are weak or unrepresentative, place the traditionally accepted theory of sovereign debt in crisis. Global egalitarians must be critical of norms regarding debt repayment that seem to place large burdens upon the young and the poor, who may have benefited little or not at all from historically incurred debt obligations. There appear to be alternative rules for international debt creation and discharge that ensure that orderly and well-functioning credit markets can exist alongside better protection of the interests of the less advantaged. Global egalitarians ought to favor them.

A Realistic Utopia

The international monetary system offers an example of an arena in which "middle-range normative reasoning"—which lies between normative reasoning that seeks to identify the obligations of actors in abstraction from an empirical context and normative reasoning that seeks to identify the obligations of actors in the existing context—and realistic utopianism—normative reasoning that is attentive to constraints of feasibility but seeks to be imaginative in identifying what is feasible—are both essential. An adequate account of the demands and prospects of justice in the international arena requires such reasoning. Reasoning of this kind shows that international monetary arrangements that more fully cohere with the interests of justice are both possible and different from those that currently exist.

Acknowledgments

I would like to thank Christian Barry, Andre Burgstaller, Joseph Carens, Julia Harrington, Jacob Kramer, Andrew Kuper, Thomas Pogge, and Lydia Tomitova for their helpful suggestions and comments.

References

Bank for International Settlements. 2002. "72nd Annual Report of the Bank for International Settlements" (July). Basel.

Bhagwati, Jagdish. 1998. "The Capital Myth: The Difference Between Trade in Widgets and Dollars." *Foreign Affairs* (May/June).

Bordo, Michael, Barry Eichengreen, and Douglas Irwin. 1999. "Is Globalization Today Really Different Than Globalization a Hundred Years Ago?" National Bureau of Economic Research Working Paper No. 7195 (June).

Cohen, Gerald A., ed. 1988. *History, Labour, and Freedom: Themes from Marx*. New York: Clarendon Press.

Commission on Global Governance. 1995. *Our Global Neighborhood*. New York: Oxford University Press.

Cornia, Giovanni Andrea, Richard Jolly, and Frances Stewart. 1987. *Adjustment with a Human Face*. Oxford: Clarendon Press.

Das, Mitali, and Sanket Mohapatra. 2002. "Income Inequality: The Aftermath of Stock Market Liberalization in Emerging Markets." Columbia University Department of Economics Discussion Paper # 0102-42; available at http://www.columbia.edu/cu/economics/dis cpapr/DP0102-42.pdf

Dworkin, Ronald. 1981. "What Is Equality? Part 2: Equality of Resources." In *Philosophy & Public Affairs*, 185–243.

Ezekiel, Hannan. 1998. "The Role of Special Drawing Rights in the International Monetary System." In *International Monetary and Financial Issues for the 1990s*, vol. 9, 71–80. Geneva: UNCTAD.

Furman, Jason, and Joseph Stiglitz. 1999. "Economic Crises: Evidence and Insights from East Asia." *Brookings Papers on Economic Activity* 2:1–114, 128–35.

Gulati, Iqbal. 1980. *International Monetary Development and the Third World: A Proposal to Redress the Balance*. New Delhi: Orient Longman.

James, Harold. 1996. *International Monetary Cooperation since Bretton Woods*. Washington, D.C.: International Monetary Fund.

Sen, Amartya. 1992. *Inequality Re-Examined*. Oxford: Oxford University Press.

Soros, George. 2002. *On Globalization*. New York: Public Affairs.

Stiglitz, Joseph. 1998. "Must Financial Crises Be This Frequent and This Painful?" McKay Lecture, World Bank, Pittsburgh, Pa., September 23; available at www.worldbank.org/html/extdr/extme/js-092398/mckay.pdf

———. 2002. *Globalization and Its Discontents*. New York: Norton.

Unger, Roberto M. 1996. "The Really New Bretton Woods." In *The Financial System under Stress: An Architecture for the New World Economy*, edited by Marc Uzan. New York: Routledge.

Wade, Robert, and Frank Veneroso. 1998. "The Gathering World Slump and the Battle over Capital Controls." *New Left Review* (September/October).

12

THE OWNERSHIP MODEL OF BUSINESS ETHICS

DAVID RODIN

Private corporations are today among the most economically powerful institutional actors in the world. In any discussion of institutions and international justice it is therefore natural to consider the role and moral obligations of corporations, their managers, shareholders, and employees. A significant consensus has developed in recent decades among many academics, NGOs, government agencies, and business leaders that private corporations have moral obligations to a set of "stakeholders" beyond their legal owners. These may include employees, customers, suppliers, the community, and even the environment and future generations. Numerous NGOs and some corporate leaders claim that corporations require a moral "license to operate" from the community, which entails being a good "corporate citizen." A whole academic and advisory industry devoted to "corporate social responsibility" has been established, as well as high-profile international initiatives, such as Kofi Annan's Global Compact.

This emerging consensus, however, is fundamentally challenged by an argument expressed in its most pungent form by the Nobel Prize–winning economist Milton Friedman (Friedman 1999). According to Friedman the moral obligation of managers to stakeholder groups other than shareholders is extremely limited. He believes that it is generally not permissible for managers to forgo legally acquired profits for moral reasons. His argument is simple: managers are employed as agents of the owners of the corporation. Their legal and moral obligation is to manage the assets of the shareholders so as to maximize shareholder returns. If they manage assets so as to fulfill "social responsibilities" and thereby fail to maximize returns, they are wrongfully appropriating resources that do not belong to them. As Friedman says, managers "can do good—but only at their own expense" (1999, 252).[1]

---

[1] Elaine Sternberg puts the point even more strongly, claiming that managing for social responsibility is tantamount to theft: "Managers who employ business funds for anything other than the legitimate business objective are simply embezzling: in using other people's money for their own purposes, they are depriving owners of their property as surely as if they had dipped their hands into the till" (2000, 41).

What is striking about this argument is that it suggests that the institutional relationship between managers and owners profoundly affects the nature and distribution of ordinary moral obligations. Managers are not required to do—indeed, they are required not to do—certain things that would be morally obligatory if they were acting outside the institutional structure, or managing their own assets.

In an intriguing chapter of his book *World Poverty and Human Rights*, Thomas Pogge presents an argument that (although not presented in this context) can be read as a response to Friedman's challenge (see Pogge 2002, ch. 3). His aim is to question the moral efficacy of social arrangements, such as the manager-owner relationship and the institution of nation- states, in altering the pattern of our moral obligations. Managers, suggests Pogge, cannot escape the normal claims morality makes on us by reference to the fact they are acting on behalf of the asset's owners. Nor can owners escape such claims by appointing managerial agents.

In contrast to Pogge, I will argue that social arrangements like the owner-manager relationship can appropriately alter the distribution of moral obligations and responsibilities in business. But in contrast to Friedman, I will argue that these relationships do not alter the distribution of moral obligations in such a way as to make ethical obligations irrelevant to corporations. On the contrary, I will sketch what I take to be a promising new model for grounding an account of corporate ethics—the ownership model of business ethics. This model develops a middle way between the two canonical theories of business ethics, the stakeholder and shareholder value theories, and it has important advantages compared with these two theories.

Pogge's argument is rooted in a form of structural critique of moral codes. He claims that a moral code can be shown to be incoherent and in prima facie need of revision if it contains a counterproductive loophole. By this he means roughly that the code provides incentives for an ideal adherent (one who is fully informed and committed to complying with the code) to act in ways that defeat the overall purpose of the code. If a code incentivizes behavior that is regrettable, all things considered, by the lights of the code itself, then other things being equal the code ought to be revised.

One of the examples Pogge uses to illustrate this claim is the agency model of business management. He asks us to imagine that our father owns an apartment block inhabited by elderly tenants who have lived there for many decades and enjoy a strong sense of community. An opportunity arises to increase financial returns on the building by evicting the tenants and converting the apartments into luxury flats. Pogge supposes that the prevalent ethical code endorses the following judgments: (1) it is impermissible for the father acting on his own behalf to undertake the conversion; (2) it is permissible for a lawyer appointed by the father to maximize returns on the building to undertake the conversion; and (3) it is permissible for the father to appoint the lawyer on these terms.[2]

But Pogge argues that a code endorsing this set of judgments is incoherent in that it contains an inherently regrettable loophole. For the father is able to avoid an important moral obligation by effecting what amounts to a merely cosmetic change in social arrangements—having the lawyer administer the conversion rather than doing it himself. Pogge supposes the conversion to be intrinsically regrettable by the code's own lights, yet the code provides an ideal incentive to effect this outcome by providing means to do so without color of wrongdoing. Broadening the argument, Pogge concludes: "We should avoid inherently regrettable ideal incentives toward creating or joining social arrangements by denying altogether the moral significance of social arrangements in matters of common decency and basic justice" (2002, 87).

Against this I will argue that the prevalent moral code governing business activities is a good deal more resilient than this. It does not contain inherently regrettable loopholes in the sense Pogge suggests. There is a coherent code of business ethics that does recognize the significance of social arrangements in apportioning moral responsibility, though spelling out what this amounts to will require a careful analysis of interacting moral responsibilities and will also require a call for some reform of corporate institutional arrangements.

Pogge considers what he sees as "a weak spot in my entire approach, because, quite generally, the claim to have found a loophole can always be countered by claiming that the relevant ideal incentive is not in fact regrettable *on the whole*" (2002, 79). In other words, though it may be regrettable in some respects that there exists an ideal incentive to hire the lawyer to evict the tenants, there may be some countervailing value embodied in the code that means it is not regrettable, all things considered, for the code to provide this incentive. He notes, rightly, that the key question about such an objection is its plausibility in light of the rationale of the code as a whole. He considers and rejects out of hand a proposal that the code is not regrettable, all things considered, because of the moral importance of hiring lawyers.

But Pogge fails to consider a much more plausible rationale, one that does in fact underlie many aspects of the moral code of private business. This is the moral importance of the benefits that accrue to society as a

---

[2] In fact Pogge stipulates that this is true of the hypothetical code he presupposes in his example. But it is clear that he takes this code to be substantially coextensive with the ethical code that is actually prevalent in society, for as he says later in the chapter, he believes his argument has the effect of upsetting "received moral convictions" (2002, 89). I therefore read the argument as engaging with the prevalent ethical code as it actually exists in our society. It should also be noted that "ethical code" here refers to a set of generally accepted ethical norms, but these need not be codified in any formal way.

whole from the practice of managing assets so as to maximize returns. Such a practice helps to achieve the most economically efficient distribution of resources, which benefits society as a whole. For example, in the case of the apartment block, maximizing returns by converting the building releases underlying capital value that may then be used for further investment. This in turn generates additional employment and tax revenue that may be used for health care, education, and other public goods. It is this societal benefit that is the rationale underlying the permission for the lawyer to undertake the conversion, and it provides a strong prima facie reason for believing that the incentive within the code to appoint a lawyer to evict the tenants is not regrettable, all things considered.

I take this observation to be part of a broader account, consequentialist in spirit, that underlies the moral rationale for the institution of competitive capitalism as a whole. Of course it could be that such a rationale is based on faulty economic analysis. Alternatively, it may be that the societal benefits in this particular case are not sufficient to outweigh the aggregate harm to evicted tenants, or that tenants have rights against being harmed in certain ways. If this were the case, then the terms of the prevalent code of business would require alteration. But the reasons for the alteration would be internal to the justificatory dynamic of the code itself and would not stem from the existence of any kind of incoherence evidenced by the existence of a loophole in Pogge's sense.

But Pogge's argument is capable of a deeper formulation. Even if it is not regrettable, all things considered, for the moral code to generate an ideal incentive to evict the tenants, it may still be regrettable, all things considered, actually to evict the tenants. If it is true that performing such an act is impermissible for the owner acting alone but permissible once the owner has appointed an agent, then there is a sense in which moral responsibility has been lost or evaded simply by putting in place a social arrangement that appears to be morally unimportant in itself. Any code that permitted this would clearly be defective.

But I do not believe that the prevalent moral code does allow the evasion of responsibility in this way. To see this, let us first draw an intuitive distinction between what we might call "minimal" and "maximal" moral obligations.

Minimal moral obligations are claims others have on us stemming from human rights and justice. Minimal obligations tend to be the most stringent form of moral obligation, in that they delineate the minimal standards for human decency—thus the term *minimal obligations*. If I violate a minimal moral obligation owed to you, then I wrong you (whether or not I harm you). Because of this, the violation of minimal moral obligations provides a ground for complaint by the object of the obligation, and for claims of compensation and redress. Moreover, it can often be appropriate to enforce compliance with minimal obligations through punishment or other forms of sanction.

Maximal moral obligations are those stemming from all other moral considerations, including positive duties of aid, charity, beneficence, commitments to moral ideals, and the virtues. Such considerations provide us with moral reasons for action, but these reasons are in some respects less stringent than those deriving from human rights and justice. Typically, maximal moral obligations are not enforced by punishment, and noncompliance does not give rise to valid claims for compensation. This is because someone who suffers as a result of the violation of a maximal obligation is harmed but is typically not wronged. In certain respects maximal obligations may even have a discretionary element. For example, an agent may, with equal moral honor, choose to structure his life around varying sets of virtues that will make correspondingly different moral claims upon him. Consider, for example, the differing moral demands incumbent on a man who has chosen the life of a dedicated teacher, diligent researcher, and committed family man compared with those incumbent on a man who has dedicated his life to delivering medical services in dangerous and war-torn parts of the globe.

Whether an obligation is maximal or minimal can depend on facts about both the subject and the object of the obligation. For instance, providing assistance to a given person may be a maximal obligation for you but a minimal obligation for me, if I have made a promise or entered into a contract to assist, or if I am a close family member. On the other hand, human rights, such as the right not to be attacked or unjustifiably deprived of my property, impose minimal obligations on all people.

The distinction between minimal and maximal moral obligations will obviously require a good deal of further clarification and explanation before it can function in a full-fledged moral theory. For example, might it not be the case that some duties of aid are also obligations of justice— for example, those that arise in situations of extreme need or rescue?[3] My intention here is not to provide such a full analytical clarification but rather to investigate how institutional arrangements affect the distribution and structure of these two classes of moral obligation, intuitively and indicatively understood. Such an investigation has the potential to be valuable however one chooses fully and finally to specify the distinction between minimal and maximal obligations, and it may even provide useful constraints that will assist in the process of drawing the distinction itself.

It is of the greatest importance for the proper interpretation of business ethics cases, such as that of the apartment block, to determine whether we are dealing with minimal or maximal moral obligations. Pogge supposes that the obligation not to evict the tenants is a minimal moral obligation.

---

[3] We will return to this question below.

"The tenants," he writes, "are morally entitled to the preservation of their community" (2002, 86). But this interpretation is doubtful. It is hard to see how the tenants could have a claim right against the owner not to evict them. What could the source of such a claim be? It is true that the tenants would be harmed by the eviction. But the question, so far as minimal moral obligations are concerned, is not whether the tenants are harmed but whether they are unjustifiably harmed, in other words wronged, by the eviction (consider how local tradesmen and shopkeepers who stand to gain from the conversion would be harmed by the abandonment of the conversion plans). The harm inflicted on the tenants might be unjustified if it violates an explicit or implicit contract, or if it violates an accepted norm (for example, one that judges the eviction of tenants to be unjustly disproportionate to the social benefits achieved from allowing owners to maximize returns on their properties). But there is no reason to suppose that such factors are at work in this case, because if they were then it would be equally impermissible for both the lawyer and the owner to undertake the conversion.

Generalizing this point, it would seem that Pogge's claim that the ethical code permits the lawyer to evict the tenants is only plausible on the assumption that the obligation to not evict is construed as a maximal, not a minimal moral obligation. Consider how, according to the prevalent moral code, lawyers and managers are not entitled to promote their client's interests through assault, murder, theft, fraud, enslavement, or other actions that violate clear minimal moral obligations. It would seem to be a general moral principle that obligations that genuinely form part of the moral minimum cannot be evaded by reference to the existence of an agency relationship. Minimal moral obligations cannot even be evaded by the existence of highly coercive command structures such as exist in military organizations (thus the generally accepted claim that "following orders" is not a sufficient exculpation for most serious moral transgressions).

Let us take this as our first conclusion about the prevalent code of business: minimal moral obligations apply equally and in all circumstances to all persons and cannot be evaded or substantially altered by social or institutional arrangements, such as the owner-manager relationship. So far as the moral minimum is concerned there is no diminution of responsibility entailed by the owner-manager relationship, for both owners and managers are bound by those requirements.

If the obligation not to evict the tenants is not a minimal moral obligation, then it must be a form of maximal obligation. Indeed, it would seem most plausible to construe it as a maximal moral obligation stemming from considerations of beneficence and virtue. Thus, though the owner would not violate the tenants' rights or relevant principles of justice by evicting them, it is something he ought not to do, all things considered, because to do so would violate the requirements of compassion, generosity, and beneficence. This observation is itself significant, for it shows that though maximal obligations are in a sense less stringent than minimal obligations they are still very significant. Indeed, it may sometimes be true—as it seems to be in this case—that a maximal moral obligation (generosity or charity) can override a minimal moral liberty (the fact that the owner has no minimal moral obligation not to evict the tenants).

Suppose I am correct to characterize the duty not to evict the tenants as a maximal moral obligation. Why shouldn't these obligations be incumbent in precisely the same way on the lawyer acting as a manager? Why should it be permissible for the manager to evict the tenants but not for the owner to do so (as the prevalent code apparently decrees)? There are two ways we may approach this question. The first is by examining constraints on the fulfillment of maximal obligations implicit within the nature of these obligations themselves. The second is by examining the moral relationship that exists between owners and managers.

Regarding the first of these considerations, it would seem to be a general feature of maximal moral obligations that they can only be fulfilled with one's own resources, not at the expense of others.[4] Obligations of charity, beneficence, generosity, and other virtues can only be properly fulfilled using resources that really are yours to dispose of. Indeed, it is hard to even make sense of what it could mean, in a moral sense, to be generous or beneficent with someone else's money. If I am an officer of a charitable organization, I might be generous in disbursing the resources of the organization; but the generosity here is the organization's, not mine. I am being generous on *behalf* of the organization, and this will only be morally laudable if I am properly mandated to use the resources in this way.

This constraint, implicit within the structure of maximal obligations themselves, seems to explain why such obligations operate differentially on owners and managers in business-ethics cases. For a manager administers property that does not belong to him, and he is entrusted with generating profits to which he is not entitled. In general it is inappropriate for mangers to use assets and profits that are not their own in order to fulfill maximal moral obligations incumbent on them (we may call this the "no Robin Hood-ing" requirement). This would appear to be the primary explanation for why it is impermissible for the owner to evict the tenants but not impermissible for the lawyer acting as manager to evict them.

One might object to this line of thought by considering the following kind of case: imagine that a company manager can save a person's life through some very small encroachment on the company's resources, letting a person use the company car to drive to hospital, for instance. It

---

[4] This is one of the intuitive principles invoked by Milton Friedman, though he does not distinguish carefully between maximal and minimal moral obligations (1999, 252).

seems clear that the manager has an obligation to render assistance in such circumstances even though this involves utilizing resources that are not his own. Yet one might think that this obligation, being an obligation of assistance, is maximal rather than minimal.

As I indicated above, obligations of assistance in emergency situations occupy a difficult gray area between obviously minimal and obviously maximal obligations. One might think that rendering significant assistance to someone when the costs are very low is in fact a minimal obligation, such that someone who fails to render assistance in these circumstances wrongs the person in need, generating in turn a claim for compensation, redress, or enforcement.[5] On the other hand, one might hold that such duties of assistance are maximal, albeit of a particularly strong and stringent kind. In this case one will need to provide a more complex analysis of the case. The most natural interpretation is that company owners implicitly authorize managers to use company resources to render assistance in such emergency cases. In which case, to the extent that the act of assistance or generosity involves the use of resources that belong to owners, it is properly described as the *owner's* act of assistance or generosity, and it is the owners who have fulfilled the maximal obligation. Suppose, however, that the owners do not permit their resources to be used in this way. We still believe that the manager morally ought to render assistance. In this case we will say that the manager has justifiably infringed the owners' right not to have their resources appropriated without their consent. If the owners are really so mean as to demand compensation, the manager would be morally obliged to pay it. In this case the manager genuinely has fulfilled the maximal obligation himself, but because he has assumed a moral liability to pay back the resources used or render compensation we can also say that he has fulfilled the obligation using his own resources.[6]

The second consideration (which has often been emphasized in discussions of business ethics) refers to the set of obligations implicit within the agent-principal relationship. These stem from the fact that an agent, such as a manager, has contracted or promised to administer the principal's affairs in accordance with his wishes, and more generally to act in the principal's best interests. One might be tempted to reason on the basis of such considerations as follows: contractual and promissory obligations are a component of justice and as such they form part of the moral minimum. But because minimal obligations are more stringent

---

[5] Spain, France, Germany, Greece, and several other jurisdictions impose some form of legal duty to assist.

[6] This dialectic has obvious relevance to the question of how managers and owners of corporations ought to respond to radical poverty in markets in which they operate, or how pharmaceutical companies ought to respond to medical emergencies in developing countries. Much will turn on how low the cost of assistance must be before the obligation becomes overriding, and whether directness or proximity to those in need makes a moral difference.

than maximal obligations, they trump them in cases of conflict, and it is this fact that explains why the lawyer is not simply morally permitted, but indeed morally required, to evict the tenants.

But we must be very careful with this line of thought. Even if we accept that contractual and promissory obligations are components of justice and therefore part of the moral minimum, clearly not all minimal obligations are of equal strength or importance. As we have already seen, minimal obligations stemming from human rights consistently override whatever obligations one may have as an agent to maximize the interests of the principal. This would only be explicable if some forms of minimal obligation have an importance that can override contractual and promissory obligations.[7] More important, it is not clear that minimal obligations do always override maximal obligations. We have already seen how maximal obligations can in certain circumstances override minimal Hohfeldian liberties. It may be the case that certain maximal obligations are so important that they can override even some weak forms of minimal obligation.[8]

So the simple argument that casts contractual obligations as minimal obligations and sees them as overriding all maximal obligations is insufficient in itself. It would seem, in contrast, that these two forms of consideration are best seen as functioning in concert. The fact that maximal obligations can only appropriately be fulfilled with one's own resources is sufficient to establish a moral liberty for managers to act in ways that would ordinarily be ruled out by maximal considerations. The existence of contractual and promissory obligations (though not necessarily sufficient in themselves to defeat maximal obligations genuinely relevant to an agent) functions to establish a moral presumption in favor of preferencing the interests of the principal over those of others, where there is a liberty for the agent to do so.

---

[7] There are two ways one might conceive of the relationship between contractual and promissory obligations and human rights. One may think of human rights as overriding the contractual and promissory obligations stemming from the agency relationship. Alternatively, one might think of human rights as placing limits on the nature of the obligations one is empowered to acquire through the process of contracting and promising. For example, it may be that human rights and justice function as an implicit backdrop and constraint to all contractual and promissory relationships (including the agent-principal relationship), such that one simply is not empowered to acquire a valid obligation that contradicts basic human rights and justice.

[8] Warren Quinn gives the example of a lifeguard working for a private client. Quinn is inclined to suppose that if the lifeguard has to choose between saving his client or five drowning strangers, he should save his client and allow the five strangers to drown (1989, 293). But if we change the example so that the contractual obligation is trivial—buying the client an ice cream—then most would feel that it is permissible to infringe the contractual obligation to save the five, even if one believes the contractual obligation to be morally minimal (implying that the client has been wronged and requiring, for example, the lifeguard to provide compensation or apology to the client for financial loss suffered as a result of his justified infringement).

It is worth pointing out that this account does not imply that maximal moral considerations have no role to play in the moral deliberations of managers acting as agents. It is rather that the role played by maximal considerations is modified by the existence of the agency relationship. For example, in the apartment-block case, if we accept that evicting the tenants genuinely contradicts important maximal obligations by being ungenerous and cruel, then the lawyer thereby assumes the obligation to bring this to the attention of the owner and to lobby the owner not to permit the eviction. At the limit, a manager may be obligated to resign if it is clear that he is being asked to participate in an activity that is morally objectionable for maximal reasons. What a manager cannot do, on this account, is utilize the resources of the business, or the owners of the business, to fulfill maximal obligations as if they were his own. This account would seem to explain why the lawyer acting as an agent is not only permitted but also morally required to evict the tenants, even though it would be impermissible for the owner to do so on his own.

But now it would seem that we are once again saddled with the problem that Pogge identified at the outset. If it is impermissible for maximal moral reasons for the owner to evict the tenants but it is not impermissible for the lawyer to evict the tenants, then it would seem that the owner could evade his maximal moral obligations without color of wrongdoing by simply appointing the lawyer. It would seem that this involves a regrettable loss of moral responsibility, especially given the moral importance of the maximal obligations concerned.

In reality, however, there is no loss of moral responsibility. To think otherwise is to misunderstand the nature of the relationship between owners and managers, or more generally the nature of the principal-agent relationship. The mistake is to think that because it is permissible for the lawyer to evict the tenants, it follows that it is permissible for the owner to appoint the lawyer on such terms that he would be permitted or obligated to do so.

On the contrary, the principal is responsible for setting morally appropriate terms under which an agent will manage his affairs. Thus if an owner is subject to a moral obligation pertaining to his asset, then he has a further obligation to ensure that any agent managing this asset does so in a way that is consistent with that moral obligation. Moreover, the principal will typically retain ultimate supervisory and executive control over the agent's decisions and actions. Thus we often say of the agency relationship that the agent acts on *behalf* of the principal and the principal acts *through* the agent. Maximal obligations are therefore not lost in the principal-agent relationship, because they are fully retained by the principal.[9]

[9] This retention of responsibility on the part of the principal is exceptionally robust. It may even exist when the agent performs acts without specific instruction by the principal.

The appropriate image for understanding the nature of a principal's responsibility is ownership of a machine. Owning a commercial asset, such as a business, is like owning a special kind of machine whose function is to generate outputs of greater value that its inputs. Like any machine, a business brings with it a collection of rights and responsibilities for the owner. Rights clearly include first call on the profits generated. But responsibilities come with those rights, and they include the obligation to ensure that the business machine does not cause unjustified harm to others, and that its products are utilized in accord with the requirements of both the moral minimum and the moral maximum. To take a simple example, owning a car brings with it the right to keep the profits generated by its commercial use, but it may also bring with it important obligations and responsibilities. These will include the obligation not to use the car in a way that endangers others, and to take reasonable steps to ensure that others do not use it dangerously. Ownership may also generate maximal obligations. For example, if my car is the only one in town, then I may acquire an obligation that I would not otherwise possess to drive a sick child to hospital. Ownership of a business generates moral rights and responsibilities in precisely the same way.

Thus Pogge's example of the apartment block, designed to demonstrate the incoherence of the prevalent moral code, has instead enabled us to elucidate a robust account of that code which accords with our pretheoretical intuitions. It is an account in which moral responsibilities are indeed sensitive to institutional arrangements, such as the agency relationship, but where neither minimal nor maximal obligations are lost or diminished.[10] We might summarize these results as shown in table 1.

This analysis may be viewed as an elementary model of the distribution of moral responsibility in business ethics. Call it the ownership model of business ethics. Note how the model occupies a plausible middle ground between the two dominant theories of business ethics, the shareholder

---

Thus, if I have a troublesome colleague in the department and I hire a thug known to have committed contract killings in the past and tell him to "just deal with the problem," then I will be guilty in both law and morality if he proceeds to kill the colleague. There are, obviously, limits to the responsibility of principals. If an agent acts in bad faith and without instruction, and moreover the principal has taken sufficiently stringent measures to oversee and supervise the agent's activities, then the principal may have no responsibility at all for the actions of the agent.

[10] Of course, much of what is most interesting in Pogge's book as a whole is that he believes that the moral maximum is much more minimal than we have tended to suppose. Many obligations that have been thought of as more or less discretionary positive duties to assist others are in fact much more stringent moral requirements rooted in human rights and justice. But this argument must stand on its own merits—it can receive no support from the loophole argument. If we are persuaded by Pogge's account of the moral minimum and come to see the obligation not to evict the tenants in these terms, then we will ipso facto have reason to believe that the lawyer acting as agent is not morally permitted to undertake the conversion.

DAVID RODIN

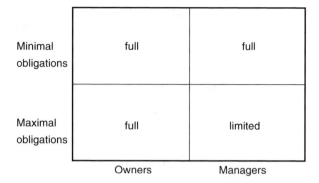

	Owners	Managers
Minimal obligations	full	full
Maximal obligations	full	limited

TABLE 1. The Ownership Model of Business Ethics

value theory and the stakeholder theory. According to the shareholder value theory, owners and managers are subject to a thin set of minimal moral obligations, but maximal obligations (the bottom line of the matrix) are almost entirely omitted. At best maximal obligations are viewed as discretionary commitments that owners of a business may use company profits or dividends to achieve, but that play no appropriate moral role in the management or governance activities of the company itself.[11]

In contrast, stakeholder theory gives prominence to maximal obligations, but its focus is almost exclusively on the obligations of managers rather than owners (the right-hand column of the matrix). According to stakeholder theory, managers are morally required to utilize the resources of the firm to serve the interests of all stakeholder groups, of which the owners are but one (see Evan and Freeman 1999). But viewing business ethics in this way has several counterintuitive consequences. The first is that this view ignores the special rights that owners have to the profits generated by the firm and the special responsibilities that accompany these rights. I have argued that both the rights and the responsibilities are implicit in the moral nature of ownership. The second is that it ignores the constraints on the maximal moral action of managers—the fact that it is morally inappropriate for managers to fulfill maximal obligations with resources that are not their own.

The ownership model suffers from none of these shortcomings. It accounts for our pretheoretical intuitions about the distribution of moral

---

[11] Maximal obligations may play a purely instrumental role in management decisions according to shareholder value theory. Thus, if undertaking activities perceived in society as "morally good" brings net financial benefits to the firm—for example, by generating good will with customers—then managers may appropriately undertake them. But it is clear that such considerations can play no recognizably moral role in management deliberation on such an account.

responsibility in institutional business settings, and does so without any regrettable loss of moral responsibility. It would seem to be a robust and promising model for the development of business ethics.

It might be objected, however, that this model has been developed in the context of small businesses where the relationship between owners and mangers is a reasonably direct one. Suppose we wanted to generalize this model into a general theory of business ethics appropriate also to large publicly listed corporations? Would the ownership model still be appropriate?

One difficulty stems from the insertion of the legal corporation as an intermediary between the shareholders and managers of a business. In law a corporation is conceived as an artificial person that is itself the owner of the assets of the business. What shareholders own is a legal entitlement to a share of the corporation's profits. Because of this it is an open question whether the relationship between managers and shareholders is an agent-principal relationship at all, for on some accounts it is the corporation itself that is the principal.

Notice, however, that my argument for the limited nature of managers' maximal responsibilities does not depend on their agency relationship being with the owners or shareholders. If the principal of the agency relationship is the corporation itself, this will not alter the fact that it is morally inappropriate for managers to fulfill maximal obligations with resources that are not their own. This suggests that the much-discussed question of whether shareholders and managers are really in an agent-principal relationship is not in fact the crucial issue so far as this question is concerned.

A more serious difficulty concerns the status of the shareholders themselves. How appropriate is the ownership model to a large modern corporation where shareholding is highly distributed and the ability of individual shareholders to affect the activities of the company is extremely minimal? Imagine, for example, that instead of owning an apartment block outright, the father owns shares in a large property company that is proposing to convert one of its buildings and evict the elderly community. The father may feel that there are moral reasons prohibiting the owners of the company from undertaking such action, yet he may recognize that as a small shareholder he has no ability to change the company's policy. Reflecting on the principle that "ought implies can," he may conclude that a shareholder in his position has no responsibility for the eviction. The situation is even worse for the large number of shareholdings held in mutual funds or other investment vehicles, where shareholding is transitory and the ultimate owners may not even know the content of their portfolio at a given time.

Here it would seem we are genuinely faced with a dilution of moral responsibility as a result of institutional arrangements. For the shareholders of modern publicly listed corporations have no effective way of communicating their moral preferences to managers and ensuring that they are effectively implemented, whereas managers, as we have seen, are prohibited from exercising maximal moral obligations using the resources of the corporation without the explicit consent of the owners. It may appear that this is intrinsically morally regrettable, and indeed calls into question the moral viability of the institution of the large public corporation.

Now Friedman argues that there is no diminution of responsibility implicit in the modern corporation because shareholders can always use their company dividends to fulfill individual maximal obligations independently of the activities of the corporation. But this claim ignores the fact that there are certain maximal moral obligations that only arise, or arise in different forms, in the corporate context and cannot be appropriately fulfilled by individuals acting alone. For example, there may be certain forms of assistance that corporations are uniquely positioned to provide (think of a drug company holding a patent on AIDS medication), and there are some goods that Microsoft can achieve as a corporation that even an immensely powerful and wealthy shareholder like Bill Gates cannot achieve as an individual. Similarly, corporate activity may create harms that cannot be properly compensated or redressed by shareholders acting as individuals.

If one is persuaded by the moral analysis of the ownership model, then it would seem that the tendency of the large modern corporation to erode maximal moral obligations in this way is one of the great unresolved problems of business ethics. I would like to conclude by indicating three potential responses to this problem.

The first seeks to deny that there really is a problem. It takes as its starting point the observation that the social institution of the large publicly listed corporation can hardly be described as a trivial or cosmetic change from the model of the small business owned by an individual or a family, envisioned in our example of the apartment block. The differences are profound, and many have significant moral implications because of the potential benefits they can bring to society. For example, today's giant corporations can reap huge economies of scale that lower the cost of goods for consumers and create wealth for shareholders. Moreover, there are some products that could literally only have been created by organizations of this scale and structure (think, for example, of the Boeing 747 or an Intel microprocessor). Now it is true that the scale of private corporations can be replicated by state-owned enterprises, but their desirable dispersal of risk over private individuals and access to the deep capital resources of equity markets cannot be so easily replicated. These are all significant goods that there are moral as well as prudential reasons to bring about.

Accordingly, one may attempt to argue that insofar as the institution of the corporation entails the diminution of certain maximal obligations, such as the personal virtues of kindness, compassion, and generosity, this is not morally regrettable, all things considered. For these losses are compensated by important social gains.[12] Indeed, one might suppose that the loss, insofar as there is one, is not regrettable at all, for it simply represents the transition to a set of institutional virtues more appropriate to the economic sphere: efficiency, rationality, and dedication to maximizing returns.

It must be doubted, however, how far this line of thought can take us. It is difficult to regard an institutional arrangement that replaces the virtues of kindness and generosity with those of simple profit maximization as not entailing some profound form of moral loss, even if one accepts that it may lead to utilitarian welfare gains for society as a whole.

A second strategy would be to attempt to claw back some of the manager's lost competence to act in accordance with maximal moral obligations in large publicly listed corporations. One potential way to do this would be by permitting, or perhaps even requiring, managers to use what we might call a "principle of interpretative charity" when managing the assets of shareholders. This would specify that in the absence of a reliable way for shareholders to communicate their moral preferences to managers, managers are entitled to administer the corporation in accordance with the maximal moral commitments that they can reasonably and honestly attribute to their shareholders. Such an approach is consistent with the call made by many NGOs for managers to use the resources of their corporations to do good irrespective of whether they have a clear mandate from shareholders to do so.

But it must be recognized that there are substantial dangers implicit in this proposal. For corporations are vastly powerful institutions, yet the managers controlling them are largely trained in technical matters and are, as a group, highly conservative: they are still overwhelmingly white, male, and upper-middle class. If they were given a mandate to use the resources of corporations to achieve the maximal moral goods that they may reasonably and honestly attribute to their shareholders, they would be exposed to significant temptations to use those resources to fulfill their own conception of the maximal moral good. Given the narrow social class represented by managers, those conceptions may be idiosyncratic, distasteful, or even dangerous.[13] Managers would require extraordinary moral imagination and integrity to keep their own conceptions of

---

[12] Of course, any such account would have to include a firm insistence on the minimal obligations of managers and shareholders, in order to prevent the enormous power of large modern corporations being used to inflict unjustified harm.

[13] Of course, something of the same problem arises with all private philanthropy. But private philanthropists are at least constrained by the fact that they must utilize their own resources for their philanthropic schemes. Moreover, the exercise of maximal obligations by shareholders urged by the ownership model avoids this problem to a significant degree. Because pension funds and mutual funds have replaced wealthy individuals as the most

maximal obligations distinct from those reasonably attributable to their shareholders. Even granting such qualities, they would certainly require stringent oversight and accountability in exercising these powers. It is difficult to see who would be better suited to provide this oversight than the shareholders themselves or those properly authorized to perform the function on their behalf, namely, the board of directors.

This leads naturally to the final response, which is less conceptually innovative than the last, but which instead invites a program of practical institutional reform to corporate governance mechanisms. This approach insists that responsibility for maximal moral obligations rests inalienably with the owners of business assets. The problem is not with the ownership model of business ethics but rather with the governance structures of corporations themselves. The basic goal of such structures should be to align ownership and control, so that managers are accountable to owners not only for the financial performance of the corporation but also for the minimal and maximal moral character of its activities.

How might this be achieved? There are two broad mechanisms through which shareholders can affect the policies of corporations. The first is through their election of the board of directors; the second is through the buying and selling of shares, which determines market capitalization and indirectly the cost of equity capital, two critical determinants of corporate success. Both mechanisms need to be strengthened and reformed if the moral vision of the ownership model is to be given effect.

There is a vast literature on both topics, and I can only make some very indicative comments here. It is interesting to note, however, that reform of corporate governance is already high on the agenda of shareholders, managers, and government regulators. So the ownership model of business ethics provides further normative motivation for a movement that is already substantially under way. Since the birth of the shareholder activism movement in the 1990s and the corporate scandals of the early years of the new century, numerous corporate governance initiatives have been proposed to protect the interests of shareholders by increasing their control over management behavior. Many of these same reforms may simultaneously be used to empower shareholders to communicate their moral preferences to management and oversee their implementation. But in general the moral dimension of corporate-governance reform needs to be more explicitly recognized. There need to be explicit mechanisms for moral policies to be debated by the board of governors and proposed and voted on by shareholders. Shareholders themselves must become more aware of the moral responsibilities of ownership and be more prepared to become proactively involved in corporate-governance activities. Already

important owners of equity in most markets, the social profile of the ultimate shareholders of large corporations is now much closer to that of society as a whole.

many NGOs lobby shareholders directly in an attempt to change a corporation's policy.

But given the nature of modern shareholding, active and effective participation in corporate-governance activities will never be a realistic possibility for most small investors. For this reason the various ethical-investment initiatives are of the greatest importance. The ethical-investment industry is still in its infancy; it is small and highly fragmented, and many of its products and indices are ethically crude. But it is also the fastest-growing segment of the mutual-fund industry in many markets. If the ethical-investment movement were ever to reach sufficient scale and appropriate structure, it would have the potential to be a powerful mechanism for shareholders to affect the moral activities of corporations by raising the cost of capital for corporations that do not conduct themselves in accordance with the moral preferences of shareholders.

The chief requirement for this to occur (beyond the support of the share buying public) is the existence of accessible, standardized, and impartial data on the ethical aspects of corporate activity. At the moment numerous different ethical standards, investment criteria, and indices compete for investor attention. Most of these are based on a particular conception of what constitutes "ethical behavior" on the part of corporations. Yet it is unlikely that any of these particular standards will ever gain universal acceptance among investors because people differ in their moral commitments and, as we have already seen, certain differences in the conception of the maximal moral obligations are entirely appropriate.

What seems to be required is the existence of a third-party rating agency that can assess the performance of corporations along a number of different ethical criteria. It could measure such factors as support of the disadvantaged, treatment of employees, the manufacture of dangerous products, and so forth. The criteria themselves could be specified at a very fine-grained level involving hundreds of criteria and subcriteria. The data pertaining to these criteria would need to have the following features. First, the data would need to be produced in such a way that shareholders are able to weight the different criteria according to their own moral preferences and commitments to generate a personalized moral profile for their investment activities. For example, one investor may be morally opposed to the manufacture of weapons but less concerned about greenhouse-gas emissions, whereas another investor may have the opposite concerns. Second, the data must be capable of being aggregated across a portfolio of shares or a managed fund, so that the portfolio or fund as a whole can be assessed according to an investor's personal moral profile. Finally, the data must be standardized and easy to use, and the providers must be universally recognized as legitimate and trustworthy. In other words, what is needed is an analogue in the arena of ethical assessment to the standard providers of credit-risk assessment, Moody's and Standard & Poor's.

None of these ethical reforms will be quickly or easily achieved, and their ultimate effectiveness is not guaranteed. But what is clear is that appropriate reform will not be achieved without the right theoretical account of the distribution of responsibilities in business ethics—in what ways managers and owners ought to respond to maximal and minimal moral considerations. On the argument of this essay, it would appear that the ownership model of business ethics is a strong contender for providing such an account.

References

Evan, William, and Edward Freeman. 1999. "A Stakeholder Theory of the Modern Corporation: Kantian Capitalism." In *An Introduction to Business Ethics*, edited by George Chryssides and John Kaler, 254–66. London: Thomson Business Press.

Friedman, Milton. 1999. "The Social Responsibility of Business Is to Increase Its Profits." In *An Introduction to Business Ethics*, edited by George Chryssides and John Kaler, 249–54. London: Thomson Business Press. First published in 1970.

Pogge, Thomas. 2002. *World Poverty and Human Rights*. Cambridge, Mass.: Polity.

Quinn, Warren. 1989. "Actions, Intentions, and Consequences: The Doctrine of Doing and Allowing." *Philosophical Review* 98, no. 3: 287–312.

Sternberg, Elaine. 2000. *Just Business: Business Ethics in Action*. Second edition. Oxford: Oxford University Press.

13

THE PREVENTIVE USE OF FORCE:
A COSMOPOLITAN INSTITUTIONAL PROPOSAL

ALLEN BUCHANAN AND ROBERT O. KEOHANE

Since September 11 fears of terrorism and weapons of mass destruction have fueled a vigorous worldwide debate about the preventive use of force. Preventive use of force may be defined as the initiation of military action in anticipation of harmful actions that are neither currently occurring nor imminent.[1]

This essay explores the permissibility of preventive war from a cosmopolitan normative perspective, one that recognizes the basic human rights of all persons, not just citizens of a particular country or countries. We argue that within an appropriate rule-governed, institutional framework that is designed to help protect vulnerable countries against unjustified interventions without creating unacceptable risks of the costs of inaction, decisions to employ preventive force can be justified.

In our proposal, states proposing preventive war would have to enter into a contract with a diverse body of states as a condition for authorization of their actions. Both proponents of action and those opposing it would be held accountable, after the fact, for the accuracy of their prior statements and the proportionality of their actions. This institutional arrangement is designed to improve the quality of decisions on the preventive use of force. It does so by insisting that these decisions take place under rules that create incentives for honest revelation of information and responsible conduct, and that they be made by agents that are comparatively morally reliable.

The key to ensuring the fairness of rules governing the preventive use of force is accountability. Our proposed scheme promotes accountability through a combination of *ex ante* and *ex post* mechanisms. Prior to taking preventive action, states will be required to enter into a contingent contract that imposes two requirements. First, they must make an evidence-based case for preventive force to the UN Security Council. Second, they must agree in advance to submit themselves to an evaluation by an impartial body after the preventive action occurred. This body will

---

[1] The notion of an "imminent" attack is somewhat vague but is usually understood to include not only situations in which missiles or warplanes have been launched but have not yet struck their targets, but also situations in which forces have been mobilized with apparently aggressive intent.

be charged with determining whether the empirical claims that were employed to justify the preventive action were true. If the *ex post* evaluation undermines the intervening states' justification for acting, the contract would provide for sanctions against them. If the *ex post* evaluation vindicates the recourse to preventive force, then the contract would impose sanctions on those members of the Council who opposed the proposed action. If preventive action were blocked by a majority vote of the Security Council or a veto by one of the permanent members, those seeking to engage in preventive action could then make their case in a different body—a coalition of democratic states—with its own institutionalized mechanisms for accountability. Although our goal is to develop an institutional framework for decisions concerning the use of preventive force, we believe that our general approach can also be used to develop a framework for making decisions concerning humanitarian military intervention to stop presently occurring massive violations of basic human rights. We focus more narrowly on preventive force for two reasons: the preventive use of force involves special risks and is thus more difficult to justify; and the Bush administration's recent claims that the right of self-defense includes the permission to engage in the preventive use of force have made this of urgent practical importance.

Four Views on the Preventive Use of Force

Four distinct positions in the current debate on preventive force have emerged: the Just War Blanket Prohibition; the Legal Status Quo view; the National Interest view; and the Expanded Right of Self-Defense view. Clarifying these views and identifying their shortcomings helps to illuminate the distinctive features of our proposal.

The Just War Blanket Prohibition. The dominant view in the just war tradition has been that preventive force is strictly forbidden. Force may sometimes be justified in cases in which an attack has not already occurred but is imminent—when, for example, an enemy is mobilizing his forces with clear aggressive intent or when missiles or warplanes have already been launched but yet not struck their targets—but there is generally thought to be a *blanket prohibition* on preventive action (Walzer 1977).

The Legal Status Quo. States' preventive use of force is generally regarded as prohibited in contemporary international law unless they have received collective authorization by the UN Security Council. Article 2(4) of the UN Charter requires "all states" to refrain "from the threat or use of force against the territorial integrity or political independence of any state," unless authorized by the Security Council (Articles 39, 42, 48) or in self-defense against an armed attack (Article 51). According to the Legal Status Quo view, this highly constrained stance on preventive force ought to be maintained. Preventive force should be used only with Security Council authorization.[2]

The National Interest. Realists hold that states may do whatever their leaders deem necessary to serve the best interests of the state. According to this view, leaders of states may disregard universal moral principles when they conflict with the national interest. More specifically, they may employ force, including preventively, if they deem it necessary for the pursuit of state interests.[3]

The Expanded Right of Self-Defense. The Bush administration's "National Security Strategy" articulates a fourth position. It expands the definition of self-defense to include preventive action: "While the United States will constantly strive to enlist the support of the international community, *we will not hesitate to act alone, if necessary, to exercise our right of self-defense by acting preemptively against such terrorists, to prevent them from doing harm against our people and our country* [emphasis added]" ("National Security Strategy of the United States of America September 2002," 6). The Bush administration's "National Security Strategy" asserts that states possess a right of self-defense that entitles them to take preventive action.

None of these four views provides an adequate model for governing the preventive use of force. Adherence to the Just War Blanket Prohibition is too risky, given the widespread capacity and occasional willingness of states and nonstate actors to deploy weapons of mass destruction covertly and suddenly against civilian populations. In addition, this view requires states to refrain from acting even when they could prevent massive human rights violations at little cost.[4] The National Interest view is also unacceptable. Indeed, it repudiates all progress that has been made

[2] In the absence of authoritative judicial determination, international law is subject to a variety of interpretations. Some might hold that under current international law preventive action can be legitimate because the Genocide Convention obligates states/parties to take action to prevent genocide. However, this claim is contestable because, according to Article 103 of the UN Charter, the prohibition against preventive use of force trumps all other treaties, including the Genocide Convention. It might also be held, on the contrary, that preventive force is not permissible under international law even with Security Council authorization, except in order to respond to a "threat to international peace and security." For our purposes, it is not necessary to take a stand on these legal questions. We merely follow most authorities in treating the legal status quo as prohibiting preventive use of force without Security Council authorization, but permitting it if such authorization has been provided.

[3] For the classic statement, see Morgenthau 1985, 12. Advocates of the National Interest view need not be moral skeptics; instead they may hold that state leaders have one supreme moral obligation—to serve the national interest—and that this obligation overrides all other principles of morality. Those who espouse the National Interest view may disagree among themselves, of course, as to whether a policy of recourse to preventive force, or any particular decision to use preventive force, is in fact likely to serve the national interest or be detrimental to it.

[4] We explore the flaws of the Just War Blanket Prohibition in more detail below.

in constraining the international use of force. The problem is not simply that the national interest is such a malleable concept that its invocation is likely to provide a rationale for aggression and a recipe for destructive international instability, but that by reducing the grounds for the preventive use of force to self-defense, this view conceives of the potential aims of preventive action too narrowly. It fails even to consider the possibility that there are circumstances in which the preventive use of force would be justified to protect the rights of persons other than one's fellow citizens.

The Expanded Right of Self-Defense view must also be rejected. Allowing states to use force on the basis of their own estimate that they may be attacked in the future, without provision for checks on the reliability and sincerity of that judgment, would make the use of force too subject to abuse and error. Like the National Interest view, it also focuses only on the welfare of those within one's own state, thereby providing no basis for the preventive use of force on behalf of others.

The Legal Status Quo view is quite attractive when compared to the three views described above, since it allows preventive action, including its use to protect persons beyond one's borders, while also providing checks on the judgment of any particular state or group of states seeking to use it. But when compared to a fifth alternative—the Cosmopolitan Institutional view—the Legal Status Quo view appears far less compelling. The normative foundation of the Cosmopolitan Institutional view is cosmopolitan in the sense that it takes the human rights of all persons seriously. By basic human rights we mean the most widely acknowledged rights that are already recognized in the major human rights conventions. These include the right to physical security of the person, including the right against torture, and rights against at least the more damaging forms of discrimination on grounds of religion, gender, race, or ethnicity, as well as rights against slavery, servitude or forced labor, and the right to the means of subsistence.[5] A commitment to protecting and preventing massive violations of human rights provides a prima facie justification for preventive force as a last resort.

These commitments of the cosmopolitan perspective are far from novel. Indeed, they are central to the just war tradition and the current international legal order's allowing human rights to limit state sovereignty. The distinctiveness of the Cosmopolitan Institutional view lies in

---

[5] The position we endorse is sometimes called Moderate Cosmopolitanism, which allows one to give a limited priority to the interests of one's own nation and does not require strict impartiality. It is a liberal form of cosmopolitanism, since it emphasizes the basic human rights of all persons. One could imagine other kinds of cosmopolitanism, such as Marxism, that forbid discrimination on grounds of nationality, but do not focus on human rights. For a philosophical justification for the assumption that there are human rights, see Buchanan 2003.

how it incorporates these normative commitments with an effective *accountability regime* for responsible decision-making concerning the preventive use of force.

A cosmopolitan accountability regime involves both substantive standards and processes. The substantive standards include traditional just war principles, including competent authority, proportionality, noncombatant immunity, realistic likelihood of success, and avoidance of excessive force against enemy combatants. Unfortunately, the chief deficiency of just war theory lies not in its principles but in the failure of the just war theorists to take seriously the need for institutionalizing them in a way that provides incentives for agents to apply them impartially and on the basis of good information. Current international law does institutionalize the important just war principle of competent authority: the requirement that the use of force must be authorized by the Security Council, except in cases of self-defense (when there is no time to consult the Council).[6] And in this sense, the Legal Status Quo view can be seen as an important advance from an anarchic situation in which states unilaterally decide whether to use force. But this way of institutionalizing the use of force is seriously inadequate, at least when it comes to the preventive use of force.

The Cosmopolitan Justification for Preventive War

We begin with the assumption that it can be morally permissible to use force to stop *presently occurring* massive violations of basic human rights. We then argue from this assumption that there is at least a prima facie case for the moral permissibility of using force to *prevent* massive violations of basic human rights.[7] The core justification for using force to stop rights violations as they are occurring—the need to protect basic human rights—can also justify the use of force to prevent rights violations.[8]

---

[6] The humanitarian law of war can be seen as an imperfect institutionalization of some of the most important *jus in bello* principles of just war theory. However, given the distinctive risks of the preventive use of force, special institutional arrangements are required for responsible decisions to use force preventively, over and above better compliance with rules of humane warfare that are designed to apply to all uses of force.

[7] The prima facie argument seems to imply that preventive action to protect basic human rights is not only permissible but also obligatory. However, since we seek to advance a feasible proposal, our discussion of institutional arrangements does not assume such an obligation. The successful implementation of the accountability regime we propose might be an important step toward the more ambitious goal of institutionalizing an obligation to prevent massive violations of basic human rights.

[8] By beginning with the assumption that the use of force is sometimes permissible to stop massive violations of basic human rights already under way, we are of course implicitly rejecting the absolute pacifist view that the use of military force is never justified because it inevitably involves harm to innocent persons. We share this assumption with the four perspectives that we criticize.

Reflection on two scenarios will help to flesh out the prima facie case for this proposition. In the first case, a group is *already* in the process of releasing a weaponized, extremely virulent, lethal virus into the heart of a major city. Surely, it would be justifiable to intervene forcibly to stop them from releasing more of the deadly concoction. In the second scenario, the intelligence agencies of a state have consistent information from many reliable sources that a group that has deliberately killed civilians in the past has in its possession a weaponized, extremely virulent, lethal virus and plans to use it against a civilian population. Suppose further that the current location of the virus is known but the city at which it is targeted is not, and that once the virus leaves its present location it will be very difficult to track. Let us also stipulate that the current location of the virus is in the remote stronghold of the group and that a preventive strike can destroy the virus without killing any persons who do not belong to the group. Under these circumstances, the need to protect basic human rights supports preventive action, regardless of whether the rights endangered are those of our fellow citizens or foreigners. Reflection on such examples supports the conclusion that preventive action can be ethically permissible.

It is crucial to emphasize that this prima facie justification for the preventive use of force does not apply to all cases where harm may be prevented but only to situations in which there is a significant risk of sudden and very serious harms on a massive scale. Such a risk is inherent in weapons of mass destruction but not exclusive to them. Genocides may also erupt suddenly.

In situations characterized by incrementally increasing violence, such as in the former Yugoslavia, however, the case for preventive war is much less compelling. Action to respond to aggression or acts of ethnic violence can feasibly be taken in such contexts with far less uncertainty regarding the need to act after the first human rights violations have already occurred. Thus the force of the prima facie argument is limited and focused. It does not purport to show that force may be used whenever it is likely to stop massive violations of basic human rights.

What the Cosmopolitan Institutional view and the Legal Status Quo view have in common is the assertion that there are some cases in which preventive action ought to be permitted. The prima facie argument for prevention sketched above provides a needed moral foundation for both of these positions.

A Critique of the Just War Blanket Prohibition Argument

Those who endorse the blanket prohibition characteristic of the just war tradition could point out that the prima facie argument ignores a crucial point about preventive force: it is directed toward someone who has not committed a wrong. Thus preventive action violates the rights of its target. Unless this moral objection can be met, both the Cosmopolitan Institutional view and the Legal Status Quo view must be rejected.

This objection is unconvincing, since it rests on a false assumption about the right not to be attacked. There is, trivially, a right not to be attacked *unjustly*. But to assume that this includes the right not to be attacked unless one has already committed, or begun to commit, a wrongful harm is to beg the question at issue—namely, whether preventive force can ever be morally justified.

Reflection on the right of self-defense suggests that preventive action need not violate the rights of the target. At common law, an individual may use deadly force in self-defense if a reasonable person in his circumstances would judge that he is in danger of death or serious bodily injury. Of course, other conditions must be fulfilled as well, including the avoidance of excessive force. The point, however, is that there are circumstances in which it is justifiable to use lethal force even if the target against which it is applied has not yet caused harm. If this is the case, then it may also be permissible to use lethal force in cases where a reasonable actor would judge that the behavior of another person or persons poses a serious threat of death or serious bodily harm even if an attack has not yet begun.

In the case of individuals, there is much to be said for restricting the legal right of self-defense so as to require the reasonable belief, by the agent exercising the right of self-defense, that an attack is already under way. This restriction is reasonable in contexts in which there are a well-functioning police force and legal system that serve to reduce the risk that individuals will be attacked by their fellow citizens. In the international arena there is nothing comparable to an effective police force, and the stakes are often much higher, since millions of people may be killed by a sudden deployment of weapons of mass destruction. Under these circumstances the restrictive interpretation of the right to self-defense seems inadequate. It seems much more plausible to assert that the use of force to prevent great harm can be justified, even if that harm is neither presently occurring nor imminent.

In the second scenario described above, the terrorist group has not yet launched an attack, and the harm it seeks to inflict is not literally imminent. Yet it is incorrect to say that the group has done nothing. It has *wrongfully imposed an especially high risk of serious harm on others*, through its past actions, its current planning to carry out a lethal attack, and its expression of a willingness to kill noncombatants. The group's actions, plans, and avowed intentions have put innocent people at risk for great harms.

Reflection on the law of conspiracy suggests that using force against someone who has not yet committed a wrongful harm need not violate his rights. The elements of conspiracy include a "specific intention" to do wrongful harm and an "agreed plan of action" to produce the harm. The "specific intention" requirement rules out mere unfocused malevolence as a trigger for criminal liability, while the requirement of an "agreed plan of action" satisfies the condition that a crime must include an act, not merely a guilty mind. There is nothing morally repugnant about the idea of using force against conspirators simply because they have not yet performed the act they have planned. We can dismiss the simplistic allegation that it cannot be right to use force against him because "he hasn't done anything" once we acknowledge that the conspirator has indeed done something by agreeing to a plan to produce wrongful harm. One plausible explanation of why it can be justifiable to use force against someone who has a "specific intention" and an "agreed plan of action" to do wrongful harm is that he has *wrongfully imposed a risk of serious harm on others*. It is a wrongful imposition of risk if those put at risk have neither voluntarily accepted the risk nor deserve to be subjected to it. The crucial point is that when someone has wrongfully imposed a risk, it can become morally permissible to do things to alleviate the risk that would otherwise be impermissible. This is not to say that one may do whatever is necessary to alleviate the risk. As with the use of force generally, the principles of proportionality, avoidance of excessive force, and demonstration of proper regard for the rights of innocent persons must be observed. Whether the use of preventive force is justified in such cases will depend, as with self-defense against an imminent attack, upon whether it is reasonable to conclude that the target of prevention has wrongfully imposed a dire risk on others.

The analogy with the law of conspiracy and of self-defense takes us only so far, however, since it shows only that if similar conditions were satisfied in the case of a state or a terrorist group, it would be justifiable to use force to arrest and punish them. Whether it can be justifiable to use deadly force against them depends on the additional assumption that the wrongful act they plan to commit will be *sudden and will cause massive violations of human rights*. In such cases, the use of military force will often be necessary to alleviate these threats.

One might object that the idea of alleviating an unjustly imposed risk through preventive action justifies inflicting harm only on the one who has imposed the risk, whereas preventive action will inevitably involve a risk of harm to others. As we have already acknowledged, preventive military action (unlike ordinary acts of law enforcement) will almost invariably risk harm to the innocent. This is equally true, however, of intervention to stop a presently occurring genocide and of interdiction, and even of the least controversial cases of self-defense against an aggressive attack. Unless one is willing to embrace an absolute pacifist position that rules out the use of military force in self-defense, the fact that a preventive response to the wrongful imposition of dire risk may involve harm to innocent persons does not necessarily render it morally illegitimate.

Given that military action typically involves much greater risk of harm to innocent persons than ordinary policy action against conspirators, the threshold of expected harm needed to justify preventive military action should be high. From a cosmopolitan perspective, an appropriate threshold is the occurrence of *massive violations of basic human rights.* As noted earlier, by "basic human rights" we mean the most widely acknowledged rights that are already recognized in the major human rights conventions. The requirement of massive violations of *basic* human rights sets a very high threshold for preventive action.

Advocates of a blanket prohibition on preventive force have one last arrow in their quiver. They can argue that prevention carries special risks that are not present in the case of armed responses to actually occurring attacks. The appeal to hypothetical examples such as that of the sudden release of a deadly virus, it might therefore be argued, glosses over an important distinction between the justification of a particular action and the justification of a rule allowing that type of action. Even if preventive action would be morally justified when certain highly ideal conditions are satisfied, it does not follow that we should replace current restrictions on preventive force with a more permissive rule.

The prima facie moral argument for preventive action asserts that preventive action may be undertaken to remove or mitigate a wrongfully imposed dire risk. However, for a dire risk to lead to severe harms, a long causal series of events must typically be completed. Even if the probability of each event in the causal series is high, the probability of the harm will be much lower, since it is the product of all the probabilities of the events in the series. Thus suppose that the causal series anticipated by the potential preventer consists of events A, B, C, and D and that each event has a probability of .8. The anticipated harm (the massive violation of basic human rights) will occur only if the whole series of events occurs; but the probability of this is the product of the probabilities of each of the members of the series: .4096. If the probability of individual events is lower, the joint probability is dramatically reduced. Furthermore, if events are *uncertain*—that is, probabilities are unknown—it is impossible to calculate precise probabilities.

It is not enough to show, the objector would conclude, that there are some circumstances in which preventive action would be morally justified. If these cases are few—and if there is a significant risk that those contemplating preventive action may err in determining whether those circumstances obtain—then perhaps preventive action should be prohibited altogether, as traditional just war theory holds.[9]

This argument from the special risks of prevention to a blanket prohibition is fatally incomplete. It overlooks the fact that acceptable

[9] In one sense, this objection points out the obvious: that tradeoffs exist in policy between timely action and certainty about the necessity of action. The longer one waits, the more information one is likely to gain; but by the same token, one's ability to affect the situation may be reduced. Britain and France had better reason in 1939 than in 1936 to regard Germany as a threat to their security, but the cost of averting the threat was higher in 1939.

risk reduction can be achieved not only by a blanket prohibition but also by a more permissive rule embedded in an appropriate institutional framework. Indeed, a blanket prohibition comes at a high cost, since it rules out action to prevent massive violations of basic human rights even when the costs of prevention are very low and the likelihood of its success is very high.

A blanket prohibition rule also tends to reduce the effectiveness of coercive diplomacy, which may often be the most promising means of preventing terrible harm as a result of foreseeable future aggression. Coercive diplomacy can be defined as "bargaining accompanied by threats designed to induce fear sufficient to change behavior" (Lauren 1994, 23). It includes deterrence but is more comprehensive, since it also incorporates what Thomas Schelling once called "compellance"—inducing an adversary not merely to refrain from some action but to engage in an action that it would not otherwise undertake (Schelling 1966, 69–78). For most states, most of the time, illegality is viewed as a cost, if only because of damage to reputation. If preventive force is illegal, states will be less likely to use it and efforts at coercive diplomacy through the threat of preventive force will be less credible.

A Critique of the Legal Status Quo View

The Legal Status Quo (Security Council authorization) view and the Cosmopolitan Institutional view both reject the blanket prohibition. Each holds that we can effectively mitigate the special risks of prevention by creating institutional safeguards. Although reliance on Security Council authorization is superior to a blanket prohibition, it is not the best institutional alternative.

The first and most obvious moral flaw of the legal status quo is the moral arbitrariness of the permanent member veto. From a cosmopolitan standpoint, there is no justification for this radically unequal distribution of decision-making authority. The veto seriously impugns the legitimacy of the legal status quo.

Second, the use and anticipated use of the veto can block preventive actions that we have morally compelling reasons to undertake. As the Independent International Commission on Kosovo argues, and as the secretary-general of the UN acknowledged at the time, the case for military action to prevent (further) ethnic cleansing of Albanians in Kosovo was very strong, but no resolution to intervene was proposed in the Security Council because it was known that Russia (and perhaps China as well) would veto it (Independent International Commission on Kosovo 2001).

Third, the legal status quo lacks provisions for holding the decision-makers who propose preventive force (and those members of the Council who must approve it) accountable for their actions. There is subsequently very little assurance that only morally defensible interventions will be authorized. Without standards for when preventive action is justified and without accountability mechanisms to increase the probability that those standards are met, authorization is likely to be unprincipled rather than guided by a proper concern for human rights.

These flaws constitute a strong prima facie case for rejecting the Legal Status Quo view—but only if a superior alternative is feasible. We have seen that none of the three conventional alternatives—the Just War Blanket Prohibition, National Interest, and Expanded Right of Self-Defense views—is adequate. If the current legal status quo ought to be abandoned, it must be for a new arrangement that provides more, not less, accountability.

The Risks of Preventive Action

Even though preventive military action is sometimes justified, it creates a number of serious risks, two of which are of special concern with respect to preventive action, even if they are not unique to it. The first is that self-interest masquerading as concern for the common good may lead to decisions that are unjustifiable. The second is that preventive action will undermine existing beneficial institutional norms constraining the use of force. Each of these risks is particularly worrisome since predictions that violence may occur are generally more subject to error and bias than observations that it is already occurring.

These risks indicate the need for institutional safeguards to make decision-making regarding the preventive use of force more responsible. The more effective these safeguards are, the more the probability of abuse will be reduced, and the more justified it will be to undertake preventive action to cope with massive violations of basic human rights. By reducing the risks of abuse, institutional safeguards can make preventive action more feasible on a greater range of issues, promoting basic human rights.

Institutional safeguards therefore take the sting out of the fact that there is no unique, nonarbitrary threshold of probability of harm needed to justify prevention. We cannot reduce the risk of unjustified preventive action to zero, but we can lower it sufficiently so that preventive action can become a more useful tool of policy. Our institutional analysis in the next section is designed to show that this can be achieved.

Cosmopolitan Institutions for Accountability

We advocate three principles for designing institutions to govern the use of preventive force. The first is *effectiveness:* the institution should effectively promote the responsible use of force to prevent massive violations of basic human rights, regardless of whose rights are threatened. One way to achieve this is to design institutions governing the preventive use of force in which decisions to use force preventively are made by agents who are, comparatively speaking, morally reliable, and who are provided incentives to make these decisions responsibly.

Only those states that have decent records regarding the protection of basic human rights should be allowed to participate in institutional processes for controlling the preventive use of force. Those who have demonstrated respect for human rights over a considerable period of time are generally more reliable decision-makers regarding the use of force for protecting human rights than those who have not. We call this the comparative moral reliability criterion.

Yet even agents that are morally reliable, comparatively speaking, may act unreliably unless they are provided with incentives that induce them to make decisions on the basis of the best available information, and to take actions that are consistent with cosmopolitan principles. In particular, incentives are needed to counter the tendency of those proposing the preventive use of force to overestimate the risk to be averted and the tendency of others to shirk responsibilities to protect basic human rights.

Our second design principle also flows from a core commitment of the cosmopolitan ethical perspective: *mutual respect* for all persons. Being willing to help protect the basic human rights of all persons is one important way in which we show respect. Showing respect also entails being willing to justify one's actions to others. Arrogant dismissal of others' views without providing reasons and evidence is inconsistent with this principle.

Within democratic societies, this principle of mutual respect means that people wielding power and the means of coercion must respond to queries about their use from those who ultimately must authorize these actions—members of the society in question. Those who wield power must also offer justifications of their actions to those who are affected by them, including those who are not members of their societies. In the words of the Declaration of Independence, they must show "a decent respect to the opinions of Mankind."

Our third principle of institutional design, *inclusiveness*, reflects the values of both effectiveness and mutual respect. Effectiveness in world politics depends on the independent actions of many states. Therefore, the principle of effectiveness suggests at least a presumption in favor of maximal inclusiveness, unless countervailing considerations intervene. In addition, the principle of mutual respect implies that institutions should be as inclusive as is feasible, given their goals, since all are entitled to equal regard.

In many cases effectiveness, mutual respect, and inclusiveness will point in the same direction. But it is worth noting that there can be a conflict between promoting effectiveness by selecting agents that possess comparative moral reliability, and inclusiveness. Inclusiveness argues for giving all states access to participation in institutional processes for controlling the preventive use of force, whereas the need to enlist agents who have a sincere commitment to and a sound understanding of human rights favors restricting participation. How the tradeoffs between inclusiveness and comparative moral reliability are made is of crucial importance for institutional design, as indicated by our discussion below of possible arrangements for a democratic coalition to supplement the authorization processes of the Security Council.

The Concept of Accountability and the Preventive Use of Force

No single state can be counted upon fully to take into proper account the interests of others, particularly when considering the use of military force. Therefore, processes by which states, or nonstate actors, can hold states accountable are essential if the parochial concerns of the most powerful states are not to be allowed to prevail over broader interests and shared values.

Standard definitions of accountability emphasize both information and sanctions. "A is accountable to B when A is obliged to inform B about A's (past or future) actions and decisions, to justify them, and to suffer punishment in the case of eventual misconduct."[10] Accountability operates both *ex ante* and *ex post*. Those states that propose to use force preventively must, under cosmopolitan principles, consult with other states and make their intentions known to international society more generally before using force. Having used force, they must provide information, answer questions, and subject themselves to sanctions according to rules that have been established in advance.

Inclusion of sanctions (including punishments) is crucial, since there will be little incentive to comply with the requirement to answer questions and provide justifications unless those to whom the action is to be justified can sanction those in power. In addition, accountable institutions require specification of the standards to which agents are to be held accountable, those to whom they are to be accountable, and a willingness on the part of agents to provide information and answer questions about their behavior.

For a cosmopolitan view, the most fundamental standard of accountability is that states must act in ways that are designed to respect and protect the human rights of all persons. They are only to use force or to authorize its use for the sake of preventing violations of human rights. In addition, justified preventive action must include standards for *how* preventive force is to be applied so that it reflects the cosmopolitan commitment to basic human rights.

Prominent among the substantive standards for determining the way in which preventive action may be conducted will be the traditional *jus in*

---

[10] Schedler 1999, 17. The word "punishment" could be interpreted in too formal and restrictive a way. We accept this definition only with the proviso that it refers more broadly to a *penalty*.

bello principles—that harm to innocents should be minimized, force must be proportional to the end to be achieved, excessive force is to be avoided, and unnecessary suffering should not be inflicted on enemy combatants. To institutionalize adequately these standards requires mechanisms that help to ensure that they are applied correctly and that there are effective sanctions to increase compliance with them.

To determine whether these standards are met, information is required. Thus the second component of a defensible accountability system is provisions for *the sharing of information*. A state proposing to use force must share its information about the risks of large-scale human rights violations that would result from inaction as well as the risks of action, especially regarding harm to innocent persons. The information that it provides must be comprehensive enough for other states to make independent judgments on the costs and benefits of the preventive use of force.

Procedures that ensure information sharing are necessary for providing the appropriate incentives for action. Without such procedures, states could pretend to be using preventive force to protect human rights while in fact acting to preserve their hegemony in a region, to protect weak regimes with which they are allied, or to gain economic advantages. The requirement of information sharing is designed, therefore, not only to correct false beliefs but also to reduce opportunistic use of force. Information sharing is therefore required by the design principle of effectiveness. It is also required by the principle of mutual respect, since mutual respect is evidenced by a willingness to share information with equals rather than to demand deference from those regarded as inferior in the capacity to understand issues and make decisions.

Introducing *sanctions* for the violation of standards is the third element of an accountability system. It is also the most difficult to institutionalize. Different societies hold different values, and states are likely to privilege their own interests, so it is infeasible to rely on voluntary compliance. World politics is often seen as a "self-help" system in which each state is responsible for its own security (Waltz 1979). Without sanctions, rules for the regulation of the preventive use of force would almost certainly be ineffective. Unless there are sanctions for violations of the requirement to share information, some states will misrepresent the facts, exaggerating the probability of the harm that they propose to prevent. Unless there are sanctions against those who use excessive force, states are likely to discount the harm their forceful actions will inflict on others. Without effective sanctions, the institutions will be ineffective, since in the absence of sanctions, "the strong do what they can and the weak suffer what they must" (Thucydides 1982, 351 [bk. 5, para. 84]).

Standards, information, and sanctions are all crucial to accountability, but they leave open the question, To whom should agents who are considering wielding military force be held accountable? We have already suggested that a cosmopolitan view entails a presumption in favor of inclusiveness. In addition, the design principle of mutual respect creates a presumption that participation in institutional processes for the use of force to protect the human rights of all should be open to all. This presumption could be rebutted, however, if the effectiveness of the accountability regime requires restricting participation to those agents that are *comparatively* morally reliable.

Ex Ante *Accountability*

With respect to a state's proposal to engage in the preventive use of force, *ex ante* accountability requires that all of the issues and options (including nonmilitary options) be discussed, and that states that question the necessity of the intervention have the opportunity to interrogate those who propose it. Consistent with the principle of mutual respect, rational persuasion must be employed. Reliance on principled rational persuasion also means that parties speaking in favor of or against preventive military action must acknowledge that their decisions will have precedential value for future decisions. Both the party contemplating intervention and those who must ratify its decision must therefore acknowledge at least a prima facie obligation, on future occasions, to follow the principles that they have invoked to defend their actions, regardless of the identities of the intervener and the target of intervention. In this sense, the expectation that current decisions will have precedential value for future decisions serves as a kind of veil of ignorance, making the procedure conducive to fairness and therefore to mutual respect (for a more general argument, see Keohane 2001, 1–13; see also Brennan and Buchanan 1985, 30; Frohlich and Oppenheimer 1992). Even if a very powerful state may not expect to be a target of future preventive action, it may worry that the principles it employs to justify or to oppose preventive action will be used by other powerful states to justify their own preventive uses of force.[11]

Mutual respect also requires that all participants in the process of deciding on the preventive use of force must have equal standing to pose questions to the potential intervener and offer arguments against intervention. In addition, there is at least a strong presumption against according weighted votes or veto power.

Finally, the process of deliberation *ex ante* must involve the participation of a group of states with diverse interests. Too much uniformity of interests among the participants would run the risk of bias, perhaps even turning the regime for accountability into a tool for domination. Protection of the human rights of all requires diversity of perspectives.

---

[11] In the World Trade Organization states behave in this way. They are reluctant to put forward legal arguments to defend their own practices that could be used in the future by other states to justify protectionist measures.

Ex Post *Accountability*

It is quite possible that what is discovered after even a successful military attack will not justify the actions that were taken. *Ex ante* accountability is therefore not sufficient; provisions for *ex post* accountability are also essential. The attacking states must come back with a full report to the body that authorized their actions. They must also allow an impartial commission appointed by that body to have free and timely access to all places in the country controlled by the attacking states in the course of the preventive action. That is, they must facilitate the generation and publicizing of the best available impartial information about the actual effects of preventive use of military force.

Evaluation of the results of the preventive military action would focus on the consistency of the acting states' behavior with the statements they made in the *ex ante* accountability process. Two issues are particularly important:

- Was the information gained *ex post* about the risk-imposing actions of the target consistent with the statements made by the states proposing action *ex ante*?
- Were the military actions of the attacking states consistent with their assurances *ex ante* that their actions would be proportional to the objectives being attained? The justification of military action on the basis of risk only justifies action necessary to remove or significantly reduce the risk. It should ultimately be up to the authorizing body, not to the attacking states, to decide how far military action needs to go to attain the agreed objectives.

With respect to the justification of an attack, two contrasting inferences might be drawn from information gathered after the war: one, on the whole, the *ex post* investigations support the assessments of risk made before the attack; or two, on the whole, the *ex post* investigations fail to corroborate those assessments. Of course, there would be gradations of judgment between these two poles.

If the situation corresponds more closely to situation one, the attacking states would indeed have performed a public service for the world by eliminating or reducing the threat that weapons of mass destruction would be used or that large-scale violations of basic human rights would be inflicted by some other means. These positive contributions would be counted against their financial obligations. Indeed, it would be presumed that those states that had not shouldered the risk of preventive military action would bear special responsibility for financial support in rebuilding the target country should the preventive use of force have caused extensive damage. Insofar as feasible, they would also bear responsibility for peace enforcement. That is, under these conditions those states that had not supported preventive military action would be sanctioned as "free riders," who were informed about the threat but refused to act in a timely manner. Although the economic obligations of such free riders would be limited by their economic capabilities—poor and weak states would not be unduly burdened in any case—they would, in this situation, be *greater* than those imposed on states with comparable resources that supported the military action.[12]

However, if the *ex post* review concludes that the preventive action was unjustified, the attacking states and their supporters would be held accountable. They would have to face sanctions for their actions in much the same way that states participating in the international regime are liable for their infringements of its rules. They would be required to compensate those who suffered harm from the preventive action and to provide full financial support for operations that restore the country's infrastructure and enable it to govern itself effectively. Furthermore, the intervening parties would not be allowed to control the political situation in the conquered country, or to determine the allocation of aid or the awarding of contracts to firms offering services for the reconstruction effort. If states know *ex ante* that these rules are in place, incentives for opportunistic interventions aimed at domination rather than protection of human rights will be diminished.[13]

A crucial component of our proposal is an impartial independent commission, appointed by the authorizing body (such as the Security Council). This commission would have prompt access to the conquered country and would determine the magnitude of reconstruction aid needed. It would also determine the allocation of responsibilities to provide the necessary funds.

One particularly attractive feature of the *ex post* accountability requirement is that it provides the intervening state with a powerful incentive to comply with the just war principle of using the minimum of force sufficient to achieve the goal of prevention. This requirement places the burden of evidence on the intervening state: it must be able to show that its *ex ante* judgments in support of preventive action were valid, and this requires that evidence to substantiate those judgments be available for all to see *ex post*. Were the intervener to use excessive force, this could destroy the needed

---

[12] The analogy of conscientious objection may be helpful. Conscientious objectors may avoid military service but are expected to subject themselves to at least equivalent burdens and risks as those who do carry arms, by serving as medics, for example.

[13] The Fourth Geneva Convention relative to the Protection of Civilian Persons in Time of War of August 12, 1949, and other provisions of international law specify the obligations of occupying powers. These include ensuring respect for basic human rights, including restoration and maintenance of law and order and provision of food and medical care to the population. Under our proposal these obligations would not be diminished, but occupying powers whose actions had been judged by the *ex post* review to be unjustified would have their ability to make decisions severely constrained.

evidence. *Ex post* accountability thus institutionalizes an important just war principle in such a way as to create incentives for compliance with it.

Similarly, the knowledge that its actions will be subject to an impartial review would give the intervening state an incentive to minimize harm to noncombatants, especially if significant penalties would follow upon a finding that the harm to noncombatants was excessive. These would primarily consist of compensation to those harmed or their families, but might include other sanctions as well.

The key to this mechanism of accountability is a *contingent contract* that applies *both* to states seeking to use force preventively and to states opposing the preventive use of force. States would agree that after the conflict they would abide by the judgments of the authorizing body on the validity of their *ex ante* arguments. They would also agree that, should this judgment go against them and the independent commission determine a level of compensation, they would pay such compensation (subject perhaps to an appeals procedure). It should be emphasized that states opposing preventive action would also be liable to pay compensation if *ex post* discoveries confirmed the claims made *ex ante* by the states advocating preventive action and disconfirmed their own *ex ante* objections. In other words, the contract is double-sided and does not discriminate against potential interveners.[14]

Such a contractual arrangement would decrease the incentives for dishonesty on the part of both proponents and opponents of preventive action in their *ex ante* presentation of evidence. A major problem facing all but the most powerful states, and all publics, is that they do not have access to privileged intelligence information, particularly with respect to closed societies and dictatorships such as North Korea and Iraq. They are therefore subject to being deceived about the real state of affairs. And since they are aware that they do not have access to much information, they may become unreasonably skeptical of proposed interventions (see Akerlof 1970).

Another advantage of this contractual arrangement is that it would limit abuses of victory in a preventive war. When interventions result in large-scale damage, decisions about how to reconstruct the country, including those relating to its political-economic system and control of its resources, must be made in consultation with the authorizing body. When the states engaged in preventive military action have succeeded in their objective—the elimination of the risks for which they claimed to go to war—they must subject their plans for postwar reconstruction and prevention of recurrence of the risks to the authorizing body.

---

[14] Here it might be objected that the strongest states might agree *ex ante* to pay compensation if an *ex post* review found their preventive actions to be unjustified, but simply fail to pay up. To avoid this problem, assets could be escrowed *ex ante*. Such an arrangement was used in the agreements that ended the U.S.-Iran hostage crisis in 1981 and that established the U.S.-Iran Claims Tribunal. See Carswell and Davis 1985, 201–34, and document in appendix D, 405–22.

All states could stand to gain from the implementation of the accountability safeguards that we have described. States not expecting to use preventive military force would gain more reliable information before having to make decisions on its authorization by a collective body such as the United Nations. States expecting to use preventive force could hope to gain credibility for their claims, and therefore be likely to generate broader support for preventive military actions that are justified. And all could benefit from the combination of inducements to avoid dysfunctional deadlock and abuses of authority.

Alternative Institutional Models for Accountability

In this section we discuss three alternative arrangements that might reasonably satisfy the requirements of cosmopolitan accountability. None of these arrangements may be politically feasible at present, even though we have sought to design them in a way that takes a nonideal world of primarily self-interested states as a given. We hope that people of goodwill and sophistication may be interested in refining and implementing them, or institutions inspired by them. These suggestions therefore fall somewhere between mere thought experiments and proposals that could be implemented under current conditions.

Institutional Model 1: Accountability without the Veto

The first model relies exclusively on the Security Council but creates mechanisms for *ex ante* and *ex post* accountability and removes decisions about preventive force from the scope of the Council's permanent member veto. The veto could still be exercised in other Council deliberations, but it would be abolished in the case of decisions whether to use preventive force.

On this model, the provisions for *ex ante* accountability described above would structure the Council's deliberations, if time permitted. If nine members of the Council voted in favor, a proposed preventive action would go forward, subject to an impartial *ex post* review as described. The requirement of a supermajority of nine votes appears reasonable, since it ensures that a diverse group of states would have to agree to the action.

If a state or group of states uses preventive force prior to Council authorization on the grounds that there was no time to seek it, then they would also be subject to an impartial *ex post* review. Such a review would also determine whether it had been reasonable to go forward without prior approval by the Council. Should the review determine that they were not justified in attacking without prior approval, they would be subject to sanctions at least as severe as those imposed on attackers who received authorization under false pretenses.

There are three major arguments in favor of dropping the veto for these decisions. First, it has no ethical standing, since it is a political artifact of the era in which the UN was founded, and offends against the presumption of equality implied by the design principle of mutual respect by giving disproportionate power to some states. Second, removing the veto reduces the inertia in the present system, making it more likely that force could be used preventively when its use would be morally compelling. Third, abolishing the veto would encourage states that resist the use of preventive force to propose constructive alternatives. The lack of a veto would make it necessary for states to persuade others that the preventive use of force is not necessary. In some cases this would require that they present alternatives to its use. At present, those who wield the veto need not persuade, they can simply dictate the outcome.

Despite these attractions, any proposal that includes abolishing the permanent member veto will meet insuperable political resistance to its implementation in the foreseeable future. States that now possess the veto are unlikely to relinquish it, and no one else can make the proposed change. Moreover, it is especially unlikely that they would relinquish the veto over something as important and controversial as the preventive use of force. Even if the permanent members saw some merit in the proposal to relinquish the veto only in decisions concerning preventive use of force, they might fear a slippery slope leading to the loss of the veto in other areas. Finally, there is a danger that removing the veto for states wielding significant force could create military conflict between the United Nations and a great power, which would be a disaster.[15] This alternative for institutional reform, then, is the least feasible of the three alternatives.

Institutional Model 2: Accountability Despite the Veto

A less radical and correspondingly more feasible model would create mechanisms for *ex ante* and *ex post* accountability as in model 1 but leave the permanent member veto in place.[16] On this second model, the Security

---

[15] I. L. Claude likens the UN Security Council veto to "a fuse in an electrical circuit," reflecting the wise conviction that "in cases of sharp conflict among the great powers the Council ought, for safety's sake, to be incapacitated" (Claude 1962, 160).

[16] Article 51 of the UN Charter states that Members of the United Nations that respond with force to an armed attack shall "immediately" report their actions to the Security Council. Our institutional model 2 goes significantly beyond Article 51 in three ways: it expands the scope of a reporting requirement beyond the case of self-defense against an actual armed attack to cover preventive force; it specifies that the report must be made by an impartial body and must explicitly address issues of fact and of reasonableness in the justification of the use of force; and it attaches penalties in the case of an unfavorable report. Article 51, in contrast, allows the party using force to report on itself, specifies no criteria of evaluation for the report, and mentions no consequences of an unfavorable report.

Council would have to approve military action by the procedures currently in the Charter. The Council would appoint an impartial body to determine whether the intervener's *ex ante* justification for preventive action is confirmed *ex post*.

Such an arrangement might reduce the likelihood that vetoes would be used, since those states reluctant to endorse preventive action would at least be assured that the results would be impartially reported, with provisions for penalties in the case of malfeasance. In other words, they would not be issuing a "blank check" to those initiating force preventively. To that extent, the second model's provisions for accountability would alleviate the problems that the veto poses. However, it should be emphasized that for *ex post* accountability to work, it would also be necessary for the Council to create suitable penalties to be applied in the case of a negative *ex post* evaluation.[17] Model 2, like model 1, builds on the existing UN structure, but is more feasible than model 1, since it does not require those with the veto to relinquish it.

Nevertheless, even the measures proposed in model 2 might seem to be too costly for the leader of a coalition for prevention. Why should the coalition leader accept these constraints if it is to bear the principal costs of military action? The answer is that only by accepting constraints, *ex ante*, could the coalition leader make credible its justification for preventive force and its own promises regarding its conduct during and after the conflict.[18] And credible promises are essential to induce other members of the Security Council to grant authorization for the use of preventive force. Furthermore, securing a broad coalition *ex ante* can provide valuable insurance for the interveners, since they could otherwise be stuck with bearing the full cost of reconstruction if political conditions in the occupied territories worsen after a successful military operation. States that do not

[17] This necessity raises the problem of an *ex post* veto by the intervening state or states of the findings of the impartial commission or penalties implied by those findings. This problem could be solved by adapting a suggestion recently made by Thomas Franck, who points out that Article 27 provides that "decisions of the Security Council on procedural matters shall be made by an affirmative vote of nine members." That is, on procedural matters, the veto is inapplicable. *Ex ante* the Council could decide that votes on the composition and report of the impartial commission, and on any recommendations for penalties, would be considered procedural. (Professor Franck's proposal concerns specification of what constitutes a "material breach" regarding UN resolutions concerning Iraq. See Franck 2002.)

[18] When the United States invaded Iraq in 2003 without Security Council authorization, the Bush administration's chief justification for doing so was to destroy weapons of mass destruction, which it said were present in that country. It can be argued that as of seven months after the invasion began, the United States has failed to show either that there were weapons of mass destruction in Iraq at the time of the invasion or that there was good reason to believe that they were present. If this still appears to be the case after all the evidence is in, the problem of achieving credibility for the preventive use of force will be even greater in the future. The case for the *ex ante* and *ex post* accountability mechanisms we propose will be all the stronger.

consent to the use of force in the first place are likely to demand a high price for being involved in the postconflict reconstruction.[19]

Although superior to model 1, model 2 is also unsatisfactory. It avoids the impracticality of model 1, but keeping the permanent member veto comes at a high price, because the veto is both morally arbitrary and facilitates a lack of accountability. The veto gives those who wield it little incentive to persuade others by principled argument or to offer constructive alternatives to the use of force. So long as the decision whether to use preventive force rests exclusively with the Security Council as currently constituted, there will be no recourse against deadlock produced by arbitrary and self-interested use of the veto.

Institutional Model 3: A Role for a Democratic Coalition

The third and most defensible institutional alternative is to implement the Security Council–based accountability mechanisms described in model 2 but supplement them with a supporting role for a coalition of reasonably democratic states. By democratic states we mean those with constitutional, representative governments, competition for elected positions through reasonably fair elections, and entrenched basic civil and political rights. A fairly wide range of political institutions and cultures can meet these minimal requirements. There is no suggestion that democratic states include only U.S. or Western European–style democracies. The point is simply to exclude states that are unambiguous violators of human rights.

Of course there is disagreement as to precisely how these elements of democracy are to be understood. For our purposes, however, there is no need to enter into that debate. Our proposal is to begin with a core group of states whose democratic credentials are uncontroversial, such as the members of the European Union plus states such as Australia, Canada, Chile, Costa Rica, Japan, South Africa, and South Korea. Unlike NATO, the coalition that intervened in Kosovo in 1999, such a coalition would be open to states from all regions of the world. Indeed, we expect that most of its members would not be from Europe or North America. The initial members would be authorized to admit additional countries through a transparent process utilizing publicly stated criteria for membership. Consistent with our overall argument, the democratic coalition would itself need institutionalized procedures for accountability, both with respect to admission to membership and for substantive decisions.

From a principled standpoint, creating a democratic coalition is attractive because it would reinforce the role of states that meet our standard for comparative moral reliability. This is not to say that we

---

[19] The United States gained Security Council approval for the first Gulf War in 1991, but not for the invasion of Iraq in 2003. Other countries paid approximately 80 percent of the cost of the former conflict; so far, the United States is paying over 80 percent of the costs of the latter.

believe that democracies always, or even typically, act in ways that are consistent with cosmopolitan morality. Indeed, a key premise of our institutional proposals is that all states often behave in parochial and self-interested ways. We believe, however, that when democracies violate cosmopolitan principles, they are more likely to be criticized by their citizens for doing so, and will be more likely to rectify their behavior in response. They may not be morally reliable agents, but *comparatively* they are more reliable than autocracies.

The third model is feasible, since formal UN action would not be necessary to implement it. Indeed, if a large and diverse cluster of democracies proposed it, no single state could easily block it. The democratic coalition would be based on agreements among its members—not necessarily through a formal treaty. Over time, its practices could become part of customary international law. Furthermore, recent experience with respect to the Anglo-American war against Iraq suggests that democratic countries are capable of making independent judgments about the proposals of a superpower, even when faced with the prospect of bilateral sanctions. Chile and Mexico, for instance, refused to support the resolution authorizing war against Iraq put forward by the United States and United Kingdom in February and March of 2003.

In international law, recognition of new states is awarded by existing states, acting individually or through institutions such as the United Nations. Those entities that are indisputably sovereign states have the authority to determine which other entities will be treated as sovereign. Likewise, the initial core of the democratic coalition would be self-designated states whose credentials as stable democracies are unassailable. They would then develop membership criteria that would determine which other states would be eligible. These criteria would be public, developed and applied through transparent, accountable processes. An additional advantage of a democratic coalition is that accountability is much more institutionalized within democratic societies than in authoritarian ones.

The incentives for joining the democratic coalition would be substantial. Submitting to the coalition's deliberations could enable states proposing the use of military force to gain legitimacy for their actions without Security Council authorization. Furthermore, the accountability arrangements of the coalition would increase the credibility of its arguments, thereby enabling it to gain allies who would share the costs of military action and reconstruction. And other members would receive valuable recognition as democratic states that are regarded as sufficiently trustworthy to participate in important decisions regarding the use of force. More important, they would gain decision-making authority, both with respect to legitimizing the preventive use of force and for determining which other states should be allowed to join. There would also be a powerful incentive to help initiate the coalition or, if others initiated it, to join early, since the original members would have more say in determining the rules under which the coalition would operate.

The principle of mutual respect implies that the rich members of the democratic coalitions would have to offer poorer democracies better treatment than is now the case with respect to both trade and aid. Members of the democratic coalition would extend trade privileges to one another, beyond the requirements of the World Trade Organization, and the richer members would offer particularly generous aid to the poorer ones.[20]

The democratic coalition would not replace the Security Council. Instead, if a state or group of states proposed preventive action to the Council and was unable to gain its authorization, it could then present its case to the democratic coalition. The democratic coalition would have its own *ex ante* and *ex post* accountability processes that might differ in detail from those of the Security Council under model 2, but that would likewise be designed to approximate as closely as feasible the design principles for a cosmopolitan accountability regime.

The third model, then, includes two parts. The first is the existing Security Council arrangement, including the permanent member veto, but importantly modified to include *ex ante* and *ex post* accountability mechanisms. The second is a distinct body for decisions concerning the use of preventive force, consisting of a coalition of democratic states, geographically unrestricted in membership, and designed to go into operation only in the event of deadlock in the Security Council.

The most obvious advantage of model 3 is that it provides for the possibility of responsible decisions to use force when the Security Council fails to do so. But another, equally important advantage is that the possibility that a decision will go to the democratic coalition provides an incentive for the Security Council to act more responsibly. Model 3, then, remedies the chief deficiency of model 2 without requiring the impracticality of abolishing the permanent veto as in model 1. If model 3 were adopted, permanent members of the Council would be more reluctant to veto proposals for preventive action without good reasons and substantial support, if doing so would transfer decision-making authority to an arena in which they did not enjoy veto power—and in which they might perhaps not be represented at all.

Conversely, the continued operation of the Security Council, with strengthened institutions for accountability of the sort we recommend, could make the idea of a democratic coalition more attractive. It would reduce the likelihood that resort to the democratic coalition would be overused, creating a schism between the democracies and the other members of the UN.

The third institutional model creates healthy competition with the UN system without bypassing it altogether. More specifically, the democratic

---

[20] We are indebted to Michael Doyle for the suggestion that led to this proposal.

coalition provides an incentive for the permanent members to use the veto more responsibly and for all members of the Council to realize that they no longer enjoy an absolute monopoly on the legitimate authorization of preventive use of force.

None of these schemes could function effectively without prior agreement on a threshold criterion for predicted harm to be prevented. We have argued that a starting point for such a threshold is the idea of massive violations of basic human rights. To create a workable criterion would require gaining agreement among the participants in these institutions on a minimal list of basic human rights. The problem of specifying when "massive" violations of basic human rights have occurred would be more difficult. There would, however, be clear cases—for example, where the threatened harm is the detonation of a nuclear bomb in a densely populated area. A solution to this problem would presumably involve a combination of prior agreement on levels of risk sufficient for triggering serious consideration of preventive action and a developing case law that would provide further specificity over time.

The concept of accountability is crucial in thinking about more adequate institutional procedures for decisions concerning the use of force. States advocating preventive war should be subjected both to *ex ante* and *ex post* accountability. *Ex ante*, they must be able to persuade other states of the merits of their case for military action. *Ex post*, their actions must be subjected to scrutiny and potential sanctions.

Our view might be seen as unduly constraining to states that might otherwise engage in justified preventive intervention. This is indeed a possibility, but it must be emphasized that our argument is *comparative*. Our system for cosmopolitan accountability is less constraining than what we take to be the most plausible of the competing views, the Legal Status Quo view, since our proposal merely envisages a democratic coalition as an *additional* channel for authorization.

Even the most powerful states wish others to view their actions as legitimate. They need allies when undertaking military action and supporters to provide policing assistance, civilian infrastructure, and financial support in the aftermath of war. By meeting the requirements of the cosmopolitan accountability regime, a state proposing preventive military action would gain legitimacy by submitting to the rule of law, and credibility by allaying the suspicions of other states that the justification given for prevention was not sound or that prevention was a pretext for conquest. The cosmopolitan accountability regime should be attractive, then, not only to those wishing to constrain states bent on preventive action but also to those seeking to engage in it.

This is not to say that we regard our proposal as feasible in the short run. There is, as Machiavelli noted, "nothing more difficult to take in hand, more perilous to conduct, or more uncertain in its success, than to take the lead in the introduction of a new order of things" (*The Prince*

[1532], ch. 6). Considerable discussion and refinement would be necessary for our accountability regime to be accepted by states. Countries in the global South will have to be reassured that the rich countries are really following cosmopolitan principles of mutual respect. Potential interveners will have to come to recognize that the advantages of accountability outweigh constraints on their freedom of action.

Even the process of discussing accountability in this way would be an advance, by focusing attention on the problem of eliciting accurate information in situations of potential military conflict.[21] Such discussions could themselves enhance the reputational and credibility costs of *ex ante* dissimulation. Over time, we hope that our proposal could provide an intellectual resource for reformers seeking to promote effective multilateral action, with safeguards against its abuse. Establishing an institutionalized system of accountability for preventive war would constitute a progressive step in international governance.

Acknowledgments

The authors are grateful to J. L. Holzgrefe for stimulating conversations that helped to generate this essay. We have benefited from comments on presentations of this essay from participants at colloquia held at the Woodrow Wilson School, Princeton University, February 19, 2003; the Faculty Colloquium, Sanford Institute of Public Policy, Duke University, February 24, 2003; Duke Law School, March 19, 2003; the University of Sydney Law School, August 22, 2003; Columbia University Law School, October 28, 2003; and the University of California Law School, November 17, 2003. We thank Michael Byers, Neta Crawford, Ruth Grant, Henry R. Nau, Joseph S. Nye Jr., and two anonymous reviewers for valuable written comments on an earlier draft. We are particularly grateful to Christian Barry and Joel Rosenthal for their extensive and perceptive suggestions. We are grateful for research support from the Triangle Institute for International Security–Duke University project "Wielding American Power," funded by the Carnegie Corporation of New York and its International Peace and Security Program.

References

Akerlof, George. 1970. "The Market for Lemons." *Quarterly Journal of Economics* 84, no. 3 (August): 488–500.
Brennan, Geoffrey, and James M. Buchanan. 1985. *The Reason of Rules: Constitutional Political Economy*. New York: Cambridge University Press.

---

[21] We are indebted to Jeremy Waldron for this point.

Buchanan, Allen. 2003. "Human Rights." In *Justice, Legitimacy, and Self-Determination: Moral Foundations for International Law*. Oxford: Oxford University Press.

Carswell, Robert, and Richard Davis. 1985. "Crafting the Financial Settlement." In *American Hostages in Iran: The Conduct of a Crisis*, edited by Warren Christopher et al., 201–34. New Haven: Yale University Press, for the Council on Foreign Relations.

Claude, I. L. 1962. *Power and International Relations*. New York: Random House.

Franck, Thomas. 2002. "Inspections and Their Enforcement: A Modest Proposal." *American Journal of International Law* 96 (October): 899–900.

Frohlich, Norman, and Joe A. Oppenheimer. 1992. *Choosing Justice: An Experimental Approach to Ethical Theory*. Berkeley: University of California Press.

Independent International Commission on Kosovo. 2001. *Kosovo Report: Conflict, International Response, Lessons Learned*. New York: Oxford University Press.

Keohane, Robert O. 2001. "Governance in a Partially Globalized World." *American Political Science Review* 95, no. 1 (March): 1–13.

Lauren, Paul Gordon. 1994. "Coercive Diplomacy and Ultimata: Theory and Practice in History." In *The Limits of Coercive Diplomacy*, edited by Alexander L. George and William E. Simons. Boulder, Colo.: Westview Press.

Morgenthau, Hans J. 1985. *Politics Among Nations: The Struggle for Power and Peace*. 6th edition. Revised by Kenneth W. Thompson. New York: Knopf.

"National Security Strategy of the United States of America September 2002." Available at www.whitehouse.gov/nsc/nss.pdf

Schedler, Andreas. 1999. "Conceptualizing Accountability." In *The Self-Restraining State: Power and Accountability in New Democracies*, edited by Andreas Schedler, Larry Diamond, and Marc F. Plattner. Boulder, Colo.: Lynne Rienner.

Schelling, Thomas C. 1966. *Arms and Influence*. New Haven: Yale University Press.

Thucydides. 1982. *The Peloponnesian War*. Translated by Richard Crawley. New York: Modern Library.

Waltz, Kenneth N. 1979. *Theory of International Politics*. Reading, Mass.: Addison-Wesley.

Walzer, Michael. 1977. *Just and Unjust Wars*. New York: Basic Books.

14

APPLYING THE CONTRIBUTION PRINCIPLE

CHRISTIAN BARRY

1. Introduction

This essay examines a methodological problem related to the application of a principle that is given substantial (and sometimes decisive) weight in most people's assessments regarding what (if anything) is owed, and by whom, to those who suffer from acute deprivations—shortfalls persons suffer in their health, civic status, or standard of living relative to the ordinary needs and requirements of human beings. The principle, which I shall refer to as the "contribution principle," holds that *agents are responsible for addressing acute deprivations when they have contributed, or are contributing, to bringing them about.* In the real world, it is often difficult if not impossible to determine with much confidence whether and to what extents different individual and collective agents (a person, a development bank, or a national government, and so on) have contributed to acute deprivations, and it is therefore unclear whether those who grant substantial weight to the contribution principle should take these agents to have responsibilities to remedy them, or how weighty they ought to hold them to be. This problem can only be fruitfully addressed by examining the appropriateness of different standards—which I shall call *standards of application*—that might be appealed to for determining agents' responsibilities in contexts where it is difficult or impossible to determine whether and to what extents different agents have in fact contributed to, are contributing to, or will have contributed to acute deprivations. These standards include the burden of proof, the standard of proof, and the admissibility of evidence for assessing which agents have contributed (and how much they have contributed) to acute deprivation.

People are generally aware of the importance of these standards in the context of legal and scientific inquiry, but they tend not to reflect upon their significance for assessing ethical responsibilities. As a result, people often seem lazily to import standards of application from criminal legal contexts into this domain, asserting, for example, that they lack ethical responsibilities to remedy acute deprivations unless their contribution to them can be proved "beyond a reasonable doubt." This is problematic, I shall argue, because the standards that are arguably appropriate for applying criminal legal norms are extremely implausible when applied to norms for determining other ethical responsibilities. I shall indicate how adopting more plausible standards for applying the contribution principle would very likely lead adherents of this principle to interpret their ethical responsibilities with respect to acute deprivations much more broadly than they appear to do at present.

2. The Contribution Principle

Although other principles are often invoked in debates concerning responsibilities for addressing acute deprivation, the contribution principle seems generally to be taken to have special significance.[1] All participants in the debate concerning access to antiretroviral medicines for the treatment of those suffering from HIV/AIDS, for example, seem to agree that, were it to be shown that certain actors have substantially contributed to these deprivations, it would be their responsibility (though perhaps not *solely* their responsibility) to try to remedy them. The pains that various actors, such as pharmaceutical company executives, government ministers, and WTO officials and trade representatives, have taken to show that they have *not* contributed to these problems, or that more substantial contributions have been made by others, further emphasize the importance that is attached to this principle.[2]

Talk of an agent's "contribution" to some or other problem admits of many different interpretations, with different implications for practice (see Bennett 1995). Since this essay focuses on a question that will arise in applying the contribution principle under *any* plausible interpretation, however, I shall bypass these difficult interpretive issues and, to fix ideas, simply stipulate the following definition: Agent A contributes to Agent B's deprivation *if and only if*:

(a) A's conduct was *causally relevant to it*;
(b) A's conduct did not merely allow a causal sequence that had antecedently put B under threat of acute deprivation to play out, but rather *initiated, facilitated, or sustained* it.[3]

---

[1] I discuss the plausibility of this claim in Barry (forthcoming).

[2] Responsibilities with respect to acute deprivation to which one contributes are often held to have three features. First, they are thought to be especially *weighty*: there are strong moral reasons to refrain from contributing to others' acute deprivation regardless of any further connections that we may have to them, so that we cannot easily appeal to considerations of *cost* to ourselves to excuse our failure to act on them. Second, they bind a *broad range of agents*: these reasons are applicable not only to individual persons but also to collective agents, such as corporations and states, which may otherwise not be held responsible for preventing acute deprivation. Third, they are *broad* in scope: they apply to these individual and collective agents with respect not only to what they *directly* do to others but also to what they indirectly do to others through creating and maintaining shared social rules and practices that can themselves contribute to acute deprivation.

[3] This type of interpretation is developed by Foot (1994) and Kamm (1983). This interpretation has a clear evaluative component, since assessments of whether the alternative to B's deprivation is that he or she would have avoided it through agent's aid will depend on

Both (a) and (b) clearly require further analysis. I shall here interpret condition (a) to require that A's conduct was a necessary element in a set of actual antecedent conditions that was sufficient for its occurrence.[4] The key distinction in (b) is between causally relevant conditions that allow an antecedent sequence to play out and causally relevant conditions that initiate, facilitate, or sustain the sequence. A's causally relevant conduct merely allows a sequence to continue rather than initiating, facilitating, or sustaining it *if and only if* (1) there is a high antecedent probability, independent of what A might do, that B will suffer acute deprivation, (2) B suffers acute deprivation, and (3) had B avoided suffering the acute deprivation, it would have been through A's assistance.

3. Standards for Applying the Contribution Principle

In some cases, it will be relatively easy to determine whether or not some agent has contributed to acute deprivation. In many other cases, however, things will not be so clear. Indeed, it is often difficult (if not impossible) to tell conclusively (or even with great confidence) whether and to what extent some agent has contributed to particular acute deprivations, and there are very few claims regarding the contributions of different agents to acute deprivations that cannot be plausibly contested. The plausibility of different explanations of some hardships is often obscured by the fact that each side in a debate—regarding the contribution of the International Monetary Fund's (IMF) structural-adjustment programs to poverty in developing countries, for example—tends to be *fully* convinced of the implausibility of their opponent's position. Anyone who is tempted to give weight to the contribution principle in his or her practical delibera-tions, then, must address the following question:

> Q1. In cases where it is unclear whether or to what extent some agent (A) has contributed to the deprivation of another agent (B), how should A conceive of his or her responsibilities to B?

It is clear that how Q1 is answered will substantially affect the practical meaning of this principle and the behavior of agents who are committed to it. To examine the considerations that are relevant to answering Q1, let us imagine the following case: A relatively poor developing country (which we shall call G77), asserts that a wealthy developed country (which we shall call G1) has undertaken a policy that has contributed to acute deprivations among its citizens. Because of this, G77 argues, G1 has

---

prior moral judgment regarding A's and B's entitlements. See McMahan (1998) for further elaboration and defense of this interpretation.

[4] See Wright (1985) and Honoré (1999, 94–120) for discussion of the applications of this conception of causation in legal contexts.

strong contribution-based reasons to undertake efforts to alleviate these problems and to avert further deprivations that their past conduct will otherwise cause in the future. To help fix ideas, let us suppose that Policy P refers to the policy of unilaterally deciding when and to what extent monetary policy should be tightened in response to domestic inflation or other national macroeconomic concerns. And let us further suppose that G77 claims that G1's decision to raise interest rates in response to fears about inflation in its domestic economy has contributed to its debt crisis, with severe consequences for its most vulnerable citizens.[5] Let us call G77's assertion regarding G1's responsibility Claim D. To evaluate Claim D we must determine whether G1's conduct was a *cause* of these deprivations, and whether its conduct initiated, facilitated, or sustained a causal sequence that led to the suffering of citizens in G77, rather than merely allowing an antecedent threat to play out.

We may lack confidence in our ability to make these determinations. Evidence of Policy P's overall causal impact on G77, for example, will perhaps be inconclusive. And even if we are confident that Policy P was a causally relevant condition for the deprivations of citizens in G77, it may be unclear whether these citizens were antecedently under threat or whether they would have avoided these deprivations only if G1 had provided assistance to them.[6] Evaluating Claim D in contexts in which substantial factual uncertainties of this kind are present will require us to distinguish three different *standards of application* for the contribution principle:

1. *The burden of proof:* Who has the *burden* of proof in this case? Must G77 (or some other agent) show that Policy P contributed to the deprivations in question? Or must G1 show that it has not done so?
2. *The standard of proof:* What evidential *threshold* must be reached for it to *count* as proven that Policy P did or did not contribute to deprivations amongst G77's people?
3. *The constraints on admissible evidence:* What kinds of *evidence* will be taken to corroborate the thesis that Policy P has contributed to deprivations amongst G77's people?

How each of these standards is specified will often be quite consequential. The placement of the burden of proof will determine whether or not G1 is

---

[5] The mechanisms by which this claim could be true may be complex. It might be, for example, that the effect of the debt crisis on G77 was further mediated by other policies undertaken by G1 (such as demanding the repayment of loans that they and other agents had extended to G77), or also by institutional arrangements—such as rules governing the management of sovereign debt, that G1 has played some role in shaping.

[6] Even when we are confident that certain agents have contributed to acute deprivation, we may be uncertain about *how much* they have contributed. I shall not address this important issue here.

taken to bear responsibility in cases where we cannot determine with any confidence whether or not Claim D is (or is likely to be) true. If the burden is on G1, it will be held to have contribution-based responsibilities with respect to these deprivations if it cannot demonstrate that Claim D is false or unlikely. If the burden is on G77, substantial evidential uncertainties will make it impossible for it to establish that G1 has contribution-based responsibilities. Similarly, the higher the standard of proof, the harder it will be for G77 to establish Claim D, and the lower the standard of proof, the easier it will be for G77 to establish it. Likewise, the broader the range of evidence taken to corroborate Claim D, the easier it will be for whichever party bears the burden of proof to do so. The narrower the range of evidence that is admitted to establish this claim, the harder it will be for this party to do so.

4. Establishing Fair Standards of Application

Unfairly allocating the burden of proof, lowering or raising the standard of proof too far, or broadening or restricting the range of admissible evidence too much will lead to unjustified costs for G77 or G1. But how can we determine whether any particular way of specifying these standards is fair? The first thing to note is that there is no obviously correct answer to this question, nor is there any neutral or natural way of specifying these standards that can serve as a default. It clearly depends upon the context of the inquiry and the goals of the practice within which it is undertaken. Take, for example, standards of application with respect to establishing whether some agent's conduct was a cause of someone's acute deprivation. The appropriateness of different standards of application for establishing a causal connection between some chemical substance and a medical condition may vary, depending upon whether we are engaged in scientific inquiry, criminal or civil legal proceedings, or ethical reflection. It is not (as is sometimes supposed) that different conceptions of causation must be employed in these cases but that the distinct aims of these inquiries and the point of the practices in which they are embedded may admit or require different specifications of the standards of application. In a criminal trial in which some agent A is being tried for having released a chemical which, it is alleged, has caused serious health problems among children at a neighboring school, most would insist that high evidential thresholds be employed for determining the causal links between the substance and the harm, and that the burden of proof be placed with the prosecution. We might further insist on very strict constraints on admissible evidence, perhaps allowing only epidemiological studies to count as evidence of causation. In a civil trial in which some Agent A is being tried for a similar offence, however, establishing a "preponderance of evidence" that the chemical released by A has contributed to the children's health problems would provide adequate grounds for attributing liability to him. And we might also allow a broader range of evidence, such as studies of the effects of the chemical on animals. And if the question is whether further such chemical releases should be legally authorized, it is not implausible that even slight evidence that these releases harm children should suffice to disallow them.[7]

When we engage in ethical reflection, meanwhile, the mere suspicion that one may have been involved in causing some harm often provides sufficient reason to act to address it. If, for example, A suspects that the chemical he has released may have causally contributed to children's health problems, he might reasonably take himself to have an ethical responsibility (although not a legal or enforceable one) to contribute toward meeting the costs of he treatment of their problems—or at least to have more reason to do so than he would have in the absence of his suspicion that he may have contributed to their condition. And this may be true where it is impossible to determine whether the "preponderance" standard is met, *or even when we know that it has not been met.*

That reasons for specifying standards of application one way or another would seem to depend on our purposes should not really surprise us. The same is true, after all, of standards for assessing reasons of all kinds, including reasons for belief. Robert Nozick (1992, 85), for example, has suggested that for everyday belief, the rule that "we should not believe some statement H if some alternative statement incompatible with H has a higher credibility value than H does" provides a sufficient standard of credibility. More stringent standards of credibility, however, must be applied in science, where "a statement may be required to reach a certain level of credibility, not simply to be more credible than any incompatible alternative." Nozick also warns that once stringent standards for assessing reasons (such as those required in science) are known, they tend to be extended to other contexts where—due to the energy, time, and resources that would have to be devoted to employing procedures that satisfy them—they are inappropriate. Further, he cautions against "concluding that someone is being irrational simply because his reasons do not meet the most stringent standards we can formulate. They may meet the standards appropriate to their context" (85). We must be similarly cautious about extending standards of application, which are appropriate in legal proceedings, to other areas of practical deliberation.

During the confirmation hearings of (now) Justice Clarence Thomas, in which evidence that he had sexually harassed Anita Hill was introduced, there were several instances in which commentators argued that, because the evidence was not sufficient to prove that he had committed these offenses "beyond a reasonable doubt," there were no grounds for

[7] See Carl F. Cranor (1990, 1993) for interesting discussions of the standards relevant for determining the toxicity of substances in basic scientific research and governmental regulation.

opposing his confirmation. Were he involved in a criminal trial, such concerns may have been entirely appropriate, but it is highly questionable whether these standards were appropriate in the context of confirmation hearings for a prospective member of the highest federal court (see Dworkin 1991). Recognizing the general point that different standards of application may be more or less appropriate depending on the context, however, does not immediately help us resolve our assessment of G1's responsibilities with respect to G77—especially if the truth (or likelihood) of Claim D cannot be shown with much confidence. For that, we must know more about the *kinds* of contextual features that are relevant for specifying standards of application and have a clearer sense of which of these features best characterize this type of case.

We can sharpen our discussion of these contextual features by representing different standards of application in terms of the relative importance that they attach to avoiding what are commonly called "Type 1" and "Type 2" errors.[8] In the case of Claim D, a Type 1 error would occur if G1 were falsely taken *to have* contributed to the deprivations among G77's citizens. A Type 2 error would occur were G1 to be falsely taken *not to have* contributed to these deprivations.

Different specifications of standards of application will result in different probabilities of these types of errors. In characterizing any such set of standards, then, some view must be taken of the relative costs of these types of errors. Stringent standards of proof and restrictions on admissible evidence in criminal proceedings, for example, reflect a strong aversion to Type 1 errors—expressing the conviction that falsely criminalizing the innocent is more costly than allowing many crimes to go unpunished. The "preponderance" standard in civil procedures also expresses an aversion to Type 1 errors—reflecting a willingness to err on the side of failing to allocate resources to those who have been injured by inordinately risky conduct or products—but it is much less stringent and foreseeably engenders only a higher probability of Type 1 errors and a lower probability of Type 2 errors.

In order to identify some of the contextual features that are relevant to the case of G1 and G77, then, it may be worthwhile to consider some of the reasons that might plausibly be offered for requiring different standards of proof in criminal and civil legal contexts, and also the kinds of cases in civil law that have encouraged many tort theorists and even some courts to depart more radically from traditional tort procedures.[9]

---

[8] For formal description of types of errors, see Witte and Witte (2001).

[9] Given the diverse goals that criminal and tort law have been taken to serve, the reasons for the differences in evidential standards are quite complex and have been the subject of substantial disagreement among legal theorists. For more thorough discussions of these themes, see Feinberg (1970), Ripstein (1999), and Honoré (1999).

These standards seem to vary because of the overall social *costs* of different kinds of Type 1 and Type 2 errors. Consider the attitudes toward Type 1 errors in tort law and criminal law, respectively. One reason for the stringency of standards of proof in criminal law is connected to the potential costs that are imposed on the *agent* who is erroneously identified as a lawbreaker. In criminal trials, defendants are faced with the prospect of losing their rights, liberties, and perhaps even their lives. Moreover, by identifying them as "criminal offenders," society *expresses* an assessment of them and an attitude toward them—that their conduct is paradigmatically blameworthy—that can be seriously damaging to others and their own sense of themselves.[10] Because of its strong expressive function, falsely accusing an agent of criminal offences carries an additional cost, namely, that the agencies that are acting in the name of justice act unjustly. In criminal cases, it is the state that brings the case against the defendant. We care that the state agencies representing us not only bring about desirable end states but also take special precautions not unduly to harm individuals through what they *do*, even when this may lead them to allow still greater harms that are brought about by others. Because of these costs, we do not typically want to imprison someone for exposing others to a chemical unless we are confident—on the basis of the soundest available evidence—that the exposure contributed to the medical condition in question.

This is not the case with civil law. Its core evaluative concepts— "tortious" or "wrongful"—do not carry the same stigma as "offence." As Bernard Williams (1995, 391) has put it, "Someone might say that in an absolutely ideal world all and only guilty criminals would be prosecuted, but there could be no world in which it was only successful plaintiffs whose cases were heard. Tort, by its nature, must be more like a system for the allocation of costs than the criminal law is" (see also Coleman and Ripstein 1995). Although the potential costs to the agent who is falsely held to have wronged another may be significant, they will involve only compensation, not the loss of a broader range of liberties.[11] If our concern is with making legally binding decisions for the allocation of costs for treating the children's medical conditions, a "preponderance of evidence" that the chemical released by A has contributed to the harms may make it reasonable to shift these costs (at least in part) to A.[12] The agency of the state is also involved in tort law, but in a way that can

[10] Feinberg (1970) argues that criminal punishment is expressive in two ways: it allows society to distance itself from the wrongful conduct and also allows it to claim to be vindicating the claim of law.

[11] The fact that those who live in societies that maintain a system of tort law can often insure themselves at reasonable cost against the risks that they may impose on others may further lessen the potential personal costs of Type 1 errors.

[12] This idea is interestingly explored by David McCarthy's (1996) discussion of the case of "curable cancer."

plausibly be seen as changing the potential costs of different types of error. The judiciary plays an adjudicative role, but private individuals and collective agents typically bring civil cases against defendants. Even when states are litigants in civil suits, they do not claim, as in criminal cases, to be vindicating the claims of law.

Further, in the context in which we are faced with a decision regarding the regulation rather than the punishment of some activity, such as whether A should be legally permitted to continue to release the chemical in question, we may feel justified in relaxing the standards of proof and broadening the range of admissible evidence even further. Even if, on balance, we think the benefits of A's activities outweigh its costs, and that requiring A to pay compensation to those who may be adversely affected by them would be counterproductive, it may still be incumbent upon us to offset these costs.

Unlike criminal and civil proceedings, or even regulatory action, assessments of ethical responsibility do not single out agents for sanctions that are backed by the coercive force of the state or any other "official" agency. All that is at stake is ethical censure, and even this need not take the form of blaming A for his conduct, or seriously impugning his character. We may simply conclude that, because he has contributed to the deprivation, he is obliged to share the costs of alleviating it, or at least to desist from releasing the chemical. If we consider it socially necessary for A to continue to release this chemical without paying compensation, and we wish to uphold legal permissions for him to do so, then we must at the very least explore the possibility of developing mechanisms of shifting the costs from the children, perhaps by instituting a general social-insurance scheme, or some other means of cost spreading.

It is also important to note that some legal and political theorists have recently argued that in certain circumstances further lessening the standard of proof, broadening the range of admissible evidence, and even shifting the burden of proof have seemed to many to be appropriate in legal contexts too. Several authors have recommended, for example, that the burden of proof be shifted in civil law in contexts where the causal links between potentially risky chemicals and injuries are uncertain (uncertainty about general causation), in cases involving multiple defendants each of whom has produced substances that are harmful to humans but where it is uncertain whose injuries have been caused by particular producers (identity uncertainty about specific causation), or in cases where it is known that a chemical causes a particular injury in a certain percentage of cases of that injury but it is not possible to distinguish the cases caused by the chemical from those caused by other factors (probabilistic uncertainty about specific causation).[13] The view that the

---

[13] I have borrowed these terms for different types of uncertainty from Feldman (1995), who provides a helpful discussion of these issues as they arise in the context of product

range of evidence that should be deemed admissible in these contexts should be substantially broadened has also been advocated.[14]

These proposed departures from traditional standards of application in civil law reflect a recognition that the goals of this social institution—such as allocating resources to those who have been injured by exposure to risky chemicals and requiring injurers to compensate those they have harmed—may be better served by different standards in these special contexts. Some have gone even further to suggest that, with respect to some domains, the goals of tort law may be better served by abolishing it altogether in favor of a social insurance, or some other scheme. As Arthur Ripstein (1999, 21) puts it, "It may be that a widespread social insurance scheme would actually approximate corrective justice better at the micro level than does the current tort system. Regulatory regimes may do more to make sure that people internalize the costs of their choices."

Another consideration that may be relevant to relative willingness to allow Type 1 and Type 2 errors is related to the costs to those *subjects* who go "uncompensated" due to Type 2 errors. If subjects who typically go uncompensated due to Type 2 errors are generally left very badly off, and we believe that these errors occur very frequently, we may have reason to revise our standards of application. It is important to note that the magnitude of these costs will depend on other features of the social system, such as whether it provides a system of social insurance that will cover the costs of treatment for them. And it seems plausible that the appropriateness of different standards of application may vary depending on changes in these background features. As noted above, in cases where Type 2 errors can be avoided only by substantially increasing the risk of costly Type 1 errors, we may have reason instead to offset the costs to uncompensated subjects through social insurance or some other scheme of cost spreading.[15]

In evaluating the relevant standards of application for assessing Claim D, then, we must establish the relative importance of the overall social

---

liability. Feldman proposes that the burden of proof should be shifted or plaintiffs should receive proportionate 50 percent recovery if they can demonstrate "strong" uncertainty regarding causation.

[14] See, for example, Cranor (1993) and Mayo and Hollander (1991). These proposed reforms are quite controversial (see Geistfeld [2001]). Indeed, since the U.S. Supreme Court's decision in *Daubert v. Merrell Dow Pharmaceuticals*, courts have increasingly relied on epidemiological evidence in establishing causation. Similar debates concerning the admissibility of different types of evidence advanced in support of causal claims have taken place in debates concerning the permissibility of affirmative action. See Adams (2001) and the references cited therein for discussion.

[15] Indeed, it may be, as Robert Goodin (1982, chap. 8) has argued, that when causes are complex and intertwined, it typically costs more than it is worth to try to disentangle them to establish personal responsibility, and that in such contexts a no-fault system is superior to a fault system for allocating costs.

cost of Type 1 and Type 2 errors. If it is believed that the cost of Type 1 errors to G1 is substantially less than the potential cost of Type 2 errors to G77, for example, we ought strongly to consider adopting standards of application that are far more tolerant of Type 1 than of Type 2 errors in assessing Claim D, and vice versa. But what are the relative costs of Type 1 and Type 2 errors in the case of G1 and G77? Consider first the cost of a Type 1 error to respondents such as G1 (for example, if Claim D is falsely found to be true). This cost will depend on how well off G1 is, how badly off the claimants are (for example, the deprived parties in G77), and how much it will cost for G1 to alleviate their deprivations.[16]

These costs may be monetary, involving the transfer of resources, but they might also involve the extension of special privileges and rights to G77—such as tariff-free access to G1's markets—or perhaps G1's efforts to increase the quantity of funds available to G77 at lower rates of interest.[17] But what other costs might G1 bear? Claim D implies nothing about *legal* sanctions for G1, nor need it imply anything regarding G1's *blameworthiness* for adopting Policy P. Claim D is relevant only for the purpose of determining who ought (morally) to bear the burden of the cost of addressing deprivations in G77, and whether different institutional reforms that effectively remedy them would place morally objectionable burdens on G1. We can judge G1 to have responsibilities to alleviate deprivations in G77 on the basis of the principle of contribution regardless of how well meaning and generally unobjectionable G1's reasons for adopting Policy P, provided that their failing to take precautions not unduly to expose G77's citizens to hazardous risk was causally relevant to their deprivation. The costs of Type 1 errors to G1, while certainly not negligible, need not necessarily be terribly severe.

But what of the costs of Type 2 errors to the subjects that might wrongfully go uncompensated—in this case the deprived parties in G77? Since, by hypothesis, G77 is a poor country, those who suffer from acute deprivations within its territorial domain will—due to resource and other constraints—likely remain very badly off (indeed, in life-threatening situations) if they go uncompensated. This, of course, depends on the assumption that the world that G1 and G77 inhabit does not possess *formal* mechanisms (such as a global system of social insurance) or informal arrangements (such as a generally known and complied-with norm of providing assistance to the acutely deprived) that reliably meet the costs of addressing acute deprivations within G77.

---

[16] Other considerations that may also be relevant concern whether there are other parties on whom G77 can make similarly justified claims, and whether G77's own negligence played a substantial role in the deprivation of its citizens.

[17] For a valuable discussion of measures to offset the deleterious effects of monetary decisions in powerful countries, and their relevance to global distributive justice, see Reddy (2003). For an account of the effects of U.S. monetary policies in the 1970s, see James (1996).

Given the relative costs to G1 and G77 of Type 1 and Type 2 errors, I conclude that there is a strong prima facie case for specifying standards of application for applying the principle of contribution *that expresses a willingness to err in favor of the acutely deprived subjects*, whether they are the party alleging that they have been harmed or the party against which such claims have been made. I shall call this norm the "*vulnerability presumption principle.*" While implausible as a principle for specifying standards of application in a criminal (and most likely in most civil) legal contexts, or as a principle for assessing ethical responsibilities more generally, the vulnerability presumption principle seems clearly superior to stringent standards of proof and evidence with respect to the determination of ethical responsibilities to address acute deprivations.

5. The Vulnerability Presumption Principle: Three Objections

I anticipate that the vulnerability presumption principle will be subject to sharp criticism. And although I cannot here provide an exhaustive defense of the principle or fully work out how it might inform our deliberations about practical dilemmas in the real world, it is worth briefly discussing three deep objections to the line of argument that I have presented.

The first objection is that the plausibility of my assertions regarding the potential costs of Type 1 and Type 2 errors to G1 and G77 (and thus about the relevant standards for assessing Claim D) depend on artificially restricting attention to costs of these types of errors to G1 and G77 *in this particular case*. An honest accounting will focus on the overall long-term social costs of standards of application that engender different prevalence rates and distributions of these types of errors.[18] And such an accounting may well find that the costs to G1 and other well-off agents will be quite substantial, since the G77s of the world will constantly put forth to the effect that that they have contributed to deprivations within their territories. Indeed, this may have the perverse effect that badly off countries disown their *own* responsibilities for these deprivations through wild assertions regarding the contributions of outsiders. It may be, for example, that countries will blame their debt crises on Policy P even when their own poorly conceived domestic policies are mostly to blame.

This objection articulates a valid concern, but it does not seem to me decisive, because it downplays the ongoing costs of more stringent standards of application. Maintaining very stringent standards of proof and constraints on evidence with respect to contribution will not only

---

[18] This objection was put to me by Jedediah Purdy and Sanjay Reddy.

disadvantage G77 with respect to Claim D but also systematically disadvantage *all* badly off populations who have or may have been adversely affected by the conduct of powerful governments and other actors.[19] Indeed, even if less stringent standards of application lead to a rapid increase in claims regarding the contribution of powerful countries to the deprivations within the territories of the weak countries, this may have the desirable consequence that powerful countries will find it in their interest to promote the development of shared formal institutions or informal norms that prevent and reliably respond to acute deprivations, and allocate the burdens of alleviating them more equitably.[20] In the case of Policy P, for example, new issues of special drawing rights, which function in part as a hard-currency line of credit available to all member countries of the International Monetary Fund, or the development of a global economic security council whose role is to prevent and alleviate acute deprivations would both reduce the incentives for weaker countries to advance claims against more powerful countries and diminish the plausibility of such claims (see Reddy 2003; Soros 2002; Commission on Global Governance 1995).

The second objection is that my discussion has treated ethical reflection on responsibilities for acute deprivations as if it were, like criminal or tort law, a practice with well-defined goals that can be served better or less well by specifying its standards of application in different ways. But ethical reflection, it may be argued, is not like these other practices in the relevant sense. The argument would be that ethical reflection provides a standpoint from which to evaluate these practices, but the practice of ethical reflection should not *itself* be subject to this kind of evaluation. This objection also has some merit, since the "purpose" of the practice of ethical reflection and argument cannot be characterized in terms of a well-defined set of goals in the way that law might be. Yet, like law, ethics is concerned not only to evaluate but also to provide conduct-guiding structures of values and norms that shape the behavior of individual and collective agents. And like law, ethical theories generally specify aims and objectives that their adherents ought to promote. It would seem odd indeed if these theories are exempt from being evaluated in terms of their success in promoting the aims and objectives that—by their own lights —matter (see Parfit 1993, chap. 1; Pogge 1990; Hare 1981). If an ethical

---

[19] It is noteworthy that developing countries lack mechanisms by which they can formally complain and seek compensation that is caused by the grave negligence of international financial institutions and donor countries. This contrasts with the rights of individuals in the Anglo-Saxon legal system, in which they can even sue financial consultants for negligent advice. Kunibert Raffer (2003) has recently advocated an international arbitration panel to assess such claims.

[20] As discussed above, the existence of reliable mechanisms for addressing acute deprivations reduces the cost of Type 2 errors.

theory includes a conception of responsibility for alleviating acute deprivations and this conception gives substantial weight to the principle of contribution, it is implausible that adherents of the theory would be unconcerned by the fact that they are employing standards of application that undermine one of its central aims—to encourage agents to take precautions to avoid contributing to acute deprivations, and to try to alleviate them when they have done so.

The third objection is that I have been tacitly appealing to some further principle that gives more weight to the less well off and discounts the costs to the well off in ranking the desirability of different outcomes. I have, it might thus be argued, emphasized the importance of what one might call the "security interests" of the badly off at the expense of the "liberty interests" of the well off, assuming that we are justified in, to borrow Judith Thomson's language, disrupting the plans of the well off when doing so would enhance the security of the badly off. However, this is not the case. If an ethical theory incorporates the contribution principle, it presumably does so because it holds that conduct which contributes to acute deprivations is seriously wrong—so wrong, in fact, that considerations, including cost to oneself and observance of one's special obligations, which are normally held to have great moral weight can be overridden. The vulnerability presumption principle expresses the strong disvalue that any such theory attaches to contributing to acute deprivations. Moreover, an ethical theory that gives precedence to the contribution principle already gives substantial weight to peoples' so-called liberty interests. Unlike what David Miller (2001) has called the "capacity" principle, which requires that those who can alleviate acute deprivations most easily must do so regardless of their connection to them, the principle of contribution sharply limits the conditions under which those who suffer hardships can disrupt others' plans and shift the costs of alleviating their deprivations onto them.

6. Conclusion

Few rallied to the call when the Commission on Macroeconomics and Health recently estimated the cost of developing a comprehensive program to reduce the ill health of the global poor and called upon wealthy nations to contribute $22 billion toward the $57 billion additional annual cost of scaling up its program in 2007, suggesting that "lack of donor funds should not be the factor that limits the capacity to provide health services to the world's poorest people."[21] It may be that this kind

---

[21] See Sreenivasan (2002) for discussion. Other widely reported estimates of the cost of addressing acute deprivations include the so-called Zedillo High-Level Panel of 2001 (UN 2001), which set the cost of the extra resources needed to achieve the Millennium Development Goals at US$65 billion per year. To get a sense of proportion regarding these expenditures, note that the total Overseas Development Assistance (ODA) currently

of neglect can be explained by the fact that people often act for self-interested reasons and tend, often unconsciously, to interpret and apply their moral values in ways that will not threaten their own interests. Their behavior can also be partly explained in terms of what Amartya Sen (2002b, 23f.) has called "correspondence irrationality," in that people often act "without thinking," reason lazily about what to do, and are prone to weakness of will.

These are not the only possible explanations, however. Widespread commitment to the contribution principle, it may be argued, helps to explain why few well-off agents feel themselves responsible for addressing acute deprivations. Would a *conscientious* application of the contribution principle lead to the conclusion that these agents lacked such responsibilities? Many have thought so, because they assume the truth of the following conditional: If (1) there is conclusive evidence that well-off agents *have not* contributed to acute deprivations or (2) *conclusive* evidence that they *have* contributed to acute deprivation is lacking, then the contribution principle entails that these agents lack weighty moral reasons to address such deprivations. Some have argued vigorously that, whether or not the conditional is true, the antecedent is false, since there *is* conclusive evidence that well-off agents have contributed to acute deprivation—whether through unfair trade practices, by shaping the policies of international financial institutions through enthusiastic participation in the global arms trade, or via other means (see Pogge 2002; Sen 2002; Stiglitz 2002). This essay has shown, however, that the assumption that agents bear little responsibility with respect to acute deprivations unless there is fairly conclusive evidence suggesting otherwise cannot be sustained. To think otherwise, I have argued, requires a commitment to a view of standards of application that, while not implausible in some legal contexts, cannot be defended in the context of determining ethical responsibilities for addressing acute deprivations. Although it is true that the contribution principle would entail that well-off agents would lack moral reasons to address acute deprivations *should* there be conclusive evidence to the effect that they have not contributed to them, the conditional is nevertheless false, since the truth of the second disjunct does not entail the consequent. And since the first disjunct rests on an extremely dubious empirical claim, many well-off agents that are committed to the contribution principle have reason to revise their behavior significantly.

provided by the high-income countries and multilateral organizations is now roughly US$50 billion a year. All developed countries together spend only $4.31 billion (2002), one-sixtieth of 1 percent of their combined gross national incomes, on meeting basic needs in the developing world (http://millenniumindicators.un.org/unsd/mi/mi_series_results.asp?ro wId = 592).

Acknowledgments

I am indebted to Thomas Pogge and Sanjay Reddy for conversations that helped me to develop the ideas presented in this essay and to Bashshar Haydar, Andrew Kuper, Jedediah Purdy, Lydia Tomitova, Katja Vogt, and Jeremy Waldron for their very helpful criticisms of an earlier version of it.

References

Adams, M. 2001. "Causation and Responsibility in Tort and Affirmative Action." *Texas Law Review* 79, no. 3:643–702.

Barry, C. Forthcoming. "Understanding and Evaluating the Contribution Principle." In *Real World Justice*, edited by A. Follesdal and T. W. Pogge. Dordrecht: Kluwer.

Barry, C., and K. Raworth. 2002. "Access to Medicines and the Rhetoric of Responsibility." *Ethics & International Affairs* 16, no. 2:57–70.

Bennett, J. 1995. *The Act Itself*. New York: Oxford University Press.

Coleman, J. L., and A. Ripstein. 1995. "Mischief and Misfortune." *McGill Law Journal* 41, no. 1:91–141.

Commission on Global Governance. 1995. *Our Global Neighbourhood*. Oxford: Oxford University Press.

Cranor, C. F. 1990. "Some Moral Issues in Risk Assessment." *Ethics* 101, no. 1:123–43.

———. 1993. *Regulating Toxic Substances: A Philosophy of Science and the Law*. New York: Oxford University Press.

Dworkin, R. 1991. "Justice for Clarence Thomas." *New York Review of Books* 38, no. 18. http://www.nybooks.com/articles/article-preview?article_id=3100

Feinberg, J. 1970. "The Expressive Function of Punishment." In *Doing and Deserving: Essays in the Theory of Responsibility*, 95–118. Princeton: Princeton University Press.

Feldman, H. L. 1995. "Science and Uncertainty in Mass Exposure Litigation." *Texas Law Review* 74, no. 1:1–48.

Foot, P. 1994. "Killing and Letting Die." In *Killing and Letting Die*, edited by A. Norcross and B. Steinbock, 280–89. Second edition. New York: Fordham University Press.

Geistfeld, M. 2001. "Scientific Uncertainty and Causation in Tort Law." *Vanderbilt Law Review* 54, no. 2:1011–37.

Goodin, R. E. 1982. *Political Theory and Public Policy*. Princeton: Princeton University Press.

Hare, R. M. 1981. *Moral Thinking*. Oxford: Clarendon Press.

Honoré, T. 1999. *Responsibility and Fault*. Oxford: Hart.

James, H. 1996. *International Monetary Cooperation Since Bretton Woods*. Washington, D.C.: International Monetary Fund.

Kagan, S. 1991. "Précis of *The Limits of Morality.*" *Philosophy and Phenomenological Research* 51, no. 4:897–901.

Kamm, F. 1983. "Killing and Letting Die: Methodological and Substantive Issues." *Pacific Philosophical Quarterly* 64:297–312.

Levi, I. 1980. *The Enterprise of Knowledge.* Cambridge, Mass.: MIT Press.

Mayo, D., and R. D. Hollander, eds. 1991. *Acceptable Evidence: Science and Values in Risk Management.* New York: Oxford University Press.

McCarthy, D. 1996. "Liability and Risk." *Philosophy and Public Affairs* 25, no. 3:238–62.

McMahan, J. 1994. "Killing, Letting Die, and Withdrawing Aid." In *Killing and Letting Die*, edited by A. Norcross and B. Steinbock, 383–420. Second edition. New York: Fordham University Press.

———. 1998. "A Challenge to Common Sense Morality." *Ethics* 108, no. 2:394–418.

Miller, D. 2001. "Distributing Responsibilities." *Journal of Political Philosophy* 9, no. 4:453–71.

Nozick, R. 1992. *The Nature of Rationality.* Princeton: Princeton University Press.

Parfit, D. 1984. *Reasons and Persons.* Oxford: Oxford University Press.

Pogge, T. W. 1990. "The Effects of Prevalent Moral Conceptions." *Social Research* 57, no. 3:649–63.

———. 2002a. *World Poverty and Human Rights: Cosmopolitan Responsibilities and Reforms.* Cambridge: Polity Press.

Raffer, K. 2003. "Some Proposals to Adapt International Institutions to Developmental Needs." In *The Role of International Institutions in Globalisation: The Challenges for Reform*, edited by J. Chen, 81–101. Northampton: Edward Elgar.

Reddy, S. G. 2003. "Developing Just Monetary Arrangements." *Ethics & International Affairs* 17, no. 1:81–94. Included in this collection as "Just International Monetary Arrangements."

Ripstein, A. 1999. *Equality, Responsibility, and the Law.* New York: Cambridge University Press.

Scheffler, S. 2001. *Boundaries and Allegiances.* New York: Oxford University Press.

Sen, A. K. 2002a. "How to Judge Globalism." *American Prospect* 13, no. 1:A2–A6.

———. 2002b. *Rationality and Freedom.* Cambridge, Mass.: Harvard University Press.

Singer, P. 1972. "Famine, Affluence, and Morality." *Philosophy and Public Affairs* 1, no. 3:229–43.

Soros, G. 2002. *George Soros on Globalization.* New York: Public Affairs.

Sreenivasan, G. 2002. "International Justice and Health: A Proposal." *Ethics & International Affairs* 16, no. 2:81–89.

Stiglitz, J. 2002. *Globalization and Its Discontents.* New York: Knopf.

Summers, L., and L. H. Pritchett. 1993. "The Structural-Adjustment Debate." *American Economic Review* 83, no. 2:383–89.

U.N. 2001. *Report to the Secretary-General of the High-level Panel on Financing for Development [the Zedillo Report]* (25 June 2000). New York: United Nations.

Unger, P. 1996. *Living High and Letting Die.* New York: Oxford.

Williams, B. 1995. "What Has Philosophy to Learn from Tort Law?" In *The Philosophical Foundations of Tort Law,* edited by D. G. Owen, 487–99. Oxford: Clarendon Press.

WHO. 2001. *Macroeconomics and Health: Investing in Health for Economic Development.* Report of the Commission on Macroeconomics and Health. Geneva: WHO Publications. Also available at www.cmhealth.org/ and www.cid.harvard.edu/cidcmh/CMHReport.pdf

Witte, R. S., and J. S. Witte. 2001. *Statistics.* Sixth edition. Fort Worth: Harcourt, Brace, Jovanovich.

Wright, R. W. 1985. "Causation in Tort Law." *California Law Review* 73:1737–828.

15

GLOBAL JUSTICE AND THE LOGIC OF THE BURDEN OF PROOF

JUHA RÄIKKÄ

To shift the *burden of proof* to one's opponent is a strategic move used in all kinds of disputes. This is a common strategy in scientific argumentation, but undoubtedly it appears most commonly in legal, ethical, and political debates. An intelligent arguer attempts to avoid the burden of proof and achieve a position in which she is presumed to be right until proven otherwise. The harder it is to prove how things really are, the more important it is to shift the burden to one's opponent. In the heat of a debate this shift may go unnoticed. As a result, a party who in fact has the burden of proof may win a dispute just because her opponent does not pay sufficient attention to the dynamics of the burden. For example, there are many professional politicians who seem also to be professionals in shifting the burden of proof. But this should not be taken to indicate that shifting the burden is merely a rhetorical trick, since reasons can be presented that rationally persuade us that the burden of proof *should* be shifted in the discussion.

The question of who has the burden of proof is often important in practice. We must frequently make decisions and act on the basis not of conclusive evidence but of what is reasonable to presume true. A paradigmatic example of this is of course the trial, in which a person is presumed innocent and must be freed unless proven guilty, but there are many similar situations outside a purely legal framework. However, it is not always easy to see exactly what is reasonable to presume in a given context. Sometimes people disagree not only about how things are but also about what the reasonable presumption is. Consequently, it happens that a given practical question must be solved by referring to principles that explicitly or implicitly determine, at least partly, where the burden of proof should rest. In this essay, I consider the role of the logic of the burden of proof in a debate on global justice. In particular, I ask how the logic of the burden of proof is seen or could be seen by those who defend conservative positions in a debate—that is, such positions as "there is no moral obligation to reduce poverty beyond borders," "some forms of discrimination on the basis of citizenship is perfectly acceptable," and so on (see, e.g., Kekes 2002). I argue that defenders of conservative positions tend to shift the burden of proof in an unjustified way.

The Moral Irrelevance of National Boundaries

Since the early 1970s, several philosophers have argued that we are not morally justified in discriminating against foreigners, especially against people in developing countries. Perhaps the best-known early critics of *national discrimination* are Henry Shue (1980) and Charles Beitz (1977), who have defended the rights of the people of poor countries in many forums. Because the discriminatory practices continue in the sense that there are huge differences in people's standard of living (for example, in 2002 there were 1.2 billion people living on less than a dollar a day), the objection presented by Beitz and others is still relevant and popular. The argument against discrimination on the basis of one's nationality is grounded on the view that "a moral person ignores morally irrelevant differences in those actions that affect others." Since it seems that a "person's nationality, like his race, sex, and religion, is in itself an irrelevant difference," a question arises of how, then, "can national boundaries make any moral difference in regard to obligations to aid in the satisfaction of basic needs and to oppose the violation of basic rights" (Goldman 1982, 437). Thus, to put it simply, the objection against national discrimination seems to be as follows: Although discrimination on the basis of nationality may be justified to a lesser extent than the present differential treatment, proponents of discrimination have not shown a morally relevant property that would justify discrimination to its present extent. Millions of people are left to starve in developing countries. This being so, discrimination to the present extent is not justified. Therefore, the morally right course of action is to stop discrimination and help people much more than is currently done. (*How* exactly this could and should be done is not an issue here.)

The traditional objection against national discrimination can be met by three different strategies, each of which denies a different premise of the objection against discrimination. Of the following strategies, A is the tactic most often explicitly used, but C is probably the most common implicitly accepted one.

> *Strategy A.* It is true that those who defend discrimination have the burden of proof to identify a property that justifies discrimination, but they have met this burden by having already identified the property. Therefore, discrimination is morally justified.
> *Strategy B.* It is not true that those who defend discrimination have the burden of proof to identify a property that justifies discrimination. On the contrary, those who object to discrimination have the burden of proof to show that there is no property that justifies discrimination.
> *Strategy C.* It is true that those who defend discrimination have the burden of proof to identify a property that justifies discrimi-

nation, and it is also true that they have not yet met this burden. However, since the question is still open, the proper course of action is to continue discrimination.

Presumably, strategy A is not convincing. It does not seem that a property that would justify extreme discrimination on the basis of one's nationality has been identified in any meaningful sense. The nature of associative ties between conationals or the greater extent to which conationals are affected by each other's decisions may be morally relevant and justify some differential treatment, but it is questionable whether these features justify discrimination to its present extent. In any case, it is assumed here that strategy A is not convincing, or not fully convincing anyway, although it is not possible to consider separately every instance of this strategy, defended by David Miller (1995) and many others.

Strategy B is also problematic. Since there *cannot* be perfectly conclusive evidence for the nonexistence of a property that would justify discrimination, the burden of proof is on the side of those who believe that there is such a property. In order to shift the burden to others they must commit to presenting reasons for their belief. It renders the dialogue irrational to grant that those who do not believe there is a property that would justify discrimination have a burden of proof to show that there cannot be such a property—even if there is no way, even in principle, to meet this burden. As Nicholas Rescher (1977, 30) has put it, a rational discussion presupposes that the "adducing of supporting considerations must be something that is not made in principle impossible under the circumstances." Thus, strategy B seems dubious, too, although it should be admitted that there is nothing impossible about "proving" that no property justifying discriminations exists, so long as the *standard of proof* does not demand perfectly conclusive evidence.

Strategy C is probably the best means for defending discrimination. Strategy C does not include the mistakes made in the alternative strategies. It may be justified to infer that it is reasonable to presume that there is a property that justifies discrimination from the premise that we do not have sufficient evidence that there is not such a property. Since we do not know whether there is such property and since the debate is still continuing, perhaps it is justified to presume that there is, after all, such a property and to act on that basis. Whether this kind of reasoning is justified depends on how one is able to answer the following two critical questions. First, is there a justification for thinking that the question is still open? After all, the discussion has lasted many years, and there is not any agreement that a property that would justify discrimination exists. Second, is there a justification for not stopping or reducing discrimination on nationalist grounds if the question is still open? No doubt, much depends on what should be understood by "open question." But let us begin by introducing the notion of "conservative presumptionism."

"The One Who Asserts Must Prove"

According to the doctrine that I will call "conservative presumptionism," it is reasonable to believe anything one happens to believe as long as there is not a sufficient reason to believe otherwise. Conservative presumptionism can justify the view that since the question of whether there is a property that would justify national discrimination is still open, it is reasonable to presume that discrimination is justified. Put simply, the argument goes as follows. Most people believe that discrimination on the basis of nationality is justified, and everyone is justified in maintaining such beliefs in the absence of a sufficient reason for thinking otherwise. Since the case is still open, it follows by definition that there is not yet a sufficient reason to think otherwise—that is, there is not yet very strong evidence that discrimination on the basis of nationality is wrong. Therefore people are entitled to believe that discrimination against people in developing countries is justified, and to act provisionally on such basis and continue discrimination at the present level.

In order to make sense of conservative presumptionism, we must distinguish the so-called "evidential burden of proof" (E-burden) from the "initiating burden of proof" (I-burden). Roughly, an I-burden is a burden to support one's view within the dialogue if the view is presented first; an E-burden is a burden to produce further evidence when a sufficient reply is made to one's claim (cf. Rescher 1977, 27). The I-burden remains on one side throughout the discussion, while the E-burden can shift from side to side. It is clear that a party in the dialogue may have an I-burden but not an E-burden, or vice versa. If, for example, you were to put forth the claim that there is no property that would justify national discrimination, you would have the I-burden to prove this view. After presenting evidence for your view, it might appear that there is indeed no property that would justify discrimination. At this stage, your opponent has the E-burden. After her reply, however, it could appear that there is a property that would justify discrimination, and you would then have the E-burden to show that she made a mistake. Therefore, you have not necessarily met your I-burden, even though it can appear that you have: if your opponent manages to meet her E-burden, you have not really met your I-burden. According to conservative presumptionism, your opponent is justified in keeping her view until you have really met your I-burden (that is, until she is unable to rise to your challenge). When a case is open, any *action* should proceed from the view that the one who does not have an I-burden is right.

Conservative presumptionism—"she who asserts must prove"—is a widely accepted rule, and many influential theorists have endorsed it. C. L. Hamblin writes that "there is a presumption in favour of existing institutions and established doctrines, and against anything paradoxical, that is, 'contrary to the prevailing opinion'" (1993, 172). In Douglas

Walton's view (1989, 28), "someone who sets out to disprove a proposition that is widely accepted or popularly presumed to be true will have to mount a strong argument if he is to meet a reasonable burden of proof that would convince an opponent in reasonable dialogue." According to a textbook on argumentation theory, "people have a very general burden to *have* good reasons for what they say"; more specifically, "people have a burden to *present* some reasons when they make accusations or statements that run counter to common opinion" (Fogelin and Sinnott-Armstrong 1991, 319). Of course, conservative presumptionism is not an epistemic doctrine. It does not claim that having a belief is itself evidence for the truth of the content of that belief. All that it says is that the opponents of widely held beliefs have the initial burden of proof. Thus, it is the *critics* and not the defenders of nationalistic discrimination that have the burden of proof. (In affluent countries nationalistic discrimination against poor countries is clearly accepted, although on a global scale a "common opinion" may be different.)

However, conservative presumptionism is not a morally neutral doctrine, and its acceptance may imply substantive moral conclusions. This is hardly surprising, since the view that one is justified in presuming that national discrimination is morally acceptable if one happens to believe that it is morally acceptable is clearly a substantive moral view. Although there has been some tendency to think that conservative presumptionism is a purely formal rule (cf. Feinberg 1973, 110; Katzner 1970, 257), this view is implausible. *Formal* principles are completely *presumption-free* principles. Consider the following five principles. The first two are formal, while the remaining three are not, because they set presumptions that are relevant when deciding how to act.

1. *Formal principle of justice.* Treat those who are equal in relevant respects equally and treat those who are unequal in relevant respects unequally.
2. *Formal principle of equality.* Treat those who are equal in relevant respects equally.
3. *Material principle of equality.* Always justify departures from equal treatment; always presume that the cases are equal.
4. *Material principle of inequality.* Always justify departures from unequal treatment; always presume that the cases are unequal.
5. *Conservative presumptionism in justice.* Justify both departures from equal treatment when cases seem to be equal and departures from unequal treatment when cases seem to be unequal; presume that the cases are equal when they are thought to be equal and that the cases are unequal when they are thought to be unequal.

Obviously, conservative presumptionism is an *alternative* to the material principle of equality (and to the material principle of inequality). If the material principle of equality is a correct or accepted principle, those who defend national discrimination would have an I-burden of proof (not only an E-burden), and it would be right to stop discrimination until a good reason is provided for why discrimination is justified. It is a moral choice whether one thinks that the presumption is in favor of the status quo or in favor of change. Of course, a person who thinks that the presumption is always in favor of the status quo *may* support egalitarian politics and global equality if it *happens* to be a case that people in affluent countries generally are egalitarians. They are not, at least not on global issues.

The problem with conservative presumptionism is not that it asserts presumptions from moral (or axiological) grounds. It is perfectly acceptable to do so. If we do not know whether a revolver is loaded or not, it is reasonable to presume that it is loaded. This is because presuming that the revolver is loaded is safer than presuming the opposite. If we do not know whether a person is guilty, it is acceptable—indeed, obligatory—to presume that she is not guilty. The presumption that a person is guilty could violate the value of not condemning innocent persons. In both these cases people usually agree on what the justified presumptions are, since they share moral values. Even if parties disagree whether the revolver is loaded or whether a person is guilty, they agree on who has the burden of proof and that the burden is asymmetrical (unequally distributed). Those who propose counterintuitive claims must offer very strong evidence in order to shift the burden of proof to their opponents (Walton 1991, 54).

The problem with conservative presumptionism in the debate on global justice is that without explicitly presenting any moral reasons, it asserts presumptions from moral grounds even if there is *no agreement* about what these moral grounds might be. Conservative presumptionism seems to rely on the following principle: one is justified in believing anything one happens to believe, so long as there is not a sufficient reason, based on strong evidence, to believe otherwise *and* one is justified in supporting any social practice one happens to support, so long as there is not a sufficient reason to support another practice, even if this might mean that one determines the solution of a moral disagreement without first providing a moral argument for one's position. This is an easy way to oppose reforms in international structures.

In social criticism conservative presumptionism and the material principle of equality are both substantial moral doctrines and, in the final analysis, either of them (or some other alternative) can be acceptable. Conservative presumptionists are right when they argue that we must start from something, but the question remains whether we should start from conservative presumptions—*when this has implications for action*. What is clear is that we are not justified in accepting conservative presumptionism and rejecting the material principle of equality without a moral argument. As Allen Buchanan (1992, 655) has argued, a central question of modern political philosophy is whether the material principle of equality is justified. In general, conservative presumptionism might be a very wise doctrine. However, regarding issues like global justice, which are strictly related to political action, conservative presumptionism is just one alternative among many. If it becomes an acceptable doctrine in the context of global justice, this must be because there is a *moral argument* that proves it. At the moment we lack such an argument (cf. Räikkä 1997).

Open and Closed Questions and the Burden of Proof

Under what conditions is it justifiable to think that the question of whether there is a property that would morally justify discrimination on the basis of one's nationality remains open? On the one hand, it does not make much sense to claim that there should not be any open questions at all. *Some* questions should count as open questions. Consider a case where a person encounters an argument according to which it is morally right to beat one's children, and she cannot find any mistake in the premises of the argument or in the logical deduction of the conclusion (which she nevertheless rejects). It is clear that she has *no* obligation to accept the conclusion immediately and start acting on that basis (cf. White 1981, 50–52). She is justified in holding the question open and continuing to act as if the argument were wrong. (Here conservative presumptionism might be acceptable, since it does not seem to conflict with any important value and the issue is not controversial.)

On the other hand, however, it is surely not acceptable to hold a question open indefinitely. There should be a point at which we should treat some questions as closed. To grant that a question could remain open indefinitely is to accept a dogmatic (irrational) conservatism, which does not allow any social changes (if one also accepts conservative presumptionism). If the argument that the extreme discrimination against people in developing countries is not justified does not appeal to a person, it does not follow that she is free to maintain her position without argument forever—that is, there should be a point at which she should either reply or change her mind. The problem is determining exactly when a person has considered the question sufficiently. At what point is it right to conclude that the question is closed and act accordingly?

There are many methods of determining when a given question is no longer open. When a question closes, parties have an answer as to whether or not the (original) I-burden was met. The winner is the one who did not have the E-burden in the final stage of argumentation, just before closing the question. The most common methods of closing the question are the following three:

(1) *Formal method.* A question is to be held open until the discussion stops according to some formal criterion.

(2) *Consensual method.* A question is to be held open until parties have achieved agreement on the solution of the question.
(3) *Rational method.* A question is to be held open until it is rationally solved.

The formal method is used in courts of law. A court's deliberation stops when all the available evidence is presented and when there are no more arguments that can be offered in the determined period of time. The consensual method is common in political negotiations. For example, negotiations concerning suitable levels for salaries do not usually end until parties have achieved consensus. The rational method is typical in scientific research, where a question must be held open until it is answered in a rational way, meaning that the answer is objectively or intersubjectively justified. A scientific question may be left open for a long time; there is no formal criterion that would determine the deadline. On the other hand, a scientific question could be closed before consensus is achieved. In science a question may get a rational answer even if that answer does not garner immediate general support. Of course, people are free to discuss scientific questions even if those questions are "closed" in the sense that there is already a good answer to a question and that *action* could be justified on the basis of that answer. (For instance, one may ask whether some chemical really causes cancer even if we have strong evidence that it does and the use of the chemical can be forbidden on that basis.)

In science a party who has an E-burden may believe that it is still unclear whether the I-burden has been met, even if it were rationally determined that the I-burden has (or has not) been met. Thus, formal, consensual, and rational methods cannot be reduced to one another, although it is clear that both formal and consensual decisions may be rational as well.

Rescher (1977, 43) and Walton (1991, 76) have argued that rules determining the burden of proof should be formulated so that "it can be determined, after a finite number of moves in the dialogue, whether the burden has been met or not." Obviously, then, rules determining the burden of proof establish not only what is to be presumed but also *how long* this presumption should be maintained.

Presumptions can be strong and the burden of proof heavy in two senses. The presumption is strong whenever there is a need for exceptionally weighty evidence in order to change the presumption. The presumption is also strong whenever it takes an exceptionally long time to win the dialogue from the point of shifting the E-burden to one's opponent. From a conservative point of view, much evidence is required to prove that things are not as they seem to be, and when the evidence is presented, it takes a long time to reach the conclusion that the I-burden has been met. Questions can be open in two senses. A question is open when it is unclear whether or not the I-burden has been met. A question is also open when it makes sense to ask the question again even if the I-burden was met. Questions of global justice are open in this latter sense: there cannot be final solutions, and there must be space to examine the global practices again and again. From a conservative point of view, however, questions are open also in the former sense. (The longer the questions are open in the former sense, the better for a conservative.) According to conservatives, it is not justifiable to change the holder of the I-burden during the discussion (which keeps on going), and in effect, those who are criticizing existing institutions have an I-burden, practically speaking, forever (that is, until the currently existing institutions are no longer the existing ones).

Those who think that the question of whether a property that would justify national discrimination exists is still open seem to think that the *consensual* method is the appropriate one for determining how long to maintain the conservative presumption that national discrimination is justified. On rational grounds the question looks closed. According to the consensual method, a question is open until an agreement has been reached, and clearly there is no agreement whether discrimination on the basis of one's nationality is justified. Therefore, the question is open. An important point is to see whether a question is open or closed. We should not ask what people *should* believe; instead, we should ask what they *do* believe. A person who thinks that discrimination on the basis of nationality is justified is free to continue doing so until a general consensus (whatever that means) has been reached in favor of the contrary view. Clearly, this may take a very long time, and it has taken a very long time already: the fight for global equality has a long history.

No doubt, another way one may try to justify the view that the question of whether discrimination on the basis of nationality is justified is open is by claiming that so far there has been *no rational answer* to that question. This view, however, is not plausible. Many intelligent theorists have studied for years the question of whether there is a property that would justify discrimination on the basis of nationality, and even if we could now say that discrimination is justified to some extent, it is questionable that it is justified to the present extent. (Some people think that it is, some people do not.) It is tempting to conclude that presumably there is no property that would justify extreme discrimination, which causes hunger and diseases in developing countries.

Of course, those who think that extreme discrimination is justified believe that this thought is rational. This is a necessary psychological presupposition for having such a thought, but the fact that some believe it is rational to think that there is a property that would justify national discrimination—to the present extent—does not imply that it really is rational to think so. No doubt, it is *possible* that there is such a property, and it might even be reasonable to continue research in that field (that is, the question may be open in that sense), but still it is not rational to expect that one will find it. Therefore, those who think that the question of whether there is a property that would justify discrimination is still open are committed to the consensual method for determining how long presumptions are to be kept in the debate on global justice.

The problem is that it is anything but clear that the consensual method is appropriate in this debate. There is nothing wrong with the consensual method as such. For example, in politics it can be reasonable to keep questions open until agreement is achieved, since in politics agreement is valuable in itself. In political negotiations it does not matter much whether the level of salaries is right "in fact"; all that matters is that the parties agree that it is. In the debate on global justice, however, the aim of the discussion seems to be more than mere agreement. The parties of the discussion do not think that they are merely negotiating. They think that they are defending the "truth," or at least a justified conception of global affairs. Thus, it seems that we must ask whether it is *rational* to think that the question whether discrimination is justified is open. As argued above, presumably it is *not* rational to think so. Rationally speaking the question seems to be closed. It seems that the consensual method is required to defend the view that the question of whether there is a property that would justify national discrimination is open. Probably the appropriate method for deciding the issue is not the consensual method but the rational method. If this is so, those who defend conservative positions in a debate have a problem.

Conclusion

I have argued that a plausible way to meet the objection against discrimination on the basis of nationality is to hold that since the question is still open, one is justified to continue discrimination. However, those who wish to accept this form of defense have to rely on dubious assumptions. First, they are committed to the view that one is justified to believe anything one happens to believe as long as there is not a sufficient reason for believing otherwise, even if this might mean that one determines the solution of a moral disagreement without any moral argument. Second, they are committed to holding that they should maintain the conservative presumption that discrimination is justified until the disagreeing parties have achieved a *factual agreement* on the solution of the question of whether discrimination is justified. Taken together, these assumptions have very conservative implications, as the debate on global justice indicates. Nothing has happened, although the criticism is of long standing and new arguments have been presented by authors like Peter Singer (2002), Thomas Pogge (2001; 2002), and Nigel Dower (2003).

It has become common to think that the most important questions regarding the logic of the burden of proof center upon what is meant by "sufficient evidence" for shifting the burden to one's opponent. However, the above discussion tends to show that, at least regarding questions of global justice, it is equally important to find out who has the initial burden of proof and how long this initial burden remains on one side. It has also been common to claim that burden-of-proof rules are similar in law and in "less strictly organized types of argumentation," that is, "in certain important respects" (Walton 1988, 245). While this may be true, it cannot be emphasized enough that the logic of the burden of proof in less strictly organized argumentative situations, as in the debate on global justice, also differ from the logic of the burden of proof in law in a crucial way. In the debate on global justice, there are no shared values that would uncontroversially determine what the reasonable presumption is and who has the burden of proof. Nor are there formal rules that would stop the debate and announce the winner at a specific point.

The implications of my argument are not radical. If the argument presented is correct, and if there are not more promising arguments for the conservative position, then we must conclude that the national discrimination to the *present extent* is not justified, and we should start to *act* immediately to reduce global poverty. In short, if I am right, we are not morally justified to *wait* anymore.

Acknowledgments

I would like to thank Christian Barry, Thomas Pogge, Susanne Uusitalo, and Jukka Varelius for helpful comments.

References

Beitz, Charles. 1977. *Political Theory and International Relations*. Princeton: Princeton University Press.
Buchanan, Allen. 1992. "Distributive Justice." In *Encyclopedia of Ethics*, 655. New York: Garland.
Dower, Nigel. 2003. "The Ethics of Globalisation or the Globalisation of Ethics?" In *Global Order and Governance*, edited by Harto Hakovirta, 99–125. Turku: Figare & Safir.
Feinberg, Joel. 1973. *Social Philosophy*. Englewood Cliffs: Prentice-Hall.
Fogelin, Robert, and Walter Sinnott-Armstrong. 1991. *Understanding Arguments*. Fort Worth: Harcourt Brace Jovanovich.
Goldman, Alan H. 1982. "The Moral Significance of National Boundaries." *Midwest Studies in Philosophy* 7:437–53.
Hamblin, C. L. 1993. *Fallacies*. Newport News: Vale Press.
Katzner, Louis. 1970. "Presumptivist and Nonpresumptivist Principles of Formal Justice." *Ethics* 81:257–58.
Kekes, John. 2002. "On the Supposed Obligation to Relieve Famine." *Philosophy* 77:503–17.
Miller, David. 1995. *On Nationality*. Oxford: Clarendon Press.

Pogge, Thomas. 2001. "Priorities of Global Justice." *Metaphilosophy* 32:6–24.
———. 2002. *World Poverty and Human Rights*. Cambridge: Polity Press.
Räikkä, Juha. 1997. "Burden of Proof Rules in Social Criticism." *Argumentation* 11:463–77.
Rescher, Nicholas. 1977. *Dialectics*. Albany: SUNY Press.
Shue, Henry. 1980. *Basic Rights: Subsistence, Affluence, and American Foreign Policy*. Princeton: Princeton University Press.
Singer, Peter. 2002. *One World: The Ethics of Globalization*. New Haven: Yale University Press.
Walton, Douglas. 1988. "Burden of Proof." *Argumentation* 2:233–54.
———. 1989. *Question-Reply Argumentation*. New York: Greenwood.
———. 1991. *Begging the Question*. New York: Greenwood.
White, Morton. 1981. *What Is and What Ought to Be Done*. New York: Oxford University Press.

16

EXTREME POVERTY AND GLOBAL RESPONSIBILITY

BASHSHAR HAYDAR

There is no doubt that a significant number of people in the world today live under conditions of extreme poverty. Those people lack secure access to basic goods, such as food, water, and health care, owing to their meager economic resources.[1] Everybody agrees that those are horrible conditions and that it is, therefore, extremely important that something be done to alleviate them. There is no agreement, however, as to who is supposed to do what and when in order to achieve this goal. Providing an answer to this question depends, at least in part, on determining who is responsible for extreme poverty in a given situation and what the degree of their responsibility is.

Generally, responsibility has been attributed at either of two levels. At the first, responsibility for extreme poverty in a given location is attributed to domestic conditions—institutions, policies, decisions, practices, and values—that exist and operate in that location. At the second, the tendency is to attribute responsibility for extreme poverty to global factors, such as the set of global institutions and the practices and policies of various international actors. Given these two tendencies, we can imagine a full spectrum of views regarding the responsibility for extreme poverty depending on the relative weight each of these views assigns to domestic factors versus global factors.[2]

It is important to start with some clarification of the notion of responsibility. I take the claim that an agent is responsible for some harm to mean that the agent has special obligation to alleviate that situation or prevent it from taking place. One way to distinguish an agent who has special obligation to alleviate some harm from those who do not have such obligation is that less weight should be given to the former's appeal to cost in order to justify her not taking steps to alleviate the harm

---

[1] According to the World Bank (2000), about 2,800 million people live below US$2/day and about 1,200 million of these live below US$1/day.

[2] It should be pointed out that the distinction between domestic and global factors does not neatly capture all factors that might have an impact on poverty. Suppose, for example, that country A invaded country B and that the invasion partially explains the existing levels of poverty in B. So far as B is concerned, the invasion is obviously not a domestic factor. But, at the same time, the invasion does not count as a global factor. The responsibility for the invasion is that of country A and not necessarily that of the global order.

in question.[3] In this regard, one can identify at least two kinds of factors that might contribute to determining the degree of responsibility of an agent for a bad situation. The first kind has to do with the way and extent to which the agent is related to the production of that situation. Does the agent, for example, bring about, intend, merely allow, or foresee the outcome? The second kind has to do with the type of bond that exists between the agent and those affected by the harm in question. Is the agent, for example, a friend, a family member, or a guardian of the persons affected by the bad situation?

1

How, then, should we go about determining the relative degree of responsibility of domestic versus global factors for extreme poverty in a given situation of extreme poverty? One possible way of comparing the degree of responsibility of the global order with that of the domestic order is to compare two hypothetical scenarios. In the first scenario, we keep the domestic order fixed and try to evaluate the impact of adopting an optimal global order on extreme poverty. By "optimal global order" I have in mind a global order that reduces extreme poverty more than any alternative order. In the second scenario, we keep the existing global order fixed and try to evaluate the impact of an optimal domestic order on extreme poverty. Thus, the first scenario involves an optimal global order, and the second involves an optimal domestic order. Accordingly, in a given case of extreme poverty, the global order would be considered more responsible than the domestic order to the extent that there would be less extreme poverty under the first scenario than under the second.

It is difficult to determine what would count as an optimal global or domestic order with respect to extreme poverty. It is also difficult to determine the extent of reduction in extreme poverty under each respective scenario. Nevertheless, it could be argued that given the huge resources that are available to rich countries, an optimal global order would go a long way toward eliminating extreme poverty. This might be achieved, for example, by a general scheme of taxation that transfers funds and resources to poor countries with the aim of eliminating extreme poverty. Thus, we should expect great success in alleviating extreme poverty under the scenario that involves an optimal global order and an actual domestic one.

The same, however, could also be true in certain cases under the scenario that involves an optimal domestic order and an actual global one. There might be cases where optimizing the domestic order is

---

[3] This account of responsibility is similar in certain respects to what David Miller (2001) calls "remedial responsibility." It differs from it, however, in the way it treats the role of cost to the agent. See also section 3 below for a discussion of the relation between responsibility and appeals to cost.

sufficient to eliminate extreme poverty. In other words, under each scenario, there might be a situation where extreme poverty would be eliminated. It does not follow, however, that in such cases global and domestic orders share equal responsibility for extreme poverty. First, it might be possible for *any* one country to escape poverty within a suboptimal global order if it has an optimal domestic order while other poverty-stricken countries have suboptimal domestic orders—without it being possible for *all* currently poverty-stricken countries to eliminate poverty if all of them have optimal domestic orders. The fact that not all could avoid poverty if all adopted optimal orders would affect the share attributed to the global order for each.[4]

Second, it could be argued that the method suggested above of determining the relative degrees of responsibility for extreme poverty wrongly assumes that the domestic order should be treated in the same way as the global one when it comes to determining the level of responsibility for extreme poverty in a given case. This symmetry in treatment could be rejected on the ground that the domestic order has special duties toward people in its domain and hence bears the primary responsibility for their predicament. Instead, it might be proposed that the share of extreme poverty for which the global order is responsible is that portion that would persist even under optimal domestic order. Yet, there is a problem with this way of determining degree of responsibility of the global order, even if one accepts the claim that the domestic order should bear primary responsibility for alleviating poverty—since the global order itself may be partially responsible for the fact that the domestic order in question is not optimal with respect to reducing extreme poverty.

So far we have been trying to identify possible methods of determining the relative degree of responsibility of the global and domestic orders in situations of extreme poverty without making any distinctions as to the way in which the order under consideration is causally linked to the situation of poverty. But it might be argued that the share of responsibility that should be attributed to an institutional order for extreme poverty depends to a great extent on the nature of its connection to it. At the level of individual agents, a distinction is usually made between what one does or brings about, on the one hand, and what one merely allows or lets happen, on the other. An agent is usually said to be more responsible for what she does than for what she merely allows. The same could also be applied to political, social, and economic institutions. Thus, it could be maintained that institutional orders are more responsible for what they do than for what they merely allow to happen.

I will focus on the issue of whether the global order brings about or merely allows existing levels of extreme poverty by examining Thomas

---

[4] This possibility has been pointed out to me by Christian Barry.

Pogge's recent contribution on this topic. I argue that although Pogge builds a plausible case for the claim that the global order brings about, and not merely fails to prevent, extreme poverty, the moral and empirical complexity of the situation leaves room for doubting his conclusion. I conclude, however, that it is enough that there be a reasonable chance —though not conclusive evidence—that the global order brings about the existing extreme poverty to reduce considerably the moral weight of its privileged participants' appeal to cost in order to justify not taking steps to alleviate poverty.

2

Accepting a distinction between what an institutional order brings about and what it merely lets happen implies at least three possible ways in which an institutional order (IO) might relate to a given condition C. First possibility: IO brings about C. Second possibility: IO allows, but does not bring about, C. Third possibility: IO neither allows nor brings about C. The third possibility obtains when there is no alternative feasible institutional order under which C would not obtain. The second possibility obtains when there is some alternative feasible institutional order under which C would not take place. It is not clear, however, what needs to be true in order for the first possibility to obtain: it is difficult to identify the criterion that would permit us to say that the institutional order in question does not merely allow a given condition but also brings it about.

One possible suggestion for distinguishing between what the global institutional order brings about and what it merely lets happen is to appeal to some pre-institutional comparative benchmark. It might be argued that the present global order causes extreme poverty, and not merely fails to prevent it, if such poverty would not have existed in a global state of nature. There are, however, several difficulties in employing such a comparative benchmark. First, it is not clear whether the state of nature applies only to global institutions or also to domestic ones. Should we, in other words, imagine as part of a global state of nature that there are no nation-states, on the ground that nation-states could be perceived as part of the existing global order? Second, it is not clear at what point to introduce the hypothetical global state of nature. Are we supposed to consider what would happen if there were no global order as from the present moment? Or are we supposed to consider what it would be like had there never been such an order at all? The obvious difficulties involved in answering these questions suggest that any attempt to distinguish between what the global institutional order brings about and what it merely lets happen by appealing to a pre-institutional benchmark would be very problematic.

It might be suggested that we should look at how the bringing about/ letting happen distinction is drawn at the level of individual moral agents and generalize it to institutional orders. But even at the level of individual persons it has proven difficult to come up with an objection-proof criterion for drawing the distinction between what someone brings about and what she merely lets happen. Despite these difficulties, one can come up with examples where it seems that some distinction between what an agent brings about and what she merely allows underlies a confident attribution of different levels of moral responsibility. Consider, for example, the following pair of cases. In the first case, Mary, in order to avoid a certain amount of cost to herself, has pushed John into the water where she knows that he will drown (unless rescued by her). In the second case, Mary, in order to avoid the same amount of cost to herself, refrains from rescuing Henry, whom she notices, while merely passing by, to be about to drown (unless rescued by her). We would take Mary to be clearly more responsible for the drowning of John than for the drowning of Henry. It is plausible to maintain that what makes Mary more responsible for John's predicament than for Henry's is that the former, unlike the latter, is brought about and not merely allowed by Mary.[5]

Similarly, despite the difficulty of coming up with a general criterion for distinguishing what an institutional order brings about and what it merely lets happen, we can identify cases where such a distinction has a clear and indisputable weight in the assignment of moral responsibility to institutional orders. This type of analysis is employed by Pogge in his defense of the moral relevance of distinguishing between what an institutional order brings about and what it merely lets happen. Pogge offers a set of scenarios to illustrate his view. In all of these scenarios, the focus is on a group of persons who avoidably suffer from a deprivation or shortfall of essential nutrients V. The shortfall is avoidable in the sense that there is a feasible alternative institutional order under which the shortfall would not occur. Pogge provides the following six scenarios to illustrate his view:

> In scenario 1, the shortfall is officially mandated, paradigmatically, by the law: legal restrictions bar certain persons from buying foodstuffs containing V. In scenario 2, the shortfall results from legally authorized conduct of private subjects: sellers of foodstuffs containing V lawfully refuse to sell to certain persons. In scenario 3, social institutions foreseeably and avoidably engender (but do not specifically require or authorize) the shortfall through the conduct they stimulate: certain persons, suffering severe poverty within an ill-conceived economic order, cannot afford to buy foodstuffs containing V. In scenario 4, the shortfall arises from the private conduct that is legally prohibited but barely deterred: sellers of foodstuffs containing V illegally refuse to sell to certain persons, but enforcement is lax and penalties are mild. In scenario 5,

---

[5] One important way in which the difference in the level of responsibility reveals itself is in the fact that Mary's appeal to cost in order not to rescue John (the first case) would have less moral weight than her appeal to cost in order not to rescue Henry (the second case).

the shortfall arises from social institutions avoidably leaving unmitigated the effects of a natural defect: certain persons are unable to metabolize V due to a treatable genetic defect, but they avoidably lack access to the treatment that would correct their handicap. In scenario 6, the shortfall arises from social institutions avoidably leaving unmitigated the effects of a self-caused defect: certain persons are unable to metabolize V due to a treatable self-caused disease—brought on, perhaps, by their maintaining a long-term smoking habit in full knowledge of the medical dangers associated therewith—and avoidably lack access to the treatment that would correct their ailment. (Pogge 2002, 41–42)

Pogge argues that the level of institutional responsibility for the resulting shortfall cannot be the same in all of these scenarios. It is obvious, for example, that the institutional order is more responsible for the shortfall in scenario 1 than in scenario 6. Pogge seems also to indicate that the aforementioned difference in the degrees of responsibility is partially due to the fact that the shortfalls in scenarios 5 and 6 are not being brought about by the social institution but are only being allowed by it.[6]

It is helpful to go back to the task of assessing the relative responsibility of the domestic and global orders for extreme poverty in the light of Pogge's distinctions. Those in favor of assigning lesser responsibility to the global institutional order might argue their case by maintaining that the global order is related to extreme poverty either in the same way an institutional order relates to the shortfall in scenario 5 or in the way it relates to it in scenario 6. Let us consider scenario 5, in which the genetic defect of the disadvantaged persons is a necessary condition for their predicament and this feature makes the institutional order not highly responsible for their predicament. Similarly, it could be argued that the global order is not highly responsible for extreme poverty that exists in a given country whenever the poverty in question is due to meager natural resources in that country.

There is, however, an obvious problem with the above analogy between genetic defects in scenario 5 and the lack of natural resources in a given country. Although the location of natural resources is a natural fact, the ownership and use-rights of these resources are not. They are, rather, part of the global order that regulates and governs the use, exchange, and profit from such resources.[7] But suppose that the analogy between genetic and natural resources holds. We would then need to determine the conditions in which extreme poverty in a given country is due to the lack of natural resources in that country. It is not enough that the extreme poverty in question could be reduced or eliminated with more natural resources, since this would not establish that the country's

<hr>

[6] It should be mentioned that Pogge (2002, 42) also emphasizes the role of implicit attitudes of social institutions toward the shortfall in determining the institution's degree of responsibility.

[7] For more on this point, see Beitz 1999, 136–43.

comparatively smaller share of natural resources causes it to do worse than other countries. It is necessary to establish a stronger correlation between the lack of natural resources and extreme poverty for this conclusion to hold true. It is doubtful, however, that one can find in our world such a correlation between extreme poverty and meager natural resources.[8]

The case for maintaining that the global order is not highly responsible for extreme poverty appears to be stronger in analogy with scenario 6, in which the disadvantaged persons are themselves responsible for their predicament. Their long-term smoking is a necessary condition for their inability to metabolize nutrients V. It should be kept in mind, however, that the behavior in scenario 6 is not sufficient for the existence of the predicament since the predicament could be avoided under some feasible alternative institutional order. If this feature makes the institutional order not highly responsible for the predicament, it could be argued that the global order is not highly responsible for extreme poverty in a given country so long as the behavior of the people suffering from this poverty constitutes a necessary condition for their predicament. Thus, one could argue that the global order is less responsible, for a given case of extreme poverty, to the extent that the adoption of nonoptimal domestic institutions and practices is a necessary condition for the existence of the extreme poverty.

There is, however, a clear disanalogy between the lack of nutrients V in scenario 6, on the one hand, and extreme poverty, on the other. While it is postulated that each person in scenario 6 is responsible for her smoking habit, the same is obviously not true of persons living in extreme poverty: one only has to think of children suffering from extreme poverty. Their case is more analogous to the case of a person who cannot metabolize nutrients V due to the smoking habits of her mother (or some stranger). The latter case (call it scenario S) does not fall either under scenario 5 or under scenario 6: the predicament of persons in scenario S is neither self-imposed nor naturally caused. The question then is how to rank the level of responsibility of the institutional order in this type of case. One option is to treat them like cases of scenario 5 on the grounds that it should not make a difference whether the predicament is due to some natural defect or to the irresponsible behavior of others. In both types of case, the responsibility of the institutional order in question is the same.

One might, however, provide a different answer. For cases of type S, it might be argued that the responsibility of the institutional order should rank higher than that of the institutional order in scenarios 5 or 6, if one accepts that it is the primary responsibility of an institutional order to protect innocent people from the wrongful behavior of others. But one

---

[8] A comparison between poor but resource-rich Africa and relatively well off but resource-poor Japan, South Korea, and Taiwan provides some evidence for the above claim.

might wonder in response to this rationale why such primary responsibility does not extend to protecting innocent persons from the effects of natural defects or misfortune. There seems to be no reason why the responsibility should not extend to cases of type 5 as well. It is important to add here that what falls under the primary responsibility of an institutional order might differ between the domestic order and the global one. It could be argued that the domestic order has a more special and stronger obligation toward people within its domain than does the global order. For example, it could be argued that although it is a primary responsibility of the domestic institutional order to protect persons in its domain from the wrongful behavior of others as well as from natural disasters, it is not part of the primary responsibility of the global order to do either.

Setting aside the problem of children and other possible innocent victims of local or domestic nonoptimal practices, let us consider again the claim that the relationship between the global order and a given case of extreme poverty could be analogous to the situation in scenario 6.[9] If the analogy holds, it would intuitively reduce considerably the responsibility of the global order for the poverty. The evidence one needs to obtain in order to establish that the above analogy holds must at least show that certain domestic practices constitute a necessary condition for extreme poverty. It need not show, however, that these domestic practices are sufficient for extreme poverty.

We can look for such evidence by investigating the correlation between nonoptimal domestic practices and extreme poverty. Such correlation could be investigated by identifying countries with nonoptimal or bad domestic practices and seeing the extent to which these same countries have higher levels of extreme poverty than other countries with more optimal domestic conditions. If it is found that countries with nonoptimal domestic practices tend to have significantly higher rates of extreme poverty, then we could say that the correlation in question is established.

It might be argued, however, that establishing a correlation between nonoptimal domestic conditions and extreme poverty does not relieve the global order from a high degree of responsibility for extreme poverty. Pogge has provided two such arguments. In the first argument, he draws on an analogy with teaching.[10] He points out that although great variations in the performance of students taking the same course show that these variations must be due to "student-specific factors," such as the amount of effort each one of them puts into her studies, this does not

[9] Instead of simply setting aside the case of children, one might alternatively try to come up with an acceptable notion of collective responsibility that would cover all cases of individually innocent victims of domestic nonoptimal practices.

[10] Thomas Pogge, "Severe Poverty as a Human Rights Violation." In *Freedom from Severe Poverty as a Human Right: Who Owes What to the Very Poor*, edited by Thomas W. Pogge (Paris: UNESCO, forthcoming).

show that the quality of teaching does not affect the overall performance of the students. Despite the individual variations among students, the quality of the teaching, argues Pogge, can still be a major factor in explaining the overall performance of the class. The same applies to extreme poverty. Variations in the levels of extreme poverty in different countries show that these variations must be due to country-specific factors, such as the kind of domestic institutions and practices each of them has. This does not show, argues Pogge, that the global order does not play a major role in explaining the overall levels of extreme poverty. Hence, it does not show that the global order is not responsible for that poverty.

Although Pogge may not want to build much on the student analogy mentioned above, it is instructive to examine it more closely. Suppose that of two students who take the same course, one passed while the other failed. Pogge's point is simply that we cannot infer solely on the basis of this information that the teacher is not to be blamed for the student's failure. But what is it that we need to show in order to confirm or deny the teacher's culpability? Such culpability would be established if we can show, for example, that the teacher's performance was below a minimally acceptable standard and that the failing student would have passed the course had the teacher's performance met that minimum. Notice that the teacher's culpability cannot be established simply by showing that there is an alternative possible teaching performance under which the failing student would have passed the course. Suppose the student would have passed had the teacher put great effort into teaching beyond what is required of her under these circumstances. Not putting in such effort does not constitute valid ground for blaming the teacher for her student's failure. It is not easy, however, to determine the minimally acceptable level of performance for teachers. Moreover, what constitutes such a level might differ in different cases and contexts. What is minimally required or expected of a university professor is quite different from that expected of an elementary-school teacher. Much less personal attention is required from the former relative to the latter.

How does all of this apply to the relationship between extreme poverty and the global order? Following the student analogy, and in order to establish that the global order is to be held responsible for extreme poverty, we need to show that the global order has failed to meet a minimally acceptable standard. But it is not clear how this standard should be characterized. The task of identifying this minimum seems to be even more difficult in this case than in the case of teaching. In the case of teaching, we can at least start with the assumption that teachers have some special obligation toward the academic performance of their students. We can also rely on various teaching traditions as well as on comparisons between different teachers from the same tradition. It is not clear, however, that the same applies to the global order. Of course, it could be argued that, even though the global order might not have a special obligation toward those living in extreme poverty, it does not follow that it meets a minimally acceptable standard with respect to this matter. It could be maintained that the global order fails to meet such standards if extreme poverty could easily be avoided or alleviated under an alternative global order that does not impose a comparable burden on others.[11] But, even if we accept the latter claim, this does not help us in settling the question at hand—namely, whether the global order brings about, or merely allows, extreme poverty.

In addition to the student analogy, Pogge provides a more direct argument against the claim that establishing a correlation between nonoptimal domestic practices and extreme poverty is sufficient to show that the global order does not bring about extreme poverty but merely allows it. This correlation is not sufficient, argues Pogge, because it is possible that the global order itself is seriously responsible for the fact that the domestic practices are not optimal. In order to account for this possibility, we need to assess the degree of responsibility of the global order for the nonoptimal domestic practices. Thus, if we accept the moral relevance of the bringing about/letting happen distinction at the level of institutional orders, we should provide a way of distinguishing cases where the nonoptimal domestic practices are brought about by the global order and cases where these practices are merely allowed by it. This, however, takes us back to the difficult task of providing a criterion for distinguishing between what an institutional order does and what it merely allows.

The difficulty of providing such a criterion does not, however, rule out the possibility of identifying examples where it is clear that an institutional order brings about and not merely allows a certain condition. Pogge provides an example of this sort concerning the relationship between the global order and nonoptimal domestic practices. He points out that the global order permits the selling of natural resources by those in power in a given country regardless of their legitimacy. It also permits them to borrow money from other states and from international lenders in the name of the country under their control. These privileges encourage corruption and provide incentives for undemocratic acquisition of power, which in turn plays a pivotal role in creating and maintaining the conditions that are responsible for extreme poverty in these countries. The fact that the present global institutional order confers these privileges cannot, argues Pogge, be considered part of what the global order merely lets happen. Rather, it is analogous to knowingly buying stolen goods and hence constitutes a sort of collaboration in the crime itself (Pogge 2002, 141–44). Without getting into the details of Pogge's example, we can agree, in principle at least, that if the current resources and borrowing

---

[11] For further discussion of this claim, see section 3 below.

privileges contribute to extreme poverty, then the present global institutional order that confers such privileges is doing harm and not merely failing to prevent harm from occurring.

Changing the current system of international resources and borrowing privileges might have a positive impact on good domestic governance, which in turn could have a positive effect on reducing levels of poverty. It is not clear, however, what the extent of this effect would be or how much time it would take to achieve it. Some might still maintain that the chief sources of domestic inefficiency are themselves deeply domestic. Different views on this issue remain viable because of the empirical complexity of the matter at hand. The same is true, for example, for the debate concerning the impact of colonialism. One can present a plausible case for the claim that colonialism did cause considerable and long-term damage to the colonized countries. Still, the complexity of the facts and factors involved, including the counterfactual histories one needs to consider, makes it difficult to arrive at a clear and indisputable confirmation and assessment of the damage done by colonialism. Similarly, with all the complexity, it becomes difficult to show indisputably that the global order is bringing about and not merely allowing a considerable amount of extreme poverty.

3

How, then, should we proceed in view of these uncertainties and complexities? Recall that the need to determine whether the global order brings about or merely allows extreme poverty is motivated by the need to assign the appropriate level of responsibility of the global order for such horrible conditions. Determining the appropriate level of responsibility is itself motivated by the need to answer the question of who should do what, and when, in order to alleviate extreme poverty. If it turns out that the global order brings about considerable portions of the existing extreme poverty, then there is a strong moral requirement for those who uphold or benefit from the current global order to change it and compensate those who are harmed by it. The greater the responsibility of the global order for extreme poverty, the weaker becomes the appeal to cost (made by those who benefit from that order) as justification of the failure to make the changes required to alleviate the poverty.

The relation between levels of responsibility and the plausibility of appeals to cost can be put as follows. People can appeal usually to cost in order to justify their failure to alleviate some harm. Thus, Mary can be granted a moral permission not to rescue Henry from drowning on the ground that the rescuing could cost her an arm. However, Mary would be morally required to rescue Henry had the rescuing been of no or negligible cost to her. The weight of an appeal to cost seems to be determined by three main factors. The first factor is the amount of cost to the agent relative to the amount of harm alleviated. Generally speaking, the higher the ratio of cost incurred to harm alleviated, the more plausible the appeal. The second factor is the degree of responsibility of the agent for the harm in question. It is in regard to this factor that it matters whether the harm to be alleviated is brought about by the agent or is merely something the agent allows to happen. Thus, if Mary initially pushed Henry into the water, her appeal to cost in order to be granted moral permission not to rescue him would be considerably less convincing. The third factor has to do with whether there is special relation or obligation between the agent and the victim. Thus, Mary's appeal to cost would have less weight had she been Henry's wife or had she been a lifeguard on duty.

Given these three factors, the task of determining the weight of an appeal to cost in a given case can be summed up as follows. First, we determine the ratio of cost incurred to harm alleviated. Then we check the second and the third factors in order to determine whether this ratio would keep its full weight or receive a certain degree of reduction. The smaller the ratio of cost to harm alleviated (the first factor), the less the need to determine the situation with regard to the second and third factors.[12] So, for example, if Mary can rescue Henry with negligible cost to her, she would be morally required to do so regardless of whether she pushed him or happened to be his wife.

Applying this reasoning to the issue of the global order and extreme poverty, we can say that the smaller the ratio of cost incurred to poverty alleviated, the stronger the moral requirement to alleviate the poverty in question, and the less important it is to determine whether the global order brings about or merely allows the existing extreme poverty. Thus, suppose that the amount needed to alleviate extreme poverty is not more than 2 percent of the global gross domestic product of rich developed countries. In this case, the ratio of cost (2 percent) to harm alleviated might be low enough to generate a moral requirement to alleviate extreme poverty by those who do well under the current global order, independently of the second factor or of whether the poverty is brought about or merely allowed by the global order.

Suppose, however, one adopts a moral view that gives the second factor a decisive role in determining the weight of an appeal to cost. According to this view, even minimal cost would grant an agent permission not to alleviate serious harm, so long as the harm is not brought about by the agent who is appealing to cost. Only when the harm is brought about by the agent would an appeal to cost fail to generate moral permission not to alleviate the harm in question. Thus, according to such a view, even a cost of 2 percent of the GDP of rich countries would morally permit them not to alleviate extreme

---

[12] The degree of reduction depends on the degree of emphasis that is put on each of the three factors. Different moral views might give different weights to each of these factors.

poverty, so long as it has not been brought about by these rich countries. But what if we are in a situation where it is not clear whether the harm to be alleviated is brought about, or merely allowed, by the agent in question? If the harm is serious and the cost of alleviating it is quite low, then not alleviating that harm would be running the risk of causing serious harm. This would clearly be morally unacceptable—we do strongly require people to take measures in order to avoid the risk of bringing about harm to others, whenever these measures are not too costly. Similarly, if the complexity of the situation makes it difficult to determine conclusively whether the global order brings about or merely allows the existing extreme poverty, then this uncertainty must negatively affect the weight of an appeal to cost by those benefiting from the current global order. If there is a reasonable chance that the global order is bringing about extreme poverty and if the cost of alleviating it is not high, then those who uphold and benefit from the global order clearly are morally required to alleviate that poverty. Otherwise, they would be failing to take measures to avoid the risk of bringing about harm to others when the cost of adopting these measures is quite low.[13]

Acknowledgments

I am grateful to Lina Choueiri and Christian Barry for valuable comments on previous drafts of this essay.

References

Barry, Christian. 2005. "Applying the Contribution Principle." Included in this collection.
Beitz, Charles. 1999. *Political Theory and International Relations.* 2nd edition. Princeton: Princeton University Press.
Miller, David. 2001. "Distributing Responsibility." *Journal of Political Philosophy* 9:454–64.
Pogge, Thomas W. 2002. *World Poverty and Human Rights: Cosmopolitan Responsibilities and Reforms.* New York: Polity Press.
World Bank. 2000. *World Development Report 2000.* New York: Oxford University Press.

---

[13] For extensive discussion and defense of this view, see Barry 2005. Barry builds his case on an analogy with legal practices.

17

THE NEW LIBERAL IMPERIALISM: ASSESSING THE ARGUMENTS

JEDEDIAH PURDY

This essay is an attempt to take the idea of empire seriously as an element in normative political theory. The sudden reappearance of "empire" as a doctrine to be taken seriously had some of the thrill of the forbidden. Who would dare to endorse imperial ambitions as good for their country or, more heretical still, good for the world? Iconoclasm, though, is a short-lived pleasure. Now that the concept of empire has gone from pariah status to buzzword, the time has come to attempt some rigor in characterizing and assessing the arguments for empire.

As the idea of empire has become fashionable, it has acquired many putative meanings, some military and political, others economic, and still others concerned with cultural power. The aim of this essay is not to define empire for all purposes, but to examine the most plausible and, arguably, influential arguments for a new imperial policy, chiefly in the realms of political and military power. These arguments are united by their appeal to broadly liberal, although not necessarily democratic, values. They are significant not least because they probably constitute the only imperial doctrine that most people at present are likely to accept. Although by no means all advocates of the doctrine can be styled "liberals" in their domestic political contexts, the doctrine's recourse to liberal values makes "liberal imperialism" an appropriate rubric for it.

What Makes an Imperial Doctrine Today

What makes today's liberal imperialism an imperial doctrine is its commitment to the political inequality of countries. This inequality is not restricted to contingent differences in power, but includes differences in competence for self-governance. Competence, in this sense, includes both the *capacity* for self-governance, a matter of the practical where-withal to maintain a decent social order, and *qualification*, or legitimacy, as measured by some combination of liberal and democratic norms. The normative consequence of political inequality among countries is that some may legitimately make and implement important decisions concerning the governance of others. Imperial policy thus represents either a selective or a categorical rejection of two contemporary axioms of political legitimacy, which may be fairly termed Wilsonian: national sovereignty and democratic self-determination.

One can distinguish between "weak" and "strong" imperial policy according to the manner and degree of this rejection. Weak imperial policy is premised on the political inequality not of peoples but of *governments*, holding that some governments do not command the respect of others because they are unfit representatives of the peoples they claim to govern, whether for procedural reasons—for instance, because they are not democratically accountable—or for substantive reasons, because they participate in impermissible abuses against some of their citizens or subjects. Weak imperialism thus claims not that a people whose government may be thwarted or overthrown is *incapable* of self-rule, but that its self-rule has been frustrated by its own government, and must be won back for it by the intervention of another government. This distinction corresponds to a distinction in the Wilsonian axioms: the sovereignty of a government does not always protect the self-determination of a people. Where a government is despotic, the shield of its sovereignty may stand in the way of its people's self-governance. Many saw NATO's 1999 Kosovo action as crystallizing the claims of weak liberal imperialism, protecting a people within a state from the depredations of the state. The doctrine of weak liberal imperialism also formed one rationale for the American-led invasion of Iraq in 2003, whose aim was frequently given as the liberation of the Iraqi people.

Strong imperialism goes further, insisting on the political inequality not just of governments but of peoples. Its basis is typically sociological, having to do with a subordinate people's preparedness to govern itself peacefully and sustain orderly institutions (or, more robustly, democratic and liberal ones). On this view, one people may do more than unseat another's government to restore to the people its proper sovereignty: it may also exercise ongoing power over basic collective decisions, in the name of some interest that is claimed to trump the people's sovereignty itself. If weak imperialism seemed heterodox in the 1990s, strong imperialism until recently would have been heretical. It is a return to the doctrine of John Stuart Mill, who wrote with India in mind that "rule by a foreign power is as legitimate as any other mode" when it is to the ultimate benefit of the ruled.

An initial difficulty is worth noting in the relationship between the two Wilsonian axioms, sovereignty and democratic self-determination. Overtly imperial projects today, such as the invasion of Iraq, tend to find their initial justification in a doctrine of weak imperialism—they claim to suspect sovereignty, but not democratic self-determination, as the sovereign governments that are constrained or overthrown are far from democratic. On the strength of the Kosovo precedent and the ascent of the norm of democratic legitimacy to general (at least nominal) acceptance, violating a country's sovereignty for the announced purpose

of bestowing democracy on its population often wins, so to speak, as
many points as it loses. This advantage is fleeting, however, if the imperial
power does not quickly and soundly establish democracy, which will in
many cases prove impossible or so inexpedient that the imperial power
deems it unacceptable. When it becomes clear that democracy is not
rapidly forthcoming, and that the country's direction will remain substantially in the hands of its imperial occupier, overseer, or sponsor, then
the imperial project can no longer rest its normative claims on weak
imperialism. The practice increasingly corresponds to the doctrine of
strong imperialism, and the imperial power must insist that overriding
democratic self-determination is justified by some other value or values.

Justifications for Imperial Policy

Because it begins as an exception to principles that, however unevenly
practiced, are widely accepted as normative polestars,[1] an imperial policy
today must rest on other basic values, which justify the exception.
Defenders of imperial doctrine, now and often in the past, have presented
three kinds of considerations that, it is claimed, outweigh the Wilsonian
axioms.

The first is an account of global security: what the security of all
nations consists in and how to protect it. This is an old concept, which has
taken new force from the increased scale of today's potential threats. In
the eighteenth century, the chief activity that international law recognized
as a threat to all was piracy, the occasion of the United States Marines'
famous action at Tripoli. Today terrorism, roughly defined as politically
motivated attacks on civilians by nonstate actors,[2] is a candidate to
become the piracy of the twenty-first century: the universally proscribed
activity that may be hunted wherever it takes refuge. The second kind of
threat that today's imperial policy recognizes is the possession of certain
kinds of weapons: chemical and biological weapons because they are
nominally banned but more specifically because certain countries alleg-

---

[1] There is, of course, ample tension between these two principles to begin with; but the
fact remains that national sovereignty is the most basic principle of legitimate international
action, while the democratic self-determination of peoples is, for all its persistent violations,
the only widely accepted standard of domestic political legitimacy, and one to which nearly
every regime at least pretends. Although they are far from requiring one another, they do
belong together both for their common axiomatic status and because they together formed
the core of both Wilsonian liberalism and anti-colonial independence movements, two of the
defining ideological families of the last century.

[2] I am deliberately omitting the question of whether there should be a category of state
terror, and if so how it should be defined. I do so not because I consider it insignificant, but
because it has not entered significantly into the prudential arguments in favor of liberal
imperialism. Certain forms of what may be called state terror against a state's own subjects
fall within another argument for liberal imperialism: the prevention of severe human rights
abuses within a state. The important question of one state's actions against the citizens of
another state does not enter into this essay.

edly cannot be trusted to keep such weapons out of the hands of terrorists; and nuclear weapons because certain countries allegedly cannot be trusted not to use them, to make first use of them, or to put them in the hands of terrorists. In combination, terrorists and so-called weapons of mass destruction present the potential of devastating attacks on civilian populations, although the degree of the threat is hard to judge because it has been so profligately invoked. The implication of this prospect is that global security may require that entire regimes be brought forcibly to heel. Iraq is now a matter of record on this score, and with the first precedent in place, the principle is at once very potent and of indeterminate proportions.

Considerations of global security might be called, in a way that is only mildly stylized, the ultimate in prudential reasoning. Such considerations aim at avoiding disaster and securing the sometimes fragile preconditions of other kinds of interests. The second kind of consideration has much more to do with affirmative conceptions of human flourishing. It begins from an idea of what the most basic and general human interests are, and proposes that the domination of one people by another, at least for a time, may be necessary to achieve them. The historical version of this view most likely to be intelligible to us is the liberal nineteenth-century conception expressed with some eloquence and full conviction by John Stuart Mill and his father, James Mill. On this view, peoples whose social orders were premised on superstition and tyranny would have to spend some time under the hard-nosed but beneficent tutelage of more advanced nations, which had themselves realized liberal values and could now enforce and cultivate them abroad. At the end of the tutelage, the subject peoples would emerge into the full historical daylight of self-government, commerce, and reason.[3]

This idea has undergone a chastened period, embarrassed in politics by successful anti-colonial movements, and in the realm of ideas by both theoretical and historical explorations of its implication in the repudiated abuses of the colonial period. Of late, though, it is newly robust. The

---

[3] A fine introduction to the views of the senior Mill is Mill 1975. In his discussion of "The Civilization of the Hindus," for instance, Mill observes "the necessity of regarding the actual state of the Hindus as little removed from that of half-civilized nations" (231); reckons that "despotism and priestcraft taken together, the Hindus, in mind and body, were the most enslaved portion of the human race" (237); and quotes with approval Adam Smith's judgment that Asian "despotism is more destructive of leisure and security, and more adverse to the progress of the human mind, than anarchy itself" (249–50). John Stuart Mill, in his chapter "Government of Dependencies" in *Considerations on Representative Government*, wrote more systematically: "[Rule by a foreign power] is as legitimate as any other [mode of government] if it is the one which in the existing state of civilization of the subject people most facilitates their transition to a higher stage of improvement. There are . . . conditions of society in which a vigorous despotism is in itself the best mode of government for training the people in what is specifically wanting to render them capable of a higher civilization" (Mill 1993, 415).

practice of nation-building has moved to the fore of American and, often in consequence of American-led military actions, multilateral policy. The promise of such policy is that, given a period of tutelage, peoples emerging from oppressive governance or chaos can secure and preserve liberal and democratic institutions, and enter into the ordered liberty of modern life. Different inflections of this view unite a spectrum of politicians and commentators who advocate making war abroad and provisionally governing subject peoples to foster American-style freedom, from archconservatives and longtime imperialists such as William Kristol and Paul Wolfowitz to newly converted believers in this vision of American mission such as President George W. Bush.

The third kind of consideration is deontological. It is usually expressed in the idea that certain kinds of actions are absolutely prohibited, and that when someone does them, others have a right or, alternatively, a duty to intervene and prevent them. In the political shorthand of the last decade, this is the Kosovo scenario. In the second half of the twentieth century, genocide became the exemplary prohibited act, whose evil overrides all other considerations of legitimacy (if not considerations of convenience, as the world's indifference to murder in Rwanda suggested). The nearest historical analogies are cannibalism and human sacrifice, which were the prohibited horrors that the Spanish gave as reasons for conquest of Native American populations; but such actions were never the sole or overwhelming reason for an invasion, as was true of genocide in Kosovo.

These three kinds of considerations—prudential reasons, reasons of flourishing, and reasons of prohibition—correspond to deep human interests, and represent serious reasons for dissatisfaction with the Wilsonian axioms. The history of the last twenty years has done much to make these considerations seem more vital and viable than they had recently appeared. The fall of Marxist-Leninist governments across Eastern Europe and the then Soviet Union seemed mightily to confirm that people everywhere really do want the same things: personal liberty and security, a measure of comfort and opportunity, and the privilege of feeling at home in a "normal country" (the poignant term of post-Milosevic Yugoslav leader Vojislav Kostunica) whose economic and social order falls somewhere near that of the United States or Western Europe. Widespread attention to the "global culture" of mostly American images and phrases that new communications technology spread in the 1990s reinforced the idea that, given the choice, all cultures would converge on a roughly American set of tastes and aspirations. The extraordinary intellectual self-confidence of the neoliberal program of market-oriented economic reforms in the 1990s completed the picture: people everywhere wanted the same things, and there was one, scientifically mandated way to secure them, which the neoliberal program presented in some detail. By the time the United States invaded Iraq, it seemed intuitive to many that Iraqis would seize upon the unseating of

Saddam Hussein as an opportunity to become American, or at least Arab-American.

Reasons of prohibition, too, loomed larger in the 1990s as the idea of human rights—inviolable and universal protections against state and sometimes against private violence—grew in importance. The Kosovo intervention capped a period in which groups such as Amnesty International and Human Rights Watch became essential custodians of public conscience. In the same period, the relentlessly reported ethnic wars of the Balkans and the Rwanda massacres drove home that genocide, enshrined after World War II as the ultimate abuse of human rights, had not been consigned to the past. Public moral language increasingly became the language of human rights, so that by the time of the Kosovo intervention objections based on sovereignty had come to seem legalistic and even morally obtuse.

As for considerations of global security, the terrorist attacks of September 11, 2001, significantly reoriented American foreign policy and domestic attitudes. Americans now are much more likely than five years ago to view the world as bristling with dangers *for them*, and to support their government in responding aggressively to actual or perceived threats. This is, of course, a matter of the security interest of one nation, which may be quite a different question from the requirements of global security; but the scale of American political, economic, and military power means that an American emphasis on the security threat posed by terrorism inevitably draws global attention (sometimes sincerely, sometimes opportunistically) to the same concern.

All of these trends have been reinforced by the manifest failures of many postcolonial states. Human rights abuses, the harboring of terrorists, and the relentless quashing of human flourishing were variously characteristic of the authoritarian, kleptocratic, or anarchic countries that dotted the Middle East, Central Asia, and sub-Saharan and northeastern Africa in the 1990s. The end of colonialism in the middle of the twentieth century was supposed to be a harbinger of progress. Wilsonians and other anti-colonialists expected national sovereignty and democracy to coexist and elevate both the dignity and the prosperity of former colonial subjects. The widespread thwarting of this expectation made increasingly plausible the idea that respecting the sovereignty of failing or abusive, nondemocratic governments was a species of criminal neglect.[4]

---

[4] It is worth noting that the failure of many postcolonial regimes does not in itself mean that the preceding colonial rule was a good thing, whose passing was to be regretted. Nor, more pertinently, does such failure indicate that independence was inherently unviable for those countries. The bipolar manipulation of governments and anti-government insurrections during the Cold War was a disaster for many newly independent countries. While those countries faced terrible disadvantages apart from the Cold War, we will never know whether some might have done much better free of the proxy battles of those decades.

All of this created great potential for new or revived imperial arguments, which found their moment in American politics in the eighteen months following September 11, 2001, when talk of American empire moved from the margins of political and scholarly agitation to the center of public debate and political decision. The Bush Doctrine (crystallized in the official statement of "The National Security Strategy of the United States of America September 2002"), taken at face value, is a statement of liberal imperial policy that makes its case for American military supremacy and unilateral intervention by way of all three classes of consideration that I have described: an appeal to security asserting that terrorism and "weapons of mass destruction" together form a new and urgent kind of threat; an appeal to absolute prohibitions in its invocation of human rights principles to justify intervention; and an appeal to human flourishing that envisions a world in which peoples live freely and peaceably after liberation from their present tyrannical governments, sometimes but not always after a period of American tutelage. In this view, the special American relationship to liberal and democratic principles, combined with the unique capacity of a solitary superpower, exempts us from the constraints that govern other nations and imposes the responsibility of action on us.

Historical Lessons on the Hazards of Empire

That said, how to assess the new imperial arguments? Anyone who thinks this question important owes the new imperialists a debt for the inadvertent favor of making it explicit. As a beginning, I suggest two ways of enriching the discussion while acknowledging that today's imperial programs respond to genuine moral and political problems, and are formulated in good faith as regularly as any other program of political action. The first approach is to deepen the historical context in which to view the idea and practice of empire, which is often, and somewhat opportunistically, discussed without attention to its complex precedents. The second is to engage with the imperial arguments on their own ground: the quality of the reasons they provide for overriding the Wilsonian axioms. A sufficient assessment of the present imperial program must include an assessment of those reasons, and any alternative requires an alternative account of them.

The historical tack is perhaps the less telling of the two, but it should address an asymmetry of historical awareness in the contemporary discussion of empire. The sudden revival of the great forms of argument for empire, even in sometimes slapdash form, has not been accompanied by a symmetrical revival of the tradition of anti-imperial argument. An observer whose knowledge of these issues came entirely from the contemporary debate might come naturally to one of two mistaken conclusions: first, that objections to empire are simply expressions of fastidiousness on the part of those who decline to confront a messy and dangerous world; or, second, that although racism, violence, and exploitation were indeed the sins of earlier empires, the contemporary imperial program, because cleansed of those defects, is not objectionable as earlier empire might have been.

The benefit of even a superficial acquaintance with the liberal and humanitarian strains of justification for the British Empire, or the illiberal and humanitarian defenses of Spanish conquest, is the recognition that today's imperial apologists are not novel in either their good intentions or their willingness—even eagerness—to give reasons for their programs. Nor does this fact mean that past criticism of imperialism was premised on a misunderstanding, a failure to recognize that the East India Company and everything that followed it pursued a civilizing mission. The recently fashionable caricature of previous centuries' imperialism as mere rapine has made it too easy for today's imperial planners to ignore their ideological ancestry. It has also, paradoxically, strengthened the hand of revivalists of the old imperial ideas, who make much of the rediscovery that imperial administrators oversaw legal systems and railroads as well as plunder and repression—facts allegedly fatal to the allegedly naive critics of empire.

At least one historical strain of anti-imperialism that remains instructive today was perfectly compatible with the fact that imperialists saw themselves as pursuing a moral mission. Indeed, this form of anti-imperialism took strength from that fact. It is also, and perhaps more saliently, unweakened by the recent historical developments that have cleared the way for the new enthusiasm for empire. I have in mind a form of skepticism about moral reasoning in politics whose modern form was pioneered by two thinkers who were at grips with the imperial projects of their own times: Michel de Montaigne and Edmund Burke.[5] The skepticism that united them across two centuries and a modest but significant body of water had two foundations, the less important one epistemic and the more important based on a theory of human motivation. Their epistemic point was, then as now, familiar if not uncontroversial: that people systematically err in their judgment of the moral and empirical

---

[5] Montaigne's view of these matters is expressed in two of his essays, "Of Cannibals" (1995a) and "Of Coaches" (1995b). Burke's extraordinary speeches on imperial policy are well represented in Burke 2000. Particularly illuminating are "Speech on Fox's East India Bill" and "Speech in Opening the Impeachment of Warren Hastings," although there is much to learn in Burke's "Speech on Conciliation with America," which treats imperial policy in a different context but with a remarkable unity of concern. Anyone who believes that racial attitudes are historically determined and excused might also read the letter to Miss Mary Palmer, in which Burke writes of his long defense of India, "I have no party in this business, Miss Palmer, but among a set of people who have none of your lilies and roses in their faces, but who are of the images of the great Pattern as well as you or I. I know what I am doing; whether the white people like it or not" (2000, 374).

considerations relevant to their decisions and, moreover, systematically overestimate their capacity for such judgment and so fail to give due weight to the likelihood that they are in error. Both believed that it was, therefore, prudent to reduce one's estimate of the degree of rationally motivated control one had over one's own life and actions. For Montaigne, the partial abdication of the sovereign subject was to both the customs of his time and a certain playful embrace of uncertainty; for Burke, it was in favor of tradition and political authority.

Their more distinctive idea was that erroneous judgment was self-reinforcing and self-amplifying, *because it was exciting and satisfying.* Self-certainty and self-righteousness, on Montaigne's account, were constant temptations, because the mind hungered to fix on certainty even though it could not reliably produce truth. Moreover, self-righteousness led to cruelty, the willful and self-conscious infliction of violence, because it provided a moral license to act against others without hesitation, and the pleasure of such action produced an appetite for more. Burke's picture was similar: grand principles and dramatic moral and political visions produced a kind of intellectual and aesthetic excitement that overwhelmed ordinary prudence and carried one forward like a powerful stimulant. Acting under the influence of such ideas, people self-confidently carried out acts of violence and domination against others, only to discover that domination produces its own satisfaction, and a taste for unconstrained power for its own sake. Burke called the temptation of visions and ideas the passion of zealotry; the temptation of power he called the passion of tyranny.

Montaigne and Burke are best remembered for their opposition to forms of European extremism: Montaigne to the sectarianism of the Wars of Religion, and Burke to the elements of the French Revolution that led to the Terror. Both, however, saw imperialism as the optimal setting for the forms of dangerous conviction they feared, a theme that Montaigne explored in meditations on Spanish violence and cruelty in the Americas and Burke in the great parliamentary speeches that capped his fourteen-year crusade against the depredations of the East India Company. Placed in power over a remote people, whose cultural and moral lives were unfamiliar, opaque, and easily misapprehended, it was easy to conclude that the subjects were, in Montaigne's term, "barbarians," so terrible and unintelligible as to fall outside the circle of one's own moral considerations. Moreover, Burke emphasized, imperial governors ruled unconstrained by the habits of decency, toleration, and prudence that formed the backdrop of any ongoing form of life. Wrenched out of their own habitual constraints, and unintegrated into those of their subjects, they were men without borders, able to give their hazardous appetites maximum play. Such people were entirely likely to do more harm than good wherever they were set down, and when they returned to the home country, they were inclined to impose their tyrannical habits on the domestic political culture. The fact that empire produced an imperial ruling class that applied its habits of governance to the imperial capital is one of the critical but neglected reasons that empire was long assumed to be incompatible with republican government.

This set of considerations should provide a valuable check on any form of imperial self-confidence. It is a moral argument about the hazards of empire, which does not assume that empire is amoral and rapacious, but argues that empire's hazards inhere in the shape it gives to moral reasoning and political judgment. Although its textual sources are several centuries old, that fact represents the nexus between the development of this thought and the rise of two of the great recent empires. Anyone who would set it aside as anachronistic would have to show why its premises are outmoded—not a simple argument after the run that zealotry and tyranny have enjoyed in the twentieth century, both in and outside the colonial and postcolonial countries. Those who would set it aside as false would have to account for the same phenomena over a longer period.

The Logic of the Imperial Exception

This tradition of argument, though, provides only a piecemeal and prudential argument against any particular imperial project—and, indeed, against any application of moral reasoning in the exercise of power. For a more systematic assessment of the contemporary imperial program, it is necessary to consider it by reference to its specific claims to justification rather than by way of a general precaution about the hazardous conjunction of justification, power, and distance.

Recall that I suggested earlier in this essay that contemporary justification for imperial projects invokes three kinds of considerations: absolute prohibitions, the requirements of global security, and the nature and preconditions of human flourishing. The most powerful counterarguments to today's imperial doctrine assert that the doctrine rests on a misreading of those three considerations.

On the axis of global security, at least two arguments suggest that imperial policy is inferior to respect for sovereignty as a basis for international order. The first would note that the Bush Doctrine is premised on the idea that the United States can remain the world's sole and dominant superpower, either indefinitely or until its liberalizing and pacifying mission has succeeded and made it unnecessary. On this premise, the United States is and will remain the authoritative interpreter of when global security requires imperial intervention in otherwise sovereign states. Even if American judgment is sometimes imperfect, the United States will occupy the status of Hobbes's Leviathan, establishing rules that, because all are forced to follow them, are superior to any situation in which rules are effectively uncertain because their enforcement is impossible or uneven. To deny this view, one would have only to believe that American military domination is not comprehensive even now, when Chinese and Indian military-economic growth are only getting under way and Russia is at a nadir; it would not even be necessary to speculate about the challenge those powers might pose within a century to a Pax Americana. If even now, let alone in two or three decades, other countries are likely to take on themselves the judgment as to when security putatively requires intervention—and there will be plenty of room for opportunism in this judgment—then promulgation of the Bush Doctrine will not solve the problem of a Hobbesian world by creating a Leviathan, but intensify the problem by licensing competing Leviathans to jostle for position outside of even the highly imperfect rules of sovereignty.

The second argument is even simpler. It would ask whether, at this stage in the proliferation of nuclear weapons, the threat of unilateral American intervention is in fact likely to dissuade prospective members of the nuclear club, or to hasten their efforts. At the time of writing, it is arguable that the lesson to small countries from the American encounters with Iraq and North Korea (not to mention Pakistan) will turn out to be that we punish those who pursue nuclear weapons and fail, but reward those who succeed. The incentives of such a principle are, to say the least, not unambiguously against proliferation.

The most interesting area for dispute, though, and the one in which normative political thought seems prima facie most likely to make a distinctive contribution, is human flourishing. Let us stipulate, for the moment, that some version of the Bush Doctrine's assertion is true: people everywhere want security, personal liberty, and prosperity (although they may have quite distinct specific goals in mind under these general headings). The Bush Doctrine stakes its case on the idea that these values can be effectively implanted by imperial intervention. The basis of this idea, on the strength of the evidence so far from Iraq, is the belief that top-down American competence and bottom-up local spontaneous order will meet to produce a market economy, stable democratic institutions, and a civil society that protects basic liberty and security.

Taken at face value, this is a view about a most basic philosophical issue: how freedom unfolds in history, or, put less grandly, what the preconditions of modern freedom are. Any strong form of the Bush Doctrine view of this issue depends in turn on two presuppositions that are, at a minimum, controversial. The first might be called the harmony of liberal ends: the belief that free markets, democratic political arrange-ments, and increasingly individualistic social orders are all mutually reinforcing, and together uphold personal liberty and security. The neoliberal policy reforms of the 1990s were premised on a similar idea, and in several cases, notably Indonesia and Argentina, doctrinaire liberalizing reforms in economic policy induced political crises with illiberal political results, arguably including an increase in the influence of Indonesian Islamist parties. It is well established that electoral support for illiberal and quasi-fascist political parties is often concentrated in the small merchant and middle classes that constitute a market economy. Even more straightforwardly, the phenomenon of so-called illiberal democracy is now so notorious as to provide a kind of catchphrase for American reasons for disfavoring direct elections in most of the Arab Middle East, where it is reckoned that the polls would favor illiberal Islamist parties (as they did in the hurriedly canceled Algerian election of 1994).

The second controversial presupposition of the Bush Doctrine is that nationalism is substantially irrelevant to political outcomes, and hence the provenance of reform matters much less than its content. If a given reform would be attractive when issued by a local government, it will be equally attractive when handed down by an occupying power or the client regime of that power. This belief may well be possible, today, only for Americans, whose habitual confidence in the universality of their values, practices, and institutions is a source of both visionary good and visionary harm. There is no particular reason, though, to doubt that the inevitable resentment and opportunism of a period of transition will not be the more potent insofar as they are directed at a government perceived as alien. If true, this means that the pervasive conflicts between, say, popular elections and liberal government or market reforms and liberal political culture will be more pronounced and explosive when nationalist resentment provides a vocabulary for both discontent and ambition. The universality and power of nationalism as a political motivation is perhaps the most salient single difference between the circumstances of previous imperial powers and the situation of the United States today.

Let us suppose that neither proposition is true in the degree that the Bush Doctrine presupposes: that persistent tensions among the elements of liberalizing reform can push countries in illiberal directions, and that national sentiment is persistently important. If these qualifications are accurate, they give reason for skepticism about whether overtly imperial policy in fact fosters the kind of flourishing that the Bush Doctrine envisions. But the reason for hesitation is greater than that: assessment of an imperial policy's claim to promote human flourishing cannot be restricted to the prospects of the countries under direct imperial occupation or influence; it must also extend to the prospects of other countries whose domestic politics are reshaped by response to imperial policy. Anecdotal and statistical accounts of the sharp increase in anti-American resentment worldwide in the last two years are now legion. What is not yet clear is whether this resentment will strengthen the hands of, for instance, nationalists in the Chinese government, military, and middle classes who view the United States as the successor to the colonial powers of the nineteenth century, and look forward to a moment when China will

challenge the American imperium for dominance in the Pacific; Hindu
nationalist parties that denounce economic liberalization as neocolonial-
ism and Western-toned cultural change as corruption, and have driven
India's nuclear development as a symbol of the country's status on the
world stage; Iranian fundamentalists whose people resent them but
may resent an American occupying army next door more, and so
forth. Precedent, though, is not encouraging: anti-colonial nationalism
strengthened the hands of authoritarians in many mid-century colonial
countries, while the association of free markets with American domination inspired nominally state-socialist regimes; the combination often
inflicted considerable costs in terms of human flourishing, and the
motives were the same that the United States is sowing now. A policy
must be judged not only by its success or failure in its intended effect,
but also by its other consequences, including the inflection it gives to
global politics.

These are all reasons for skepticism about the claims of today's
imperial policy-makers. Considering them also clarifies what would be
necessary in formulating an adequate alternative. One would need not
simply to invoke the Wilsonian axioms, but to weigh them and their
alternatives against an account of this moment in history: where the most
significant hazards and opportunities lie along the three axes of protecting
global security, promoting human flourishing, and preventing impermissible atrocities. A lucid picture of these considerations gives a proper scale
for assessing any particular proposal, and helps to check the usual
hazards of normative political reasoning: dogmatism about familiar
rules, obsession with specific problems to the exclusion of broader
concerns, mistaking one's own convenience for the universal interest,
and clinging to an idea because of the excitement or emotional satisfaction it provides rather than its merit. It is arguable that American imperial
policy, now in an early stage of explicit expression, has suffered from
several of these hazards: obsession with a few symbolically significant,
hostile enemies, and one terrible event—the attacks of September 11,
2001; the assumption that American concerns are automatically global
concerns, and the consequent reorientation of global political attention to
an imprecisely formulated antiterror campaign; and the excitement of the
crusading war, exemplified in President Bush's fist-pumping announce-
ment that "I feel good" moments before he declared the beginning of the
Iraq invasion. Adherents of the Bush Doctrine, of course, have no
monopoly on these vices; but these vices are suggestive of hazards specific
to imperial policy.

I have suggested one starting point for an account of organizing
concerns: the prospects of broadly liberal political and social development in rapidly changing countries such as India and China, which alone
contain almost half the world's population outside the wealthy Euro-
American zone, and which hold tremendous potential both for human

flourishing and for an illiberal and belligerent future. These developments are not susceptible, even as a purely pragmatic matter, to imperial intervention; but they are significantly affected by whether the United States behaves, and is perceived, as an attractive model of liberal modernity or as an arrogant and threatening power.

Procedure and Prudence

A last word is in order about the claimed intellectual and moral virtue of the imperialists: realism. Their iconoclasm toward Wilsonian pieties, and their willingness to concentrate attention on the worst regimes and most alarming prospects in world politics have won them credit for clear-eyed maturity, especially amid the suspicion that American foreign policy in the 1990s was characterized by slovenly and unearned complacency. The institutions and procedures of the mid-twentieth century are inadequate for today's world, the imperialists insist, and a harder and less-compromising attitude must replace it.

Do their observations support their conclusions? At least some of the attraction of imperial policy is written into two persistent modern paradoxes. The first of these is the perversity of proceduralism. From criminal law to legislative process to the machinations of the United Nations Security Council, the quintessential modern check on power is a procedural requirement that certain steps precede any action, whether jailing a criminal defendant, passing a draconian (or benevolent) law, or undertaking a war. The purpose of such procedures is to protect liberty and security against arbitrary and self-interested uses of power; but inevitably the procedures also thwart good projects and protect the wicked, sometimes specifically in ways that further the abuse of power, whether by holding up campaign finance reform in the United States by decades or by helping to preserve the Khmer Rouge or the Iraqi Baath party. From this perversity comes an inevitable impulse to override the procedures, grab the levers of power, and do the (perceived) right thing. Acting on that impulse brings in train all the dangers of unchecked power that occasioned procedural constraints in the first place. The present imperial program represents a grand procedural exception, which is by its nature redolent of clear moral perception and decisive action, but is necessarily a high-stakes gamble that the violated procedures either were unnecessary or can be readily repaired or improved. Those who argue for keeping the procedures in place are not naive or obtuse about the reasons for action; they have calculated the gamble differently, and they may be right.

The second modern paradox is captured in Rousseau's notorious remark that those who will not choose their own freedom "must be forced to be free." The imperial promise is to bring subject peoples over the last barriers to self-emancipation, when they can be set free with confidence that they will make choices that preserve their freedom. The decision to force others into freedom comes readily in a time founded on radical breaks with the past in the name of progress, and particularly from the United States, founded and refounded on such breaks in its founding revolution and its Civil War, and populated by people who broke with their own pasts in immigrating to it in the first place. The decision is, however, not always possible or appropriate. Such a project supposes that freedom supplied from outside has the same meaning and staying power as freedom achieved from within the politics and history of a country, which there is reason to doubt. It supposes also that the system the outside power imposes is the one that the locals would freely develop of their own accord; that is, that modern freedom has only one shape, which there is also reason to doubt. And it supposes that the act of imposition itself, with whatever violence and disruption it brings, will not irremediably corrupt what follows it. Many top-down revolutions have ended disastrously in attempts to force people into freedom; while much of their failure may have come from a mistaken conception of freedom, some at least resulted from the same questionable suppositions that today's imperial policy displays. There is no reason to expect imperial projects to be immune to the same hazards.

Imperial undertakings, then, are not amoral but supremely morally ambitious, and a large part of their hazard consists precisely in their moral quality. They are, in salient respects, attempts to break out of the constraints our period has accepted as part of its freedom, which include a fair amount of hypocrisy and frustration, and the cynicism that accompanies those. Although their supporters present them as square-on confrontations with the worst facts about human nature and world politics, imperial policies are also evasions of other obdurate facts about the dangers of power and the limits of politics. As exceptions they are hazardous. As governing principles, they have potential for disaster.

Acknowledgments

I would like to thank Christian Barry, Mary Campbell, Owen Fiss, and Sanjay Reddy for their helpful comments on earlier drafts.

References

Burke, Edmund. 2000. *Burke on Empire, Liberty, and Reform*. Edited by David Bromwich. New Haven: Yale University Press.

Mill, James. 1975. *The History of British India*. Abridged and with an introduction by William Thomas. Chicago: University of Chicago Press.

Mill, John Stuart. 1993. "Government of Dependencies." In *Utilitarianism, On Liberty, Considerations on Representative Government*. Rutland, Vt.: Everyman.

Montaigne, Michel de. 1995a. "Of Cannibals." In *Complete Essays of Montaigne*, translated by Donald M. Frame. Stanford: Stanford University Press.

———. 1995b. "Of Coaches." In *Complete Essays of Montaigne*, translated by Donald M. Frame. Stanford: Stanford University Press.

INDEX

Note: "n" or "and notes" after a page numbers indicates a note on that page.